PSYCHOLOGY LIBRARY EDITIONS:
CHILD DEVELOPMENT

Volume 20



# CHILD'S PLAY

# CHILD'S PLAY

## Developmental and Applied

Edited by
THOMAS D. YAWKEY AND
ANTHONY D. PELLEGRINI

Routledge
Taylor & Francis Group
LONDON AND NEW YORK

First published in 1984 by Lawrence Erlbaum Associates, Inc.

This edition first published in 2018
by Routledge
2 Park Square, Milton Park, Abingdon, Oxon OX14 4RN

and by Routledge
711 Third Avenue, New York, NY 10017

*Routledge is an imprint of the Taylor & Francis Group, an informa business*



*British Library Cataloguing in Publication Data*
A catalogue record for this book is available from the British Library

ISBN: 978-1-138-74142-3 (Set)
ISBN: 978-1-351-27384-8 (Set) (ebk)
ISBN: 978-1-138-29766-1 (Volume 20) (hbk)
ISBN: 978-1-138-29772-2 (Volume 20) (pbk)
ISBN: 978-1-315-09907-1 (Volume 20) (ebk)

# CHILD'S PLAY: DEVELOPMENTAL AND APPLIED

Edited by

Thomas D. Yawkey
*The Pennsylvania State University*

Anthony D. Pellegrini
*University of Georgia*

LAWRENCE ERLBAUM ASSOCIATES, PUBLISHERS
1984 Hillsdale, New Jersey London

Lawrence Erlbaum Associates, Inc., Publishers
365 Broadway
Hillsdale, New Jersey 07642

**Library of Congress Cataloging in Publication Data**
Main entry under title:

Child's play.

Bibliography: p.
Includes indexes.
1. Play. 2. Child psychology. I. Yawkey, Thomas D.
II. Pellegrini, Anthony D.
BF717.C43 1984 155.4'18 83-20769
ISBN 0-89859-300-X

Printed in the United States of America
10 9 8 7 6 5 4 3 2 1

# Contents

# Foreword

James E. Johnson
*The Pennsylvania State University*

> *All purely material research conducted by a human scientist is pure inquisitive behavior—appetitive behavior in free operation. In this sense, it is play behavior. All scientific knowledge . . . arose from playful activities conducted in a free field entirely for their own sake . . . Anybody who has seen in his own activities the smooth transition from inquisitive childhood play to the life-work of a scientist could never doubt the fundamental identity of play and research.*
>
> —Konrad Lorenz
> Psychology and Phylogeny
> 1976

Within the past 15 years we have witnessed a dramatic increase in empirical research on the play of children, both in terms of research articles published in professional journals and in research-based books on play such as the present volume. A major focus of this research has centered upon the role of play in development—in what ways does play influence development, or consolidate or reinforce it, or simply reflect the child's developmental history? In a complementary vein, there has been interest in another important way of examining child's play. That is, how do play behaviors themselves develop? What are the antecedent conditions and behavioral correlates of various forms of play at different developmental levels and for different populations? What is the conceptual relationship between play and other epistemic-ludic behaviors, such as reality testing, exploration, insightful tool use, learning, humor, metaphor comprehension, ritualistic behavior, or language itself?

This surge of research productivity has certainly hammered the last nails on the coffin of the Schlosbergian condemnation of the study of play on the grounds that the construct is vague, superfluous, and scientifically useless. As we have seen, conceptual and methodological advancements over the years (and a fair amount of true grit) has rendered play more and more empirically manageable. As a consequence, it has become more scientifically respectable to conduct research on child's play.

A major purpose of the present book is to bring together in a single volume, work that reflects the wide range of interests that social and behavioral scientists have in play, development, and the environment. The book had its beginnings during the 1982 American Educational Research Association meetings in Montreal when Professors Yawkey and Pellegrini informally began contacting leading scholars in the area of play research to ask them to contribute to a book devoted to both basic research and applied developmental or educational concerns. Moreover, the intent of the book would be to refine and extend concepts and methodologies within and beyond one's usual area of study. The idea was that this formula and direction would yield novel information and fresh insights. After diligent and painstaking organizational and editorial work by Professors Yawkey and Pellegrini, not to mention the excellent contributions of the authors and co-authors of the nineteen chapters of the present volume, we have an excellent product that encompasses a wealth of topics concerning structural, functional, and pragmatic aspects of play during early childhood and childhood, and a product that includes strong emphasis on methodological as well as substantive content concerns.

The empirical and theoretical research and scholarship compiled in this volume reflect a common theme. The works may be said to have evolved within a common framework that the study of play is relevant and indeed necessary for fully comprehending human development. Some of the researchers represented may be primarily interested in play as expressive behavior and others in play for its constitutive role in development. In both cases, play is held to provide a foundation for ontogenetically later occurring interpersonal and intrapersonal qualities and characteristics. Accordingly, the significance of the study of play extends over the life course, well beyond infancy and early childhood. Self-fulfilling adult behaviors in occupational or leisure realms can have their roots traced to fully developed childhood play. The chapters of this text suggest Lorenz's notion of continuity across the life stages, and are a testimonial to Researcher the Player.

It is hoped that the chapters of this book will inspire a new generation of research extending knowledge both in theoretical and applied areas. As a book as this would suggest, a critical mass in the area of research has been reached validating and legitimatizing play as an important area of empirical study. On the other hand, to be sure, there are yet many within our ranks still swayed by Schlosbergian prejudices about play. For these less informed or hard-nosed among us who still condemn play research as frivolous, let us keep up the momentum displayed in these pages and accept the challenge to obtain even higher levels of excellence and methodological rigor in the years ahead. In the past, play research has been accused of being the "ugly duckling" of the behavioral sciences. We are now approaching the point where more will see the "beautiful swan" we have known play to be all along.

# 1 Selected Introductory Notes on Child's Play As Developmental and Applied

Thomas D. Yawkey
*The Pennsylvania State University*

## Introduction

Although child's play and play-related actions such as exploration and humor have been of import to researcher and practitioner alike for centuries, interest in them as cognitive entities and for systematic research study has mushroomed since the publication of Jean Piaget's (1962) book on this subject. In this seminal work, Piaget identifies pretend or ludic play as a necessary ingredient for cognitive development of human organisms from infancy to adulthood. First, pretending and cognizing both carry necessary elements of symbolic representation that more or less differ qualitatively and quantitatively depending on the situation and, more currently, on context.

Second, in stressing the significance of the pretend function to past, present, and future cognitive development and the interrelationships between logical and pretend thought functions, Piaget also describes a qualitative and quantitative shifting from more to less assimilative thought as children increase with age. Piaget hypothesizes that this shift may rest with emerging cognitive capacities developed inherently within the pretend play act itself (e.g., the ability to decenter). For example, in a cognitive sense the youngster through pretend play begins to view his relations to and with others as reciprocal rather than unidimensional. Constantly and continually interchanging thought with others through ludic play actions, the youngster decentralizes himself and coordinates internal relationships derived from desparate points of view. In ludic play, for instance, the child gathers together different experiences and creates combinations from them in and through ludic functioning. In pretend play, the youngster easily rearranges his representational thinking with objects, ideas, situations, and contexts and meshes them with ongoing play actions in relative and pluralistic ways.

Even though research in pretend play is in its developmental infancy and researchers acknowledge no common definition of or set of constructs universal to it, Piaget's views on ludic and logical functioning and their necessary interrelationships give a concrete foundation and certain legitimacy to research endeavors in this field. Piaget's thoughts provide the descriptive spark and the rich reservoir of fuel for exploring, researching, and uncovering a dimension of development that was largely concealed and hidden in theories of human behavior (Reilly, 1974). This textbook draws together current research and thinking about pretend play and ludic-related functioning in children at largely early- (and middle-) childhood levels. It also provides a rich base of literature in both the theoretical nature and applied functioning of ludic play and play-related capacities.

Accordingly, three conceptual problems undergrid this work. These broad conceptual problems, each forming a section of this book, follow:

1. Does pretend play, as a cognitive entity, contribute to development and growth of individuals in Western and non-Western settings and with normal and handicapped populations? In a related sense, can the methodological problems be resolved in order to provide solid bases for further systematic study of pretend play and specific ludic capacities as developmental capacities and/or in social context with normal and handicapped youngsters from Piagetian as well as from other psychological perspectives?
2. Can cognitive actions antecedent to, those presumed necessary for, and those that selectively accompany playful productions (in relative and pluralistic ways), such as, exploration, novelty, and humor be differentiated from pretend play in order to further understand and investigate them in systematic ways? In a related sense, how can these differentiations between exploration, novelty, humor, playful attitudes toward objects for associative fluency, and pretend play be operationalized for purposes of systematic research and greater understanding of them as independent and contextual entities in cognitive development?
3. Is there a current and substantive research base for play actions, and how might play actions be used in applied programs to promote or facilitate possible growth? What product and process outcomes might be anticipated in using play in applied modes?

## THEORETICAL PRETEND PLAY

The chapters in this section focus on the nature and origins of pretend play largely as a cognitive entity from cultural, social, and cross-cultural perspectives and with normal and handicapped children. In addition, the authors examine methodological concerns and theoretical propositions relative to pretend play in context and from selected psychological perspectives.

In responding to conceptual problems underlying pretend play, Athey provides a clear foundation and concrete set of perspectives on how it is viewed historically and in present times. Athey notes that past and present theories of play provide baselines and relevant attributes for its understanding. In similar fashion, however, these classical views have actually contributed to the neglect of play because they focused largely on its "causes." Both play and its causes contributed to viewing it as a peripheral action to the mainstream of development and to society in general.

Sutton-Smith and Kelly-Byrne distinguish between the major theories of play by focusing on their special characteristics rather than definitional utility. Their insightful and inductive analyses of these special or structural characteristics of play theories are viewed as and arranged along a bipolar continua that is marked by equilibrating and disequilibrating points. The inherent bipolar nature of play is in fact one of the sources of methodological problems in experimentally investigating child's play.

Schwartzman and Quinn and Rubin discuss pretend play actions and selectively identify problems of methodology in the context of research on play with cross-cultural, cross-class, and handicapped populations. Schwartzman develops selected relationships between children's pretend play and social class and cultural variables by: (1) examining cross-cultural and cross-class studies; and (2) responding to the theoretical problem of pretend play as "deficit" or "difference" using research results from these studies. Schwartzman responds to the current problem of pretend play as deficit or difference using ethnographic data and results and examines the major assumptions concerning children's pretend play in social-class and cross-cultural contexts. Quinn and Rubin integrate current research on play behaviors of children showing intellectual, physical, and emotional handicaps. The authors note that exploring play behaviors of the handicapped provide: (1) baselines for the study of normal children's play actions; (2) a developmental progression to understand play of the handicapped; and (3) selected conditions that effect the growth of play in atypical populations. In addition, Quinn and Rubin in very explicit fashion describe methodological weaknesses of current play studies such as exploration versus play and suggest ideas for further research in play with the handicapped.

McCune-Nicolich and Fenson critically examine selected methodological issues basic to investigating early pretend play in children. By providing examples of methodological variations from their previous research studies and of problems of definition, McCune-Nicolich and Fenson pinpoint relevant research concerns such as the roles of decentration and decontextualization. These authors also address possible confounds in the experimental paradigms used by researchers to investigate pretend play in very young children. These critical problems related to research paradigms rest, for example, with additional factors of settings, materials, and the children themselves. Finally, McCune-Nicolich and Fenson clearly focus attention on methodological aspects of assessment and screening with normal and handicapped youngsters.

Copple, Cocking, and Mathews explore object or material-based symbolic acts in order to determine the nature of cognitive actions fundamental to pretend play of preschool children. Because pretend play evolves through interaction specific to situations and players, Copple, Cocking, and Mathews analyze verbalizations accompanying children's object choices that can provide insight into their cognitive functioning. From analyses of data, results show that young children can display representational criteria for pretend object use. The preschooler seems to attend to attributes of objects that are relevant to their functions in the play context. In addition, preschoolers through their communicative acts show that they can reflect on object choices and recognize their own personal processes of evaluating and pretending.

Fein studies the self-building potential of pretend play by analyzing and insightfully integrating content propositions from George Herbert Mead's ideas of pretense and structural principles from the interactionist theory of symbolic play. This analysis and integration provides a potential framework for examining the young child's views of his changing self. In the analysis and extension, Mead's notions of role taking comprising covert and overt role-playing behaviors can be ordered into a hierarchical series of play stages that ultimately evolve into higher-level role-reversals (i.e., when a child plays a role with a partner as a complementary other). In the process, communication is generated in the play context and the data provide clues to cognitive attributes of self and others. Through repeated role reversals, Fein's analyses show that the social self becomes organized, differentiated from, yet related to, others in social context and content.

## PLAY-RELATED ACTIONS

This section explores play-related actions, such as exploration, novelty, and humor (which can under certain conditions accompany playful productions) as well as playful attitudes toward objects for purposes of associative fluency. Second, the authors in the section determine similarities and contrasts with pretend play and explore methods and procedures for systematic research of these play-related actions as independent capacities and in social context.

The chapters by Wohlwill and Henderson center on exploration as a play-related action. Wohlwill masterfully distinguishes between exploration and pretend-object play through behavioral attributes and identifies relationships between play and exploration. In discussion of temporal relationships between exploration and play, Wohlwill identifies selected functions of play materials and shares results of a study that suggests that these temporal interrelationships (between exploration and pretend-object play) may rest, in part, on choice and use of materials. In similar yet distinct ways, Henderson's core thesis is that social situations may effect what is explored and how it is explored. In reviewing the empirical literature on social context, Henderson expertly identifies basic assumptions of exploration and analyzes it in social contexts of object, structure, and function. In addition, the effects that parents, other adults, and peers have on children's exploration are described.

Ellis conceptually analyzes play behavior from varying systems of interpretation generated to explain these and other functional behaviors in the context of physical and social environments. Hypothesizing that play provides data to the player who possesses these novel cognitive configurations with internal rewards, Ellis describes the impact of collative properties of stimuli, for example, novelty and complexity on play behaviors. The analysis clearly focuses on the property of novelty that alerts the child to play and subsequently maintains his interest in it. The author outlines a "progression to and in play" that enables children to employ their physical and social milieu for rewarding stimuli.

McGhee argues quite convincingly that humor, a form of intellectual play with ideas, has intersecting cognitive elements with play, but is a different type of playful production. In addition, he explores cognitive aspects of humor development and, in a similar vein with Ellis, the role of incongruity. In reality assimilation and fantasy assimilation, two separate cognitive ways that individuals come to understand incongruous events, McGhee argues for the latter symbolic process as central to humor. Derived from McGhee's research studies, four cognitive stages of humor development are also explained and examined.

Pellegrini summarizes selected studies of facilitating young children's associative fluency and extends them in his own research by differentiating between explorative and pretend play behaviors. In observing that the child's ability to form relationships about objects and show playful attitudes toward them are bases of associative fluency, Pellegrini contends that creative uses of conventional objects may vary according to his familiarity with attributes of and his attitude toward them. Pellegrini's results show that associative fluency can be facilitated through training: (1) exploration of objects' attributes by responding to descriptive, then convergent and divergent classification questions; and (2) abilities to classify objects divergently. In concluding his sound analysis, Pellegrini notes that exploration of as well as divergent thinking about objects result in increased associative fluency in young children.

## PLAY AS APPLIED ACTIONS

In the final section of this text, the various chapters examine and extend selected substantive research on pretend play for purposes of applied programming with young children. In developing implications for application from investigations, the utility of play for growth of young children is employed in varying settings (e.g., elementary classrooms and preschools, counseling sessions, and hospitals) and differing situations (e.g., fantasy, grammatic, and individual play tutoring).

The chapters completed by Glickman and Curry and Arnaud argue logically for justifying play as a means for education in public elementary schools and for development in preschools. Through a survey of results of play research, Glickman develops implications of play as constructive bases for elementary school programming. In addition, he weaves his sound argument around the purposes of public education from historical and philosophical perspectives. Throughout his narrative, it becomes apparent that play could be employed as a basis for curriculum programming in elementary education. However, the public who supports the elementary schools must conceptually and practically reconsider the purposes of education of young and older children in order to increase the roles of play and its powers for cognitive, social, and motor growth and learning.

With similar justification and intent to harness the powers of play, Curry and Arnaud view it as significant utility for developmental preschools. With implications drawn from their own research and related studies, Curry and Arnaud develop methods to facilitate pretend play for optimal social, intellectual, and physical growth of young children. Realizing that pretend play varies as a function of the child's developmental level, previous experiences, and present classroom climate, they masterfully consider three aspects of play facilitation (i.e., environments, adults, and peers).

Both L. Guerney and Bolig view play and its various forms as facilitators of young and older children's growth in counseling and hospital settings, respectively. L. Guerney draws expertly from classical views and current research studies to explain the significance of play and shows clearly how play forms can contribute to therapeutic intervention with children in counseling settings. From therapeutic and varying psychological perspectives, she summarizes play theories (e.g., psychoanalytic, release therapy) and client relationships (e.g., theraplay, behavioral). Enligntening also is L. Guerney's description of roles, functions, methods, and strategies used by the counselor for purposes of child diagnosis and client intervention (e.g., limit setting and play materials).

Bolig's chapter reviews selected possible effects of hospitalization and functions of play in this setting. The play elements used in hospitals share some of the same attributes of nondirective play therapies including ameliorative functions and serve multiple roles depending on the hospital's philosophy. Bolig notes the type of child's illness (or condition) requiring hospitalization is the primary consideration for play programming (e.g., children in psychological and/or physiological stress and those that are bedridden or isolated). In recognizing the needs of children and the philosophy of the hospital, Bolig describes several types of play programming that may assist their recuperation.

Williamson and Silvern and Mann in their respective chapters both employ pretend play as a potential facilitator of selected cognitive abilities in young children. Williamson and Silvern thoroughly review classical and current research studies and argue convincingly for the effects of play on young children's growth. Focusing on the potential effects of dramatic fantasy play, Williamson and Silvern's results show that it can facilitate language learning in young children. Novel experimental procedures, measurement of language learning, and experimental control of possible confounds are novel in this study on play tutoring.

In assessing symbolic play as a preschool instructional strategy, Mann explores different effects of using: (1) unrealistic as opposed to realistic props in facilitating children's concept development and divergent thinking; and (2) two prop conditions on these behaviors during rehearsal. Drawing on related research, Mann hypothesizes that the more abstract the children's make-believe the greater should be the enhancement of representational skills and the more accurate his recall. In using realistic props in the rehearsal condition, the major result was that children's successful performance in enacting stories predicted their ability to recall stories and to think creatively about the story's content. This was not the case for unrealistic props and this condition appeared to require greater use of covert representational abilities for concept formation and divergent thinking.

## ACKNOWLEDGMENT

The author's research and writing on constructivist play, cognition, and communication are supported, in part, by grants from The United States Department of Education, The Margaret M. Patton Foundation, and Penn State's Division of Curriculum and Instruction, Professor Fred H. Wood, Chair. The views expressed in this and other documents are those of the author and do not represent the funding agencies, divisions, or institutions.

## REFERENCES

Piaget, J. *Play, dreams and imitation in childhood.* New York: Norton, 1962.

Reilly, M. (Ed.). *Play as exploratory learning.* Beverly Hills, Ca.: Sage, 1974.

# 2 Contributions of Play to Development

Irene Athey
*Rutgers, The State University of New Jersey*

The subject of play is a relative newcomer to academic thinking. A cursory inspection of the subject index of most leading texts on human development that have appeared in the last 20 years reveals few references on play. During the past few years, however, play has come into its own, and several major books have appeared, in addition to which there has been considerable research activity, some of it interdisciplinary in nature. Reasons for the earlier neglect may lie in the perception of play as an activity peripheral to the mainstream of development. Definitions characterizing play as "the aimless expenditure of exuberant energy" (Schiller, 1875), "superfluous activity taking place instinctively in the absence of real actions" (Spencer, 1896), or "any exercise or series of actions intended for amusement or diversion" (Webster's Dictionary, 1961) were hardly calculated to inspire a zeal for investigation of the subject, especially in the puritanical ethos of the late 19th century. As Ellis (1973) points out, the earlier definitions seemed to regard play as a necessary evil of childhood, possibly devoid of useful outcome for the player, and certainly of little interest to the scientist.

Part of the problem of definition has come from the fact that play is a broad concept that includes many forms of behavior, such as the imitation of adult actions, practice of skills that will be useful in later life (Groos, 1916), recapitulation of earlier stages of human evolution (Hall, 1916), or simply the expenditure of surplus energy (Spencer, 1896). In formulating their explanations of play, scholars have emphasized one or other of these characteristics, but these explanations—life preparation, recapitulation, and surplus energy—have been discarded or modified in the light of current thinking. Nevertheless, these aspects are still considered important features of play. In fact, most researchers accept the spontaneous, voluntary, active, and pleasurable aspects as critical to the definition of play, setting it off from other forms of behavior (Klinger, 1971). Some have regarded play as having no extrinsic goal and hence as inherently unproductive. However, this definition seems more difficult to defend, since many forms of behavior that are clearly playful also have outcomes of personal or social value. In view of these many difficulties, the study of play has passed from a preoccupation with definition and function to the investigation of its systematic relations to other aspects of behavior. In particular, this later view has served to blur, rather than to clarify, the distinction between work and play. There seems to be tacit recognition of the fact that this distinction is no longer useful in such well-worn phrases as "Play is child's work," and "One man's work is another man's play."

Early childhood educators were among the first to recognize the value of play to the young child's development. Since early childhood education has never been an accepted component of the formal educational structure, however, their influence has been somewhat limited. Clearly the dichotomy between work and play as useful and useless activity and the view of the preschool as less important than formal education are mutually reinforcing. In fact, it should be noted that when the importance of the early years to later cognitive development became widely recognized through the work of Bloom and others, the natural reaction of many educators was to extend the worklike activities of the elementary school downward. An equally logical conclusion would have been to reassess the value of the natural activity of early childhood, namely play, and to incorporate that activity into the life of the elementary school. That play possessed such intrinsic value was the theme of two major works by the well-known British psychologist Susan Isaacs (1940, 1966). She documented through daily observations and records of young children's behavior and language her view of the influence of play on their intellectual growth and social development. Similarly, Piaget's (1962) interpretation of play as a form of symbolic representation laid the theoretical foundation for more recent views of play as intrinsic to and necessary for later cognitive development.

Emanating from the various attempts at definition have come a number of questions or issues, more or less controversial. Some of these have been touched on previously, and others are corollaries of these: (1) do adults play, or only children?; (2) must play be purposeless, or can it have an aim over and above the pleasure of the activity itself?; and (3) can play function as work, and vice versa? In this chapter, it is assumed that, whatever definition is adopted, there is no basis for excluding adult activities from the realm of play; that play can, and often does, have a purpose or aim; and that, for some individuals at least, work and play are sometimes indistinguishable.

The more interesting question, which will form the basis for this chapter, concerns the contributions of play to various aspects of human development. The major argument will be that under favorable conditions play can make a contribution throughout the life span to every aspect of human development. This position in itself assumes that adults play, that their play may involve work, and that the play serves either a conscious purpose or a psychological function, or both. Although it is probably demonstrable that play has a role in development at all stages of the life cycle, the literature has, for reasons outlined earlier, tended to concentrate on the earlier stages, especially that of early childhood. For this reason, the review concentrates on the age range from birth to adolescence; however, this restriction should not be construed as implying that play serves no useful role in the adult years. The traditional division into physical, intellectual, language, social, and emotional development will also be used. Finally, given the broad scope of the chapter, it will be possible to touch briefly only on a few major points, since each section represents a very large topic in itself.

## PHYSICAL DEVELOPMENT

At all ages, play is closely associated with physical activity. Infants respond to the playful overtures of adults by squirming and wriggling their whole body. Much of the play of toddlers and preschoolers involves gross motor activities such as climbing, running, jumping, and moving large objects. The enjoyment of sports in the years of middle childhood and adolescence is also largely derived from the exercise of the muscular and oculomotor systems. Physical ability and energy find their outlet in play, and play in turn leads to further refinement in physical abilities.

### Infancy

Can the newborn infant be said to play? Infants vary in the amount of activity they display, but even the most active sleep a great deal. If we think of play as stimulus-seeking (as opposed to activity for the sake of satisfying some basic need), it appears that the infant engages in a great deal of both exploratory and social play (Ellis, 1973). Exploratory behavior at this age includes looking, touching, grasping, experimenting with parts of the body, vocalizing, and so forth, all of which contribute to the growth and control of the skeletal and muscular systems and to the perception and mastery of objects both in isolation and relative to one another in time and space. The initial movements may be generated during a burst of random activity, become singled out for repetition, and are sometimes accompanied by obvious signs of pleasure (Millar, 1968). Alternatively, the movement may originate in a specific purpose such as obtaining a better view of an object and thenceforth be repeated for its own sake. Piaget (1952) provides the example of an infant repeating the movement of throwing back his head "with ever-increasing enjoyment and ever-decreasing interest in the external result." Adults too may initiate such movements in their playful interactions with babies, the behavior in question then being perpetuated beyond the immediate encounter. Whatever the source, it appears that the repetition of movements, or sequences of movements, has the effect of establishing the neural pathways that facilitate performance and make these sequences readily accessible for future use. Some researchers have attempted to distinguish between the mastery of a skill and its playful deployment once perfected, but this distinction is hard to sustain in practice, since learning the skill is often pleasurable and playful practice occurs before the skill is perfected. In any event, there seems little doubt that playful repetition of a skill, perfected or not, leads to its long-term availability in the individual's repertoire of ready responses, and that the repetition serves to make the response smooth and rapid under a variety of conditions.

At the same time as the gross and fine muscles are being developed and coordinated, the oculomotor system is brought into play as the infant reaches for objects, observes motions and interactions among them, and succeeds in affecting the spatial relations of those objects. In learning to discriminate the properties of objects, the infant also learns the appropriate body response required to change these properties. In other words, the infant is learning not only about the objects themselves, but about self as an agent, about his or her own muscular system, and effectiveness in exerting his will over objects and events. Another way of thinking about this situation is to consider the infant's own body with its own natural laws as one more object that he or she must learn to discriminate from others and to understand in terms of its properties vis-à-vis those other objects. Hence it is through spontaneous play that the infant comes to define self as separate from other objects and as having properties with which he must also become familiar. This learning represents the beginning of the body image and the subsequently developed self-concept as a physical object in space and time.

## Early Childhood

Vigorous motor activity is the hallmark of the healthy child in the preschool years. It is probably from the observation of the young of both animal and human species that Schiller was led to postulate his theory of play as "the aimless expenditure of exuberant energy." However, little of the nonstop activity of the young child can be characterized as aimless, and even that which may appear aimless to the casual observer may turn out to have the function of releasing tension and affording practice for certain skills. The solitary play of the 2-year-old provides opportunities for exploring the environment, developing the large muscle system through gross motor play on bicycles and climbing frames, and for learning techniques of mastery over larger and more mobile objects and tools. Solitary play at the sand or water tray, or in quiet activities such as building with blocks or looking at pictures in a book, can also help to develop fine muscle and motor coordination as well as manipulative skills and eye–hand coordination.

Additionally, the young child's mobility and energy at this age permit the redefinition of the spatial parameters in which he or she operates.

Around the age of three the child's play becomes more social in nature, and many formerly solitary activities, as well as some new ones, are conducted in groups. Children of both sexes engage in minature versions of adult activities, often those appropriate to sex roles as defined by the society. In so doing, they are learning the requisite motor skills and behavior, and also ways of handling the tools of the culture. Growth is rapid during this period, and the child's strength increases in proportion to the gain in height and weight. Relative strength and dexterity are frequently assessed through rough-and-tumble play, in which children make bodily contact, usually without intent to harm or actual injury being inflicted. Rough-and-tumble play has been widely reported in a variety of cultures (Garvey, 1977) as well as in several animal species and is usually incorporated with other aspects of play into more complex patterns.

## Middle Childhood

The forms of play associated with early childhood give way to team games and other organized group activities, and to individual or group hobbies. These activities may require coordination of one's movements with those of other people in addition to control of objects such as bats and balls. The behavior of a physical object, once learned, is fairly predictable, but the actions and movements of other humans vary widely; indeed a wily opponent will make a point of being unpredictable. Clearly, this increased complexity demands more finely honed skills and faster reflexes than were needed in the gross motor play of early childhood.

Social activities also take the child into different environments where new skills can be learned. At summer camp, the child may learn to navigate a canoe through turbulent waters or to operate a computer or play a musical instrument. A new degree of physical coordination is called for, but these new skills in turn may transfer, thereby permitting the child to gain higher levels of expertise in old and familiar activities.

## Adolescence

With the onset of puberty, hormones are released into the body and rapid growth spurts occur, requiring new physical adaptations on the part of the adolescent. There may be considerable discontinuity with the old repertoire of skills, and new activities that more readily accommodate both social demands and the changing bodily structure may be sought out. Sports are likely to occupy a good deal of the time and attention of the adolescent, and the accomplishments at this age may form the basis for adult play activities throughout life.

## INTELLECTUAL DEVELOPMENT

Former explanations of play based on surplus energy or recapitulation of human evolution have given way to newer interpretations that postulate the need for self-expression as the critical feature (Ellis, 1973). The fundamental premise on which this dynamic theory is based is that activity is a primary need of human life, and that both perception and thought are active processes of construction. Much research conducted in the 1950s and 1960s was devoted to the demonstration of these propositions (White, 1959) and has led to the new cognitive psychology of the 1970s and 1980s. The concept of play as a dynamic, constructive activity fits neatly into this cognitive framework, and it is not implausible to suggest that the recent interest in play has something to do with the emergence of the cognitive movement. Indeed, Piaget (1962) regards play not merely as contributing to cognitive development but as itself being a manifestation of that development. To understand this statement, it is necessary to recognize that Piaget (1962) postulated "a functional continuity between the sensory-motor and the representational" and that play "especially from the point of view of 'meanings,' can be considered as leading from activity to representation [pp. 2–3]." From this viewpoint, play is a form of symbolic representation, a transitory process that takes the child from the earliest form of sensorimotor intelligence to the operational structures that characterize mature, adult thought. Hence play is itself a form of thought that is higher than sensorimotor (since it uses symbols) and also a building block prerequisite for the modes of thought that supersede it. Piaget (1962) is the only psychologist to have incorporated play into a systematic theory of the development of cognition, and his theory has provided the stimulus for some of the more recent work on play (Gilmore, 1966).

Piaget's account of the role of play in the genesis of representational thought understandably concentrates on the period of early infancy when the first manifestations of symbolic representation appear in the baby's behavior. However, his theory does not preclude, and indeed would seem to require, that earlier forms of thought are not discarded, but reappear in new forms at later stages. Since development is cumulative, play has both immediate and long-range effects on that development. Indeed, the relationship between cognitive development and play is an inherent and necessary one. Play leads to more complex and sophisticated cognitive behavior, which in turn affects the content of play in a continuous upward spiral. In the cognitive domain, play functions in four ways: (1) it provides access to more avenues of information; (2) it serves to consolidate mastery of skills and concepts; (3) through the use of cognitive operations, it promotes and maintains the effective functioning of the intellectual apparatus; and finally, (4) it promotes creativity through the playful use of skills and concepts.

Developmental psychologists, whose business it is to chart the course of cognitive learning, do not always agree on the route that is followed or the major landmarks along the way. They do agree, however, that cognitive growth involves: (1) greater ability to discriminate between information that is relevant or irelevant to a given purpose; (2) increased adeptness in using fewer cues to generate more information; and (3) higher levels of abstraction. Each of these three aspects of cognitive growth may be broken down into more specific processes, and the relationship of these processes to play has been analyzed at greater length elsewhere (Athey, 1978). In this context, we shall comment briefly on ways in which each of these aspects relates to play at different stages of the child's growth, bearing in mind that the same process becomes increasingly refined with age.

## Infancy

In common with other species, newborn humans have the capacity to attend to any object in the immediate environment, but certain objects appear to have particular salience for the infant. Brightness discriminations (Hershenon, 1964) and differential responses to heterogeneous stimuli (Miranda, 1970) are evident in neonates. An early preference is manifested for moving stimuli over stationary ones (Fantz 1970), and differential reactions to strange and familiar faces are also evident (Bower, 1966). Though many of these stimuli are generated by the infant's own random behavior or are simply produced by the environment, many others are the result of playful activity alone or in concert with adults.

A milestone is achieved when the baby begins to predict the appearance of certain objects on the basis of prior cues. These predictions or expectations form the basis for the concept of object permanence and subsequently for classificatory behavior (Piaget, 1962). Additionally, these predictions in themselves represent a level of abstraction that will make higher levels of symbolic representation possible.

## Early Childhood

The ability to classify objects and events grows rapidly during the early childhood years. Inhelder and Piaget (1969) have documented the progression from the young child's categorization of objects on the basis of spatial proximity to classificatory behavior based on defining characteristics of the objects. As the ability to classify evolves, so too does the ability to make generalizations (i.e., to transfer relevant cues to new objects or situations), thus generating more information from fewer cues. Finally, elements of the highest levels of abstraction, such as hypothesis testing, problem-solving, and creativity begin to make their appearance in the child's play (Dansky & Silverman, 1973).

## Middle Childhood

During the elementary school years, the opportunities and the time spent in play diminish considerably. There is progressive refinement of the discriminations related to physical and social objects that were initiated by the infant and preschooler, especially those relating to causal factors in the physical and social world. Deductive reasoning involving logical and mathematical concepts develops rapidly as concrete operations give way to formal modes of thought. The content of the discriminations may also become differentiated along sex and social status lines.

As operational thought becomes less dependent on immediate experience, the ability to generate more and more information from fewer cues correspondingly increases. Concepts become richer and more differentiated, and associative networks are strengthened, allowing the child to generate large quantities of information that cross disciplinary boundaries. During this period the child also develops into a fluent reader, thus opening up new vistas of vicarious experience and providing fresh material for fantasy that may in turn find expression in play activities.

Problem-solving is expected of the child during these years. Apart from the scientific and social problems presented during school hours, play activities provide the opportunity to find solutions in less formal settings to these and other problems. Personal problems especially are worked on by means of fantasy and acting out the problem.

Children are subjected to adult-imposed rules from birth, but it is only gradually that they come to appreciate the difference between laws of nature and human rules that, if not entirely arbitrary, are at least modifiable by mutual consent. This distinction forms the basis for the development of abstract social and ethical codes of behavior.

## Adolescence

The adolescent not only possesses a vast store of highly differentiated concepts and generalizations, but through his increased powers of hypothetical and deductive reasoning is able to manipulate them in thought to produce elaborate chains of "if–then" propositions providing alternative solutions, some of which may be new and creative, to a problem. This process is often called "playing with ideas" in recognition of its qualities of fantasy and freedom from consequences, attributes which have been thought by some theorists to be the essence of play (Garvey, 1977).

Although the adolescent is still interested in many things and is adding daily to his store of general knowledge, it is during this period that the major interests that lead to a choice of work and leisure time activities begin to crystallize. In other words, improvement in the cognitive abilities to discriminate, generalize, and make abstractions becomes increasingly tied to the specific areas of information to which the individual attends.

## LANGUAGE DEVELOPMENT

As was the case with cognitive development, language and play have been found to be mutually reinforcing. Whereas play clearly precedes the advent of language play is in one sense itself a form of language because it embodies a form of symbolic representation. Piaget views thought and language as separate though related systems having a common origin in the symbolic process as expressed through play and imitation. Hence, as might be expected, the ability to represent objects, actions, and feelings in symbolic play is paralleled by a corresponding ability to represent those phenomena in language (Nicolich, 1977). Both comprehension and production of language require the child to master the phonological, syntactic, and semantic rules that must be followed if intended meanings are to be conveyed (Athey, 1974). Play is instrumental in developing all these aspects of language.

### Infancy

The earliest form of language production is the babbling of the infant. It is not clear whether babbling can be considered as play, although it certainly possesses some of the qualities of repetitiveness, purposelessness, and inherent satisfaction that have been thought to characterize play. Phonetic elements of the language are repeated in many variations, some of which begin to approximate phonemic aspects of the language used in the home. Adults who respond in kind not only provide social reinforcement for babbling but probably unwittingly influence the selection of sounds toward those represented in their everyday use. This form of social play is thus instrumental in shaping the child's production. Lewis (1969) also sees this penchant for playing with sounds as the basis for later appreciation of literature in which sounds are enjoyed for their own sake in addition to their meaning.

By the end of the first year of life, the child enjoys playing with words and intonation patterns, especially those that represent in sound qualities of familiar objects or events (Jakobson, 1968).

Even early forms of children's speech such as one- and two-word sentences reflect later syntactic distinctions (McNeill, 1970). Playing with language elements such as word order, or parts of speech leads to progressive refinement of the syntactic structures (Bruner, 1974). Object permanence is complemented by the acquisition of verbal labels that identify those objects. Similarly, during play, adult comments on the properties of objects facilitates not only understanding of those objects but also the language needed to express these meanings.

## Early Childhood

Social play propels the child into situations that necessitate use of language in order to communicate intent or desire. While language production remains primitive, the young child may attempt to convey the desired meaning through sounds or intonations (Menyuk, 1969). As these modes of communication are seen to be inadequate, the child is forced into the use of more sophisticated forms of language. Fantasy play also incorporates aspects of adult speech, thereby perfecting phonemic and syntactic patterns. Similarly, the extended world of the preschooler enlarges his vocabulary and provides labels for the finer discriminations he is learning.

Even toward the end of this period not all language is communicative; there remains a considerable amount of language that seems to be produced solely for its own sake or for sheer enjoyment in the exercise (Opie & Opie, 1969). Around the age of 4 especially, children become preoccupied with rhyme, and vie with one another to produce nonsense rhymes and sequences. Again, the predilection for playing with sounds proves to be functional in preparing the child for later uses of language. It has been shown, for example, that the ability to produce rhyming words is highly correlated with early reading achievement.

Syntactic manipulations are a frequent element of play sequences during this period. The repetitive nature of nursery rhymes seems designed to provide practice in the use of syntactic categories. Bruner (1976) has also drawn attention to a form of language game which requires the rules of syntax to be followed in producing new nouns of the appropriate category.

Through play, children expand their initially narrow understanding of lexical items, and acquire the terminology to express semantic relationships that reflect their increased understanding of the physical and social environment.

## Middle Childhood

Games of this period appear, in all cultures, to be accompanied by some variation of language play. The language play forms of the playground and street have been documented by Opie and Opie (1969), who found two categories of oral rhymes, those used to regulate game relationships, and those used to express exuberance. While the former clearly have social implications, both categories contribute to the understanding of phonemic and syntactic usage. Rhymes may be used to convey other social messages such as denigration, satire, or ascendancy over others.

Although it has been generally accepted that children's syntactic development is virtually complete by the age of 6, recent research suggests that the understanding of complex syntactic structures may be a much more protracted matter (Athey, 1974). Play that employs or clarifies these structures continues, therefore, to be important. Again, language games may serve a special function in this respect.

As children acquire mastery of the semantic networks, an enjoyment of word play, puns, riddles, tongue twisters, and other forms of humor become possible. These word forms frequently involve transformations of meaning that are beyond the comprehension of the preschooler. The onset of concrete operations makes possible the appreciation of double meaning and violated expectations that are the hallmark of humor.

Serious play also contributes to the development of lexical meanings and to facility with the syntax of the language. New forms of games, such as computer games, whatever their social consequences, introduce the child to a new lexicon and (especially if he or she owns and programs a computer) to a new syntax.

### Adolescence

Older children and adolescents continue to enjoy sound play, as seen in the colorful names they devise for classmates and in such rituals as football chants, bingo, and so on. New words are coined almost daily, reflecting not only the changing social scene, but also the human penchant for inventing sound patterns that embody some feature of the unfamiliar. Meaning is not necessary for enjoyment; especially in songs and chants, meaning is conveyed through means other than words, and pleasure is dependent on neither.

Adolescents and adults also play with the syntactic and semantic elements of language. Commercials and popular aphorisms often embody this type of word play, as in the form "you can take X out of Y, but you can't take Y out of X." The sale of such books as Willard Espy's (1975) *Word Play* testifies to adults' enjoyment of syntactic and semantic substitution.

## SOCIAL DEVELOPMENT

The primary task of childhood is to be socialized into becoming an active and productive member of the culture. This means learning the basic knowledge that undergirds the society, learning the language by which this knowledge is communicated, and, last but not least, learning the system of roles and social rules that govern interaction among its members. It is this latter aspect that is referred to under the rubric of social development. Much of the learning connected with social matters is transmitted through direct instruction on the part of the home and the school. However, the informal learnings acquired through exploration and unstructured associations with peers may contribute as much or more to the child's perception of his or her role in the social network. Social development continues throughout life, but in childhood the influence of play on the course of social development is especially evident.

## Infancy

Smiling is probably the earliest form of social interaction, and studies have shown that parents' delighted response to the first signs of smiling evoke reciprocal behavior in the infant. Healthy babies rapidly learn playful ways of prolonging these satisfying sequences, thus initiating some of the earliest modes of social interaction (Garvey, 1977). Language play also involves a major social component during infancy and early childhood, as in such games as peekaboo.

## Early Childhood

A stage of parallel play in which children engage individually in the same activity is followed at the age of about three by genuine collaborative play in groups of two or more. Social play is defined by Garvey (1977) as "a state of engagement in which the successful, non-literal behaviors of one partner are contingent on the non-literal behavior of the other partner [p. 570]." However, at this stage some of the features that characterize the social play of later stages, such as cooperation and competition, are lacking (Millar, 1968).

As play develops, its forms are determined less by the properties of the immediate environment and more by plans constructed in conjunction with peers. Aspects of the social world and expectations about the behavior of people provide the main materials for the dramatic play that is so characteristic of this age. In fact, it is in the context of play that young children develop and test out hypotheses about possible interactions and relationships among humans (Isaacs, 1940). When social relationships pose a problem for the child, play is often the vehicle through which feelings about the problem are vented and possible solutions acted out without the danger of possibly negative consequences. In this respect, play may have a cathartic quality and may also lead to the learning of new ways for handling difficult social situations. In this sense, fantasy play may be regarded as compensatory action (Curti, 1930).

Recurrent patterns of social interaction during social play document the appearance of socially desirable characteristics such as cooperation and sharing. Indeed, the give-and-take of social interaction implies a degree of cooperation and willingness to abide by the same rules, as witnessed by a child's indignation when the partner breaks a rule. In learning and practicing these rules, the child is laying the foundation for future social behavior and amassing a store of social information that will make future communication and interaction more rapid and effective. Recent research on reading comprehension, for example, has drawn attention to its dependence on prior knowledge of social "scripts," because much pertinent information is omitted on the assumption that the readers already possess it. It could therefore be argued that dramatic play promotes not only social learning but, indirectly, reading comprehension and possibly other forms of intellectual achievement.

Dramatic play also encourages preschool children to develop concepts of different social roles and to associate relevant behaviors with these roles. Children of this age seem to prefer status roles (e.g., doctor rather than patient) (Sachs, Goldman, & Chaille, 1982) and active rather than passive roles. Play also provides the opportunity to "try on" various roles to determine their desirability or appropriateness (Greif, 1976).

After the age of school entry, the incidence of dramatic play appears to decline sharply, to be replaced to some extent by fantasy (Klinger, 1971). Social play provides both material for fantasy and a context for acting out the fantasies. Clubs and societies reinforce social rules but may, at the same time, provide an escape from adult rules when these become intolerable. Similarly, team games and sports offer an outlet for frustration while contributing to learning about social relationships.

### Adolescence

As children's experience broadens and their thought structures become more elaborated and reversible, the range of problems that can be addressed through fantasy and playful activities increases accordingly. Whereas the younger child used dramatic play as a vehicle for the solution of personal problems, the adolescent can employ powers of fantasy to the solution of worldwide social and moral problems. Where the preschooler copes with anxiety by playing "hospital," the formal–operational child may participate in a mock United Nations debate on nuclear power or world hunger.

Sports, hobbies, and other leisure-time activities may be a medium for fantasy, but they also provide the opportunity for reality testing without negative consequences. Both aspects, fantasy and reality, are necessary for valid self-appraisal that, in turn, leads to more satisfactory social relationships. In brief, most leisure or play activities of the adolescent years contribute in some way to the continuing process of socialization into the society.

## EMOTIONAL DEVELOPMENT

Western societies emphasize not only social relationships and roles, but personal qualities such as independence and initiative. Indeed, much of the social learning that takes place in childhood involves a balance between the individual's needs to develop these qualities and the demands of the society for compliance with certain prescribed norms of behavior. Play is an important medium for learning this balance, and children deprived of adequate play experience frequently find difficulty in adapting to these social demands. On the other hand, when the family and school climate is propitious, providing adequate space, materials, and benign supervision for free expression through play, the child develops a healthy attitude toward self and others as well as a zest for life and an openness to new experiences.

## Infancy

Play has been characterized by some scholars as stimulus-seeking. Certainly much of the playful behavior of the infant and young child seems designed to elicit reactions from objects or other people. All animal species, including humans, appear to require a steady diet of novel stimulation if they are to function effectively. Infants deprived of adequate stimulation develop a syndrome that includes poor health, vulnerability to infection, listless behavior, and impaired ability to learn (Spitz & Wolf, 1946). Conversely, the baby who receives loving treatment from significant others begins to form an idea of separateness from other people that is the germ of the later sense of identity (Sullivan, 1953). The bodily contact that is part of adult play with babies also builds in the infant a sense of security and belonging. When parental behavior is *consistently* nurturing, the infant learns to trust the environment and to make social predictions about human behavior.

## Early Childhood

Play can be a medium for the expression of positive feelings and for learning to handle those feelings constructively. The ability to move freely in large, well-equipped spaces and the new-found facility with language induce in the child a sense of autonomy, confirming his ability to master the environment and engendering feelings of self-worth and power. Improved manipulation of objects and tools, increased verbal and communicative ability, and widening social relations all contribute to this sense of worth.

When conditions are less than optimal, the process of establishing patterns of autonomy and initiative may take longer, or even be permanently impaired. Fortunately, play provides the setting whereby many of these problems may be resolved. In fact, the value of play as a therapeutic tool even in cases of severe emotional disturbance has long been recognized (Axline, 1947; Klein, 1975), and certain kinds of play materials such as dolls or miniature worlds have become widely used tools in the diagnosis and treatment of emotional deviation. Though a wide range of feelings may surface in the course of play therapy, the most common are those associated with aggression against the parent and attendant feelings of guilt or fear of retribution.

## Middle Childhood

The major task of the elementary school years is to learn the tools of the culture, whether these be weapons for hunting, tools for building houses, or the tools of literacy required in technological societies. Related to this achievement and perhaps equally important is what Erikson (1963) has called "the establishment of patterns of industry." It appears that the child's feelings of autonomy and initiative must now be turned to the task of mastering the tools that will provide access to a place of recognition and security within the society. Such mastery is accompanied not only by praise and extrinsic rewards, but by a profound satisfaction with the achievement. Recent research is beginning to confirm Erikson's thesis that middle childhood is a critical time for the establishment of work attitudes, and that if the opportunity is lost, the person may experience lifelong difficulty in persevering with, or deriving satisfaction from, work.

Ellis points out that children often loaf and dawdle at their tasks but seldom at their play; they take the purposes of their play seriously, and that is why they put the best of their ability into it. Fortunately, young children do not make the distinction between work and play. Consequently, if tool learning is embedded in a context of activities meaningful to them, it is not differentiated from other enjoyable tasks.

Leisure-time activities are a further source of emotional satisfaction. As the child participates in games and other social functions, the camaraderie engendered in these situations leads to a further enhancement of self-esteem and increased emotional stability. Play provides opportunities for developing qualities of leadership, followership, cooperation, competition, teamwork, perseverance, flexibility, toughness, altruism, idealism, etc., all of which contribute to the development of a positive but realistic self-concept.

## Adolescence

Many important decisions face the adolescent, most of them concerning his relationships to the society of which he is a member. Uppermost in the minds of most adolescents is the choice of a career, and this choice is frequently related to a leisure-time activity that the young person finds satisfying. This activity may represent an extension of a school subject or it may be extracurricular. In some cases, the choice of a career grows out of the hobby, while in other cases the hobby is deliberately selected as a way of furthering career plans. Second, and in some cases only slightly secondary in importance, is the choice of opposite sex companions. Given the general preoccupation in this culture with matters of sex, and the very real necessity of finding a suitable companion with whom to settle down, it is not surprising that much of the adolescent's social activity centers around these problems. In fact, play provides the major opportunities for learning about social relations involving the opposite sex and for developing an awareness of personal feelings associated with matters of love and marriage.

As noted in a previous section, the adolescent is also concerned about broader social issues. Leisure activities may include reading, attending lectures, and joining demonstrations and other forms of protest in search of solutions. Clearly, in these forms of behavior, the distinction between play and other forms of behavior begins to blur. Adolescents are capable of working with enthusiasm and dedication on their chosen projects and, as in adult scientific and artistic pursuits, the distinction between work and play is no longer feasible.

## THE INTEGRATED SELF

At any stage of development, the individual is characterized by psychological integrity. While it is convenient to study the various aspects of development as separate systems, in practice, the person acts as a single dynamic, organismic whole. There is continuous interplay among the several components: physical development enables the child to extend the range of cognitive and linguistic activity. Communication with others is made possible by the advent of operational thought and the refinement of linguistic abilities. Social interaction provides the basis for development of the sense of self and for emotional growth.

### Infancy

The infant's helpless condition and basic needs for food, warmth, and sleep are the stimulus for the provision of loving care by the parents. In providing nurturance, the parents simultaneously cater to the baby's need for human contact that is the prototype for all later social interaction. While nursing and feeding, the mother talks to the baby, matching her words to appropriate gestures and nonverbal behavior. The baby is thus exposed to a continuous flow of linguistic stimulation. Although he does not, as yet, understand the words, through voice intonation and body posture, the infant may understand the feeling tone of the message. Hence the mother's vocalizations take on social significance, are attended to selectively, and are the basis for finer discriminations than other stimuli in the immediate environment. Finally, the first social relationship provides the foundation for those indispensable qualities of trust and autonomy that are the primary characteristics of emotional health and stability.

### Early Childhood

Physical growth is more rapid during the years of early childhood than at any other point in the life cycle. The young child delights in newfound prowess, and brings a seemingly inexhaustible fund of energy to the task of exploring and learning about the environment. With the acquisition of object permanence, the child can begin the long task of developing concepts of those objects. The rapid gains in language facility contribute to cognitive attainments such as labeling, categorizing, discriminating, and generalizing. Conversely, as the child's thinking becomes more operational (in the Piagetian sense) and abstract, the linguistic modes needed to express these refinements are correspondingly developed.

Locomotion and the ability to communicate also bring the young child into new spheres of social interaction. The child's drive for autonomy and mastery of the environment inevitably lead to new patterns of behavior. The child's will may clash with the desires of others, and he/she must learn to cope with hitherto unfamiliar reactions. If children attend nursery school, they are exposed to strange adults whose behavior may be very different from that of their parents, and who make unaccustomed demands on them. Responses which have formerly seemed appropriate and have been reinforced may now have to be modified or discarded. In brief, the child must learn not only that there are alternative modes of behavior, but also what they are and under what conditions they are appropriate.

As children are finding their role in the social microcosm, they are simultaneously verifying their own sense of worth and building their self-esteem on a solid and realistic foundation. Emotional development is thus highly dependent on the other aspects and, in turn, affects them in a positive or negative direction.

## Middle Childhood

Continued increases in height, weight, and physical dexterity permit the elementary school child to engage in a number of activities not previously available. Many of these activities are conducted in groups. However, the social groupings at this period may have different characteristics than those of the early childhood years. There is a stronger team spirit, and the activities tend to be governed by social rules. Such changes are made possible by the child's attainment of higher levels of cognitive functioning. Through the operations of reversibility, children are able to derive logical and mathematical conclusions that were formerly beyond their understanding, and to apply this new knowledge to games and other social pursuits. Language is an important vehicle for cognitive and social functioning at this age. The games of this period frequently employ language play as well as cognitive strategies.

The zest that went into play in the earlier years is now directed toward the mastery of school subjects. Now that the broad outlines of the child's personality have been established and a degree of emotional maturity attained, the child is ready to master the tools of the culture and to establish working patterns that will stand him/her in good stead during the adult years.

## Adolescence

The early years of adolescence are marked by new growth spurts that may temporarily upset the equilibrium achieved in the previous stage. Physical development may outstrip the attainment of cognitive and social maturity, creating confusion in the adolescents and consternation in their parents and teachers. When physical growth leads to unrealistic expectations on the part of adults, conflict and tension may ensue.

Meanwhile, cognitive development is proceeding apace. Formal operational thought permits adolescents to engage in theoretical speculation, and thus gives wings to their fantasies. The linguistic system is now almost completely developed, and is fully utilized in both intellectual and social pursuits.

Toward the end of adolescence, a new level of integration is reached. Through successful negotiation of societal hurdles, the young person comes to realize a potential role in the society, to understand his or her own strengths and limitations, and to attain the social and moral insights necessary for effective citizenship. As all these strands come together, emotional maturity is assured. Standing on the brink of adulthood, the adolescent is ready and eager to face the challenges that life has to offer.

## REFERENCES

Athey, I. Syntax, semantics, and reading. In J. T. Guthrie (Ed.), *Cognition, curriculum, and comprehension.* Newark, Del.: International Reading Association, 1974.

Athey, I. Cognitive development through play. Unpublished manuscript, 1978.

Axline, V. M. *Play therapy.* New York: Ballantine, 1947.

Bower, T. G. R. The visual world of infants. *Scientific American.* 1966, *6,* 80–92.

Bruner, J. S. The growth of representational processes in children. In J. Anglin (Ed.), *Beyond the information given.* New York: Norton, 1974.

Bruner, J. The nature and uses of immaturity. In J. S. Bruner, A. Jolly, & K. Sylva (Eds.), *Play: Its role in development and evolution.* Englewood Cliffs, N.J.: Prentice–Hall, 1976.

Curti, M. W. *Child psychology.* London: Longmans Green, 1930.

Dansky, J. L., & Silverman, I. W. Effects of play on associative fluency in preschool children. *Developmental Psychology,* 1973, *9,* 38–43.

Ellis, M. J. *Why people play.* Englewood Cliffs, N.J.: Prentice–Hall, 1973.

Erikson, E. H. *Childhood and society.* New York: Norton, 1963.

Espy, W. *Word play.* New York: Potter Press, 1975.

Fantz, R. L. Visual perception and experience in infancy: Issues and approaches. In F. A. Young & D. B. Lindsley (Eds.), *Early experience in visual information processing in perceptual and reading disorders.* Washington, D.C.: National Academy of Sciences, 1970.

Garvey, C. *Play: The developing child.* Cambridge, Ma.: Harvard University Press, 1977.

Gilmore, J. B. Play: A special behavior. In R. N. Haber (Ed.), *Current research in motivation.* New York: Holt, Rinehart & Winston, 1966.

Greif, E. B. Sex role playing in preschool children. In J. S. Bruner, A. Jolly, & K. Sylva (Eds.), *Play: Its role in development and evolution.* Englewood Cliffs, N.J.: Prentice–Hall, 1976.

Groos, K. *The play of man.* New York: Appleton, 1916.

Hall, G. S. *Adolescence: Its psychology and its relations to physiology, anthropology, sociology, sex, crime, religion, and education* (Vol. I). New York: Appleton, 1916.
Hershenon, M. Visual discrimination in the human newborn. *Journal of Comparative Physiological Psychology,* 1964, *58,* 270–276.
Inhelder, B. & Piaget, J. *The early growth of logic in the child.* New York: Norton, 1969.
Isaacs, S. *Social development in young children.* London: Routledge & Sons, 1940.
Isaacs, S. *Intellectual growth in young children.* New York: Schocken, 1966.
Jakobson, R. *Child language, aphasia, and phonological universals.* The Hague: Mouton, 1968.
Klein, M. *The psychoanalysis of children.* (A. Strachey, trans.). New York: Delacorte Press, 1975.
Klinger, E. *Structure and functions of fantasy.* New York: Wiley Interscience, 1971.
Lewis, M. M. *Language and the child.* Atlantic Highlands, N.J.: Humanities Press, 1969.
McNeill, D. The development of language. In P. H. Mussen (Ed.), *Carmichael's manual of child psychology.* New York: Wiley, 1970.
Menyuk, P. *Sentences children use.* Cambridge, Ma.: MIT Press, 1969.
Millar, S. *The psychology of play.* Baltimore, Md.: Penguin Press, 1968.
Miranda, S. B. Visual abilities and pattern preference of premature infants and full-term neonates. *Journal of Experimental Child Psychology,* 1970, *10,* 189–205.
Nicolich, L. M. Beyond sensorimotor intelligence: Assessment of symbolic maturity through analysis of pretend play. *Merrill–Palmer Quarterly,* 1977, *23,* 89–99.
Opie, I. & Opie, P. *Children's games in streets and playgrounds.* London: Clarendon Press, 1969.
Piaget, J. *The origins of intelligence in children.* New York: International Universities Press, 1952.
Piaget, J. *Play, dreams, and imitation.* New York: Norton, 1962.
Sachs, J., Goldman, J., & Chaille, C. Planning in pretend play: Using language to coordinate narrative development. Paper presented at the annual conference of the American Educational Research Association, New York, 1982.
Schiller, F. *Essays, aesthetical and philosophical.* London: George Bell & Sons, 1875.
Spencer, H. *Principles of psychology* (3rd ed., vol. 2, part 2). New York: Appleton, 1896.
Spitz, R. & Wolf, K. Anaclitic depression: An inquiry into the genesis of psychiatric conditions in early childhood. *The psychoanalytic study of the child,* 1946, *2,* 313–342.
Sullivan, H. S. *The interpersonal theory of psychiatry.* New York: Norton, 1953.
*Webster's Third New International Dictionary.* Springfield, Ma.: G. & C. Merriam, 1961.
White, R. W. Motivation reconsidered: The concept of competence. *Psychological Review,* 1959, *66,* 297–333.

# 3 The Phenomenon of Bipolarity in Play Theories

Brian Sutton-Smith
Diana Kelly-Byrne
*University of Pennsylvania*

Whatever other changes may be going on in social science, a survey of the number of articles and books on the subject matter of play indicates an ascending curve of productivity. In a recent count that we have made within developmental psychology, the first 40 years of this century produced 142 articles on play, and the last 40 years has produced 576, with the real leap forward being in the 1970s with over 200 articles and more than 20 books with a research focus (Sutton-Smith, 1983). Almost without exception these articles have found some values in play. Play has increasingly been recognized as a serious scholarly subject throughout this century. It has been rehabilitated from prior negative attitudes by claims that it has a role in animal and human evolution, a role in human adjustment, in human learning, exploration, cognition, and creativity.

So extensive have become the claims for it, and so ill-defined the global nature of the concept itself, that it has become appropriate to speak of the idealization of play (Sutton-Smith, 1981). For whatever reasons, researchers have been more inclined to give the concept support than to define it carefully.

There are important exceptions to this criticism. The work of Berlyne (1960), Ellis (1974), Hutt (1979), and others has led to useful distinctions between exploration and play. Piaget's distinction between accommodation and assimilation is of parallel import (1961). Piaget further distinguishes between play and creative imagination. The work of various linguists (Weir, 1970) makes it necessary to recall the older concept of practice or exercise, the repeating of facts to some point of functional habituation. In sum, when we are talking about the spontaneous learning of children (or epistemic activity) we can sometimes distinguish the analytic functions of intelligence from the synthesizing functions of intelligence (exploration from construction), and we sometimes can distinguish these functions from mere practice. When it comes to mental activity, we can sometimes distinguish spontaneous analytic thought from spontaneous creative thought or the imagination. In adulthood also distinctions can be made between dreams, reverie (daydreams), and the imagination. Although it would take a major conceptual and research effort to fully sort out these various distinctions, we believe there is sufficient grounds already for *not* calling them play. This is true even realizing that it is not always easy to distinguish between them or between them and play; realizing also that in the synaesthetic world of childhood, such distinctions are not always present. Further, realizing that even when such distinctions are made, it is still possible for such additional phenomena to occur as exploratory play, constructive play, playful practice, etc.

The aim of this chapter is not to define the full range of voluntary learning behavior that might include these various kinds of activities previously mentioned, but rather to distinguish play from them by calling attention to its own special characteristics. We will seek to show that each of the major theories of play from Huizinga through Bateson, whether these theories are historical, evolutionary, psychoanalytic, anthropological, cognitive, animal, linguistic, communicational, or philosophical, contains a fundamental bipolarity. This is an extension of an earlier argument in the *Dialectics of Play* (Sutton-Smith, 1978). If we ignore whether the theorist is talking about antecedents, framing, structure, or function, but rather sort the theoretical elements into whether they contribute to the status quo of individual and social life, or whether they introduce novelty into that status quo, we find that all theories, to some extent, cover both conservative and innovative functions. In order to rid this discussion of any egregious political overtones, we talk of the first group as the class of equilibrating concepts and of the second group as that of disequilibrating concepts.

We should perhaps begin by defining what we mean by this bipolarity that we are finding so central to play, but we would rather build a case for it inductively by proceeding through the theories. Let it be sufficient to say that historically most of the earlier emphasis on play was on its imitative character. In much nineteenth century anthropological writings the children's play was seen as a template of the adult culture. Helen Schwartzman (1978) has put this down to the selective perceptual activity of male anthropologists. There might be something to that, or it might be that play in tribal cultures was inherently more conserving than play in modern society. For her part, Schwartzman (1978) emphasized that play is always a kind of transformation, a creative and novel phenomenon. So we have an older attitude to play that sees play as a reflection of and a contribution to the society as it is, and we have a newer attitude to play that sees it as a more radical and creative process. I will argue that both of these meanings are central to play, and will call the first an equilibrating concept (meaning that the individual or society is kept in balance by the activity) and the other a disequilibrating concept (meaning that the individual or society is required to deal with some novelty because of this activity).

TABLE 3.1
Bipolar Features of Play Theories

| *Major Investigator* | *Equilibrial Features* | *Disequilibrial Features* |
|---|---|---|
| Huizinga | voluntary<br>fun<br>childlike | bloody and fatal contests |
| Groos, Hall, & Freud (Erikson) | play as preparation<br>mastery, planning<br>abreaction | atavistic<br>recapitulation<br>conflict; compensation<br>repetition-compulsion<br>hallucination wish fulfillment |
| Turner, Kelly-Byrne | normative pole<br>communitas, intimacy | inversion;<br>orectic polarity |
| Piaget | cognitive consolidation | assimilation, distortion |
| Berlyne (Shultz) | specific exploration | diversive exploration<br>arousal modulation and play |
| Bruner, Singer, Saltz et al. | problem solving,<br>role reversal | creativity, imagination |
| Fagen | functional flexibility<br>specific skills,<br>bonding | dysfunctional risk |
| Geertz | metasocial commentaries | deep play |
| Weir, Kirshenblatt-Gimblett | foregrounding | nonsense |
| Bateson | metacommunication and social construction | paradox<br>negatives & reversals |
| Derrida | aporic communication | deconstruction |

## HUIZINGA

We will begin with Huizinga's work (1955) because when it appeared it was the most radical thesis ever presented on the character of play. His argument that society is generated by the same formative processes that generate play completely reversed the usual disrespect in which that subject matter was held. Whatever else may be its shortcomings, and they are considerable, his theory gave play a role in culture unrivaled in other theorizing except perhaps that of Erik Erikson (1977), where phases of child play were seen as models of adult institutions (religious, legal, artistic, etc.). Huizinga's book continues to be a center of controversy in sports, in sociology, and psychology (Gruneau, 1980).

As he describes play, it is on the one hand voluntary, it is fun, it has its own space–time context, and is characterized by fixed rules and joy. On the other hand, it is accompanied by a feeling of tension and the consciousness that it is different from ordinary life. There is a bipolarity here. When Huizinga (1955) is criticising modern professional sports, he says: "The spirit of the professional is no longer the true play spirit; it is lacking in spontaneity and carelessness [p. 197]." Really to play, he says, a man must play like a child. On the other hand, when he is describing historical examples of play, he gives us contests in pain endurance. Huizinga discusses contests in mutual bragging and execration, in scurrilous songs, in squandering marches, in fatal and bloody play, duels fought to the death. "That the majority of Greek contests were fought out in deadly earnest is no reason for separating the agony from play or for denying the play character of the former," he asserts (p. 48). Again, "It is of the utmost significance that these Roman gladiatorial combats, bloody, superstitious and illiberal as they were, nevertheless kept to the last the simple word ludus with all its associations of freedom and joyousness [p. 74]."

So, Huizinga is telling us that this thing he deals with called play can be on the one hand:

fun
voluntary
joyous
childlike
spontaneous & careless

and on the other can be:

tense
disinterested
bloody
fatal
illiberal

It is a wonderful antinomy; a conflict in description that plagues the understanding of his classic work.

## EVOLUTIONARY THINKING

If we move back historically to some of the earliest academic thinking on the subject of play we have on the one hand the stress that play, as a part of the evolutionary plan, prepares the child for adulthood. The child is immature so that he can play and can be prepared (Groos, 1901/1976). On the other hand, while he is playing he is also recapitulating earlier stages in phylogenetic history, and if he does not work through these atavisms there is the prospect that he will remain of a primitive, even criminal disposition (Hall, 1917). In short, play gets one fit for society through a whole series of stages of relative unfitness and barbaric character. It is at the same time a preparation for social grace as it is an exhibition in gracelessness.

## FREUDIAN AND POSTPLAY THEORY

Here we find the same antinomy. On the one hand the child plays to become a master of anxiety and conflict (Erikson, 1951). What has been suffered in ordinary experience must here be abreacted. Play restores the child to mental health. This is certainly an equilibrating doctrine. On the other hand, the content of play is compensation, wish fulfillment, hallucinatory, and full of symbolic content from the child's polymorphous perversibility. Here again, the content is disturbing to say the least. Here are two stories from a child that are very playful and are full of Freudian content. They illustrate both sides of the Freudian thesis. In the first story the child (male, age seven) is the victim. In the story told 6 months later the child is the victor. At the same time, the story's content is hardly culturally standard material (Sutton-Smith, 1981):

*Story 1:*

Once there was two babies and they hung from the ceiling naked and their weenies was so long their mother needed 300 and 20 rooms to fit half of it in. But they had to chop half of it off. And the baby had to go to the bathroom. So, since they didn't have no bathroom big enough for his weener to fit, so he put his weener out of the window and Nixon happened to be walking along. And he said, "Flying hotdogs, I never heard of it." And then he said, "Well, I might have one, it looks good." So the baby had to go to the bathroom and Nixon tooka BIG BITE. And there the was a trampoline, because he was in the circus, and he went through the ceiling. And then by accident he went so fast and he was holding on to the weener so hard that he went straight smack into the middle of the ocean. And then—all of a sudden—he saw a giant sea spider. And his hair standed straight up. And the baby was coming so fast he landed on Nixon's head and made the long straight-up hair into bushy curls. And then he went, "I'm going to get out of here real quick, man." And um, and then the baby saw this giant anchor and he was holding onto it. And then Nixon went so fast under water, he went like a torpedo. And he stretched the baby's weener so far that it was four thousand times the size it was. The End.

*Story 2:*

Once upon a time there were two babies. They loved, they hated spinach. So once their mother gave them a big pot of spinach, each with one fried egg on it. And they hated it *so much,* they threw it at their mother. She gave them another pot of spinach with *two* eggs on it this time and they were even madder and they threw it at their father this time. Then their mother gave them two pots of spinach with six fried eggs on it. They threw it at their sister. Then, when Nixon heard of this, he called them "The Fried Egg Family." But the baby was angry at Nixon. So when Nixon came to their house, they did nothing to him. But as he was walking out the door, the baby saw him and they stuck out their weenies and then they put their weenies to work. And when Nixon saw these things, he flipped. But then, they pulled in their weener and put 2 buns on top of them and put some catsup and spinach and then Nixon got right back up and he started to bite. All of a sudden, the babies went pissing and shot their X-Y-Z. And Nixon was so upset he almost, his heart almost cracked. But then, they had more strategy.

So when he was walking over the mountain, they made flying hamburgers and then Nixon screamed, "We're being invaded by flying hamburgers!" And then the babies made flying hamburgers shoot out missile hotdogs and then Nixon had a very good idea! And he ate it—the hotdogs. But Nixon was so dumb, those hotdogs were solid metal and when he bit on them, they cracked his teeth and he was so upset. And then a lady came and said "Will you help me across the street?" And Nixon said, "Whaaaaah." "You are weird, Man," the lady said. And then the babies had little bit more strategy. They started shooting spinach with fried eggs on top. And then New York called Nixon "The Fried Egg President." That's all. The end (p. 532–533)

## VICTOR TURNER

In recent years what Freudians have asserted on the individual level has been best paralleled on the anthropological level by Victor Turner and colleagues (Turner, 1969, 1974, 1982; Babcock, 1978). Turner sees society as inevitably in conflict and argues that festivals and play occasions, such as the Mardi Gras in which the lower orders of society rule during the festival, arise to temporarily correct the balance and to restore a sense of community where basic divisions might otherwise tear the society apart. According to him, the play world inverts the values that are to be found in the real world. Play is defined by Babcock (1978) as symbolic inversion that:

> may be broadly defined as any act of expressive behavior which inverts, contradicts, abrogates or in some fashion presents an alternative to commonly held cultural code values and norms, be they linguistic, literary or artistic, religious, social or political. Although, perhaps because, inversion is so basic to symbolic processes, so crucial to expressive behavior, it has not until recently been analytically isolated except in its obvious and overt forms such as rituals of rebellion, role reversal and institutionalized clowning [p. 14].

What is so interesting about this work is that the phenomenon of play reversal, which in Freudian psychogenic and individualistic terms might have been labelled as abreactive or as reaction–formative, or compensatory, is here shown to be a structural principle of the social order. It is argued that large classes of expressive behavior in many, perhaps all, cultural groups are given over to symbolizing in various antithetical ways some of the tensions generated by the conflicts within the normative culture. Although these symbolizations for the greater part appear to be ways of decreasing those tensions through the formations of new forms of collectivity or communitas, as Turner (1974) calls them occasionally, at critical junctures in history they may also provide the opportunity for radical behavior.

In general, however, Turner finds the effects of these social dramas to be conservative. What is important for our purposes is his suggestion that such dramas always contain both a normative and an orectic pole; they celebrate their community at the same time as they institutionalize its opposite through inverting power or through abandonment of inhibition over sex, aggression, etc.

Although the recent work of Kelly-Byrne (1982) contrasts methodologically with that of Turner, the conclusions are very similar. Here is an ethnographic and phenomenological study of the play of a 7-year-old girl. She played with this child throughout a period of 1 year, periodically taping the encounters. Unlike the therapeutic approach, she played with the child rather than diagnosed or interpreted the child's behavior. From an initial situation in which the child introduced her own reversal of the power relationships within her own family, there gradually developed a great sharing of the initiatives. Originally completely dominated by the child, she was eventually permitted to play a more active role. As the latter occurred the child increasingly introduced into the play her more intimate and personal concerns. What began as highly symbolic statements of her relationships to her mother and father developed toward frank conversations. Kelly-Byrne contends that the play arena was in fact an area of largely defensive and ambivalent behavior that, when shared by both parties, permitted bonds of mutual acceptance that in due course displaced the need for such play. Unlike Turner, who was dealing with enduring community conflicts, she was dealing with developmental conflicts that could be transcended by increasing maturity in personal relationships. In both cases, however, the play is claimed to have led to greater social bonding, to communitas, or to intimacy.

## JEAN PIAGET

With Piaget (1961) we shift to a consideration of play largely as something done by solitary individuals or between themselves and objects. On the surface there is an amazing lack of compatibility between this way of thinking about play as something to do with solitariness, and the way of thinking about it that one finds in anthropology, linguistics, and communication theory, where it is the sociality of play that is a first assumption (Sutton-Smith, 1979). Piaget's theory deals with play largely in terms of an adaptation scenario involving a polarity of subject–object relationships, within which play represents the extreme of the subjective pole. His conception of what a child is doing in play is not unlike our adult conception of what we are doing in reveries, where there is little question that the goings on are highly subjective or "distorted", to use his phrase, and not much troubled by accommodation to surrounding events (Sutton-Smith, in press).

When we ask what is the point of these pure assimilations, Piaget tells us that they consolidate the gains already made in intelligent life. The mental operations already established are here used again in a new way, thus keeping them in good shape. The child baffled by the world of which he is a part at least in his own play can guarantee himself a sense of ego continuity. Thus Piaget, like all the others, sees the content of a child's play as quite bizarre, but its function as equilibrating. In passing, one might say that this is something of a paradox within the theory because only true operations can be equilibrating in emotional terms and worth their salt for retaining and continuing to use and exercise those pre-established mental operations (Sutton-Smith, 1966, 1982a).

It is rather surprising to find psychoanalytics, symbolic anthropologists, and Piaget all describing play content as bizarre and play function as equilibrating. In all cases also the instigations are disequilibrial personal conflict (Freud), social conflict (Turner) and cognitive disequilibrium (Piaget).

## BERLYNE, SHULTZ AND OTHERS

The behaviorist case is a little harder to deal with in the present terms because most attention is given to environmental principles of stimulus arrangements (novelty, conflict, etc.) as instigators of play, and to neurological states as explanations of what then occurs. There is little attention to the play itself, although Berlyne's specific exploration versus diversive exploration (1960) and Hutt's exploration versus play (1979) begin to give us connotations of one kind of activity that is closely related to its stimulus instigators and another kind that transcends and transforms the stimulus. Exploration sounds like Piaget's accommodations to the object world, and diversive exploration and play sound like Piaget's assimilation of the world to one's own fantasies. Another way of putting it, following Shultz, is in terms of a neurological arousal, conditional on the character of the stimuli, as contrasted with arousal modulation that is under the control of the subject (Shultz, 1979). One could find across the contrasts again a state in which the child uses its intelligence upon the world as it is, and a state in which the subject departs from such worldly conditioning in a more subjective manner, the latter being play.

## BRUNER, SINGER, SALTZ, AND OTHERS

The idea of children's play as a kind of learning has probably the longest history of scholarship and belief. Current research efforts concentrate on play as a form of problem-solving (Bruner, Jolly, & Sylva, 1976) or on play as a kind of fantasy that contributes to the child's imagination (Singer, 1973) or to the child's competence at role reversibility and various other cognitive and characterological skills (Rubin, Fein, & Vandenberg, in press). The greatest body of experimental work in play over the past decades has focused in these areas. Many of the major protagonists, however, are quite skeptical about the not very reliable results they have achieved and about the view that play is actually what is occurring here. They suggest it might be rather some kind of tutorial learning.

Still, despite the disagreements, once again we have those who study play as learning and emphasize convergent cognitive results (problem-solving, learning role reversal) and those who emphasize divergent cognitive results (imagination, creativity, flexibility).

## FAGEN

In his new work, Robert Fagen (1981) presents a view that is as positive a promotion of play in animal evolution development as one finds in the work of Erik Erikson (1977) or Huizinga (1955), both of whom similarly and sanguinely promote the role of play in cultural evolution. We might add that slight as may be the results in the play and learning studies just covered, they are similarly promoted by the optimism that play will indeed turn out to make a contribution to human development.

Fagen's central theme is that play is a creative force in evolution and development. It is a biological necessity he argues for animals whose life style involves actively modifying their environmental relationships in novel ways and creating environments for their own survival. In bacteria as in plants we have adaptation through external modification. In fishes, reptiles, amphibians, and the most primitive of birds we have adaptation through the use of stereotyped behavior patterns where there are fixed environmental contingencies. All other species have to construct their own environments. In some cases, as in insects, this is done in a routine way and there is no play. In others, flexibility is required and there is play. Animal play theorists, however, differ in whether they believe play trains only for species-typical motor skills (a kind of Piagetian view) or whether they think as does Fagen that the function of play is to produce individual behavioral variability, that is, complex generalized skills for interacting with a varied and changing social and physical environment. Again, some animal theorists put the major value of play on the social bonding that results from it.

Against these contentions, however, has to be balanced the evidence that play is often a very risky dysfunctional business to its animal participators. Play can lead to prolonged separations from the caregiver, to entrapment in rocks and mud, to danger from falling, to broken limbs, and to serious injuries in playfighting. According to Fagen, the amount of risk that the species can tolerate varies with their conditions of survival probability. When these are low, play is too risky. When predation is high, food short, conditions crowded, unchanging, and competitive, there is less play. More play is associated with more territory and more food. So with the animal research we are once again left with the mystery of a bipolarity of functional and dysfunctional claims.

## CLIFFORD GEERTZ

Some years ago Geertz introduced the notion of *deep play* (1973) into the literature, which is play that is irrational to engage in because of its potential danger to life, limb, or reputation. His illustration was cockfighting amongst the Balinese. This most decorous people has an abhorrence of animality as well as a disgust about human defecating, eating, and sex. However, a Balinese favorite pastime, as he describes it, is to watch and gamble upon the outcome of cockfights that are nasty and bloody affairs. He argues that in this highly hierarchical and almost caste-bound society, the outcomes of the game can upset the status rankings as well as indulge the participants in a carnival of animality, both inversions of normal social processes. In his interpretations, the events themselves are like a moral reading of what would happen to the larger society if its checks and balances of a political and psychological sort were overthrown. The chaos of the cockfight is an indication of the chaos that would ensue. Despite the risks, therefore, he argues the lessons are worth the game.

K. Alford (1982) in her current research on dysfunctional celebrations in tribal societies examined cross-culturally has argued that there are many cases in which seasonal festivals involving sexual license, inebriation, and fighting lead to death, injury, the trampling on children, and so on.

We have seen that Huizinga provides many examples of fatal and bloody contests. In our own society we regularly consign young football players to paraplegia and boxers to brain damage. Even children's play is replete with episodes of daring, naughtiness, risk, pranks, obscenities, and sexual and aggressive play as the works in childrens' folklore make very clear (Knapp & Knapp, 1976; Opie & Opie, 1968; Sutton-Smith, 1981). If Geertz's examples of deep play are explained to college students and they are asked for modern equivalents one is surprised with the amount of risk that can be involved in their play. Here are some examples from our own college students:

drinking to excess and competitively while driving
drinking and climbing buildings
gambling with the whole of one's monthly allowance
sexual play without contraceptives
competitive drinking (''Whales Tales'')
canoeing unknown white waters
flirting with strangers
hitchhiking in the Middle East or South America
physical sports under adverse conditions (skiing, etc.)
spouse swapping and secret ''affairs,'' amongst the married

## RUTH WEIR

In linguistics the work of Ruth Weir (1970) in taping the bedtime verbal activity of her 2-year-old son has been taken as a critical event in establishing the importance of children's verbal play in their language growth. She placed a microphone next to the child's crib and strung a 30 foot cable into the next room in which the tape recorder was operating. She was then able to paint a picture of a child in his own spontaneous activity, gradually building up ever more coherent sentences, and practicing away with great repetition at his syntax and semantics almost like some grammar book. Unfortunately, in her references to his intensive activity she sometimes refers to him as exploring, sometimes as practicing, and sometimes as playing, and it is not very clear when one or the other is involved. Once again we are stuck with that vagueness about what is play and what is not play, which is typical of the whole literature on this subject.

However, if there is any preference in Weir's work (1970) it seems to be to argue that ''*Sound* is what is played with and it is done within the framework of paradigmatic and syntagmatic exercises [p. 144].'' That is, she seems to feel that if the prosodics (intonation, stress, rhyme, etc.) are foregrounded it is more likely to be play than if structure or content is what is the focus. The idea is that the sound of the language is not what we usually pay direct attention to in speaking; instead we pay attention to the meaning. When children cease to follow our will in this matter they may show an intensive and playful interest in manipulating these sounds in a variety of manners.

If the manipulation is nonsensical, then we usually can use that as an index that it is play. If it is not nonsensical, however, (and much of the Weir corpus is not) then we may well be dealing with the practicing of sounds rather than the playing with sounds.

Here is an example of nonsense verbal play from a girl who was one of the story tellers in a recent project (Sutton-Smith, 1981).

Two-year-old Cathy told us "normative" stories for 15 months. Her typical stories were as follows:

Batman dig
he went to bed
him come right up
then him mommy said "go back to bed"
and Batman got woke up again
and him mommy said "go right to bed" him mommy smack him bum
he went away
and then he went home
I finished.

However, after a year of familiarity with us she lapsed into the following "play".

Now there was a pa ka
Boon, goo
There was a dog doo doo
And he didn't like dog doo doo
Then there was a man named Snowball
And he didn't like snow
Cha cha
Doo choo
Cha cha
Doo choo
I named dog doo doo
Christopher say
Dog doo doo
Then there were a boy named Taw taw
O
Too too
There there was a Captain Blooper he had a book and he were very bad and it hurt him
Then there was a blooper pa pa
Pa pa
There was Superman coming and he hurt both of him knees
Then they were flying and they went right in the ocean and he got bite from a shark
And he didn't like when he got bite from a shark
Then kla kla toe toe

Tee tah
Caw caw caw caw caw caw caw caw caw caw caw caw caw caw caw caw caw caw caw caw caw caw caw caw caw
Now ay pah pah kla klee
Sa see
Too tee
Tah tah too tee
Chee chaw
Ta Klu
Kli klu
Kla Kla
Klu fu
Klee kla
Koo koo
Say say
Klee kla
Koo Koo
say say
Klee klee
Klip kla
Klee klee
Klip kla
She she
Fik ahh
Tangoo nah
Ka pa
Popeye the sailor man
Bad guy him be very bad to him
And I spit out a words

The point of this kind of example, for our present purposes, is that at least in the linguistic area we can contend that play can be observed in the implicit bipolarity between sensible and nonsensible meanings. Play itself plays upon the difference between sense and nonsense (Kirschenblatt-Gimblett, 1976).

## BATESON

Bateson's (1972) treatment of play as a kind of communication states the bipolar character of play more explicitly than any of the other theories. Usually Bateson is paid most attention for his discussion of metacommunication; the fact that animals and humans must give off messages to indicate that they are playing. Unlike everyday communication, which may be given off without self-announcements as to its character, play has to announce itself as well as be itself.

Thus at breakfast one can simply say "Pass the toast," and that communication usually works without further modification. However, in play one has to first say, "Let's play passing the toast." If you agree to this reframing, only then can we get on with passing the imagined toast. Following Bateson there has been much attention to such messages, to play faces, to access rituals, negotiations, negations, exaggerations, miniaturizations, minimalizations, transformations, etc. as ways of metacommunicating that play is the matter at hand.

For present purposes, the most important thing about Bateson was his stress on play as a kind of paradox. The player indicates that one thing is so, but at the same time that it is not so. I am mother, but I am not really mother. I am only playing mother. In the case of animals, there is his famous quote about dogs playfighting. Each dog must know that their playful nipping of each other is not real biting. They must know that the nip connotes a bite but not what a bite connotes. Their play stands for biting, but not what real biting stands for, which might be real damage, or real death. The even greater complexity of the matter begins to emerge when Bateson says of play that we must say the opposite of what we mean (nip not bite) when we mean the opposite (bite not nip) of what we say. These are not only logical communicational propositions with Bateson, but are based on the fact that animals have no negative so negatives must be illustrated positively by not really biting but only partially biting. On the other hand, although humans do have negatives in play they are generally dealing with matters that are not fully accessible to consciousness, and for which there are also no negatives. Here Bateson follows Freud in the view that primary process does not deal in negatives. Play must, therefore, state positively what it means negatively, and the way to do this is to state the truth in a reverse form. If the truth is that I am anxious about being a weak powerless child, then in play I can state this truth by becoming a powerful Wonder Woman. I can say the opposite (power) of what I mean (weakness), in order to mean the opposite (weakness) of what I say (power). Bateson converts the Freudian notion of reaction formation from an individual problem in symptomology to a general communicational truth. One can make more explicit the Bateson nip/bite conundrum perhaps by pointing out that our play not only is not the thing to which it refers, it is often in its own imaginative way much worse. Thus, when playing school as a 5-year-old, we not only play the teacher as he is (an equilibrating process) but we also play the teacher as a monster that he is usually not (a disequilibrating process). In order to add this wish fulfillment of the Freudian view to Bateson, we have to amend his famous statement about the nip connoting a bite and not what a bite connotes, to a nip connoting a bite, and even worse than a bite connotes.

The equilibrating part of Bateson's theory is that the child is learning the subtleties of metacommunication and, therefore, implicitly the way in which reality is socially constructed. The child is learning to be a social inventor as well as an imaginative monster.

## JACQUES DERRIDA

The gradual permeation of strict philosophy by a playful world hypothesis as contrasted, for example, with Pepper's (1961) formist, causalist, contextualist, and organicist metaphors is a story told by Jacques Derrida (1970). Strictly speaking, Derrida is not talking about play, but about the polymorphous vagary of the human sign function. For him there is no given, final, or static relation between the sign and the signified; there is only that plethora of possibilities to which our minds are heir. We cannot help considering or dreaming alternatives. In all communication there is an element of undecidability or "free play." According to Derrida (1970): "In his endeavor to understand the world, man, therefore, always has at his disposal a surplus of signification [p. 261]." Also, Derrida uses this open-endedness of our meanings to show the embeddedness of most philosophies' very selective usage of language. He deconstructs the reliance of philosophy on underlying metaphors in the language that mediates that philosophy. As some have put it, he reduces philosophy to a form of literature, and redeems literature from simply being a poor form of the truth.

To this point, Derrida need not have been talking about play. He could have been talking about the freedom of the imagination and simply using the metaphor of play to imply a notion of unboundable freedom. Many modern thinkers do that when they are not talking of play at all. Play has become a metaphor of idealization for many (Hans, 1981).

Derrida introduces us to the concept of *aporia* of self-engendered paradox in discussing the problem of the way in which the deconstruction of someone else's text is a bootstrap operation that can unravel hidden meanings in that text, but cannot escape beyond the text; one cannot move on to any more universal meanings. In Greek, the term means the unpassable path, and in his work it stands both for his inability to do anything but deconstruct and also for a kind of implicit yearning for some anarchic free play that might take him beyond the text itself. Although Derrida is not talking about play, from our prior analysis of Bateson we can believe that he has borrowed not only his notion of "freedom" from the play metaphor but also his notion of paradox. Play also is an aporic language of communication. It communicates but only in the limited circle of its own being. It also yearns beyond itself, but it is also limited to its own magic circle. Its pretense means that its path to power or beauty or wisdom is always turned in upon itself. Its freedom allows it to deconstruct any worlds (inventing monsters, etc.) but its aporia limits this "free play" to its own quite strict domain.

Although Derrida is not a play theorist and never intends to be, it is arguable that his deconstructive philosophizing more heavily uses metaphors from play's own activity then does the work of any prior philosopher, while at the same time through his application revealing even more about the disequilibrial limitations of the phenomena. His aporic communication is the kind of equilibrial bafflement within which play is contained; its deconstructive free ranging is the kind of disequilibrial possibility that it also enacts.

## AN APPLICATION TO CHILDREN'S RIDDLING

This review of 12 theories involving play has attempted to make a case that the structure of play includes an inherent bipolarity. What we wish to do now is apply this structural argument to the specific work of John McDowell (1979), a folklorist at Indiana University. To the best of my knowledge and despite certain imperfections that we have dealt with elsewhere (Sutton-Smith, 1982b), this is the best description and analysis of a genre of children's play with which we are familiar. Strangely enough, the masses of work on children's play in developmental psychology and play therapy have left us with few comprehensive descriptions as well as analyses of the matter at hand. We often get a schematic analyses and an item or two of description, but that is all.

McDowell, using a largely ethnographic approach, observed the riddling activities of a group of Chicano boys in Austin, Texas. He analyzed the phenomenon in terms of the ethnic and peer traditions of these boys. He showed how the riddles were acquired at different age levels, and then proceeded to structural, textural, and content analyses within this particular ethnic and social-class context.

In Table 3.2 we have arranged our own reanalysis of McDowell's data in terms of the equilibrial and disequilibrial aspects that we find there, quite in

TABLE 3.2
Riddling as Bipolarity

| *Social Process* | *Play Equilibration* | *Play Disequilibration* |
|---|---|---|
| Oral interrogation as socialization | oral interrogation | parody of interrogation |
| Asynchronous Power of adult | asynchronous power | by child over child |
| Interrogational Discourse | interrogation | reversal of felicity |
| Content | familiar items | made unfamiliar |
| Categorization as process | syntactic, lexic semantic and epithemic categorization | focus on non-critical attributes of categories |
| Texture | | prosodic emphasis (stress, rhyme) montonic intonation |

From: *Children's Riddling*, by John H. McDowell, University of Indiana Press, 1979.

accord with McDowell who points out many of these inherent contradictions. Few adults in relation to children are so easily removed.

When the interrogation is viewed as a kind of discourse, McDowell points out how the usual felicitous conditions of questioning are reversed. Usually the questioner seeks knowledge when asking questions. Here, by contrast with these normative conditions, the questionnaire in this playframe already knows the answer and the target of the inquiry does not. Riddles sound like questions but they are not.

Within riddles themselves there are a host of ways in which our usual expectations about categories, about word meanings, and about life events are subverted. We are led to expect that the conventional responses to particular syntax, semantics, and lexics will be observed, but they are not.

Why did the dog get out of the sun? He didn't want to be a hot dog.
What did Della wear? New Jerseys.
What's long and white and lies on the bottom of the ocean? Moby's Dick.
What's green and sings? Elvis Parsley.

In riddles, familiar content is made strange or unfamiliar. Further, when it comes to texture, riddles masquerading as straight questions have many features of poetry. They tend towards rhyme and towards isochronic stress. Unlike true questions, however, they do not inflect at the end of the sentence instead they tend to be monotonic in order not to give the listener any clues.

In sum, riddles parody authority and they parody interrogation. They subvert the usual conventional expectations of language and behavior as these are used within the questioning situation. Each level of inversion is a subset within the other, so that we end with a neat nesting of texture into structure into content into discourse into social arrangement. At each analytic level there is some kind of reversal of usual expectations, creating a multi-valent symbolic lamination, a kind of overdetermination of disequilibration that gives the riddle its potential excitement and final climactic arousal kick.

## CONCLUSION

In this work a case has been made for regarding some kind of bipolarity as essential to the structural character of play. Evidence has been derived from observing these tendencies in various theories of play drawn from quite diverse sources and from a detailed examination of the case of riddles. It is of course possible that these reflections are nullified by a special reading of the theories or the riddles being a special and exceptional case of play.

There are also considerable problems in integrating this essentially "structural" view of play, with the traditional natural science emphasis on function, and with the current interpretive science emphasis on context and on meaning. Suffice, however, if our major purpose here be fulfilled, of showing that it is not legitimate to treat play in the same category as exploration, construction, imagination, practice, and so forth. It is not the same as those kinds of epistemic activities and its character and purposes are only disguised, perhaps even bowdlerized when it is cast into the same global category of child idyllic phenomena.

## REFERENCES

Alford, K. F. *The structures of expressive acts in four cultures.* Paper given at an annual meeting of the Anthropological Association for the Study of Play, London, Ontario, 1982, April 1–3.

Babcock, B. (Ed.). *The reversible world.* Ithaca, N.Y.: Cornell University Press, 1978.

Bateson, G. *Steps to an ecology of mind.* New York: Ballentine, 1972.

Berlyne, D. E. *Conflict, arousal and curiosity.* New York: McGraw-Hill, 1960.

Bruner, J. S., Jolly, A., & Sylva, K. *Play.* New York: Basic Books, 1976.

Derrida, J. Structure, sign and play in the discourse of the human sciences. In R. Macksey & E. Donato (Eds.), *The structuralist controversy.* Baltimore, Md.: John Hopkins University Press, 1970.

Ellis, M. J. *Why people play.* Englewood Cliffs, N.J.: Prentice–Hall, 1974.

Erikson, E. *Childhood and society.* New York: Norton, 1951.

Erikson, E. *Toys and reasons.* New York: Norton, 1977.

Fagen, R. *Animal play behavior.* New York: Oxford University Press, 1981.

Geertz, C. *The interpretation of cultures.* New York: Basic Books, 1973.

Groos, K. *The play of man.* New York: Arno Press, 1976. (Originally published, 1901.)

Gruneau, R. S. Freedom and constraint. The paradoxes of play games and sports. *Journal of Sport History,* 1980, *7*(3), 68–85.

Hall, G. S. *Youth: Its education, regimen and hygiene.* New York: Appleton, 1917.

Hans, J. S. *The play of the world.* Amherst, Mass.: University of Massachusetts Press, 1981.

Huizinga, J. *Homo ludens.* New York: Beacon, 1955.

Hutt, C. Exploration and play. In B. Sutton-Smith (Ed.), *Play and learning.* New York: Gardner Press, 1979.

Kelly-Byrne, D. *A narrative of plan and intimacy.* Univ. of Michigan, 1982. Microfilm 8217137.

Kirschenblatt-Gimblett, B. *Speech play.* Philadelphia: University of Pennsylvania Press, 1976.

Knapp, M., & Knapp, H. *One potato, two potato.* New York: Norton, 1976.

McDowell, J. *Children's riddling.* Bloomington, Ind.: Indiana University Press, 1979.

Opie, I., & Opie, P. *The lore and language of schoolchildren.* New York: Oxford University Press, 1968.

Piaget, J. *Play, dreams and imitation in childhood.* New York: Norton, 1961.

Pepper, S. C. *World hypotheses.* Berkeley: University of California Press, 1961.

Rubin, K., Fein, G. G., & Vandenberg, B. Children's play. In E. M. Hetherington (Ed.). *The Carmichael handbook of child psychology.* New York: Wiley, in press.

Schwartzman, H. *Transformations: The anthropology of children's play.* New York: Plenum, 1978.

Shultz, T. R. Play as arousal modulation. In B. Sutton-Smith, (Ed.). *Play and learning.* New York: Gardner, 1979.

Singer, J. L. *The child's world of make believe.* New York: Academic Press, 1973.

Sutton-Smith, B. Piaget on play. *Psychological Review,* 1966, *73,* 104–110.

Sutton-Smith, B. *Die Dialektik des Spiels.* Schorndorf: Verlag Karl Hoffman, 1978. (a)

Sutton-Smith, B. (Ed.). *Play and learning.* New York: Gardner Press, 1979.

Sutton-Smith, B. *The folks stories of children.* Philadelphia, Univ. of Pennsylvania Press, 1981. (a)

Sutton-Smith, B. Play theory of the rich and for the poor. In P. Gilmore & A. Glathorn (Eds.), *Children in and out of school.* Washington, D.C., Center for Applied Linguistics, 1982, pp. 182–205. (a)

Sutton-Smith, B. Review of J. H. McDowell's *Children's riddling. Language and Society,* 1982, *11,* 105–151. (b)

Sutton-Smith, B. *One hundred years of research on play.* Newsletter of the Association for the Anthropological Study of Play, 1983, *9*(2), 13–17.

Sutton-Smith, B. Piaget, play and cognition revisited. In W. Overton (Ed.), *The relationship between social and cognitive development.* Hillsdale, N.J.: Lawrence Erlbaum Associates, in press.

Turner, V. *The ritual process.* New York: Aldine, 1969.

Turner, V. *Dramas, fields and metaphors.* Ithaca, N.Y.: Cornell University Press, 1974.

Turner, V. (Ed.). *Celebration: Studies in festivity and ritual.* Washington, D.C.: Smithsonian Press, 1982.

Weir, R. H. *Language in the crib.* The Hague: Mouton, 1970.

# 4 Imaginative Play: Deficit or Difference?

Helen B. Schwartzman
*Northwestern University*

Recently, a number of studies (Ariel & Sever, 1980; Feitelson, 1977; Rubin, Maioni, & Hornung, 1976; Smith, 1977; Sutton-Smith & Heath, 1981) examining relationships between children's imaginative play and culture and social class variables have appeared. The majority of these studies either suggest the need for, or test the applicability of, specific play tutoring programs for improving the social and cognitive development of "disadvantaged" children. It therefore seems time to evaluate the advantages and possible disadvantages of these investigations and programs. In this chapter an assessment of these studies is offered that suggests that many are premised on a "deficit hypothesis" similar to that outlined by Cole and Bruner (1971) and Labov (1972) in their critiques of deficit interpretations of the language and culture of certain ethnic and social class groups in the United States. Three questions are considered in the evaluation presented here: (1) what types of cross-cultural and cross-class studies are available; (2) what is the evidence presented in these reports for deficits or differences in children's imaginative play?; and (3) what types of interventions (if any) seem warranted by these studies.

## CROSS-CULTURAL AND CROSS-CLASS STUDIES

### Experiments and Structured Observations

Smilansky's (1968) investigation of children's play in Israel initiated an interest in the use of sociodramatic play for educational purposes, particularly the education of disadvantaged (i.e., nondominant culture) children. This study is certainly the most well-known and widely quoted of the investigations to be discussed here. According to Smilansky, sociodramatic play is characterized by: (1) imitative role play; (2) make-believe in regard to objects; (3) make-believe in regard to actions and situations; (4) persistence (minimum length of 10 minutes); (5) interaction (two or more children); and (6) verbal communication. On the basis of her research in day care/nursery school contexts, Smilansky suggested that certain groups of children have less facility for imaginative role play than others. In her study, children of North African and Middle Eastern parents classified as "disadvantaged" are reported to engage in this type of play with much less frequency and with less ability than children of European parents.

Smilansky (1971) went on to suggest that this research and studies of "culturally disadvantaged" children in Ohio and Illinois indicate that most disadvantaged children "do not play sociodramatic play" and will not do so unless there is "some degree of positive intervention by parents and/or teachers [p. 39]." In addition, Smilansky argues that if this type of play does not develop, children may be retarded in the development of skills and behavior patterns that are "necessary for successful integration into the school situation or full cooperation in the 'school game' [p. 42]." Sociodramatic play is said to develop three aspects in children that are essential to this school game: (1) creativity; (2) intellectual growth (and the power of abstraction); and (3) social skills. Therefore, because of the importance of sociodramatic play to children's development, Smilansky believes that adults, as parents and teachers, must intervene in order to improve the "low performance" in play that certain children exhibit. A variety of intervention techniques are described (e.g., adult modeling of sociodramatic play techniques). Smilansky reported that in both the 1968 Israeli and 1971 American studies, these interventions improved the children's ability to engage in this form of play behavior.

One of the first challenges to Smilansky's argument comes from Israel. In a large-scale observational study of children's play and games, Rivka Eifermann (1971) found that the form of play (i.e., sociodramatic) that Smilansky found to be lacking in her sample of "disadvantaged" children appeared at a later age (i.e., 6–8 rather than 3–6) for a comparable group of children in her sample. She also stated that at this later age the disadvantaged children not only developed the ability to engage in symbolic/thematic play, but they also engaged "in such play at a significantly higher rate than do their 'advantaged' peers [p. 290]."

During the 1970s a number of experimental and structured observation studies were conducted attempting to elaborate on the original work of Smilansky (Ariel & Sever, 1980; Feitelson, 1977; Feitelson & Ross, 1973; Freyburg, 1973; Lovinger, 1974; Rosen, 1974; Rubin, Maioni, & Hornung, 1976; Saltz & Johnson, 1974; J. Singer, 1973; Smith, 1977; Smith & Dodsworth, 1976). All of these studies report cultural or class differences in the quantity and/or quality of children's imaginative behavior. For example, Freyburg (1973) reports that a group of 80 urban disadvantaged American kindergarten children, who were the subjects of her study, exhibited very little imaginative play on a rating scale in free play settings prior to the introduction of a training program. Additionally, both Smilansky (1968) and Freyburg (1973) report higher degrees of aggression, bossiness, hyperactivity, and overexcitement along with extreme passivity among the disadvantaged children in their studies (Freyburg, 1973, p. 135). Freyburg also found that following the play training sessions the amount of imaginative play increased and it appeared to be more organized and integrated. It was also found that aggression and hyperactivity decreased after the training sessions.

Feitelson and Ross (1973) present similar results in a study of white, lower-middle-class kindergarten children living in the Boston area. These children were found to exhibit "surprisingly low levels of thematic play" prior to participation in a series of play-tutoring sessions and stressing adult modeling of thematic play that led to a "significant increase" in their thematic play [p. 218]. Feitelson and Ross argued that these findings suggest that thematic play must be learned by some form of modeling and that, if this does not occur, this play does not develop naturally or spontaneously in all children.

One of the problems with many of these studies, as pointed out recently by Smith (1977), is that although reporting low levels of fantasy play for disadvantaged children the investigators have not included results on middle-class children for comparison. (Comparisons, however, were possible for the Smilansky study.) Smith (1977) and Smith and Dodsworth (1976) have recently attempted to correct this problem in a study of social-class differences in children's fantasy play in England. Focal sampling of children's behavior in four nursery schools in London and Sheffield was conducted. The results indicate that children from working-class backgrounds displayed less fantasy play than middle-class children. There was, however, no difference in the duration of the play, but the number of participants in working-class children's fantasy episodes was less. Smith also states that working-class children used more replica objects in play (e.g., minature telephone, toy cups, saucers), whereas middle-class children used objects in more unconventional ways (such as using wooden blocks as cakes).

All of the preceding studies must be evaluated in terms of situational effects and experimentor bias, both of which appear not to have been considered by the investigators. For example, studies (Labov, 1972; Riessman, 1964) of lower-class children's expressive and imaginative use of language in role play and other situations *outside* of school or experimental contexts indicate that in these situations these children are highly creative, are more verbal, and display a variety of social and survival skills. The inventive use of objects in play outside of the school setting (as documented in the ethnographic literature discussed later) also suggests a need to compare contexts in children's use of materials in play. For example, it seems reasonable to suggest that lower-class children might be more constrained in their use of materials in school and less constrained out of it;[1] whereas for middle-class children the reverse might occur. In fact, this would most certainly be the case if middle-class children were placed in the neighborhoods or communities of lower-class children and then rated as to type and frequency of imaginative play expressed.

These possibilities point to the importance of considering situational effects in evaluating the findings reported in many of these studies (e.g., the disadvantaged children in Smilansky's sample may have been fearful of the new and strange school that they were attending). Most of these studies were conducted in a school or laboratory context (Ariel & Sever [1980] is an exception) and generally involved adults (who were strangers to the children) as observers, raters, or trainers. Freyburg (1973) has recognized the problems this approach poses for researchers: "Lower-class children should perhaps be observed away from school, where authority figures may be inhibitory. Use of para-professionals from the community may be essential in determining whether differences in verbal and cognitive style mask abilities among lower-class children when observed by middle-class persons [p. 136]." The work of Labov (1972) clearly demonstrates how situational factors of schoolroom and testing contexts influence the verbal productions of urban black children. Labov documents this idea nicely by conducting a standard interview used to assess language competence with an 8-year-old black child. The interviewer and child are black and from the same neighborhood and yet the boy's response is monosyllabic. The standard judgment would be that the boy is linguistically and culturally deprived. But is he? In another situation the same interviewer goes to the boy's apartment with some of his friends and initiates a conversation in dialect about a taboo subject. Here the boy becomes an animated and lively conversationalist. It must be recognized that such situational factors may be operating in the studies of children's play discussed here, and in fact there are many interesting parallels between the logic of the language deficit studies (Labov, 1972) and the logic of the play deficit studies reviewed here (see Schwartzman [1978] for an extended consideration of this point).

Two other situational effects need to be considered in evaluating these studies. Recent research by Doyle, Connolly, and Rivest (1980) suggests that peer or playmate familiarity increases "the overall amount of social interaction, and during this social interaction, the complexity of toy play [p. 222]." In most of the studies reported here the effect of this variable was not specifically considered by the researchers, and in at least one study (Feitelson & Ross, 1973) children's thematic play was rated in a solitary play situation with no mention of

---

[1]A recent study by Henninger (1980) supports this view, as the researcher found that differences between middle-class and lower-class children's free play did exist when the children were observed in the classroom, but these differences did not exist when the children were observed outdoors.

how (or even whether) these results might be comparable to interactive (two or more peers) play settings. Additionally, the effect of a program or school's educational philosophy on the type and frequency of play that develops in these contexts must also be considered when comparing observations and ratings of play across settings (Johnson, Ersher, & Bell, 1980; Tizard, Philps, & Plewis, 1976). This is especially important in evaluating Smilansky's (1968) original study, which is based on data collected in 36 kindergartens and nursery school classes, and yet no detailed information is provided about the educational philosophy (similarities or differences) of these schools.

The experimental and structured observation studies discussed previously appear to demonstrate that there are *differences* in children's play performance when they are observed in specific contexts (schools or laboratories) under specific conditions and by specific groups of people. It is not at all clear, however, that these differences represent actual deficits in these children's imaginative play abilities (i.e., deficiencies in play *competence* as opposed to *performance* [see Labov's application of this contrast to linguistic deprivation studies]). Indeed, it may be that even the differences reported in these studies are the result of deficiencies in the researchers' methodology as opposed to deficits residing in specific groups of children.

## Ethnographic Studies

The anthropological literature has also been used to support the view that children from certain traditional cultures may be deficient in imaginative play abilities. Feitelson (1977, 1979) and Feitelson and Ross (1973) have specifically developed this argument citing their own research with Kurdish Jews (1954) as well as numerous ethnographies (Ammar, 1954; Fortes, 1970; LeVine & LeVine, 1963) to suggest that children in certain rural communities as well as urban areas exhibit a paucity of imaginative or active play of any sort (Feitelson & Ross, 1973, pp. 204–205).

The reasons that adults do not model imaginative play for children in these societies are because sufficient "play props"[2] and play space are not available. Feitelson (1979) cites her own research with Jews who immigrated from the

---

[2]The importance of props and toys provided by adults for children has been particularly stressed. For example, as is suggested by Feitelson and Ross (1973):

> Crowded tenements, societies in which household implements are hand-crafted, precious, and scarce, and societies in which the small child is not entitled to private possessions or personal space of his own are clearly not conducive to the emergence of thematic play. Are not toys, whether store-bought or hand-crafted, essentially artifacts provided by adult society to be used by the child at will and without recriminations, in place of useful or precious objects whose use is denied him? It is only in affluent societies with their abundance of inexpensive mass-produced implements that useful objects can readily be left to children for use as play-props [p. 206].

Kurdish area of northeastern Iraq, where she states:"during intensive participant observation sessions over twelve months in 75 families not a single instance of toy ownership and only one of representational play was recorded [p. 9]." The studies of Ammar (1954) on Egyptian village children and LeVine and LeVine (1963) on Gusii children of Kenya have also been cited in regard to these issues. For example, Ammar (1954) states: "children's play has not felt the impact of urban influences, and one cannot find even manufactured dolls in the hands of children [p. 153]." The LeVines note that fantasy play was almost nonexistent for Gusii children.

It is important to note here that presence or absence of manufactured dolls can hardly, in the author's opinion, be taken as evidence of imaginative play. Even though Ammar (1954) states that he made "no detailed observations of play situations" he devotes an entire chapter (pp. 144–160) to a description of children's play and games. He reports that Silwa children, especially boys, play mostly competitive games and engage only infrequently in imaginative play (which he considered as transformations of objects). However, he stated that a popular play situation of girls is the representation of adult female occupations and ceremonies. According to Ammar (1954) this play involves: "making straw figures, bedecked in bits of cloth as men and women and children, and with the help of stones, building a house. All the details of an event or ritual are played out in a make-believe way. Thus marriage, circumcision, cooking, and social meetings are all imitated [p. 154]." One wonders what Ammar might have found if he had chosen to make a systematic study of children's play.

There are two factors to consider in evaluating the LeVines' study. The first is that the physical isolation of the homesteads makes it very difficult for children's groups and hence play groups to form. In this case there appears to be too much, as opposed to too little, space available. Secondly, it is worth noting that children's play is vaguely mentioned in various sections of the LeVine and LeVine monograph (1963), for example: "The yard in front of the main entrance (to the house) is the scene of many daytime activities; the grinding and winnowing of grain, the play of children [p. 26]." Unfortunately little more is said about this play.[3]

Other ethnographic studies that are said to support the view that children in non-Western culture are imaginatively disadvantaged are Mead (1975) and Fortes (1970). Mead reports that Manus children spend most of their time in energetic rough-and-tumble play activities, and very little time is spent in imagi-

---

[3]This lack of discussion may also be related to the secondary status that play is accorded in the general Whiting and Child model of culture and personality development used by Six Cultures researchers. Here play and games are given an expressive but hardly formative status. Researchers were encouraged to collect information on children's games (and recreations in general) as a source of "projective data." (See Schwartzman, 1978, pp. 184–196 for a more detailed evaluation of the Six Cultures research.)

native play behavior. Mead (1975) stated that she observed "no instance of a child's personalizing a dog, or a fish or a bird, of his personalizing the sun, the moon, the wind or the stars [p. 225]." This nonanimistic and nonimaginative orientation changes, however, when Manus children reach adulthood. Adults are said to display animistic thinking, particularly in their religious concepts, according to Mead. In this case naturalistic and pragmatic children become animistic/imaginative adults, instead of the reverse as is typical in Western society. This does not mean, however, that imagination is not displayed in this society, for in this case it seems only to be delayed. Fortes' (1970) study of Tallensi children's play is also said to demonstrate that children's play is characterized by its short duration, discontinuity, and lack of complexity in comparison to Western children's play (Feitelson & Ross, 1973). The Fortes' study will be discussed later.

## IMAGINATION: DEFICIT OR DIFFERENCE?

In contrast to this line of argument it is this writer's view that the ethnographic literature does not support the idea that rural or non-Western (or nonmiddle class) children do not or cannot engage in imaginative play activities. However, the literature is sketchy and incomplete in this area. Considering the fact that most ethnographers have not systematically studied this behavior, the reports of children's imaginative and creative abilities in play that do appear in the literature are all the more interesting to consider. This does not mean that imaginative play occurs in all societies, but this fact cannot be generalized to mean that children in most "rural communities" or in non-Western or nonmiddle-class societies exhibit a paucity of imaginative play behavior. The ethnographic literature is discussed in order to question some of the assumptions that are currently being made about non-Western children's play.

One assumption that has already been mentioned is that children who work (i.e., assume child care and other economic responsibilities at an early age) cannot play. The belief here is that children must have long undisturbed periods of time available to them for imaginative play to develop (Singer, 1973). However, there are numerous examples available in the ethnographic literature of children developing interesting ways of combining their work with their play (Bateson & Mead, 1942; Leighton & Kluckhohn, 1947; Maretzki & Maretzki, 1963; Marshall, 1976; Raum, 1940). These ways provide them with enough time to engage in play and still carry out their work responsibilities whatever they may be. In addition, it is an important way that children in these societies learn that play and work are integrated rather than separate spheres of activity. Fortes' (1970) depiction of Tallensi children's play especially supports this view as he provides vivid descriptions of how children's imaginative play events are intermixed with their work requirements.

A related series of assumptions about imaginative play also needs to be examined. This includes the view that children must have sufficient and appropriate space and toys alloted to them by adults to engage in imaginative play. Along with this it is argued that adults must model and in other ways encourage this type of play for it to develop. A form of this argument appeared early in this century in the writings of play reformers such as Gulick (1920) and Curtis (1917). These individuals were especially concerned with what they saw as an absence of play among urban immigrant and working-class children in large American cities. This lack of play was in general attributed to the phenomena of immigration and urbanization because groups were "mixed up" in cities making it difficult for camaraderie, trust, affection, and leadership to develop and also because children lacked privacy and had no specific place to play. According to Lee (Curtis, 1917): "The child without a playground is father to the man without a job [p. 15]." The playground movement developed at this time (Mergen, 1980) as a means to encourage proper play and to discourage "rowdy" behavior and to "teach children leadership and cooperation, develop skills and health and encourage imagination and creativity [p. 198]."

It has more recently been noted that space may not in itself be the crucial factor and instead a "play conducive atmosphere" is what is needed. Such an atmosphere consists of the following: (1) free access to play props; (2) availability of sufficient play space and time; and (3) encouragement of and modeling by parents or other adults of imaginative play activities (Feitelson, 1977; Feitelson & Ross, 1973).

In contrast to these views, the ethnographic literature demonstrates that in many societies children do not have their own private space (at least not interior space) nor do they have playgrounds or playtimes, or an assemblage of ready-made toys that are "theirs" alone as is typical of middle-class Western and particularly American children. In addition, in many societies children's play is not defined as an activity that needs to be watched, supervised, promoted, modeled, or otherwise encouraged by adults. However, children in these societies are able to construct active and imaginative play lives for themselves although they may do this in ways somewhat different than middle-class children do. For example, the reports on children's integration of work with play were already mentioned. Along with this there are other examples of how non-Western children construct imaginative role play situations for themselves that seem to be quite ingenious if not altogether sympathetic to the adults (particularly foreign adults) in their lives. Raum's (1940) reports of Chaga children's play satires of school and teachers are useful to consider here. The teacher's obsession, from the point of view of the Chaga, with time was symbolized by placing a great clock of sand in front of the make-believe school. Likewise, the emphasis on memorization and recitation of literature in school is parodied by children reading from "books" of vegetable leaves in the monotonous tone of the teacher. The sermons of missionaries are also satirized by exaggerating the linguistic mistakes and mannerisms of the minister. Baptism events (Raum, 1940) were also said to be favorite events for caricature, as the "minister" is able to sprinkle "his converts with water according to their deserts, while in the choice of names he selects characteristic ones, such as 'Lover of Food,' 'Stupid,' 'Dwarf,' 'Bully' [p. 258]." The ethnographic literature provides numerous examples of children's imaginative role play of this sort (Centner, 1962; Fortes, 1970; Lancy, 1974; Leacock, 1971; Maretzki & Maretzki, 1963).

Along with these descriptions, it is important to remember that there are other ways, and places and times, that children may express imagination in play. This is especially apparent when one looks at the way that children, from both rural and urban areas, use the materials available in their environments to create a variety of play things and spaces. This includes using what may seem to be useless and even dangerous space and material (e.g., a trash heap, abandoned buildings or cars) in very creative ways. Again, there are numerous descriptions of child-designed toys and play in the ethnographic literature that demonstrate that children in many cultures are able, in the words of the Maretzkis (Maretzki & Maretzki, 1963) commenting on the children of Taira in Okinawa, "to meet the minimum of equipment with the maximum of inventiveness and enthusiasm [p. 536]." Reports of South American Indian (e.g., Chama and the Guarayu of Bolivia) children's self-designed toys are available by Shoemaker (1964) and Jackson (1964). Other interesting descriptions appear in DuBois (1944); Maretzki & Maretzki (1963); Marshall (1976); Raum (1940); Centner (1962); and Leacock (1971).

Finally, another expression of children's imagination that has been greatly neglected by all researchers is children's speech play. Nevertheless, there are interesting studies on this form of play for non-Western children and nonmiddle-class children, including studies of children's play languages. Examples include pig latin forms (Centner, 1962; Sherzer, 1976), verbal dueling such as "playing the dozens" (Gossen, 1976; Labov, 1972), riddles (McDowell, 1974), vocabulary games (Haas, 1964), and children's narratives (Ager, 1975; Watson-Gegeo & Boggs, 1977). In addition, an overview of this area of research is provided by Kirschenblatt-Gimblett (1976).

The tendency of researchers to ignore or overlook children's speech play as a means of imaginative expression is particularly illustrated in a monograph by Ashton (1967) on the Sotho of Lesotho (in Southern Africa). Ashton states that the children lacked ingenuity and imagination in their play. He stated that their games "are aimless and desultory and consist chiefly of roaming about, playing hide and seek, digging in ash heaps, making slides [p. 35]" and so forth. However, in the same monograph, he describes a system of complex secret languages as well as a variety of riddles and conundrums devised by these children that does not match his depiction of them as lacking in imagination and ingenuity.

In summary, what has been documented so far by considering both the ethnographic and experimental literature is that there are differences in form, content, and style of expression of imaginative play by children. However, this literature, in the author's opinion, does not demonstrate that we are dealing with a problem of play deficiency for children from specific types of socioeconomic or cultural groups.[4]

## WHAT TO DO?

Recognizing that there are or may be differences, but not necessarily deficits, of play in children, what if anything should be done? Is it necessarily harmful to teach children new or alternative ways of playing? What if children are in the process of adapting to a new context where they might need middle-class playing skills? Shouldn't this play be made available to them?

The major argument in favor of play tutoring is that it is essential for correcting a supposed play deficiency in certain groups of children. Even if this deficiency is questioned (as it has been here) it is still possible to suggest that play tutoring is an important technique to use in order to increase acts of imaginative play among some groups and also because it improves scores on standardized tests (of creativity, language skills, etc.). Therefore, it is argued, disadvantaged children who are play tutored will improve their ability to cope in a modern world as measured by such standardized tests. In contrast to this view it has recently been suggested that it may not be the play itself that improves scores. It could be the tutoring or increased adult contact, or it may be that scores are not, in fact, improved (Christie, 1982; Smith, 1977; Smith & Syddall, 1978). However, these studies still suggest that play tutoring is probably worthwhile to use for certain children in certain preschool and other settings.

In contrast to this view there is one argument that has not been seriously considered by the advocates of play training (Feitelson, Singer, Smilansky, etc.). It may be true that play tutoring is not in itself directly harmful to children and may even be beneficial in some ways. However, such programs teach teachers as well as children. The paradox develops that at the very moment that children may be learning something useful (or at least neutral) the teachers may be learning something that is harmful. In analyzing the effect of language-tutoring programs Labov makes a point that is also relevant to play-tutoring programs. He argues that these programs may actually prove to be very damaging to children in the long run because of the problem of labeling (e.g., teachers who hear children speaking BEV (Black English Vernacular) will constantly label them as illogical or nonconceptual thinkers). In a similar fashion, the play-tutoring programs may

---

[4]Sutton-Smith and Heath (1981) have recently suggested that we may be dealing with multiple paradigms of pretense, and that these *different* paradigms (e.g., oral vs. literary) may give rise to the idea that some children exhibit play *deficiencies*.

be teaching teachers that certain groups of children are nonimaginative, noncreative, and nonconceptual. The effects of labeling (Rosenthal & Jacobson, 1968) can create more problems for these children to overcome. At the very least the possible advantages and disadvantages of such programs must be weighed before they are institutionalized.

The deficiency-tutoring approach also follows another line of reason similar to that critiqued by Labov. In both instances the deficiencies of children are thought to be related to personal deficiencies *in* the child or *in* his home or neighborhood environment. Adopting this view (Labov, 1972), programs (e.g., Head Start, play tutoring) are designed "to repair the child, rather than the school [p. 232]."

Fortunately, an approach is available to researchers and educators concerned with what to do about the issues raised in this discussion. This approach would require investigators to focus *not* on children's deficiencies but instead on their competencies. In regard to play it would be necessary to first find ways to study and assess systematically the skills and competencies that children display, especially in self-organized play. Following this the challenge would be to develop ways for these skills and abilities to be applied to school, testing, and other adult-structured contexts. Cole and Bruner (1971) suggested this reorientation sometime ago in their review of language deprivation studies. In their opinion: "The teacher should stop laboring under the impression that he must create new intellectual structures and start concentrating on how to get the child to *transfer* skills he already possesses to the task at hand [p. 874]." Cole has continued his studies in this area (Cole & Scribner, 1974), whereas Leacock (1971) and Nerlove, Roberts, Klein, Yarbrough, and Habicht (1974) have specifically examined play as a "natural indicator" of certain cognitive and social skills (e.g., self-managed sequencing of activities; abilities to understand and use volume, area, and linear measurement; reversible operations; etc.).

Apparently, however, researchers in both psychology and anthropology have not been moved by this challenge, and therefore most of the problems associated with this type of research still remain to be solved. But nagging questions recur, as cited by the Laboratory of Comparative Human Cognition (1979):

> How can it be that uneducated people (in Third World countries) or poorly educated people (in technologically advanced countries) seem incompetent at school but generally competent at home and at work? We can spculate at length about the answers to this question. . . . But a scientific approach requires that we have at our disposal tools for specifying such people's competencies and activities outside of school. . . .
>
> Our cross-cultural research leads us inexorably away from the contexts we know how to analyze into domains we have only begun to understand; to deepen our understanding we have to take non-school contexts for behavior seriously and begin to view school (and the psychological tasks that act as its proxy for analytic purposes) as part of a larger set of contexts for behaving. The more seriously we

> engage this undertaking, the more sharply we are made aware of the trouble we are in. It turns out that once we move beyond the highly constrained confines of our laboratory tasks and standardized tests, not only do we lose the technology for making statements about psychological process, we also lose the framework within which we are accustomed to *describe* intellectual behavior [p. 830].

It is the author's opinion that too much time has already been spent in enumerating and assessing children's play deficiencies, and these assessments usually occur in a narrow range of contexts, generally the laboratory or school. Instead of continuing on this course researchers should turn their attention to analyses of the competencies, skills, and abilities that children display in play. This play should be of their own device and design, and it should be analyzed in *all* the contexts in which it occurs. The fact that this will not be easy and that we will not be able to rely on traditional research designs and techniques does not mean that the research should not be done. In fact, the recurring arguments of cultural deprivation (i.e., first language, now play) demand that it be done.

## REFERENCES

Ager, L. P. Play as folklore: An Alaskan Eskimo example. *The Association for the Anthropological Study of Play Newsletter,* 1975, *2*(3), 16–18.

Ammar, H. *Growing up in an Egyptian village.* London: Routledge & Kegan Paul, 1954.

Ariel, S., & Sever, I. Play in the desert and play in the town: On play activities of Bedouin Arab children. In H. B. Schwartzman (Ed.), *Play and culture.* New York: Leisure Press, 1980.

Ashton, E. H. *The Basuto.* London: Oxford University Press, 1967.

Bateson, G., & Mead, M. *Balinese character: A photographic analysis.* New York Academy of Sciences, Special Publication, Volume II, 1942.

Centner, T. *L'enfant African et ses jeuz.* Elisabethville: CEPSI, 1962.

Christie, J. F. Play: To train or not to train? In J. Loy (Ed.), *The paradoxes of play,* New York: Leisure Press, 1982.

Cole, M., & Bruner, J. Cultural differences and inferences about psychological processes. *American Psychologist,* 1971, *26,* 867–876.

Cole, M., & Scribner, S. *Cross-cultural psychology.* New York: Wiley, 1974.

Curtis, H. S. *The play movement and its significance.* New York: Macmillan, 1917.

Doyle, A. B., Connolly, J., & Rivest, L. P. The effect of playmate familiarity on the social interactions of young children. *Child Development,* 1980, *51,* 217–223.

DuBois, C. *Peoples of Alor.* Minneapolis: University of Minnesota Press, 1944.

Eifermann, R. Social play in childhood. In R. Herron & B. Sutton-Smith (Eds.), *Child's play.* New York: Wiley, 1971.

Feitelson, D. Patterns of early education in the Kurdish community. *Megamot,* 1954, *5,* 95–109.

Feitelson, D. Cross-cultural studies of representational play. In B. Tizard & D. Harvey (Eds.), *Biology of play.* Philadelphia: Lippincott, 1977.

Feitelson, D. Imaginative play and the educational process. Paper presented at the International Year of the Child Conference, Yale University, June 21–28, 1979.

Feitelson, D., & Ross, G. S. The neglected factor—play. *Human Development,* 1973, *16,* 202–223.

Fortes, M. Social and psychological aspects of education in Taleland. In J. Middleton (Ed.), *From child to adult.* New York: Natural History Press, 1970.

Freyburg, J. Increasing the imaginative play of urban disadvantaged kindergarten children through systematic training. In J. L. Singer (Ed.), *The child's world of make-believe*. New York: Academic Press, 1973.

Gossen, G. H. Verbal dueling in Chamula. In B. Kirshenblatt-Gimblett (Ed.), *Speech play*. Philadelphia: University of Pennsylvania Press, 1976.

Gulick, H. *A philosophy of play*. New York: Scribner, 1920.

Haas, M. Thai word games. In D. Hymes (Ed.), *Language in culture and society*. New York: Harper & Row, 1964.

Henninger, M. L. Free play behaviors of nursery school children in an indoor and outdoor environment. In P. F. Wilkinson (Ed.), *Celebration of play*. New York: St. Martin's Press, 1980.

Jackson, E. Native toys of the Guarayu Indians. *American Anthropologist*, 1964, *66*, 1153–1155.

Johnson, J., Ersher, H., & Bell, C. Play behavior in a discovery-based and a formal education preschool program. *Child Development*, 1980, *51*, 271–274.

Kirschenblatt-Gimblett, B. (Ed.). *Speech play*. Philadelphia: University of Pennsylvania Press, 1976.

Laboratory of Comparative Human Cognition. Cross-cultural psychology's challenge to our ideas about children and development. *American Psychologist*, 1979, *34*, 827–833.

Labov, W. *Language in the inner city: Studies in the black english vernacular*. Philadelphia: University of Pennsylvania Press, 1972.

Lancy, D. F. *Work, play and learning in a Kpelle town*. Unpublished thesis, University of Pittsburgh, 1974.

Leacock, E. At play in African villages. *Natural History*, 1971, December (special supplement on play), 60–65.

Leighton, D., & Kluckhohn, C. *Children of the people*. New York: Farrar, Straus and Giroux, 1947.

LeVine, R., & LeVine, B. Nyansongo: A Gusii community in Kenya. In B. Whiting (Ed.), *Six cultures: Studies of child rearing*. New York: Wiley, 1963.

Lovinger, S. L. Socio-dramatic play and language development in pre-school disadvantaged children. *Psychology in the Schools*, 1974, *11*, 313–320.

Maretzki, T., & Maretzki, H. Taira: An Okinawan village. In B. Whiting (Ed.), *Six cultures: Studies of child rearing*. New York: Wiley, 1963.

Marshall, L. *The !Kung of Nyae Nyae*. Cambridge, Mass.: Harvard University Press, 1976.

McDowell, J. H. *Interrogative routines in Mexican-American children's folklore* (Working paper in socio-linguistics, no. 20). Austin, Tex.: Southwest Educational Development Educational Laboratories, 1974.

Mead, M. *Growing up in New Guinea*. New York: Morrow, 1975.

Mergen, B. Playgrounds and playground equipment, 1885–1925: Defining play in urban America. In Schwartzman, H. B. (Ed.), *Play and culture*. New York: Leisure Press, 1980.

Nerlove, S. B., Roberts, J. M., Klein, R. E., Yarbrough, D., & Habicht, J. P. Natural indicators of cognitive development: An observational study of rural Guatemalan children. *Ethos*, 1974, *2*, 265–295.

Raum, O. *Chaga childhood*. London: Oxford University Press, 1940.

Riessman, F. The overlooked positives of disadvantaged groups. *Journal of Negro Education*, 1964, *33*, 225–231.

Rosen, C. E. The effects of sociodramatic play on problem-solving behavior among culturally disadvantaged children. *Child Development*, 1974, *45*, 920–927.

Rosenthal, R.,& Jacobson, L. *Pygmalion in the classrooms*. New York: Holt, Rinehart & Winston, 1968.

Rubin, K., Maioni, T., & Hornung, M. Free play behavior in middle- and lower-class preschoolers: Parten and Piaget revisited. *Child Development*, 1976, *47*, 414–419.

Saltz, E., & Johnson, J. Training for thematic-fantasy play in culturally disadvantaged children. *Journal of Educational Psychology*, 1974, *66*, 623–630.

Schwartzman, H. B. *Transformations: The anthropology of children's play.* New York: Plenum Press, 1978.

Sherzer, J. Play languages: Implications for (socio) linguistics. In B. Kirshenblatt-Gimblett (Ed.), *Speech play.* Philadelphia: University of Pennsylvania, 1976.

Shoemaker, N. Toys of Chama (Eseejja) Indian children. *American Anthropologist,* 1964, *66,* 1151–1153.

Singer, J. L. (Ed.). *The child's world of make-believe: Experimental studies of imaginative play.* New York: Academic Press, 1973.

Smilansky, S. *The effects of sociodramatic play on disadvantaged preschool children.* New York: Wiley, 1968.

Smilansky, S. Can adults facilitate play in children? Theoretical and practical considerations. In *Play: The child strives toward self-realization.* Washington, D.C.: National Association for the Education of Young Children, 1971.

Smith, P. K. Social and fantasy play in young children. In B. Tizard & D. Harvey (Eds.), *Biology of play.* London: William Heinemann, 1977.

Smith, P. K., & Dodsworth, C. Social class differences in the fantasy play of preschool children. *Journal of Genetic Psychology,* 1976, *133,* 183–190.

Smith, P. K., & Syddall, S. Play and non-play tutoring in preschool children: Is it play or tutoring which matters? *British Journal of Educational Psychology,* 1978, *48,* 315–325.

Sutton-Smith, B., & Heath, S. B. Paradigms of pretense. *The Quarterly Newsletter of the Laboratory of Comparative Human Cognition,* 1981, *3*(3), 41–45.

Tizard, B., Philps, J., & Plewis, I. Play in preschool centers-II. Effects on play of the child's social class and the educational orientation of the centre. *Journal of Child Psychology and Psychiatry,* 1976, *17,* 265–274.

Watson-Gegeo, K. A., & Boggs, S. T. From verbal play to talk story: The role of routines in speech events among Hawaiian children. In S. Ervin-Tripp & C. Mitchell-Kernan (Eds.), *Child discourse.* New York: Academic Press, 1977.

# 5 The Play of Handicapped Children

Joanne M. Quinn
Kenneth H. Rubin
*University of Waterloo*

The purpose of this chapter is to examine the selected research concerning the play of handicapped children. Prior to so doing, however, we feel it essential to address two preliminary questions. First, and more generally, why should children's play be subjected to serious inquiry? Second, and more specifically, why should the play of handicapped children be investigated?

Answers to these questions will provide both a theoretical and empirical rationale for this chapter. Moreover, the answers will enumerate several conceptual issues that pertain to the literature on the play of exceptional children. After we address these initial questions, we will critically review the literature on the play behaviors of children with intellectual, emotional, and physical handicaps. In the final section of this chapter, we will attempt to synthesize the research findings of this diverse literature and make suggestions for future research directions.

## WHY STUDY CHILDREN'S PLAY?

For centuries, children have been observed to spend much of their time engaged in play (Groos, 1898; Spencer, 1873). However, it was not until recent years that play, as an area of serious *empirical* pursuit, received scientific recognition (Sutton-Smith, 1979). Historically, several factors contributed in delaying the study of play. First, the Protestant work ethic fostered the attitude that play was a recreational, trivial, and inconsequential behavior. Second, philosophers and social scientists have been troubled by the rather ''slippery'' nature of play; it has been a difficult, if not impossible, phenomenon to define (Rubin, Fein, & Vandenberg, 1983). Third, theorists have long disagreed about the developmental significance of play. For example, Piaget (1962) contended that play was pure assimilation, and as such, could result in no new learning. Vygotsky (1967), on the other hand, suggested that symbolic representation was the significant resultant of play behavior. Finally, until recent years there has been a notable lack of reliable and valid observational assessment indices of children's play behaviors. Despite these problems, social scientists have been so struck by this historically pervasive phenomenon that for this reason alone they have pursued the study of children's play.

The rapidly accumulating empirical data base seems to support the contention that play is a developmentally important and purposeful behavior. In recent years, it has been noted that: (1) play follows a regular developmental sequence in infancy and childhood (Nicolich, 1977; Rubin, Watson, & Jambor, 1978); (2) this sequence serves as a behavioral reflection of social and cognitive development (Rubin & Pepler, 1980; 1982; Watson & Fischer, 1980); and (3) play appears to serve as a medium for the consolidation and strengthening of newly developed skills (Cheyne & Rubin, in press; Fein & Apfel, 1979). Moreover, a number of researchers have demonstrated that training children to play in a social-pretense fashion can lead to gains in cognitive, social, and social–cognitive development (see Rubin et al., 1983; Saltz & Brodie, 1982 for recent reviews of the play-training literature). In short, play appears to be a correlate and, indeed, a cause of developmental growth in childhood. As such, the answer to why one should study children's play becomes obvious.

In addition, however, there are more practical reasons to study children's play. Recent data-based advances have important implications for the use of children's play as an assessment tool. For example, Enslein and Fein (1981) and Rubin and Krasnor (1980) have found that an observational play scale developed by Rubin (1982a,b) has temporal and intersituational reliability and stability. Moreover, significant relations between specific play forms and indices of social and cognitive development have been reported. For example, children who engage in a high degree of solitary–sensorimotor or solitary–dramatic activity during classroom free play are likely: (1) to be rejected by their peers (Rubin, 1982a; Rubin, Daniels-Beirness, & Hayvren, 1982); (2) to be rated by their teachers as socially maladjusted (Rubin & Clark, in press); and (3) to perform poorly on both intelligence and social reasoning tests (Rubin, 1982b). Conversely, children who are observed to engage in a high degree of sociodramatic play are more likely to be popular amongst their peers, to be rated as socially adjusted by their teachers, and to perform well on intelligence and social reasoning tests (Rubin et al., 1982). Given these and other recent data, it may be that observed play behaviors can provide us with useful nonlaboratory indices for assessing and diagnosing young children.

## WHY STUDY THE PLAY OF HANDICAPPED CHILDREN?

There are, at least, two answers to this question. First, the study of handicapped children's play can provide theoretical validation for the play of normal children. Because play appears to be a developmentally important concept to normal development, it is necessary to confirm its importance by examining the play of children whose development is, by definition, exceptional. Specifically, the study of handicapped children can provide further validation of the extant play scales developed for use with normal infants (Nicolich, 1977), and children (Rubin, 1982a, 1982b). It would prove most interesting to discover whether handicapped children's play is more in keeping with their mental ages than with their chronological ages. Additionally, it is important to investigate the developmental progression of handicapped children's play. This investigation may help to uncover how the various handicapping conditions interfere with and affect development, and this kind of information is critical to improved understanding and treatment of these children. The play scales previously mentioned would be useful for these purposes. Second, given particular emotional or intellectual problems, can the play treatments used with normal children (Burns & Brainerd, 1979; Saltz, Dixon, & Johnson, 1977; Smilansky, 1968) be successfully applied in populations of exceptional children? We should note that neither of these issues have been dealt with adequately in the extant literature. The nonoverlap between the study of normal versus handicapped children's play will, as the reader will note, provide us with much of our critical source material in the sections that follow.

## SOME CONCEPTUAL CONSIDERATIONS

Three issues must be brought to the reader's attention before we begin our literature review. First, theorists and researchers differ in their conceptualizations of play. The particular definition ascribed to tends to influence the purposes and methods of the research. We will not attempt to deal with the definitional problems herein, and instead refer the reader to Rubin, Fein, and Vandenberg (1983) for a lengthy discussion of this issue. Suffice it to say that different definitions must be kept in mind when comparing the results of various studies concerning the "play" of exceptional children. We shall refer the reader to these definitional variants as they become relevant in our review.

Second, the extant body of play research has been influenced by our historical views of handicapping conditions. As Rubin, Fein, and Vandeberg (1983) indicate, *intellectual impairments* have been classified traditionally as falling within the rubric of psycoeducational study and intervention; *emotional disorders* have been the responsibility of the clinical psychology and psychiatric professions;

and *physical disabilities* have been viewed as research and treatment foci for the physical/occupational therapeutic and medical communities. As a result, investigations of handicapped children's play have followed diverse paths, that is, research on mental retardation has had a remedial thrust, research in the field of emotional disorders has sought to improve diagnosis by delineating the etiological factors involved, and the literature on physical disabilities has had a medical and therapeutic orientation. Thus, at times, our review of these rather diverse areas will appear piecemeal. The different research perspectives will preclude our offering general evaluative and intervention-based statements about handicapped children as a group.

Regrettably, because of these different orientations, psychological theories, particularly *developmental* theories, have largely been ignored in the play research concerning handicapped children. Consequently, as we shall point out, the methodologies and interpretations of many researchers are flawed. Many confounding variables (e.g., sex, mental age, multiple handicaps, and institutionalization) are left uncontrolled, and many classification and play rating systems are not theoretically based. These factors make some of the research findings uninterpretable. These criticisms are explored more fully as the studies are reviewed.

Finally, to discuss such a heterogeneous population as the handicapped is indeed difficult because the handicapping conditions involve a wide range of intellectual, emotional, and physical disabilities. These disabilities are not necessarily mutually exclusive (i.e., many children are multiply handicapped). The attribution of observed differences in the play of mentally retarded versus normal children solely to the effects of cognitive impairment may be erroneous unless the researchers have controlled for the presence of emotional and physical handicaps. However, although handicaps span a wide spectrum of impairments, all handicapped children show the similar disadvantage that the condition interferes with, and sometimes alters, the expected pattern and rate of development. Their ability to explore, interact with, and master their environment is impaired. How does this impairment affect their play? Will increased knowledge about their play aid us to better understand and educate these children? These are significant questions that deserve our careful attention. The extant research does not yet allow us to answer these questions. However, we shall examine the literature critically at this time to respond to these questions.

## INTELLECTUAL IMPAIRMENT

The play of intellectually impaired children has not been studied widely. Moreover, much of the extant research is methodologically flawed and/or conceptually vacuous. We review the observational and intervention play literature concerning intellectually impaired children later.

## Free Play Behaviors of Mentally Retarded Children

Typically, play researchers observe retarded children *individually* as they interact with toys. Their behaviors are then compared with those of nonretarded children. In a nutshell, the research findings have been inconsistent. In some cases, play differences between retarded and normal children have been reported; in other cases, differences have not been observed.

Horne and Philleo (1942) matched 25 institutionalized, mildly retarded 11-year-olds on mental age with 25 nonretarded 7-year-olds. The children were observed for 30 minutes individually at play with a variety of materials. The authors indicated that the younger nonretarded children preferred constructive activities with open-ended materials (e.g., art materials) that allowed creativity and imagination. The older retarded children preferred more structured or closed-ended materials (e.g., puzzles, jacks, cards).

Tilton and Ottinger (1964) compared the toy play repertoires of 18 normal, 12 retarded, and 13 autistic children. Based on prior observations of 100 normal children engaged in free play with toys, Tilton and Ottinger devised a classification system using 10 play categories. The results indicated that normal children engaged in more "combinatorial" play (i.e., child used toys in combination with each other, e.g., block combinations, screws nut on bolt, puts cup on saucer, puts hat on doll's head or cup to doll's lips) than their retarded counterparts. Retarded children engaged in more "undefined toy usage" (i.e., touching a toy without any distinct manipulations) and more pounding activities than the normal children.

The statistical procedures used by Tilton and Ottinger to analyze their data (one way ANOVAs combined with multiple *t* tests) were inappropriate for two reasons: (1) the play categories were not independent; and (2) repeated measures were made on each subject. When repeated measures are taken on any subject, they will be highly correlated. An appropriate statistical analysis is required that takes this intercorrelation into account—*t* tests do not. These analytic criticisms led the authors (along with another colleague, Weiner) to reanalyze their data using a multiple discriminant function procedure (Weiner, Ottinger, & Tilton, 1969). Generally, the results of the reanalysis were similar to the original findings. Again, the most important discriminating category was the combinatorial toy play category.

In a more recent study, Weiner and Weiner (1974) utilized Tilton and Ottinger's (1964) play scale as an instrument to differentiate retarded children from nonretarded children. Two groups of normal children participated in the study: one group was matched with retarded subjects on *CA* (6-year-olds), and the other group was matched with retarded on *MA* (3-year-olds). The best discrimination was made between the play of the retarded children and the play of those matched on *CA*. Combinational toy play once again proved to be the most discriminating behavioral category with normal 3- and 6-year-olds engaging in these types of play activities more frequently than the retarded children.

Unfortunately, several methodological problems plague the aforementioned studies. First, the children in all three studies played only *once,* in a *novel* environment, for a short period of time. At this time, it is not known whether exceptional children deviate from the norm in acclimatizing themselves to novel settings. Second, no attempt was made by the researchers to control for toy familiarity. This oversight may have affected seriously the results of the studies. Given the conceptual distinction between exploration and play (Berlyne, 1966, 1969; Hutt, 1979; Rubin, Fein, & Vandenberg, 1983) we cannot ascertain whether the different play patterns observed are attributable simply to the novelty/familiarity of the materials provided for the children. The significance of toy novelty is demonstrated in a study by Switzky, Ludwig, and Haywood (1979). These researchers controlled for object novelty and complexity and did not find play differences between retarded and nonretarded children. All children demonstrated linear decreases in exploratory behavior and linear increases in play when they were exposed repeatedly to objects of varying complexity.

Another methodological weakness concerns the effects of institutionalization. In both the Horne and Philleo (1942) and the Tilton and Ottinger (1964) studies, socioeconomic status and institutionalization were confounded. Consequently, it was impossible to separate and evaluate socioeconomic and institutionalization effects. Further methodological weaknesses include small sample sizes and the lack of analyses for sex differences. Given that sex differences are evident in the play of nonretarded children (Rubin, Watson, & Jambor, 1978; Smith & Daglish, 1977), this latter oversight is critical.

Perhaps the most critical oversight in the play research concerning retarded children is the lack of conceptual, theoretical, and developmental considerations. For example, Weiner and Weiner (1974) expressed surprise to find significant differences between the play patterns of *normal* 3- and 6-year-olds! Suffice it to say that researchers who conduct studies of the play of atypical children would do well to become conversant with the extant theoretical and development literature vis-à-vis the play of normal children (Ellis, 1973; Rubin, Fein, & Vandenberg, 1983).

An example of the possible misinterpretation of data emanating from the lack of a developmental perspective follows. The emergence of symbolic play has long been thought to reflect cognitive growth and development. Indeed, researchers have indicated recently how symbolic play becomes increasingly complex with age (Fein, 1979; Nicolich, 1977; Rosenblatt, 1977). Such activity, because of its symbolic representational nature, is a far more advanced form of play than the repetitive muscle movements definitive of practice (sensorimotor) or functional play as outlined by Piaget (1962), Smilansky (1968), and Rubin and Pepler (1982). In fact, this contention has received some support from research conducted with exceptional populations. Wing, Gould, Yeates, and Brierly (1977) found that retarded children who displayed symbolic play had more advanced cognitive and language skills than those children (particularly autistic children) who displayed only functional or manipulative play. Yet, Tilton and Ottinger (1964) have equated these two forms of play (i.e., symbolic and functional play) in their category of "personalized uses of toys." Moreover, they have equated constructive play of blockbuilding with symbolic play (i.e., doll play) in their "combinatorial uses of toys" category. Consequently, Tilton and Ottinger, as well as others who have relied on their play scale, make the critical error of confusing and obscuring important developmental differences in the play of retarded and nonretarded children.

We should note that some researchers have suggested that retarded children do not differ from normal children in some more general aspects of their play. Hulme and Lunzer (1966), for example, found that retarded and nonretarded children equated for *MA*, sex, socioeconomic status, and homelife situation did not differ in the organizational levels of their play. Moreover, the children did not differ concerning preferences for open-ended or unstructured activities. This latter finding contradicts those of Horne and Philleo (1942). The methodological superiority of Hulme and Lunzer's study over that of Horne and Philleo (i.e., the use of extended play observations and the familiarity of the materials and play situation) makes these findings more interpretable and likely more valid.

## Play in Intervention Programs for Retarded Children

Play has been used as a process through which retarded children learn social or intellectual skills. For example, researchers have indicated that sociodramatic play training (Strain, 1974) and individual or group play therapy (Leland, Walker, & Taboada, 1959; Mehlman, 1953; Morrison & Newcomer, 1975; Newcomer & Morrison, 1974) improve such target behaviors as toy or social (cooperative) play, social skills, physical coordination, and language skills.

Several methodological problems cloud the aforementioned results. First, as Rubin (1980) and Smith (1977) have noted, much of the "play-training" literature does not allow firm conclusions to be drawn about the impact of the play experience, per se, on the outcome measures. It may well be that adult attention and tuition are at least as responsible as the play experiences for the improvement of targeted behaviors. This concern is particularly relevant to the play therapy literature in which positive outcomes may well be due to increased individual attention (Newcomer & Morrison, 1974). Researchers interested in the effects of play-training experiences would do well to control for play versus tuition outcomes (Smith & Syddall, 1979).

Second, the numbers of retarded children who participate in play training studies are small and comprised mainly of those who are institutionalized. Again, adequate controls for institutionalization must be incorporated into future research efforts with the retarded.

Finally, Wehman (1975) has criticized play therapy studies for their inability to be replicated. Descriptions of the play procedures used to invoke the changes are absent. Play therapy as reported in the literature typically involves a wide spectrum of activities ranging from puzzles and pegboards to speech imitation and self-feeding instructions that ". . . with such a broad array of materials and skills used to make up play therapy, it becomes difficult to identify the components of the process instrumental in facilitating the behavior change of the children (Wehman, 1975, p. 241)." In the future, researchers will have to exercise much stricter controls as well as report carefully and accurately the experimental procedures used to affect change.

## THE PLAY OF AUTISTIC AND PSYCHOTIC CHILDREN

This population of exceptional children is indeed engimatic. Clinicians and psychiatrists have long debated acceptable universal definitions of childhood psychosis. Several different labels have been applied to these children including "schizophrenic", "autistic", "psychotic", "pathological" and "severely emotionally disturbed". In discussing the studies in this section, we have adhered to the labels used by the various researchers in their reports. Although the labels are admittedly confusing, it is important for the reader to keep in mind that these children, however labeled, demonstrate serious distortions in the timing, rate, and sequence of most basic psychological functions (American Psychiatric Association, 1980). Their developmental pattern is *distorted,* whereas the general development of retarded children is *delayed.* This is the fundamental difference between retarded and psychotic children.

Traditional procedures have demonstrated limited and questionable utility in the assessment of children with infantile autism and psychoses. The early, severe, and pervasive disorders displayed by these children (Rutter, 1974) make diagnostic testing of them nearly impossible. This has forced clinicians and researchers alike to seek new means of diagnosis. Play has provided one of these new techniques.

One would think that because of its diagnostic value, the play of autistic children would be a well-researched topic. However, it is not. For instance, the popular contention that autistic children play in a repetitive, stereotypic, manipulative manner that is devoid of symbolic representation (Bender, 1956) has received minimal empirical support (DeMyer, Mann, Tilton, & Loew, 1967; Tilton & Ottinger, 1964; Wing, Gould, Yeates, & Brierly, 1977). Tilton and Ottinger (1964) indicated that, in comparison to normal and retarded children, autistic children spent a greater proportion of their play engaged in twirling, spinning, shaking, and mouthing toys. These activities were thus thought to be characteristic of autistic children. However, the authors warned against embracing this finding too quickly as more than a third of the autistic children (i.e., 5 of the 13) did not display any such behaviors. When these authors (Weiner, Ottinger, & Tilton, 1969) reanalyzed their data with appropriate statistical procedures, the categories of repetitive mainpulations and oral uses of toys did not differentiate the autistic children from the retarded or normal participants. Not all children diagnosed as autistic display stereotypic behaviors, and, as such, this type of activity should not be considered a universal trait of autism.

DeMyer et al. utilized maternal questionnaires to compare the play of autistic and normal children. Mothers queried were those whose autistic children participated in Tilton and Ottinger's (1964) research. The validity of the questionnaire was examined by comparing maternal responses to observations made in the earlier study. DeMyer et al. claimed that 14 autistic children were available to both studies, even though Tilton and Ottinger report only 13 autistic participants—a curious discrepancy! Nevertheless, mothers of autistic children reported less frequent amounts of mature, complex toy play, appropriate toy use, and doll play than did the mothers of normal children. Autistic children were reported to engage in more perseverative and nonconstructive play than normal children. The mothers' reports did corroborate (i.e., 72% agreement) the differences between autistic and normal children's play observed in the lab session. However, the study's results are questionable because DeMyer et al. created several new categories (e.g., doll play [clothing], dramatic play [props], dramatic play [dress-up]) that were not used in the original report. This factor seriously limits the validity of the latter study. Mothers' reports of play may, indeed, be a rich source of information, not only for exceptional children but for normal children as well. However, researchers must now concentrate on developing theoretically and empirically relevant instruments that rank play behaviors in terms of their cognitive and social sophistication.

More recently, Rutter (1974) suggested that autism involves an organically based deficit in symbolic functioning. Such an impairment should interfere with language development and the development of symbolic play (Kanner, 1973). The relationship between the more abstract parameters of symbolic representation (language) and the concrete parameters of this process (play) has only recently been explored. Wing et al. (1977) found that ". . . a complete absence of symbolic play is closely linked to the presence of typical early childhood autism, or of simple stereotypes, combined with poor social contact [p. 175]." True symbolic play was not associated with the full autistic syndrome as these children had deficiencies in both verbal and nonverbal skills.

Ungerer and Sigman (in press) found a significant correspondence between receptive language skills and levels of play. Additionally, they found that autistic children could not differentiate their actions on objects from the objects themselves. According to Piaget (1962), this differentiation skill is critical for the manipulation of symbols and symbolic play.

Another aspect of symbolic functioning involves the representation of an absent object through pantomime (e.g., pretending to comb one's hair without a comb). Bartak, Rutter, and Cox (1975), Tubbs (1966), and Wing (1971) have all found that psychotic children experience difficulty when faced with tasks that required pantomimic acts. More recently, Curico and Piserchia (1978) investigated the relations between pantomime and verbal (receptive language and degree of echolalic speech) and nonverbal (drawing and sociodramatic play) symbolic functioning. The pantomimic representations were assessed under two conditions: a verbal condition and a subsequent modeling condition. After the pantomime tasks, each child was asked to imitate nonsymbolic actions (e.g., clapping their hands). This step was carried out to ensure that all subjects could imitate actions at some level.

The authors found that the more advanced or abstract pantomimic representation scores correlated significantly with receptive language, nonecholalic speech, and self–other differentiation in drawings, even when mental age was covaried out of the analyses. High pantomimic scores were also related to the observed incidence of sociodramatic play; however, when mental age was covaried, the play measure was not significantly related to pantomimic scores.

One of Curico and Piserchia's more interesting findings was that despite an active abstract model, 62% of the children's responses to the *symbolic* acts were categorized as "concrete" or "failures." However, 96% of the responses to direct imitation of *nonsymbolic* acts were accurate. Thus, it is not the act of imitating that appears to be deficient in this population, but rather the *nature* of the act to be imitated. This finding challenges the suggestion of DeMyer et al. (1972) that autistic children fail to imitate tasks because their visual memory for the absent model is poor or relatively inaccessible. Moreover, improvement from concrete to abstract representations across the verbal to model conditions was made only by those children who engaged frequently in pretense play. It would appear that in order to take full advantage of an abstract model, an initial capacity for representation is necessary. This finding concurs with those reported by Fein (1975) and Overton and Jackson (1973) who indicated that symbolic functioning in normal children cannot be stimulated without some prior susceptibility or predisposition.

It is theoretically important to continue this line of research. By examining the symbolic functioning of children who are by definition deficient in this realm, we can learn more about the interrelated processes affected by this broad deficit. Moreover, we may gain insight into the purposes that play, drawing, language, and pantomime fulfill in the symbolic development of both normal and exceptional children.

Almost all the studies carried out on psychotic populations have failed to control for the effects of intelligence. As much of this research is aimed at improving differential diagnosis between psychosis and mental retardation, this is an obvious and critical oversight. Measures of IQ can dramatically affect the symptomology of autism (Bartak & Rutter, 1976). As a result of this oversight, few conclusions, if any, can be made regarding play behaviors that distinguish autistic children from others of comparable mental age.

Clune, Paolella, and Foley (1979) have published one of the few studies in which the relations between intelligence and the play behaviors of atypical children have been examined. Clune et al. first found that cognitive play complexity was moderately correlated with the WPPSI IQ scores of 100 normal preschoolers. These investigators next observed ten moderately and six severely pathological boys at play both individually and with their mothers. The children were observed prior to admission to a treatment school and 7 and 27 months after admissions. Clune et al. found that severity of pathology was negatively related to the cognitive complexity of play. The authors also indicated that play complexity increased significantly for all children at 7 months posttreatment. Moreover, quality of play at 7 months was predictive of personnel ratings of clinical improvement at 27 months. Finally, those children who displayed the most complex forms of play and who were less severely categorized vis-à-vis pathology at 7 months evidenced the greatest improvement at 27 months. Taken together, Clune et al.'s data indicate that a measure of cognitive play complexity can: (1) differentiate between children with differing degrees of pathology; (2) detect changes of cognitive complexity in psychotic children over time; and (3) predict training improvements 2 years hence.

Surprisingly, few researchers have examined the play of both autistic and childhood schizophrenic populations. Research in this area could eventually produce a technique to settle the debated distinction between schizophrenia and autism (Ornitz & Ritvo, 1976). There are several theories concerning how these disorders differ from one another. Rutter (1974) has suggested that the two disorders differ in the extent to which children view reality. On the one hand, autistic children are thought to be concrete, rigid thinkers who seldom participate in fantasy. On the other hand, schizophrenic children engage in extensive fantasy and delusional behavior and thinking.

Normal children at least as young as 5 years can distinguish conceptually between reality and fantasy (Morison & Gardner, 1978). It is obviously critical to know if and when this fantasy–reality distinction can be made by psychotic or emotionally disturbed children. Not only might the study of children's conceptions of fantasy–reality allow differential diagnosis to be made about pathology, it might also have ramifications for intervention procedures employed with different groups of psychotic children. For example, those fantasy play-training procedures found to produce social and cognitive gains in normal children may be totally inappropriate for emotionally disturbed children. Indeed, Nahme-Huang, Singer, Singer, and Wheaton (1977) recently discovered that schizophrenic children became increasingly aggressive and less attentive following fantasy play training. Had it been first ascertained that these children had difficulty distinguishing fantasy from reality, the authors may have been prevented from offering an intervention program that was conceptually inappropriate for their targeted training group. At any rate, until we discover when and if psychotic children distinguish between literal and nonliteral meanings, fantasy play training and other similar, well-meaning intervention efforts should be suspended.

## THE PLAY OF PHYSICALLY HANDICAPPED CHILDREN

The study of physically handicapped children has generally been dominated by a medical orientation. Consequently, the play of such children has received negligible attention. Many types of physical impairments including deafness, cerebral palsy, and muscular dystrophy have been totally ignored in this regard. Blindness, language delays, and minimal brain dysfunction have received some attention from researchers interested in how these handicaps affect play. The attention, however, has not been extremely systematic nor scientific, and, consequently, the findings are not particularly illuminating. This body of research will, nevertheless, be reviewed briefly.

### The Play of Blind Children

Several researchers (Burlingham, 1965; Rothschild, 1960; Sandler, 1963) have commented that blind preschool children seem to lack a desire to play. These children are reportedly unaccustomed to expressing and involving themselves in play. Sandler and Wills (1965) identified three major points of divergence from normal development in the play of blind children: (1) blind children appear to be delayed in exploring the environment and objects; (2) blind children do not engage in elaborate play routines with significant others; and (3) imitation of actions and role playing appear late, if at all, in these children. These delays are not surprising considering the visual components that are necessarily involved in, or at least serve as prerequisites to, these activities.

More recently, Tait (1972) found that 4- to 9-year-old blind children were more likely than their sighted age-mates to manipulate objects during free play. Interestingly, Tait did not find the two groups to differ in their production of sociodramatic play. Singer and Streiner (1966) indicated that the play of blind 8- to 12-year-old children was more concrete, ordinary, and lacking in flexibility than that of sighted children. This study, unlike that of Tait (1972), suggests that vision plays a critical role in the development of imagery and related processes, at least in the later years of childhood.

Given the extant data base it would seem particularly appropriate for researchers to become concerned with the *onset* of particular play forms in blind children. At this time we have no data that informs us whether, for example, 4-year-old sighted children engage in more advanced forms of pretense and in more sophisticated object transformations in their play than their blind counterparts. The collection of such data is clearly warranted.

Finally, there are limited data concerning the use of play as a training or therapeutic avenue for blind children. In the one study that we found in our literature search, Rothschild (1960) found it necessary to teach blind children to play before play could be used as a therapeutic tool. The problem with this therapeutic strategy is obvious. If one must teach a child to play in order to allow the expression of his/her unconscious wishes or frustrations through play, then the whole premise of the therapy (i.e., spontaneous release of anxieties) is eroded by the artificiality of the expressive means. Hopefully, in the future, researchers will be cognizant of the obvious limitations placed on exceptional children's activities as a result of their handicaps.

## The Play of Language-Delayed Children

Lovell, Hoyle, and Siddall (1968) compared the symbolic play of 10 speech-delayed and 10 normal preschoolers. The children were divided into three age groups (approximately 3½, 4, and 4½-years-old). The analysis revealed that the oldest speech-delayed children did not engage in symbolic play as frequently as the same-aged normal children, and they engaged in significantly more solitary play. It was observed that the older normal children's symbolic play was, to a large extent, structured by language and was social in nature. Because of their language delays, the older speech-related group appeared to be disadvantaged in making social contacts and engaging in complex symbolic play routines. In addition, the levels of organization and coordination (integration) in the play of the oldest speech-delayed children (4½-year-olds) was found to be less mature and advanced than that of the same-aged normal children.

More recently, Williams (1980) also found that speech-delayed preschoolers did not engage in sociodramatic play as frequently as their age-mates. Both Lovell et al. and Williams concluded that language-impaired children suffer from a broader symbolic deficit and that this deficit is reflected in their lack of pretense play. This conclusion, however, may be premature. As Rubin et al. (1983) point out, the fact that these children engaged in symbolic play, albeit less frequently, suggests a quantitative difference in performance rather than a qualitative competence deficit.

The two studies previously described can be criticized on a number of methodological issues. Perhaps most important, the researchers did not assess children's intelligence. Given that children with language delays and problems often show signs of mental retardation, the confound that intelligence presents is significant and truly precludes general conclusions about the play of language-impaired children. In the future, researchers must take the effects of intelligence into account in experimental designs and analyses. However, the findings reported in these preliminary studies do suggest some interesting and important questions that require future pursuit.

## The Play of Children with Minimal Brain Dysfunction

Generally, observations and teacher, parent, or clinical judgments are used to evaluate the presence of minimal brain dysfunction (Rapoport, Abramson, Alexander, & Lott, 1971; Silvern, 1974). Play has been used as a tool in diagnosing this enigmatic condition, though not in any formalized or systematic manner.

Children with minor neurological impairments were observed during play by Kalverboer (1977). This researcher was interested in assessing the children's behavioral and attentional organization by using the observational categories of manipulative, functional–sensorimotor, and symbolic play. The children with the greatest measured impairments showed higher levels of play organization than the less impaired children. This curious finding certainly questions the use of play in assessing neurological impairment. Obviously more research in this field is required, not only to evaluate possible differences in these children's play, but also to validate definitional criteria and diagnostic procedures used to define and diagnose this condition.

As with studies of normal, emotionally disturbed, and blind children, researchers have attempted to alter the play behaviors of children with minimal brain dysfunction (in this case, "learning disabled" children) through play tuition. Strain and Wiegerink (1975, 1976), in a series of multiple baseline studies, found that the time engaged in social play and sociodramatic play by behaviorally disordered (learning disabled) children could be significantly and reliably increased by teacher attention and reinforcement as well as by teacher-tutored sociodramatic play. These few studies suggest that play deserves more scientific attention in the remediation and education of children with minimal brain dysfunction and learning disabilities.

# CONCLUSIONS

The population of exceptional children provides researchers and clinicians alike with a rich source of data and potential knowledge. Equally as rich are the data-based advances and consequential insights associated with the recent developmental literature on children's play. A systematic blending of the two fields of inquiry could not help but to produce rewarding results; results that would not only have theoretical importance but practical utility as well. However, as we have illustrated in this chapter, thus far the two areas have proven to be strange bedfellows.

The study of play may prove, ultimately, to be very important in the diagnosis, assessment, and treatment of exceptional children. Because many of these children possess handicaps that make standardized testing nearly impossible, systematic observation of their play could provide a useful, unobtrusive diagnostic device. Moreover, play could be used as a nonthreatening and enjoyable medium for therapeutic intervention, training, and skill building.

However, prior to the implementation of play as a clinical tool, it is imperative that normative data are gathered on those different populations of exceptional children previously described. Unfortunately, many, if not most, of the studies reviewed in this chapter were flawed either methodologically, statistically, and/or theoretically. These flaws, if not remedied in the future, may well lead to errors in judgment concerning the use of play as a diagnostic or training instrument. One such error described previously was the Nahme-Huang et al. (1977) study in which schizophrenic children who had difficulty in distinguishing fantasy and reality were provided with fantasy play training. As aforementioned, the results of this study were not in the best interests of the children. The results indicate clearly that play therapy or play tuition cannot be used indiscriminately across various groups of children.

Other studies in which researchers have compared the play of exceptional and normal children have painted a picture of less sophisticated or less mature play patterns evidenced by the former group. Unfortunately, in many of these studies the effects of chronological age, sex, intelligence, institutionalization and socioeconomic status, familiarity of toys, and setting have not been well controlled. Furthermore, many of the oft-cited studies in the literature are based on very small sample sizes. All of these factors have been shown to affect the results of studies involving normal children (Rubin, Fein, & Vandenberg, 1983). Taken together, we are left with a veritable case of "The Emperor's New Clothes" when scrutinizing the extant literature.

In conclusion, we have attempted to describe the play of exceptional children herein. We have also provided the reader with suggestions for future research in this important area. Perhaps, with some tightening of our conceptual and methodological bootstraps we will, in the near future, gain significant new knowledge concerning the diagnostic and therapeutic value of play for exceptional children.

## REFERENCES

American Psychiatric Association. *Diagnostic and statistical manual of mental disorders (DSM-III): Third edition.* Washington, D.C.: The American Psychiatric Association, 1980.

Bartak, L., & Rutter, M. Differences between mentally retarded and normally intelligent autistic children. *Journal of Autism and Child Schizophrenia,* 1976, *6,* 109–120.

Bartak, L., Rutter, M., & Cox, A. A. Comparative study of autism and specific developmental receptive language disorders. *British Journal of Psychiatry,* 1975, *126,* 127–145.

Bender, L. Schizophrenia in childhood: It's recognition, description and treatment. *American Journal of Orthospsychiatry,* 1956, *26,* 499.

Berlyne, D. E. Curiosity and exploration. *Science,* 1966, *153,* 25–33.

Berlyne, D. E. Laughter, humor and play. In G. Lindzey and E. Aronson (Eds.), *The handbook of social psychology* (Vol. 3). Reading, Mass.: Addison–Wesley, 1969.

Burlingham, D. Ego development of the blind. *Psychoanalytic Study of the Child,* 1965, *20,* 194–208.
Burns, S. M., & Brainerd, C. J. Effects of constructive and dramatic play on perspective-taking in very young children. *Developmental Psychology,* 1979, *15,* 512–521.
Cheyne, J. A., & Rubin, K. H. Playful precursors of problem-solving skills. *Developmental Psychology,* in press.
Clune, C., Paolella, J. M., & Foley, J. M. Free-play behavior of atypical children: An approach to assessment. *Journal of Autism and Developmental Disorders,* 1979, *9,* 61–72.
Curico, F., & Piserchia, E. Pantomimic representation in psychotic children. *Journal of Autism and Childhood Schizophrenia,* 1978, *8,* 181–189.
DeMyer, M. K., Mann, N. A., Tilton, J. R., & Loew, L. H. Toy-play behavior and use of body by autistic and normal children as reported by mothers. *Psychological Reports,* 1967, *21,* 975–981.
Ellis, M. J. *Why people play.* Englewood Cliffs, N.J.: Prentice–Hall, 1973.
Enslein, J. P., & Fein, G. G. Temporal and cross-situational stability of children's social and play behavior. *Developmental Psychology,* 1981, *17,* 760–761.
Fein, G. G. A transformation analysis of pretending. *Developmental Psychology,* 1975, *11,* 291–296.
Fein, G. G. Echoes from the nursery: Piaget, Vygotsky, and the relationship between language and play. *New Directions for Child Development,* 1979, *6,* 1–14.
Fein, G. G., & Apfel, N. Some preliminary observations on knowing and pretending. In N. Smith, & M. Franklin (Eds.), *Symbolic functioning in childhood.* Hillsdale, N.J.: Lawrence Erlbaum Associates, 1979.
Groos, K. *The play of animals.* New York: Appleton, 1898.
Horne, E. M., & Philleo, C. F. A comparative study of the spontaneous play activities of normal and mentally defective children. *The Journal of Genetic Psychology,* 1942, *61,* 33–46.
Hulme, I., & Lunzer, E. A. Play, language and reasoning in subnormal children. *Journal of Child Psychology and Psychiatry,* 1966, *7,* 107–123.
Hutt, C. Exploration and play. In B. Sutton-Smith (Ed.), *Play and learning.* New York: Gardner Press, 1979.
Kalverboer, A. F. Measurement of play: Clinical applications. In E. Tizard & D. Harvey (Eds.), *The biology of play.* London: Heinemann, 1977.
Kanner, L. *Childhood psychosis: Initial studies and new insights.* Washington, D.C.: V. H. Winston, 1973.
Leland, H., Walker, J., & Taboada, A. N. Group play therapy with a group of post-nursery male retardates. *American Journal of Mental Deficiency,* 1959, *63,* 848–851.
Lovell, K., Hoyle, H. W., & Siddall, M. C. A study of some aspects of the play and language of young children in delayed speech. *Journal of Child Psychology and Psychiatry,* 1968, *9,* 41–50.
Mehlman, E. Group play therapy with mentally retarded children. *Journal of Abnormal and Social Psychology,* 1953, *48,* 53–60.
Morison, P., & Gardner, H. Dragons and dinosaurs: The child's capacity to differentiate fantasy from reality. *Child Development,* 1978, *49,* 642–648.
Morrison, T. L., & Newcomer, B. L. Effects of directive vs. non-directive play therapy with institutionalized mentally retarded children. *American Journal of Mental Deficiency,* 1975, *79,* 666–669.
Nahme-Huang, L., Singer, D. G., Singer, J. L., & Wheaton, A. Imaginative play and perceptual-motor intervention methods with emotionally-disturbed hospitalized children: An evaluative study. *American Journal of Orthopsychiatry,* 1977, *47,* 238–249.
Newcomer, B. L., & Morrison, T. L. Play therapy with institutionalized mentally retarded children. *American Journal of Mental Deficiency,* 1974, *78,* 727–733.
Nicolich, L. Beyond sensorimotor intelligence: Assessment of symbolic maturity through analysis of pretend play. *Merrill–Palmer Quarterly,* 1977, *23,* 89–99.

Ornitz, E. M., & Ritvo, E. R. The syndrome of autism: A critical review. *American Journal of Psychiatry,* 1976, *133,* 609–621.

Overton, W. F., & Jackson, J. P. The representation of imagined objects in action sequences: A developmental study. *Child Development,* 1973, *44,* 309–314.

Piaget, J. *Play, dreams, and imitation in childhood.* New York: Norton, 1962.

Rapoport, J., Abramson, A., Alexander, D., & Lott, I. Playroom observations of hyperactive children on medication. *Journal of American Academy of Child Psychiatry,* 1971, *10,* 524–534.

Rosenblatt, D. Developmental trends in infant play. In B. Tizard & D. Harvey (Eds.), *The biology of play.* Philadelphia: Lippincott, 1977.

Rothschild, J. Play therapy with blind children. *New Outlook for the Blind,* 1960, *54,* 329–333.

Rubin, K. H. Fantasy play: Its role in the development of social skills and social cognition. In K. H. Rubin (Ed.), *Children's play.* San Francisco: Jossey–Bass, 1980.

Rubin, K. H. Non-social play in preschoolers: Necessarily evil? *Child Development,* 1982, *53,* 651–657. (a)

Rubin, K. H. Social skills and social-cognitive correlates of observed isolation behavior in preschoolers. In K. H. Rubin & H. S. Ross (Eds.), *Peer relationship and social skills in childhood.* New York: Springer-Verlag, 1982. (b)

Rubin, K. H., & Clark, L. Preschool teacher ratings of behavioral problems: Behavioral, sociometric, and social-cognitive correlates. *Journal of Abnormal Child Psychology,* in press.

Rubin, K. H., Daniels-Beirness, T., & Hayvren, M. Correlates of peer acceptance and rejection in early childhood. *Canadian Journal of Behavioural Sciences,* 1982, *14,* 338–349.

Rubin, K. H., Fein, G. G., & Vandenberg, B. Play. In E. M. Hetherington (Ed.), *Handbook of child psychology* (Vol. 4) *Socialization, Personality, Social Development.* New York: Wiley, 1983.

Rubin, K. H., & Krasnor, L. R. Changes in the play behaviours of preschoolers: A short-term longitudinal investigation. *Canadian Journal of Behavioural Sciences,* 1980, *12,* 278–282.

Rubin, K. H., & Pepler, D. J. The relationship of child's play to social-cognitive development. In H. Foot, T. Chapman, & J. Smith (Eds.), *Friendship and childhood relationships.* London: Wiley, 1980.

Rubin, K. H., & Pepler, D. J. A neo-Piagetian perspective of child's play. *Contemporary Educational Psychology,* 1982, *7,* 289–300.

Rubin, K. H., Watson, K., & Jambor, T. Free play behaviors in preschool and kindergarten children. *Child Development,* 1978, *49,* 534–536.

Rutter, M. The development of infantile autism. *Psychological Medicine,* 1974, *4,* 147–163.

Saltz, E., & Brodie, J. Pretend-play training in childhood: A review and critique. In D. J. Pepler & K. H. Rubin (Eds.), *The play of children: Current theory and research.* Basel, Switzerland: Karger AG, 1982.

Saltz, E., Dixon, D., & Johnson, J. Training disadvantaged preschoolers on various fantasy activities: Effects on cognitive functioning and impulse control. *Child Development,* 1977, *48,* 367–380.

Sandler, A. M. Aspects of passivity and ego development in the blind infant. *Psychoanalytic Study of the Child,* 1963, *18,* 343–360.

Sandler, A. M., & Wills, D. M. Preliminary notes on play and ■ in the blind child. *Journal of Child Psychotherapy,* 1965, *1,* 7–10.

Silvern, L. B. The playroom diagnostic evaluation of children with neurologically based learning disabilities. Paper presented at the American Academy of Child Psychiatry meeting, October 1974.

Singer, J. L., & Streiner, B. F. Imaginative content in the dreams and fantasy play of blind and sighted children. *Perceptual and Motor Skills,* 1966, *22,* 475–482.

Smilansky, S. *The effects of sociodramatic play on disadvantaged preschool children.* New York: Wiley, 1968.

Smith, P. K. Social and fantasy play in young children. In E. Tizard & D. Harvey (Eds.), *Biology of play*. Philadelphia: Lippincott, 1977.

Smith, P. K., & Daglish, L. Sex differences in infant and parent behavior. *Child Development*, 1977, *48*, 1250–1254.

Smith, P. K., & Syddall, S. Play and non-play tutoring in preschool children: Is it play or tutoring which matters? *British Journal of Educational Psychology*, 1979, *48*, 315–325.

Spencer, H. *Principles of psychology* (Vol. 2, 3rd ed.). New York: Appleton, 1873.

Strain, P. Increasing social play of severely retarded preschoolers with socio-dramatic activities. *Mental Retardation*, 1974, *13*, 7–9.

Strain, P. S., & Wiegerink, R. The social play of two behaviorally disordered preschool children during four activities: A multiple baseline study. *Journal of Abnormal Child Psychology*, 1975, *3*, 61–69.

Strain, P. S., & Wiegerink, R. The effects of sociodramatic activities on the social interaction among behaviorally disordered preschool children. *The Journal of Special Education*, 1976, *10*, 71–75.

Sutton-Smith, B. (Ed.), *Play and learning*. New York: Gardner Press, 1979.

Switzky, H. N., Ludwig, L., & Haywood, H. C. Exploration and play in retarded and nonretarded preschool children: Effects of object complexity and age. *American Journal of Mental Deficiency*, 1979, *83*, 637–644.

Tait, P. Behavior of young blind children in a controlled play session. *Perception and Motor Skills*, 1972, *34*, 963–969.

Tilton, J. R., & Ottinger, D. R. Comparison of the toy play behavior of autistic, retarded and normal children. *Psychological Reports*, 1964, *15*, 967–975.

Tubbs, V. K. Types of linguistic disability in psychotic children. *Journal of Mental Deficiency Research*, 1966, *10*, 230–240.

Ungerer, J. A., & Sigman, M. Symbolic play and language comprehension in autistic children. *Journal of the American Academy of Child Psychiatry*, in press.

Vygotsky, L. S. Play and its role in the mental development of the child. *Soviet Psychology*, 1967, *12*, 62–76.

Watson, M. W., & Fischer, K. W. Development of social roles in elicited and spontaneous behavior during the preschool years. *Developmental Psychology*, 1980, *16*, 483–494.

Wehman, P. Establishing play behaviors in mentally retarded youth. *Rehabilitation Literature*, 1975, *36*, 238–246.

Weiner, E. J., Ottinger, D. R., & Tilton, J. R. Comparison of toy play behavior of autistic retarded and normal children: A reanalysis. *Psychological Reports*. 1969, *25*, 223–227.

Weiner, E. A., & Weiner, E. J. Differentiation of retarded and normal children through toy-play analysis. *Multivariate Behavioral Research*, 1974, *9*, 245–252.

Williams, R. *Symbolic play in young language handicapped and normal speaking children*. Paper presented at the International Conference on Piaget and the Helping Professions, Los Angeles, Februrary 1980.

Wing, L. Perceptual and language development in autistic children: A comparative study. In M. Rutter (Ed.), *Infantile Autism: Concepts, Characteristics and Treatment*. London: Churchill–Livingstone, 1971.

Wing, L., Gould, J., Yeates, S. R., & Brierly, L. M. Symbolic play in severely mentally retarded and in autistic children. *Journal of Child Psychology and Psychiatry*, 1977, *18*, 167–178.

# 6 Methodological Issues in Studying Early Pretend Play

Lorraine McCune-Nicolich
*Rutgers, The State University of New Jersey*

Larry Fenson
*San Diego State University*

Pretend play has received much attention from developmental researchers in the past decade because it reflects significant features of early post-sensorimotor functioning. Evidence is accumulating on the composition of play at various age levels and on sequential progressions across age. Although there is a certain robustness in these findings across studies, there are also some major differences, many of which may be attributable to methodological variation among studies. Symbolic play research is particularly ripe for methodological evaluation because of the substantial recent growth of the literature produced in different labs using diverse procedures. We are now in a position to: (1) identify a number of concerns about which decisions must be made by every researcher and practitioner who chooses to study children's play; and (2) examine the pros and cons associated with various alternative approaches. Several other reviews of play in general (Rubin, Fein, & Vandenberg, in press) and symbolic play in particular (Fein, 1981; McCune-Nicolich, 1981) have recently been published. The present review differs from these (and complements them) in focusing specifically on methodological aspects of pretend play.

This review is also intended to provide guidance to the practitioner in using play techniques for assessment purposes. Knowledge of a child's symbolic play ability can provide valuable additional information in an age range where psychometric instruments are known to be weak. The two- and three-year-old child exhibits cognitive abilities that are transitional between sensorimotor and preoperational functioning. Infant tests such as the Bayley Scales of Infant Development (Bayley, 1969) emphasize sensorimotor development and yield ceiling effects, whereas more advanced instruments (e.g., The McCarthy Scales of Child Development; McCarthy, 1972) emphasize skills characteristic of the preschool or school-age child, leading to floor effects. Symbolic play assessment, as a supplement to psychometric measures, allows determination of the extent to which the child has accomplished the transition from sensorimotor to skilled symbolic functioning. For the young nonverbal child who fails to respond to items requiring a vocal response, this additional information is particularly valuable. Similarly, handicapped children who exhibit patterns of failure in testing situations may display unexpected and usable strengths in a free play setting.

Comparison of the paradigms for studying play utilized by McCune-Nicolich (Nicolich, 1977; Hill & McCune-Nicolich, 1981) and Fenson (Fenson & Ramsay, 1980; 1981) highlights the methodological variation observed across many studies. In the McCune-Nicolich approach, the researcher typically visits the home twice; the first to become familiar with the child and the setting, the second to videotape a half-hour segment of free play. The mother and the child are seated on the floor and a bucket of toys is placed near them. The mother is instructed to let the child take the lead, not to suggest or model play behaviors, but to be responsive to the child and, in other ways, behave as naturally as possible.

In recent studies by Fenson, mother and child visit a comfortable homelike laboratory, where an initial warm-up period takes place in a room furnished with a sofa and some toys. Following the warm-up, the experimenter brings the mother and child to a room furnished as a play room with a small table and chair and a larger chair for the mother. A number of studies using various toy presentations have been conducted in this lab, but typically the experimenter makes mother and child comfortable in the room, provides toys appropriate to the particular study, and leaves to videotape a brief time period of play (3 to 10 minutes) before returning to model certain behaviors with the toys, then leaving again to videotape the postmodeling phase. Several trials of this type make up a particular session. Mothers are typically instructed to remain available to the child for comfort or reaction, but are discouraged from participating in the play activity. This paradigm can be varied in terms of toys provided and actions modeled to yield a flexible tool for studying various aspects of pretend play.

Variations between these two approaches include the major methodological differences apparent in the field. McCune-Nicolich provides a large variety of toys, some appropriate for pretend play, others not. Fenson provides a set of materials chosen for their ability to elicit certain behaviors or test the baby's ability to utilize the toys in a novel way (e.g., providing a plastic scrubber that is to be used as an apple). Although the Fenson laboratory provides a warm and comfortable testing atmosphere, it contrasts with research in the home setting. For McCune-Nicolich the mother is included as a participant in play, for Fenson, as an observer. Length of time the child is continually involved with a toy set also differs, although total observation time is in some cases similar. For Fenson, modeling is an essential component that allows clearer articulation of the child's competence than simple observation. For McCune-Nicolich, reliance on spontaneous observation in studying the child's response to the toys in a naturalistic context is highly valued, despite the level of ambiguity and variation across subjects inherent in this procedure. What effects on research outcome result from methodological differences in context, maternal role, experimenter role, available objects, and use of elicitation techniques?

The scope of variation in this research area should now be clear. In the following pages we will first address definitional issues and describe the sequence of developments in early symbolic play that has been observed despite methodological variation, highlighting scoring decisions and their implications. We will then describe the various research paradigms, indicating the effects of various methodological decisions on research outcome. Finally, we will summarize and cite new directions for the study of early pretending.

## DEFINITIONAL ISSUES

With the increasing emphasis on play among developmental researchers it has become apparent that questions concerning criteria for identifying play as a generic behavior (Weisler & McCall, 1976) as well as distinguishing symbolic play from other forms have not been clearly established. Rather, there is a tendency in the literature to assume a level of agreement that a close reading of recent studies indicates is clearly lacking. Concerning play as a generic form of behavior, Rubin, Fein, and Vandenburg (in press) recognize this confusion as they propose the following definition: ''Play is a behavioral disposition which occurs in describable and reproducible contexts, and is manifest in a variety of observable behaviors. The dispositional, behavioral and contextual markers of play, however, all will vary given the particular theoretical biases of the investigator [p. 9].'' Thus play can be recognized: (1) through a particular disposition; (2) by listing a taxonomy of acceptable play behaviors; or (3) by defining occurrences in a given context as play. The dispositional characteristics suggested by Rubin et al., taken together, provide a prototype for play that would probably be recognized by most observers:

1. Play activities are pursued for their own sake and are thus intrinsically motivated, rather than based on internal drives or external pressure.
2. In play as opposed to enjoyable work, there is attention to means that may be varied and explored rather than to outcome.
3. Rather than examining an object to learn about its properties, the player seeks to answer the question ''What can I do with this object?''.
4. Play behaviors, in contrast with instrumental behaviors are not ''serious renditions'' of the actions they represent (Rubin et al., in press). Thus, the child who drinks from an empty cup does not expect to quench thirst.
5. Play is not governed by external rules.

6. The player is actively engaged in the behavior in question.

(The reader is referred to Rubin et al. for the theoretical bases and justification for these criteria.)

Thus a play context would necessarily be relaxed and free from constraints, providing the background that allows the child to begin to direct his or her own activities in a satisfying manner. Observation of a positive affective attitude and engagement with the materials on the part of the child would suggest that a play context has been established.

## Symbolic Play

An evocative statement from Shotwell, Wolf, and Gardner (1980) described symbolic play as "The ability to represent actual or imagined experience through the combined use of objects, motion and language [p. 176]." However, ambiguity concerning the term *symbolic* has prevented general acceptance of a definition of symbolic play (Huttenlocher & Higgins, 1978). The theories of Piaget (1962) and Werner and Kaplan (1963) are universally cited by play researchers, but interpretation of their ideas varies considerably. Both theories stress the basis of symbolization in sensorimotor action, from which symbols gradually evolve until they are established as signifying elements that are separate from the elements signified. Werner and Kaplan additionally emphasized social and emotional developments in the mother–child dyad as an equal contribution to symbolic development. Each theory suggests a range of transitional behaviors that mark the path from actions that are merely sensorimotor to those that are clearly symbolic.

Whereas Werner and Kaplan emphasized language development and mentioned play only in passing, Piaget presented a series of stages that span the transition from highly realistic functional play (e.g., based on object functions) characteristic of sensorimotor stage 5, through several levels of pretending where symbol and referent are only marginally separable (sensorimotor stage 6 and symbolic stage 1), to true symbolization (symbolic stage 2) where a complete separation between signifier and signified is apparent. As representational skill develops, its influence should be apparent in both play and language, although the exact nature of this influence remains controversial (Fischer, 1980; McCune-Nicolich, 1981).

Whereas some studies have considered most or all of the behaviors identified by Piaget in defining symbolic play as equivalent, most recent studies have distinguished between more and less mature behavior (Belsky & Most, 1981; Fenson & Ramsay, 1981; Inhelder, Lezine, Sinclair, & Stambak, 1972). Some researchers have viewed only the late-occurring behaviors in this sequence (i.e., those involving complete separation of signifier and signified) as symbolic. Such higher-level behavior is usually identified by the substitution of a perceptually and functionally dissimilar object (internally represented as the signifier) for another object (internally represented as the signified) (Field, DeStefano, & Koewler, 1982; Huttenlocher & Higgins, 1978; Ungerer, Zelazo, Kearsley, & O'Leary, 1981). In interpreting play results it is therefore essential to note the specific behaviors a given researcher has included in the symbolic play category.

Certain trends that characterize the transition from the lower- to higher-level behaviors make it most appropriate to consider these behaviors as a continuum and adopt a comprehensive definition. The first trend, decentration, frees symbolic actions from the child's own body, allowing adoption of others' actions in pretend play as well as use of dolls and other people for expressing the child's pretend activities. The second, decontextualization, allows pretend play to occur with decreasing environmental support. The third, integration, leads to sequentially and, later, hierarchically organized play. Thus, various behaviors can be placed on continua defined by these trends. In addition, this comprehensive approach facilitates comparisons between children and across domains of symbolic functioning.

## SEQUENCE OF DEVELOPMENTS IN SYMBOLIC PLAY

To highlight the influence of the trends of symbolic development observed in play, consider the child of 12 months who pretends to drink from an empty cup, but neither offers a drink to her mother or a doll, nor pretends to drink from her empty hand. Six or eight months later the same child may pour imaginary tea from her extended finger, into a cup that she then sips, refills, and offers to her mother saying, "careful, hot!". Contrasts are apparent in the treatment of the object, the cup, the role of the participants (self and mother), the ability to sequence behaviors, and the mode of expressing play that involves language, action, or both.

In the early example, the child's behavior is bound to its sensorimotor origins, both in the sense that pretend is supported by present appropriate objects, and in the sense that pretend actions are confined to the child's own repertoire of daily activities, and limited to single actions involving her own body. In the more mature example, the child exhibits decentration from the self by projecting a pretend scheme onto her mother's actions. By pouring from her empty hand she exhibits a decontextualization of the symbolic action from its appropriate material object (a teapot or other vessel). Finally, by having more than one participant drink, by pretending to pour then drink, and by introducing appropriate verbal commentary, the child shows a capacity for integrating symbolic play acts into larger, more complex units, perhaps based on the dawning ability to plan play prior to performance (Fenson & Ramsay, 1980).

At present, it remains unclear how decentration, decontextualization, and integration develop over time in relation to one another because studies have not yet examined all of these dimensions in the same children. Consequently they are discussed separately in the following sections, despite the fact that the same underlying representational skill may account for the several lines of development observed. As each type of play behavior is discussed, aspects of scoring that present particular difficulties at that level will be noted.

## The Transition to Pretend

*Presymbolic Actions.* At the onset of symbolic play, children begin to show a sensitivity to the socialized functions of objects. That is, a cup is for drinking, a comb is for grooming hair, a toy truck for rolling along the ground, a spoon for stirring. However, the child's presymbolic actions, although out of the realistic context (e.g., place empty cup to lips), has a serious, action-naming quality that appears different from the somewhat later, more elaborate pretend manner of handling these objects (Escalona, 1973; McCune-Nicolich, 1981). This early form of appropriate use out of context can be observed as early as 9 or 10 months of age and corresponds to the fifth sensorimotor stage (Piaget, 1962). Fenson and Ramsay (1980, 1981) did not distinguish pretend from such nonpretend play activities, but noted that self-directed acts, such as grooming and eating, preceded object-directed acts, such as rolling a truck or stirring with a spoon.

*Self-Pretend.* According to McCune-Nicolich (1981; Nicolich, 1977), following a period of realistic action naming the child begins to exhibit awareness of the pretend nature of the play activities. This simultaneous consideration of the real action and the pretend situation it represents provides the earliest symbol–referent relationship. As Piaget (1962) noted, the symbol *is* the child's action, but what is symbolized is also the child's action. Thus, although symbol and referent can be conceptualized as separate, in action they are fused. Piaget termed this transitional, limited form of pretending the *symbolic scheme* and suggested that its onset should correspond to entry into the sixth sensorimotor stage, which is also characterized by deferred imitation and the onset of representation (Ramsay & Campos, 1978).

In order to capture the transition to symbolic play and its earliest manifestation, the distinction between early conventional gestures and initial pretend can be reliably made based on the child's affect, emotional and social tone, and the elaboration of the behavior (Escalona, 1973; Fein, 1981; Nicolich, 1977). According to Nicolich (1977), a child who smiles as a conventional gesture is performed or looks coyly at the mother is exhibiting a typical pretend emotional–social tone. For children with minimal affect, however, this index leads to an excessively conservative judgment, as noted by Hill and McCune-Nicolich (1981). Such elaborations as sound effects or exaggerated gestures (e.g., tipping the head back or making lip-smacking noises when "eating" or "drinking") suggest that the child is evoking a past real experience with similar objects, rather than merely recognizing the present object by gesture. Any of the non-literal features of play suggested by Fein (1981) can also be used to distinguish presymbolic from pretend behaviors. These include performance of activities in the absence of necessary materials, failure to carry activities to their usual outcome, treating inanimate objects as animate, use of substitute objects, and performing activities usually done by someone else.

At first, pretend behaviors are limited to the child's own everyday activities (eating, sleeping, grooming) and are enacted with the child as the only participant (e.g., feed self rather than doll or mother) exhibiting the extreme centration of early symbolization. The majority of children show this type of behavior by 13 months of age.

## Decentered Pretend

*Object- and Other-Directed Acts.* Sometime between 12 and 18 months of age most children extend pretending beyond the self by imitating the actions usually performed by others and projecting symbolic schemes, previously played only with respect to the self, to other participants in pretend (dolls, stuffed toys, adult play partners) (Piaget, 1962). Where potentially animate participants are involved (e.g., feed or groom doll or mother), the actions are considered *other directed.* Where only inanimate objects are involved (e.g., stir in cup with spoon; hammer on toolbox) they are termed *object-directed* (Fenson & Ramsay, 1980, 1981). It remains unclear whether a developmental sequence exists between object-directed and other-directed pretend. Fenson and Ramsay (1980) reported greater frequency of object-directed than other-directed acts at 13 months and approximately equal frequencies at 19 and 24 months. Shimada, Kai, and Sano (1981) observed that 71% of their longitudinal sample produced other directed acts with respect to the mother prior to exhibiting doll pretend.

*Other-Directed Active Play.* A more advanced form of decentration in which the animate participant (adult partner or doll) is apparently treated as an active agent, rather than a passive recipient of the child's action, has been observed by a number of investigators as occurring between 24 and 30 months of age (Corrigan, 1982; Fenson, in press; Lezine, 1975; Lowe, 1975; Shimada et al., 1981; Watson & Fischer, 1977). It might be expected that mother would be the first active agent to be included in the child's play. Because mother is, in fact, capable of agency, orchestrating the mother's activity would not seem to require the same degree of pretence as would be the case for dolls. Shimada, Sano, & Peng's (1979) data suggested this trend, with mother or experimenter being the earliest participants depicted as recipients, and later agents, in the child's pretend activity. A note of caution is called for here, because it is sometimes difficult to determine whether the child has indeed indicated a pretend action for the mother, or if the mother assumes, on her own, that this extension of pretend is what the child expects.

Concerning use of dolls as active agents, considerable variation is apparent in the way this type of play has been defined. Some investigators specified activities as active, (e.g., place mirror in doll's hand so it can see itself; have one doll take the temperature of another doll), whereas others determined by the child's manner of handling the objects whether the doll was considered active or passive (e.g., place cup in doll's hand rather than to its lips, have doll ''walk'' to table or bed before pretending it eats or sleeps). In addition, sometimes language was used to infer that the doll was active (e.g., attribute of feelings such as sad, hungry). Thus, the doll was considered active not only in the sense of agency or movement, but rather in the sense of exhibiting some aspect of consciousness either as an agent or an experiencer.

Difficulties with this category are highlighted both by the ambiguities in defining it and by the fact that many studies find active doll use too infrequent for analysis (Corrigan, 1982; Shimada et al., 1981) and pool this category with passive pretend. When pretend language is scored separately from pretend action, attribution of active status to the doll is more frequent in verbalization than action (Bretherton, Bates, McNew, Shore, Williamson, & Beeghy-Smith, 1981; Fenson, in press), perhaps suggesting that observers can more easily note verbal attributions of consciousness or agency than they can distinguish the child's view of the doll as active or passive, merely from motor performance. Further research is needed to clarify this potentially important developmental step. Given the low frequency of this behavior in naturalistic studies, a focused modeling strategy is called for that separates verbal from nonverbal manifestations and includes modeling behaviors in the active mode that cannot be accomplished using a passive strategy.

## Integrated Pretend Play

What criteria can be used in identifying pretend play sequences? In naturalistic studies play sequences emerge from the stream of the child's pretend and nonpretend activity and may continue for many minutes as the child repeats a simple action with variations or elaborates a complex theme, or be so brief as to be unnoticed unless repeatedly viewed on videotape. It is therefore necessary to determine which behaviors taken together form a sequence, considering both their relationship to one another and their temporal proximity. For this reason, time sampling, which involves selection of arbitrary temporal units from the stream of behavior, is ineffective in characterizing the sequential aspects of naturalistic play. An approach that brackets episodes of pretending for detailed analysis is more effective in this regard.

By 19 months of age most children exhibit simple combinations of actions in their pretend play. These have been termed *single scheme* in that the same action is directed toward two recipients (e.g., feeding two dolls) or involves use of two or more objects in succession, (e.g., drinking from two cups). By about 24 months, most children exhibit a more advanced type of multischeme combination, comprised of two or more different actions.

Nicolich (1977) found that the child's initial multischemes tended to be unordered (i.e., comprised of two actions without an essential sequential relationship e.g., feed doll, bathe doll) and that multischemes reflecting an ordered relationship were later-occurring and rare, whereas Fenson and Ramsay (1980) seldom observed unordered sequences. This discrepancy in findings can probably be attributed to procedural differences in the selection and presentation of toys. Fenson and Ramsay placed related sets of objects around the room, including such items as a doll, bed, and blanket, which encouraged children to perform appropriately ordered sequences with objects. Nicolich, in contrast, presented toys in a bucket and did not include groups of objects likely to suggest ordered sequences.

What is the basis for the child's early pretend sequences? Bruner (1970) presented an analysis of sensorimotor sequences developing between 12 and 17 months that may provide a useful analogy for conceptualizing symbolic play sequences. He reported that, prior to sequencing, the individual acts became ''modularized'', such that they could each be performed with less apparent attention on the child's part, thus freeing attention for the possibility of incorporating the behavior with other actions. He identified three forms of sequencing: repetition with variation (analogous to single-scheme sequences), integration such that the act becomes part of a larger whole, and differentiated elaboration, where an act that was previously performed in global fashion is now articulated into a clear sequence of parts. Certain ordered sequences would exemplify each of these latter processes. In putting the doll in a bed and covering it, two single acts join to establish a simple theme (integration). In telephone play, the initial gross motion of holding phone to ear while vocalizing and fiddling with the dial differentiates into the sequence of a simulated phone call. Unordered sequences appear rather strung together in comparison to such orderly combinations. However, it may be that an object, such as the doll, provides a unifying theme for the child as various objects and schemes are related to it (based partly on the nature of objects in view), suggesting some aspects of integration, others of differentiated elaboration.

A single or multischeme sequence may contain self-directed as well as decentered acts, both active and passive. In addition, substitutive and inventive acts may be included. Thus sequences can present a rich source of information concerning the child's play performance. Therefore, component acts comprising the sequence should be scored as well as crediting the child with the sequence itself. In addition, sequences can be scored for their complexity in terms of number and types of components (Corrigan, 1982; McCune-Nicolich, in preparation).

## Decontextualization: Changes in Object Treatment

As previously noted the earliest manifestation of presymbolic behavior is seen at about 10 months of age when children show knowledge of realistic meanings by performing gestures appropriate to particular objects out of their pragmatic context. Use of realistic objects as props for pretend feeding of dolls, fixing of furniture, etc. indicates an initial level of decontextualization, as real objects become amenable to self, other, and object-directed pretend activities. Subsequently children learn to substitute one object for another. Experimental studies have demonstrated a scalable sequence of such developments. First, substitutions occur with objects that are similar in appearance of function to the real object; next, ambiguous objects can be used, and subsequently children will substitute objects that have their own appropriate function in diverse activities or exhibit "invention" (Fenson, 1981) by playing without the support of objects. However, these results are based primarily on studies where one or two objects were presented to the child at a time, and the desired behavior modeled by the experimenter. Further, it is unclear at what point on the continuum the child should be credited with the separation of signifier and signified noted by Piaget and others as the hallmark of the true symbol. In more naturalistic studies both eliciting object substitution and determining what behaviors to credit remain problematic. Approaches to overcoming these problems are discussed below in a section concerning selection of materials for studying pretend play.

## Planning

Planning of symbolic behaviors prior to performance has been noted as an important milestone by several investigators (Fein, 1975; Nicolich, 1977; Piaget, 1962). McCune-Nicolich (1981) proposed that planning in play indicated a clear separation of signifier from signified. Planned acts could best be described as exhibiting a hierarchical structure where a prior internal event (the "plan" that is inferred to exist based on external behaviors) functions as "signified" and the external pretend behavior functions as a separate "signifier" element. This notion represents a generalization of Piaget's (1962) criterion of announced object substitution as indicating a developmental shift in the symbolic ability to his level 2 play that is clearly symbolic rather than functionally based.

Such a shift in symbolic ability should affect various play skills and may provide an organizing principle for the highest-level abilities defined by the trends toward greater decentration, decontextualization, and integration previously described. Thus defining a doll as agent rather than recipient of action requires transformation of the doll from a passive to active role; production of ordered multischemes requires an internalization of the required order, and use of a substitute object requires internal designation of this substitution. From a methodological perspective, study of these skills in the same subjects is required to evaluate this theoretical corespondence.

According to McCune-Nicolich, planning as a separate play variable can be inferred by announcement, search for required materials, or performance of a preparatory act prior to the pretend one (e.g., removing the doll's hat in order to comb its hair). Nicolich (1977) reported that planning was first observed in her longitudinal sample between 18 and 26 months of age. Field, De Stefano, and Koewler (1982) observed increases in prior announcement of fantasy intentions when they compared 2- and 3-year-old children. Additional study of this skill seems warranted both because of its potential as an organizing principle for higher level activities and because of its continued development in older children. If play is to be related to language in a particular study, use of verbalization to infer planning involves a potential confound, so various types of planning should be coded separately.

## PARADIGMS FOR STUDYING SYMBOLIC PLAY

Symbolic play studies have varied in the contexts chosen for data collection, the materials used, the participants, and the use of elicitation strategies. In reviewing recent studies it became apparent that they could be grouped in a manner that overlaps these individual dimensions. Certain studies aimed at description of naturally occurring development of the full range of symbolic play activities, and did not use elicitation techniques. These naturalistic studies took place in the home or homelike laboratory, and included a relatively large toy selection (Inhelder, Lezine, Sinclair, & Stambak, 1972; Nicolich, 1977; Bates, Benigni, Bretherton, Camaioni, & Volterra, 1979; Fenson & Ramsay, 1980).

Other studies have concentrated on eliciting particular play skills. Investigators studying the ability to use substitute objects that vary in prototypicality presented one or two objects, modeled appropriate and inappropriate uses, and scored matching child behaviors over several trials (Elder & Pederson, 1978; Jackowitz & Watson, 1980; Pederson, Rook-Green, & Elder, 1981; Killen & Uzgiris, 1981). Another approach has been to model sequences of behaviors with two or more toys, to investigate conditions under which children perform such sequences (Fenson & Ramsay, 1981; McCall, Parke, & Kavanagh, 1977; Shore, 1981). Fein (1975) designed a study aimed at demonstrating the influence of modeling and contextual support on the child's ability to use a substitute object.

More elaborate procedures involving presentation of brief scenes including a number of objects varying in prototypicality have recently been developed, often with the goal of establishing relationships between more advanced pretend strategies and language development. (Fenson, in press; Bretherton et al., 1981). An additional paradigm, represented by the work of Watson and Fischer (1977) and Corrigan (1982), aimed at establishing the relationship between the abilities to use active agents and substitute objects in play and language.

In the following paragraphs we shall discuss the dimensions of methodological variation represented in these paradigms and consider the effects on research outcome. We shall consider in turn the setting, materials and their organization, participants and their roles, and elicitation procedures.

## Contexts for Play

As McCall, Eichorn, and Hogarty (1977) noted, when studying a relatively unknown phenomenon "a safe strategy is to begin with the context in which the behavior is known to occur [p. 14]." The most common setting for young children's play is their own home, using their own toys, and with a parent available. A number of studies have, in recent years, contributed basic descriptive information concerning play at home (Dunn & Wooding, 1977; Fein & Apfel, 1979; Hill & McCune-Nicolich, 1981; Nicolich, 1977; Rosenblatt, 1977). Similar studies conducted in laboratories presented results of sufficient similarity to suggest that play can be effectively studied in either setting (Fein & Robertson, 1975; Fenson & Ramsay, 1980). Although no study has been conducted that allows direct comparison of results, findings by Acredelo (1981) with respect to children's success in cognitive mapping tasks suggested that adequate familiarization with the laboratory environment tended to eliminate the advantage previously observed in home performance.

If pretend play is more frequent and/or shows higher levels of development at home, this may be because these behaviors are learned in the home context and at first limited to specific objects. Performances removed from this setting and using unfamiliar objects may require more advanced decontextualization (Franklin, 1973). Some extraordinary examples of early symbolization have been reported in home-based studies. Franklin cites Valentine (1937), who observed play with an imaginary object at 11 months and an occasion when the child first bumped the doll's head, then brought it to the mother to be kissed at 15 months of age. This is an ordered sequence, possibly involving planning, occurring quite a bit earlier than usual.

Bruner (1975), who observed mothers feeding and bathing their babies in a homelike laboratory every 2 weeks from 7 months of age described one 9-month-old who first put the empty cup to the mother's mouth, then later in the session to the doll's mouth, an early example of other-directed pretend. It is also possible that certain categories of play occur earlier with reference to the child's favorite toys, or in particular situations that call these to mind for the child. Thus pretending with the child's own, familiar doll may require less decentration than playing with a doll provided by the experimenter. Informal observations by McCune-Nicholich suggest that this may be the case. Pretend feeding of mother or doll may actually first occur in real feeding sessions where mothers often accept pieces of real cookie from their babies' hands as part of the social interaction at mealtime. In the early stages the boundary between pretend and real feeding may be rather fuzzy in the natural setting.

When play is studied in the laboratory, it would seem reasonable to construct as warm and homelike an environment as possible. Most infant laboratories do strive for this goal, but it is particularly important in play. Thus provision of carpeting, comfortable chairs, child-size furniture, and freedom from office noises can all be used to simulate home conditions.

Length of play session varied in the studies reviewed from 3-minute segments (Watson & Fischer, 1977) to 20 or 60 minutes (Dunn & Wooding, 1977). Watson and Fischer reported the absence of pretend play in their initial 3 minute premodeling condition. Fenson and Ramsay (1981) successfully observed such play with a moderate-size toy set in an 8 minute premodeling period. Optimum session length varies with the size of the toy set as well as the goals of the study. Based on the studies reviewed, it would seem that an adequate familiarization period, followed by an observation period of 5 minutes (unless the child indicates disinterest or completion of use of the toys) is a minimum for meaningful data collection. If the toy set is large, additional time may be needed as the children often explore the objects individually before settling down to play.

## Selection and Presentation of Toys

Young children's play is greatly influenced by the objects that are available. Hence toy selection is critical for the success or failure of most play studies. Choosing both objects and manner of presentation must be decided in relation to the goals of the study and other aspects of methodology. The number, realism, and organization of the toys all affect the type of play behavior that is likely to be observed at various ages.

Initial pretending is more a response to object properties and an expression of the child's understanding of basic social action patterns than a result of individual invention. Thus, the naturalistic studies previously noted employed sets of objects that were realistic in appearance and could be used for household, doll, and vehicle play. Some studies also included ambiguous materials such as paper, blocks, or sticks. A typical set of such objects is as follows: doll (one or more) with removable clothes; bed or box, blanket or cloth, pillow; doll bottle, spoon, cup dish, pot or pitcher; comb, brush, mirror; mop or broom, scrub brush, sponge; large truck, smaller truck with driver, blocks; teddy bear or monkey; telephone.

In the first 3 years this set is useful in eliciting presymbolic play, self-pretend, other- and object-directed pretend, as well as multischeme sequences. Occurrence of single-scheme sequences is facilitated by inclusion of several dolls and duplicates of other materials. Some boys may avoid dolls as early as 18 months (Fein, Johnson, Kosson, Stork, & Wasserman, 1975) and thus may exhibit decentration more frequently with other animate-type toys. Stuffed animals and action figures provide a useful addition to the toy set, permitting both active and passive other-directed acts. Given children's preference for realistic objects in this age range (Fein & Robertson, 1975), little object substitution is likely to be observed with this toy set despite the presence of ambiguous materials.

The toys can be presented in a container or displayed around the room. In the latter case the child will show initial preference for toys located near the mother; in the former a period of exploration as the bucket is emptied is likely to precede more involved pretend play. Alternatively the toys may be divided into related sets (e.g., doll with bottle and blanket; vehicle with driver and blocks) and presented for separate trials (Lowe, 1975; Largo & Howard, 1979). This would tend to narrow the range of behaviors observed, because children could only relate to one another objects that had been presented together. This would lead to more homogeneity across children in the types of behavior they perform, but not necessarily the maturity of that behavior. Presentation of appropriate related object sets also increases the likelihood of observing ordered sequences.

If lower-level sensorimotor behaviors or preliminary logical play (e.g., classificatory grouping) are to be coded in addition to symbolic play, additional materials should supplement the basic set previously described. McCune-Nicholich (in prep.) included a clear plastic dumping bottle filled with small fruits, a set of nesting cups, a small pop-up jack-in-the-box, a match box that slides open and shut, and a puzzle, as well as duplicates of a number of the socially meaningful toys. These toys allow assessment of sensorimotor play involving simple and more complex manipulations of objects. In addition they tend to elicit sequences of play based more on logical thinking than the personal–social knowledge emphasized in pretending. Examples include grouping objects by kind, fitting puzzle pieces and nesting cups, constructing with blocks or cups, and means– ends sequences such as popping the jack-in-the-box or dumping and filling the bottle.

In studies aimed at specifically investigating the occurrence of the more advanced forms of play (e.g., object substitution, use of dolls as agents, complex sequences) somewhat different strategies for toy selection are called for. For example, children's tendency to use substitute objects depends on contextual support as well as object characteristics. Thus, Fein (1975) reported that even under conditions of modeling, children were more likely to perform a pretend action (feed a toy horse from a cup) if either horse or cup were realistic, providing contextual support for the substitution. Similarly, Corrigan (1982) found a developmental sequence in children's willingness to substitute one or both objects in an elicited task (washing a doll). Ungerer et al. (1981) reported that between 18 and 34 months of age children were decreasingly reliant on both perceptual qualities of objects and the use of motor acts to express pretend. These known performance conditions must be taken into account in selecting both objects and methodology for studying object substitution. In a following section the effectiveness of elicitation techniques such as modeling is discussed.

Concerning the study of the use of dolls as active agents versus recipients in pretend raises similar issues of context. In addition, because rather refined motor manipulation is needed to express the doll's agency, provision of easily manipulable figures with props or tools to scale should facilitate expression of such acts.

The use of thematically related materials seems most appropriate for eliciting children's most advanced play sequences. For example, Fenson (in press) modeled a bath scene for his subjects, using the following materials: large doll, boat, plastic block, small dish, square sponge, cup, paper towel, mirror, and a cardboard box. These materials, when presented with accompanying modeling and narration, continue to elicit more elaborate sequences as well as increases in object substitution and invention throughout the third year of life.

## Participants: Child, Mother, Experimenter

*Mother.* If the process of symbolization arises partly from social interaction of mother and infant (Werner & Kaplan, 1963), the influence of the mother as a potential participant or observer in play research where her child is the subject is an important consideration. From an affective point of view, the presence of the mother can provide a level of security for the child that allows greater ability on the part of the child to engage in exploration and play with toys (Ainsworth, Blehar, Waters, & Wall, 1978; Mahler, Pine, & Bergman, 1975). According to Werner and Kaplan, it is the child's initial desire to share the object world with the mother that motivates the child's initial attempts at communication, marking the start of the child's development toward internalized symbolic processes. According to this position the motive for early pretend play is the child's desire to try out the meanings of various actions with objects, seeking confirmation from the mother of the child's developing symbols. An additional tutorial role is assigned to the mother by El'Konin (1966), who specifies that children learn to pretend by observing pretend behaviors in adults.

If the mother is present during the play observation she may fill a number of potential roles: (1) remain present, but engaged in an unrelated activity; (2) remain attentive to the child, but uninvolved in play; (3) engage in play with the child in a responsive manner only; (4) attempt to facilitate play by modeling or suggesting activities. In all of the studies reviewed here, with the exception of Dunn and Wooding (1977) and Nicolich (1977), mothers were either engaged in activity, such as reading or transcribing their child's utterances, or instructed to remain attentive but uninvolved except for providing emotional support. There have been no studies that directly examined the effects of various conditions of maternal involvement on the incidence or maturity of pretend play.

Three studies, however, contribute evidence in this regard. A recent experimental study (Sorce & Emde, 1981) has demonstrated that children's ability to engage in exploration and play, using the mother as a secure base was dependent on her perceived emotional availability to the child rather than simply her presence. When mothers read and ignored their 15-month-old children's overtures, children inhibited play and tended to remain in proximity to the mother. In contrast, when the mother passively attended to her child rather than reading, the children showed a more positive emotional tone, produced more nondistress vocalizations, smiled more often, were generally more active, and showed their positive reaction to their mothers by both looking at them more frequently and directing more affiliative bids to them.

Dunn and Wooding (1977) studied twenty-four 18- to 24-month-old children in their homes when mothers were either working around the house or relaxing. They distinguished two levels of maternal involvement, ''joint attention'', indicating that the mother was looking at the toy the child was using and ''joint play'', indicating that the mother took part in the child's activity. For all subjects the median length of those play bouts that included some time in joint attention was longer than those where the mother did not attend to the child's activities. Of the longest bouts (those longer than 6.6 minutes) 86% included some time in joint attention. Children initiated the majority of pretend play bouts. In contrast with simple object play, when children were involved with pretend, they tended to be already in joint attention with their mothers or to seek their mothers out to share the activity with them. This lends indirect support to mothers' potential role as interpreters of early symbols. Concerning mothers initiations, these were twice as likely to focus on symbolic activities as on any other individual type of activity observed. Dunn and Wooding further observed extensive explicit teaching of symbolic activities on the mothers' part, adding additional evidence for the maternal role as facilitator of symbolic development.

McCune-Nicolich (McCune-Nicolich, in prep.; Nicolich, 1977), as previously noted, included the mother in the setting as a play partner but instructed her to let the child take the lead, responding as naturally as possible. Mothers in these studies varied greatly in the extent to which they followed these instructions. Some mothers tended to initiate heavily, others virtually ignored their child's overtures, becoming involved with one of the objects themselves. When mothers made symbolic play suggestions or modeled such play, they tended to do so at one or two levels in advance of the child's ongoing activity (Adler, 1982), suggesting a tutorial role. In these studies the babies' earliest play combinations often involved sequences where one or more activities focused on mother as recipient (feed mother, rather than doll).

What are the methodological implications of these studies? First, it is apparent that the mother's assigned role in the study can have a critical effect on the results. One would anticipate higher frequencies and potentially higher levels of play when children are observed with a mother who is allowed to respond actively to the child. If early sequences tend to include the mother, these are more likely to occur. On the contrary, if mothers are present, but kept busy with an unrelated activity, they may not be functioning as a secure base for their child's exploration, and play of all types may be inhibited. However, inclusion of the mother as a participant has pitfalls. First, mothers vary in their level of responsiveness to their children, giving children whose mothers are better players an advantage. Second, mothers may or may not inhibit their natural tutorial function. In the worst case one can imagine a play session where maternal influence was so great that independent measurement of the child's ability becomes impossible.

The mothers' role needs to be weighed along with other issues in developing the methodology of choice for a particular purpose. If optimum performance on the part of every child is the critical variable (as for example when play is used for assessment purpose), mothers should be encouraged to take a passive but responsive role for part of the session, then perhaps asked to model or suggest some pretend activities that are slightly in advance of what has been observed spontaneously. It may be that assessment of pretend play in the dyad is of greater significance and utility than independent assessment of the child if the mother indeed fills the supportive role assigned her by Werner and Kaplan. If the child's independent ability is the focus, then perhaps a trained experimenter who is able to take a limited participant–observer role should be the child's co-player, while the mother sits nearby and observes under emotionally responsive passive conditions. In any case, scoring should differentiate between child acts that are in response to a model or suggestion and those that are independent.

*Experimenter.* The role of the experimenter can be considered facilitative, neutral, or negative. If the child sees the examiner as a stranger, play may be inhibited; if as an adult who can provide attention and support, it may be enhanced. None of the studies cited provided the experimenter with an active responsive role such as that provided for the mother in the Dunn and Wooding (1977) and Nicolich (1977) studies. The roles adopted by the experimenter included one or more of the following: (1) present toys and either remain as a passive observer or leave the room; (2) model symbolic play acts; and (3) make specific play suggestions. The effects of modeling and suggestions are considered later.

Limited experimental evidence exists about experimenter influences. However, familiarity of the child with the experimenter is an important consideration in all research. Given the nature of play, one might expect the presence of an unfamiliar versus a familiar adult to be have different effects on performance. Fein and Robertson (1975) compared children's play with a familiar adult who had visited the children monthly for 7 months with play involving a stranger. Play suggestions were included in this study of 2-year-old children, which used a balanced within-subjects design. Despite a familiarization procedure that required that the child be sufficiently comfortable to exchange objects with the adult prior to beginning the session, children produced more varied and frequent pretend in response to the familiar adults. The within-session results of another study described by Fein and Robertson suggested that as the child became more accustomed to interacting with an unfamiliar examiner, pretend play became more frequent. Despite possible fatigue effects after an hour's observation and testing, subjects engaged in more pretend play during later rather than earlier toy presentations.

## Elicitation Procedures: Modeling and Suggestion

A number of researchers, concerned that spontaneous play may underestimate the competencies of many children, have sought to enhance pretend play by modeling or prompting various behaviors of interest. The goal of these procedures is to elicit emergent behaviors, which are infrequent in spontaneous play but of particular importance in signaling new forms of competence. The investigator assumes that the child will perform with understanding a wider variety and/or higher level of play than would occur spontaneously in a brief observational period, particularly in the laboratory setting where the child is faced with many novel objects and may spend more time exploring than playing.

Although it is now clear that elicitation procedures are not mandatory for studying symbolic play as once claimed by Watson and Fischer (1977), it has been demonstrated that these procedures do generally enhance pretend play. Moreover it appears that young children typically imitate only those actions that are meaningful to them, rather than mimic a model's actions in a rote manner without comprehension. This conclusion derives from the finding that age differences are preserved rather than distorted in imitative play. Elicitation techniques elevate performances at all ages, but developmental relations are preserved. In fact, modeling often magnifies differing ability levels between successive age groups (Fenson & Ramsay, 1981).

Elicitation procedures are typically of three kinds. In one type, the experimenter or model performs a single act or a series of play actions but does not suggest verbally that the child follow these examples. In a second type the experimenter suggests that the child perform a given pretend behavior but does not demonstrate the behavior in question. A third type involves the combination of these two, modeling and suggestion.

*Modeling.* Modeling procedures can be developed that create relatively ideal conditions for assessing specific abilities in play. Some studies have involved modeling of one or a few discrete acts or sequences (Jeffree & McConkey, 1976; Watson & Fischer, 1977), whereas others involved enactment of elaborate pretend scripts (Bretherton, Bates, McNew, Shore, Williamson, & Beeghy-Smith, 1981; Wolf & Gardner, 1981). Fenson and Ramsay (1981), for example, in one experiment used a series of separate trials to test the limits of young children's ability to produce multischeme combinations under the most favorable conditions possible. On each trial the child was given the opportunity to imitate the target behavior immediately after demonstration with no distracting toys in view, thus limiting memory requirements. Under these conditions many

15-month-olds imitated multischeme combinations, although their performance was attenuated relative to a 19-month-old group. Performance of both groups was higher than in two other experiments in which larger numbers of multi-schemes were modeled consecutively in a free play setting. A similar highly structured trials approach was used by Corrigan (1982) to elicit imitated language and play in 19- to 30-month-olds under varying levels of contextual support.

Thus far, published analyses of modeled scripts have used these as effective means for creating a pretend context, rather than for assessing the extent of the child's ability to reproduce and/or vary the scenes as presented, although this procedure has potential for assessment of symbolic ability in children beyond 24 months of age. In addition, modeling within the script format also permits easier detection of what might otherwise be anomalous behaviors. For example, Fenson (in press) modeled several inventive actions such as turning on imaginary water faucets over a bathtub. Subsequent replications of such actions by the children were readily identifiable. Spontaneous performance of similar actions by the child outside of the modeling context would likely prove difficult or impossible to interpret and be overlooked.

It should be recognized that as experimental structure increases, the extent to which the findings replicate free play activities probably decreases. However, for the goal of using play-like paradigms to study representational development, this issue is less important than in studies designed to describe the nature and development of play as a natural child activity. In interpreting the relationship between responses to a model and the same play behavior occurring spontaneously, it is useful to think of modeling as a form of contextual support. Every pretend behavior involves some form of internal analogue to the motor performance. Modeling may function both to motivate the child to a particular behavior and to aid in construction of the internal analogue to the action. This interpretation is in keeping with Piaget's (1962) analysis of representation as derived from imitative skills.

*Suggestion.* Some researchers have combined modeling with suggestion in either order. Sigman and Ungerer (1981) suggested first, then modeled if children were not responsive to suggestion. Fenson (in press) followed modeling with suggestions both more and less advanced than the child's performance following modeling to determine whether failure to imitate higher-level acts was due to motivation or inability. Verbal requests elicited advanced behaviors in many of the oldest children who had not displayed these actions following modeling. Younger children did not imitate the more advanced behaviors, but did comply with requests for lower-level behaviors that they had performed prior to suggestion. Additional studies combining these approaches were conducted by Largo and Howard (1979) and Watson and Fischer (1977).

Suggestion has also been used effectively without modeling. Pederson and his associates (Elder & Pederson, 1978; Pederson, Rook-Green, & Elder, 1981) found that direct requests were effective in studying the ability of 2½ to 3½-year-old children to pretend with ambiguous and inappropriate objects in a structured table-top task. Suggestion was also used effectively by Fein (1979) with younger children.

Both modeling and suggestion, either in combination or individually, have proved effective in eliciting various pretend behaviors of interest. These techniques have often prompted levels of play that exceed spontaneous performance, although there are exceptions. Fein and Apfel (1979) reported that play was inhibited when an unfamiliar examiner suggested relatively abstract object substitutions to 22-month-old children, whereas simpler suggestions made by a more familiar adult tended to be followed. McCall, Parke, and Kavanagh (1977) found that suggestion increased target behaviors in the 18 to 24 month age range, but led to lower performances at 36 months. It may be that older children are particularly inhibited by requests to perform nonsensical or counter-intuitive actions with inappropriate materials under some circumstances. As McCall, Parke, and Kavanagh point out, what infants are able to imitate is partly a function of their cognitive development, whereas what they choose to imitate involves such motivational factors as social context and the child's goals at the time.

## CLOSING NOTES

### Looking Back

Stimulated by Piagetian theory, the past decade has witnessed rapid growth in the use of pretend play as a means of assessing aspects of representation, especially in the period prior to and during the early stages of expressive language. Several useful theoretical reviews of the literature have recently appeared (Fein, 1981; McCune-Nicolich, 1981; Rubin et al., in press). The present review examined methodological practices in the study of pretend play with the goal identifying how methods influence findings.

Definitional issues were considered first. Although advances have been made since Schlosberg's (1947) observation that play is too broad a term to have any value, criteria still vary widely, depending on the theoretical stance and particular aims of the investigator. A more or less agreed upon set of criteria for pretend play, however, is emerging. Next we identified consensus measures which seemed most able to capture the major aspects of decentration, decontextualization, and integration, the three main developmental trends in pretend play. Finally, we examined a range of methodological practices revolving around the play context (home versus lab, structured or spontaneous), toys (selection and presentation), the roles of mother and experimenter (active and passive), and elicitation techniques (modeling and suggestion), and attempted to show the effects of varying strategies on the nature of play observed.

## Looking Forward

The themes of decentration, integration, and decontextualization suggest several avenues of research. First, it would be useful to know what experiences or more basic underlying developments account for specific changes in the childs play. Second, what interrelationships both in timing and manifestation can be demonstrated among these three tendencies in play development? Third, to what extent do these trends characterize areas other than play, such as language, as suggested by Werner and Kaplan (1963), or social-emotional relationships with the mother or other attachment figures?

If a single aspect of early pretend could be identified, that represents the critical next step in this research area, it is attention to the role of language in play development. Given the theoretical premise of Piaget (1962) that both pretend play and language are influenced by the developing semiotic function, aspects of play methodology related to language are of considerable interest. Fein (1981) and McCune-Nicolich (1981) summarized initial research results concerning relationships between pretend play and language.

From a methodological point of view, however, a number of issues worthy of study can be identified. To begin with, we need to know to what extent children's language skill influences their performance in pretend play in a given paradigm. If play suggestions are made, or if a scene is modeled with verbal accompaniment, language comprehension skills are called into account immediately. In scoring pretend behaviors, those accompanied by verbal commentary are more easily interpretable, providing an advantage to the more verbally skilled child. Scoring procedures for pretend have taken account of the child's accompanying language in a variety of ways, sometimes without explicit discussion of the rationale. Approaches include omitting consideration of verbalizations (Lowe, 1975), requiring verbal accompaniment to clarify pretend action (Ungerer et al., 1981), including language as evidence of pretending (Nicolich, 1977), and scoring pretend language and pretend action separately (Fenson, in press). It is clear that more specific attention needs to be devoted to the language understood and produced by the playing child as a means of developing greater insight into the emerging world of both nonverbal and verbal symbols.

## REFERENCES

Acredelo, L. P. *The familiarity factor in spatial research: What does it breed besides contempt?* Paper presented at the meeting of the Society for Research in Child Development, Boston, April, 1981.

Adler, C. M. Mother-toddler interaction: Content, style, and relations to symbolic development. Doctoral Dissertation. Rutgers, the State University of New Jersey, New Brunswick, N.J., 1982.

Ainsworth, M. D. S., Blehar, M. C., Waters, E., & Wall, S. *Patterns of attachment: Psychological studies of the strange situation.* Hillsdale, N.J.: Lawrence Erlbaum Associates, 1978.

Bates, E., Benigni, L., Bretherton, I., Camaioni, L., & Volterra, V. *The emergence of symbols: Cognition and communication in infancy*. New York: Academic Press, 1979.

Bayley, N. *Manual for the Bayley Scales of Infant Development*. New York: Psychological Corporation, 1969.

Belsky, J., & Most, R. From exploration to play: A cross-sectional study of infant free play behavior. *Developmental Psychology*, 1981, *17*, 630–639.

Bretherton, I., Bates, E., McNew, S., Shore, C., Williamson, C., & Beeghy-Smith, H. Comprehension & production of symbols in infancy: An experimental study. *Developmental Psychology*, 1981, *17*, 728–736.

Bruner, J. The growth and structure of skills. In K. Connolly (Ed.), *Mechanisms of motor skill development*. New York: Academic Press, 1970.

Bruner, J. The ontogenesis of speech acts. *Journal of Child Language*, 1975, *3*, 255–287.

Corrigan, R. The control of animate and inanimate components in pretend play and language, *Child Development*, 1982, *53*, 1348–1353.

Dunn, J., & Wooding, C. Play in the home and its implications for learning. In A. Tizard, & D. Harvey (Eds.), *Biology of play*. Philadelphia: Lippincott, 1977.

Elder, J. L., & Pederson, D. R. Preschool children's use of objects in symbolic play. *Child Development*, 1978, *49*, 500–504.

El'Konin, D. Symbolics: Its function in the play of young children. *Doshkol'noe Vosapitaire*, 1966, *12*(6), 62–76.

Escalona, S. K. Basic modes of social interaction: Their emergence and patterning during the first two years of life. *Merrill–Palmer Quarterly*, 1973, *19*, 205–232.

Fein, G. G. A transformational analysis of pretending. *Developmental Psychology*, 1975, *11*, 291–296.

Fein, G. G. Echoes from the nursery: Piaget, Vygotsky, and the relationship between language and play. In E. Winner, & H. Gardner (Eds.), *Fact, fiction and fantasy in childhood*. (New directions in child development.) San Francisco: Jossey–Bass, 1979.

Fein, G. G. Pretend play in childhood: An integrative review. *Child Development*, 1981, *52*, 1095–1118.

Fein, G. G., & Apfel, N. The development of play: Style, structure and situation. *Genetic Psychology Monographs*, 1979, *99*, 231–250.

Fein, G. G., Johnson, D., Kosson, N., Stork, L., & Wasserman, L. Sex stereotypes and preferences in the toy choices of 20-month-old boys and girls. *Developmental Psychology*, 1975, *11*(4), 527–528.

Fein, G. G., & Robertson, A. *Cognitive and social dimensions of pretending in two-year-olds*. Unpublished manuscript, Yale University, 1975.

Fenson, L. Developmental trends for action and speech in pretend play. In I. Bretherton (Ed.), *Symbolic play: The developmental of social understanding*. New York: Academic Press, in press.

Fenson, L., & Ramsay, D. Decentration and integration of play in the second year of life. *Child Development*, 1980, *51*, 171–178.

Fenson, L., & Ramsay, D. Effects of modeling action sequences on the play of twelve-, fifteen- and nineteen-month-old children. *Child Development*, 1981, *52*(3), 1028–1036.

Field, T., De Stefano, L., & Kowler, J. Fantasy play of toddlers & preschoolers. *Developmental Psychology*, 1982, *18*, 503–508.

Fischer, K. A theory of cognitive development: The control and construction of hierarchies of skills. *Psychological Review*, 1980, *87*(6), 477–531.

Franklin, M. Nonverbal representation in young children: A cognitive perspective. *Young Children*, 1973, *29*, 33–53.

Hill, P. M., & McCune-Nicolich, L. Pretend play and patterns of cognition in Down's syndrome children. *Child Development*, 1981, *52*, 611–617.

Huttenlocher, J., & Higgins, E. T. Issues in the study of symbolic development. In W. A. Collins (Ed.), *Minnesota symposium on child psychology* ■. Hillsdale, N.J.: Lawrence Erlbaum Associates, 1978.

Inhelder, B., Lezine, I., Sinclair-deZwart, H., & Stanbark, W. Les debuts de la function symbolique. *Archives de Psychologie,* 1972, *41,* 187–243.

Jackowitz, E. R., & Watson, M. W. The development of object transformations in early pretend play. *Developmental Psychology,* 1980, *16,* 543–549.

Jeffree, D., & McConkey, R. An observation scheme for recording children's imaginative doll play. *Journal of Child Psychology and Psychiatry,* 1976, *17,* 189–197.

Killen, M., & Uzgiris, I. C. Imitation of actions with objects: The role of social meaning. *Journal of Genetic Psychology,* 1981, *138,* 219–229.

Largo, J. A., & Howard, J. A. Developmental progression in play behavior of children between nine and thirty months, II: Spontaneous play and language development. *Developmental Medicine and Child Neurology,* 1979, *21,* 492–503.

Lezine, I. The transition from sensorimotor to earliest symbolic function in early development. *Research Publication A.R.N.M.D.,* 1975, *51,* 221–232.

Lowe, M. Trends in the development of representational play in infants from one to three years: An observational study. *Journal of Child Psychology and Psychiatry,* 1975, *16,* 33–47.

Mahler, M., Pine, F., & Bergman, A. *The psychological birth of the human infant.* New York: Basic Books, 1975.

McCall, R. B., Eichorn, D. H., & Hogarty, P. S. Transitions in early mental development. SRCD Monograph No. 171, 1977, *42,* 3.

McCall, R., Parke, R., & Kavanagh, R. Imitation of live and televised models by children one to three years of age. *Monographs of the Society for Research in Child Development,* 1977, Vol. 42 (5, Serial No. 173).

McCarthy, D. *McCarthy Scales of children's abilities.* New York: Psychological Corporation, 1972.

McCune-Nicolich, L. Toward symbolic functioning: Structure of early pretend games and potential parallels with language. *Child Development,* 1981, *52,* 785–797.

McCune-Nicolich, L. *Symbolic play: developmental sequences in the first three years.* Book in preparation.

Nicolich, L. McCune. Beyond sensorimotor intelligence: Assessment of symbolic maturity through analysis of pretend play. *Merrill-Palmer Quarterly,* 1977, *23*(2), 89–101.

Pederson, D. R., Rook-Green, A., & Elder, J. L. The role of action in the development of pretend play in young children. *Developmental Psychology,* 1981, *17,* 756–759.

Piaget, J. *Play, Dreams & Imitation.* New York: Norton, 1962.

Ramsay, D., & Campos, J. The onset of representation and entry into stage 6 of object permanence development. *Developmental Psychology,* 1978, *14,* 79–86.

Rosenblatt, D. Developmental trends in infant play. In B. Tizard, & D. Harvey, (Eds.), *Biology of play.* London: William Heinemann Medical Books, Ltd., 1977.

Rubin, K., Fein, G. G., & Vandenberg, B. Play. In E. M. Hetherington (Ed.), *Carmichael's manual of child psychology: Social development.* New York: Wiley, in press.

Schlosberg, H. The concept of play. *Psychological Review,* 1947, *54,* 229–231.

Shimada, S., Sano, R., & Peng, F. *A longitudinal study of symbolic play in the second year of life.* RIEEC Research Bulletin, RRB 12, 1979, Gakugi University Koganei, Tokyo, Japan.

Shimada, S., Kai, Y., & Sano, R. *Development of symbolic play in late infancy.* RIEEC Research Bulletin, RRB 17, 1981, Gakugi University, Koganei, Tokyo, Japan.

Shore, C. *Getting it together.* Unpublished doctoral dissertation, University of Colorado, Boulder, Colorado, 1981.

Shotwell, J., Wolf, D., & Gardner, H. Styles of achievement in early symbol use. In M. Foster, & S. Brandes (Eds.), *Symbol as sense: New approaches to the analysis of meaning.* New York: Academic Press, 1980.

Sorce, J., & Emde, R. N. Mother's presence is not enough: Effect of emotional availability on infant exploration. *Developmental Psychology,* 1981, *17,* 737–745.

Ungerer, J. A., Zelazo, P. R., Kearsley, R., & O'Leary, K. Developmental changes in the representation of objects in symbolic play from 18 to 34 months of age. *Child Development,* 1981, *52,* 186–195.

Valentine, C. W. A study of the beginnings and significance of play in infancy (II). *British Journal of Educational Psychology,* 1937, *8,* 285–292.

Watson, M. W., & Fischer, K. W. A developmental sequence of agent use in late infancy. *Child Development,* 1977, *48,* 828–836.

Weisler, A., & McCall, R. B. Exploration and play: Resume and redirection. *American Psychologist,* 1976, *31,* 492–508.

Werner, H., & Kaplan, B. *Symbol formation.* New York: Wiley, 1963.

Wolf, D., & Gardner, H. On the structure of early symbolization. In R. L. Schiefelbush, & D. D. Bricker (Eds.), *Early language: Acquisition and intervention.* Baltimore, Md.: University Park Press, 1981.

# 7 Objects, Symbols, and Substitutes: The Nature of the Cognitive Activity during Symbolic Play

Carol E. Copple
*Whittaker Corporation*

Rodney R. Cocking
*National Institute of Education*

Wendy S. Matthews
*College of Medicine and Dentistry of New Jersey*

## Introduction

The emergence of symbolic play activity marks a critical milestone in cognitive development, falling as it does between a period in which the child's play with objects reflects merely relational activity in which an object is explored in a myriad of ways relative to other objects in the child's environment (e.g., by rolling a ball along a flat versus inclined surface) and a later period when the child can combine a sequence of symbolic acts to create an elaborate unfolding of conceptually tied symbolic actions. Commonplace events such as a child's extending a tray of poker chips to her playmate and saying "The cookies are ready" seem simple enough. Increasingly, however, the multideterminant nature of symbolic play is being recognized as evolving through the interaction of various characteristics of the *situation* and the play *participants* (Fein, 1975; Golomb, 1977; Matthews, 1977).

Matthews (1977) studied symbolic activities that transpire during interactive free play in preschool children. She directed her attention toward those symbolic acts by which fantasy sequences are initiated and identified six modes by which the preschool child transforms a reality situation into a symbolic one. In three of the modes, referred to as *Material,* children use objects symbolically, referring to them in ways that transform the objects into something other than what they are in reality (e.g., "This [counter] is an oven"). In the other three modes, termed *Ideational,* no tangible referent is involved in the fantasy (e.g., "Pretend I'm a lady, OK" or "We're about to have fireworks"). Instead of relying on objects, the pretense or symbolic activity stems exclusively from the imaginations of the play participants.

Playmate familiarity influences the mode of symbolic activity (Matthews, 1977). Matthews examined the proportion of material to ideational fantasy initiations across play sessions and found that when children have not played together much they tend to rely more heavily on material modes, utilizing objects often in the course of their symbolic actions. As they become further acquainted, however, the ideational modes increase and the children come to rely less on the objects in the play environment.

Although Matthews' work was not developmental in nature, others have wondered if a developmental progression might be seen in children's use of material and ideational modes in symbolic play. Field, DeStefano, and Koewler (1982), in a cross-sectional developmental study of fantasy play involving children from approximately 1½ to 5½ years of age, found evidence of a developmental progression. Citing Fein (1975), Field et al. concluded that "fantasy play that has an 'anchor support' from the object may require less symbolic activity than [for example] the representation of a person 'removed from the features of the immediate environment' [p. 511]."

The intent of the present chapter is to explore aspects of material-based symbolic acts for what they reveal about the cognitive activity underlying symbolic play in the preschool years. Specifically, we were interested in children's choices of object-substitutes when the functional uses of these objects are systematically varied with choice options favoring different object properties. Investigations already have been conducted on children's choices of object-substitutes on the basis of the physical similarities between the object-substitute, or "signifier," and the actual object, or "signified," to use Piaget's terms. Other studies have examined the functional properties of object-substitutes, as will be pointed out in the course of the discussion. The aim of the research that we undertook and will describe later was to go further than these previous studies and examine the verbalizations that accompany the children's object choices. We regard these verbalizations as holding the cues to the cognitions upon which the children's representational choices were based.

## Transformations and Prototypicality

In a study of object substitution during pretend play, Fein (1975) systematically varied the "prototypicality" of play objects. The boundary characteristics by which a play object could count as some "real object" varied according to the number of cognitive transformations required by the child to achieve a mental representation sufficient to effect a symbolic act, such as "feeding a horse." For example, feeding a toy horse from a clamshell would require a "single substitution" of the shell for a food container. However, feeding a highly schematic horse-shape from the clamshell would require a "double substitution" of both the horse-shape and the clamshell. Fein found that it was easier for young children to transform one object than two within a symbolic play act, and that having one highly prototypical or realistic object seemed to provide support for the symbolic use of a second object that was less realistic.

Object substitution in children's play was also investigated by Golomb (1977). In a reality-oriented puzzle situation, she presented children with the task of making a mannequin. Pretense situations were also employed in the study, such as asking the children to pretend that a baby had just awakened and needed something to eat. In both the puzzle and pretense situations a selection of objects was available to the children, ranging from suitable to highly unsuitable. Although there is no assurance that the "range of suitability" of objects was equal, either within or across situations, the findings suggest that children's object transformations are not only different in pretense and realistic games, but that they reflect a certain "lawfulness" in terms of object choices.

Focusing on the children's responses to the object options, Golomb was able to consider more fully the thought processes underlying the children's use of the objects in pretend play. Golomb had children continue to choose among the object options as one by one preferred substitutes were successively eliminated. The protocol material revealed that children's responses to less than suitable object substitutions included hesitations, evasiveness, explicit rejections, amusement, and various forms of symbolic transformations. Although requiring children to continue to choose substitutes until all options had been exhausted had the disadvantage of detracting from the ecological validity of the pretense situation and possibly weakening the make-believe set, the advantage of the procedure was that it allowed the observer to see regularity in the order to children's judgments of object suitability, as well as their reactions to progressively dissatisfactory alternatives for representing the object.

Ungerer, Zelazo, Kearsley, and O'Leary (1981) were also interested in the effect of the similarity between "real" and substitute objects. They wondered, for example, if children would increasingly show the ability to move away from a physically similar signifier (toy telephone) and utilize a physically dissimilar object (e.g., a wooden block) in representing a signified object such as a telephone. They also questioned whether the functional requisites of the symbolic act could override the child's need for a physically similar object in favor of a functionally-approximate one that was physically dissimilar. In structured play situations, Ungerer et al. (1981) found that young children between 18 and 34 months of age "depended more on the physical similarity between signifier and signified . . . than on the object's functional action properties [p. 194]." This finding might reflect nothing more than an inclination to take a likeness when a likeness is offered, however. How a child might behave symbolically under the constraint of a particular functional demand but in the presence of two equally dissimilar objects was not explored in the Ungerer et al. study. This issue will be addressed in the research undertaken for this chapter by the present authors.

Attributes of both form and function were systematically varied in a study by Jackowitz and Watson (1980). From a developmental analysis, they found the earliest stage of object substitution involved the utilization of materials that were highly similar to the signified object both in form and in function. In a subsequent stage, either physical or functional dissimilarity could be tolerated with equal ease: a toy telephone could be represented by a toy banana (similar form, dissimilar function) or by a walkie-talkie (which they regarded as a dissimilar form that had a similar function). Only in a later stage could a dissimilarity in both form and function be tolerated simultaneously within a symbolic act.

In conceptualizing the research to be reported in this chapter, we were interested in exploring further the nature of the child's choices of object substitutes. Some of the background literature will help to clarify our rationale. Fein (1975), for example, has talked in terms of the prototypicality of an object. Researchers and theorists in linguistics and memory are converging on a model in which there are degrees of prototypicality within a given category rather than a perceptual template of some kind that is a single unchanging picture of what an object looks like (Brown, 1977; Rosch, 1973, 1975). In the case of the concept of cup, for instance, the notion is that individual cups may vary in their prototypicality to the degree that they are representative of the category. It is reasonable to assume that with development there are changes in the nature of the child's mental prototypes themselves, as well as changes in how these prototypes affect such behavior as object choices, drawing, and other representational activities.

## REPRESENTATION AND SYMBOLIC PLAY

Developmental differences aside, a fuller understanding is needed of the nature of the representations underlying children's object use. It was our hypothesis that children do not carry a fixed image of a given object for which they seek the closest approximation possible in play. Rather, from observational reports and data (Matthews, 1978), we were led to believe that children choose an object for pretending on the basis of the role the object will play in their particular fantasy situations. This is obviously true at the practical level. For example, if a group of children want a spaceship they can board, they will pick an object that is at least child-size and perhaps large enough to contain one of them. However, what is of more interest is whether an anticipated *imaginary* function would make a difference as well. That is, when there is no immediate *physical* necessity in taking Object A over Object B, would the function the child is imagining for the object make a difference? For example, if a child is considering a pretend sequence in which she/he will pour into a cup, it does not matter in a practical sense whether or not the "cup" is concave because there is no liquid. Does it matter to the child? If the property of concavity matters for situations in which the cup is to hold an imaginary liquid but not for other situations, such as pretending to wash the cup, this fact would indicate that differentiation according to function is part of the mental activity of the imagining process.

Fein and Apfel (1979) also noted the lack of information on the extent to which children's pretend enactments reflect differentiated object combinations. Looking at the very earliest period of pretending (12–20 months), they sought evidence of differentiation of object use according to the *recipient* of the action. For instance, would a tool used for pretend feeding be used for all sorts of recipients, or would tools and recipients be selectively matched? Fein and Apfel found selectivity among objects according to whom the child was feeding in the make-believe situation. In our own research, we were interested in investigating children's selectivity among objects on the basis of the use to which the objects would be put within a particular fantasy play context.

Elder and Peterson (1978) studied developmental differences in children's reliance on the presence of a substitute object and the importance of similarity of the object and its referent. The investigators did not separate object features critical to performing a given function from perceptual features that were incidental to the use function. Hence, the Elder and Peterson study left a question unanswered: To what extent does the child judge correspondence between referent and substitute according to the function the object will have in make-believe play?

## Function and Prototypes

We were interested in examining this question in a systematic way, and we chose children's dramatic play situations as the vehicle. Two groups of subjects were involved in two contrasting fantasy scenarios. The same object would be needed for one purpose in one scenario and for an entirely different purpose in another scenario. For example, half of the subjects would need a spoon for stirring make-believe lemonade and half would need it for scooping imaginary ice cream. We reasoned that if the children made different spoon choices depending on the differing functions, this would suggest that the children were operating with prototypes or representations that were at least partially *function-specific*.

## Language Representation and Symbolic Play

We were interested in what the children said and did along with their object choices. These behaviors potentially provide insight in several ways. Suppose a child says, "This will be my phone. Pretend it has a dial." The message reveals, first, something about the child's idea of what a phone should be like, at least in the given context. By looking at what many children say or do in the same situation, we might discover some interesting regularities. For example, do children often mention physical features that are irrelevant to the demand characteristics of the pretense situation (e.g., "Pretend it's black like a phone")? With respect to the function criterion, do children focus on physical features that are relevant to the present requirements or are they equally likely to note functional features of the object that would currently be irrelevant (e.g., a dial when the scenario only calls for answering the phone)?

Second, in the preceding telephone example, we find the child actively bridging the gap between the idea of what an object should be like and what is at hand. In this case, the idea is expressed overtly in a verbalization. Although such verbalizations may be partially or primarily for the benefit of other persons, they may also be seen as manifest forms of a kind of mental activity that takes place in solitary play as well, though often covertly. At the least, it seems safe to assume that underlying such verbalizations is awareness of a gap between the substitute and that which it depicts and a consciousness of pretending that the object looks different.

To summarize the objectives of the current study, we examined whether children would discriminate in their choices of objects according to the purpose the object was to serve in pretend play, given specific functional demand characteristics. We were interested in the verbalizations and gestures that transformed the selected objects into the props required for performing the make-believe situations, and therefore incorporated these behaviors into our investigation as well. That is, when the child chose an object that did not ostensibly have the feature needed to serve the function the scenario demanded, we expected that it would often be supplied verbally or gesturally. Within the age range of the study (3 years, 11 months to 5 years, 5 months) we did not expect differences in the basic tendency to select object substitutes according to function. Our interest was in the emergence of children's *awareness* of their own evaluating processes in selecting objects for symbolic use. This reflectiveness was expected to emerge in children's comments, both unelicited and elicited during an interview with the experimenter.

## AN EXPERIMENTAL APPROACH TO THE STUDY OF OBJECT FUNCTION IN SYMBOLIC PLAY

### Method

*Subjects.* Eighteen boys and twelve girls who were enrolled in two preschool programs participated in the study. Ranging in age from 3-11 to 5-5, these children were divided into two groups of subjects that were matched for age, sex, and preschool program. Script I was used with one group and Script II was used with the other, as described in Table 7.1.

*Setting.* Children were brought to a small laboratory room on an individual basis. In this setting, they engaged in dramatic play sessions with a female

TABLE 7.1

| *Warm-up Items*<br>*Prototype* | *Functional Emphasis* | *Materials* |
|---|---|---|
| Newspaper | Reading | Magazine page |
| Pack of gum | Separating sticks of gum | thin, narrow strips of plastic |

| *Play Episode Items*<br>*Prototype* | *Functional Emphasis*<br>*Script 1* | <br>*Script 2* | *Materials*<br>*Script 1* | <br>*Script 2* |
|---|---|---|---|---|
| Spoon | Scooping | Stirring | ½ eggshell | Wooden rod |
| Pitcher | Pouring | Carrying | Pitcher with spout | Pitcher with handle |
| Bowl | Holding fruit | Holding water | Colander | Lucite flowerpot |
| Envelope | Readability | Openability | Index card with writing | Clear vinyl glasses case |
| Shoe | Wearing | Tying | Milk container with top cut off | Pegboard with string between two holes |
| Phone | Talking | Dialing | Toy dog bone | Metal pinwheel mounted on a board |

experimenter who was familiar to all of them. Initially, the experimenter and the child sat at a child's table and talked in order to establish the play situation. A toy cash register was nearby on the table, and behind the experimenter were various boxes, drawers, and cupboards where the child was told there would be objects they could use in the games. Each of the drawers of the chest, doors to the cupboard, and the various boxes was distinguished by different colored circles.

The play interactions were videotaped through one-way windows between the small play room and the control booth. The technology of this laboratory was sufficient to ensure high quality audio recording of the children's verbalizations.

*Procedure.* The experimenter invited each child, one at a time, to join her in playing a game. As she and the child entered the playroom, the experimenter suggested that they pretend to be storekeepers. She pointed out the cash register and permitted the child to play with it. Following a brief introductory period, the experimenter began one of the two "scripts" that was randomly assigned to the subject. The experimenter took the lead in indicating general and specific points of the plot for the play, including the need for various objects. Two warm-up items were given during this introductory period (see Table 7.1). The warm-up items were similar to the subsequent coded trials, as can be seen. These warm-up items were designed to draw the child into the make-believe set and to assure that the child understood the expectations of the situation. In both warm-up and actual trials, the experimenter's requests for various objects were made in a casual manner, with the experimenter indicating to the child the content of the pretend episode and the place in which an appropriate object might be found; for example:

> "Now let's pretend Mr. McGhee is in the store. He says he wants to look around a bit and then he'll have some ice cream. We'll need a spoon for scooping out some ice cream. In the box with the white dots there should be a bunch of things. OK? See what you find in there that will make a good spoon". (Script I)

The contrasting portion of Script II was very similar except that the use for which the imaginary spoon was being requested was stirring lemonade instead of scooping ice cream. In each case, the seemingly critical attribute for Script I would differ from that of Script II. In the case of the spoons, for example, a long sticklike piece is suited for stirring whereas a concave object would be better for actual scooping (see Table 7.1). In Table 7.1 the uses for which the objects were requested in Script I and Script II are shown.

Figure 7.1 shows the six objects that were in the box the child had to sort

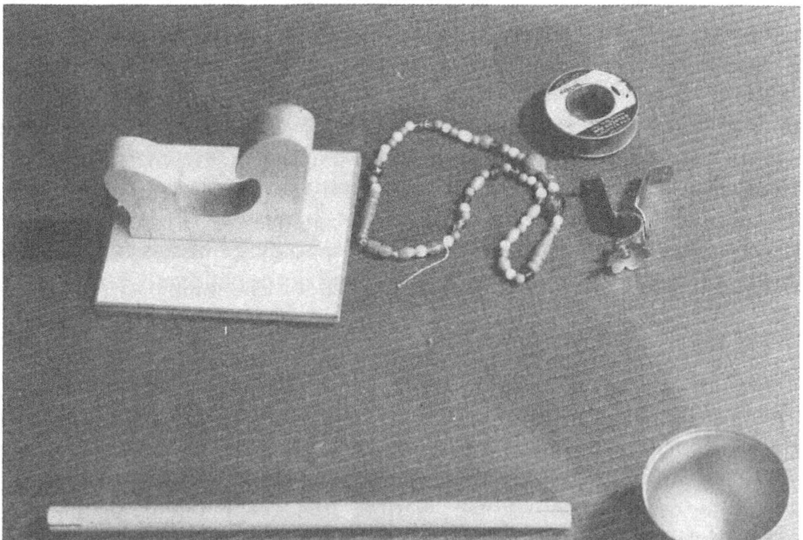

FIG. 7.1. Spoon: Target and distractor items.

through to find a spoon. The primary candidates for choices of spoons are the plastic eggshell (Script I) and the rod (Script II), both in the foreground. The four other objects were included as ''distractors'' in order to reduce the likelihood of the children's picking the target object by chance.

The situation was not designed as one in which the children would be passive and mute. It was important that they be involved as contributors to the pretending as much as possible given the constraints of the experimental situation. Embellishments of the make-believe premise by the children were welcome and occurred frequently.

*Interview.* The child was asked to demonstrate the target function after making each object choice. For Script I, the following was said: ''Here's the ice cream box (experimenter handing child a cigar box). Now, you give Mr. McGhee some ice cream.'' In Script II, the child was asked to demonstrate the use of the object that had been selected, as follows: ''Now, you get the lemonade ready for Mr. McGhee. It isn't mixed yet.'' Even if the child had not chosen the function-related object, the procedures allowed individual modification of the object through action in performing the target function. For example, if in Script I the child had chosen the wooden rod (stirrer), she or he might give evidence of attending to the target function by using a scooping motion.

The experimenter prompted the child in the following manner if the object's use was not demonstrated: ''Show me how you would use that; show me how you would use that as a ______ (spoon for scooping ice cream, etc.)''

A verbal interview followed the child's demonstration of each object's use. When Script I was the basis for the play scenes, the child was asked: ''Is that a good spoon for scooping ice cream? Is there anything not good about it? Is there anything we need to pretend was different to make it a better spoon for scooping ice cream?'' When Script II was used, the experimenter asked the child comparable questions regarding the suitability of the object for stirring lemonade.

In this part of the procedure, the child was given the opportunity to describe attributes of the chosen object that made it suitable for performing the target function. This procedure also afforded the child the chance to note and discuss object discrepancies even if a nontarget object were chosen, that is, an object other than one we judged appropriate for performing the specified function. Thus, there was ample opportunity to learn the child's rationale for the object choice and to observe how the selection would be used. A nontarget object could be used to serve the requisite function by the child's supplying verbal modifications or transforming the object through actions.

*Coding and Scoring Protocols.* Each trial was coded as either a target or a nontarget object choice. In a few cases, objects were chosen in combinations. If the child failed to choose the target object on a given trial, coders next evaluated whether or not the child gave evidence of attending to the demand characteristics of the make-believe situation by attending to the target function. A trial was coded as "attending to the target function" on the basis of certain *verbalizations* or *actions*. Verbalizations indicating that the child had the target function in mind were usually comments about the relevant property; for example, "This ('shoe') should have shoelaces" or "This ('bowl') shouldn't have holes." The child could also show attention to the target function through action; for example, choosing the dog bone as the phone for dialing by putting the dogbone to the ear as a make-believe receiver and making a dialing motion in the air.

The verbal data were examined in two additional ways. The first of these was a division of comments on the objects into two categories: those noting its *suitability as a substitute* (i.e., similarity to the referent, as in the comment "This ['shoe'] has string") and those comments noting its *shortcomings as a substitute* (i.e., difference between the object and the referent, as in the comment "This ['spoon'] needs a handle").

The verbal protocols were also examined in terms of qualitative categories, with a focus on the *reflectiveness* children exhibited in approaching the object substitution situation. The verbal categories that emerged from this examination are reported extensively in the following section.

## RESULTS AND DISCUSSION

### Awareness of Object Suitability

On 65% of the object choices, children selected the target object, that is, the object best suited by its features for the make-believe situation. If the children were responding by chance alone, the percentage of the trials on which the target object would be selected is 16.6%. Even when only the two likeliest objects are considered (e.g., the rod and the plastic eggshell), the expected percentage of trials on which the target objects are selected is 50%. The obtained percentage of 65% is averaged across the six experimenter requests.

The percentages of target object selections ranged from 50% for the phone to 86% for the spoon. Later in this discussion we shall consider factors that might account for the variation across objects in the numbers of children choosing the target object. At this point, we simply wish to note that there was a high degree of such variation. The hypothesis that children would make different object choices depending on the function the object was to serve in the make-believe play scenario was clearly upheld with some objects and less so with others. Overall, however, this hypothesis received support. We also found, as expected, that children exhibited their sensitivity to the anticipated function through their verbalizations and actions. When children picked an object other than the target, they nearly always showed that they were attending to the described function, either verbally or behaviorally or both. On 92% of all trials children showed by their verbalizations or gestures that they were understanding and attending to the functions for which the various objects were to be used.

Verbalizations focusing on the object's *suitability* as a substitute were nearly twice as common as behaviors that took note of a *shortcoming*. This difference was found even though the experimenter asked each child, "Is there anything you think should be different, anything that is *not* good for a ______? Is there anything we'd need to pretend for it to be a good ______?"

A significant interaction was found between age and the tendency to focus on object suitability ($\chi^2 = 4.96$, $p < .05$). Older children showed the tendency to note object similarities more than younger children, whereas object shortcomings were noted equally across ages.

## Spontaneous Comments on Making Object Substitutions

Children freely commented on their object choices. They spoke of the appropriateness of objects for the intended use, of problems with the objects as substitutes, of the lack of satisfactory choices, and of the difficulty in making up their minds. Such commentary, as a whole, reflects the fact that choosing objects for use in pretending is not an automatic process. Instead, selecting props for play is a reflective process in which the play participant maintains a self-awareness regarding his or her symbolic play activity. It is true that the tendency to ponder choices is probably heightened by the experimental setting, in spite of our efforts to provide a casual, make-believe framework. Comments indicative of reflection and self-awareness have been noted to occur in the course of interactive free-play as well (e.g., Matthews, 1978). It may be the case that covert comments are equally commonplace in solitary play.

The types of things children say when making object substitutions, we suggest, reflect the nature of the cognitive activity underlying their choices as well as the extent of the children's reflectiveness about their representational efforts. The principal types of verbalizations of this sort that we identified are the following:

1. *Verbalizing satisfaction with object*
   A. Conveys satisfaction in finding an appropriate object *without commenting on why it is suitable.*
   Examples:
   "Ah, *there* is an envelope."
   "I found the bowl that would be good."
   "This is a good phone."
   "That's not a spoon, but it could be a spoon."
   "That's what I could find that looks most like a shoe."

B. Conveys satisfaction in finding appropriate object, *commenting on why it is suitable.*
   Examples:
   "This has shoelaces."
   "I think this is a shoe. You know why? (demonstrates that it can be worn). That is why."
   "This is a shoe because it's got string."

2. *Verbalizing what's wrong with object(s) chosen*
   A. Conveys dissatisfaction with object(s) rejected *without commenting on what's wrong.*
      Examples:
      "There's no shoe."
      "Too silly. This can't be a shoe. No."
      "Not this one. This can't be good . . . not this, not this, not that, not that, and not this (about each object but the chosen one)."
      "I don't see anything."
      "This is not a good bowl."
      "This is not a shoe (laughing)."
      "Is this the telephone? No, probably not."
   B. Conveys dissatisfaction with object(s) rejected, *commenting on what's wrong.*
      Examples:
      (Looking for bowl for fish). "This (colander). No! No! No! No! No! The water will come out. This is better (flower pot)."
      (Looking for shoe for tying). "It doesn't have any string."
      (Looking for pitcher for pouring) "This one doesn't have a handle (pointing to the spout on other pitcher; confused about word). Needs to have a handle."
      (Looking for bowl for fish) "I know which one that would not be a good one. This one (colander) would not because it has holes in it. The water can get out."

3. *Verbalizing dissatisfaction with object chosen*
   A. Conveys some dissatisfaction with object chosen by *commenting on what's wrong.*
      Examples:
      "Maybe this into a ______. I know how to make one of these into a telephone (holds object to ear)."
      "This would be better with a handle (referring to pitcher with spout, selected for pouring water)."
   B. Conveys some dissatisfaction with object chosen by *modifying it* (and commenting on modification).
      Examples:
      "Here's one part (bone for telephone receiver). I can't find the other part in here (finally adds dial)."

"This one (milk carton 'shoe') doesn't have one (a shoelace). Poke a hole in it and we could take this (lace from peg board 'shoe'). Get this for a shoelace."

"What's this? (looking at the bone 'receiver')? Can't be it. It has to be—it could go here, like that (puts 'receiver' beside 'dial')."

"We need to put this (picks up 'scooping spoon,' mumbling, then "stirring spoon'). Hm-m-m, you have to put that together somehow (puts scoop at end of stirrer; finally, puts scoop back). I'm pretending something's right here."

4. *Pondering choices verbally*

A. Verbalizes that more than one object has appeal.

Examples:

"This or that?"

"Let's see; which pitcher should I take?"

"I don't know which one."

"I can't find the goodest one."

"There are two pitchers."

"Could this be a phone . . . ? (Experimenter: "Could it be?") . . . I don't know."

"Is this it? No. This? No. This could be it."

"I see two pitchers."

B. Talks while choosing, "thinking aloud."

Examples:

"Envelope? (look at object) Yes."

"Look in there and see what would be good for a shoe (looking in drawer). Good for a shoe, good for a shoe. Is this? (puts shoe on foot). It probably will."

"Where is the telephone anyway? Is this the telephone? No, probably not."

## METACOGNITION AND SYMBOLIC PLAY: THE VALUE OF VERBAL DATA

Comments of the type previously described are of considerable interest in what they tell us about preschool children's use of objects in pretend play. First, it is clear from these spontaneous remarks that the children have standards about what constitutes a suitable substitute object in a given situation and that the children make their choices after considerable reflection. A request by an adult for an object substitute in make-believe was readily accepted by all the children, but they did not seem to think that any object would do equally well. The children went through an evaluation process, sometimes very explicit, considering the available objects with respect to the criteria they were seeking to meet.

Second, the children's comments include thoughts about *why* a given object is a good choice, *why* a rejected object is not desirable, and what is less than ideal about a chosen object, although it may be the best available. Sometimes children talk about how difficult it is to decide between one object and another or express their dissatisfaction with all the available choices. On occasion we hear them ask themselves aloud whether or not a given object will do. In some of these remarks the children show an awareness of their own evaluating processes or of the representational task. These are particularly interesting in light of recent interest in the emergence of metacognition. In many of the verbalizations we see the child doing what might be thought of as transforming the object and imposing a new identity upon it. At the least, children show a tendency to use a verbalization to bridge the gap between the object as it is and as it should be for the play episode. It is worth noting that similar verbalizations have been observed in other activities where children are representing something in the world. In art, for example, investigators have found that children frequently make spontaneous comments to supplement their drawings or clay constructions (Cocking & Copple, 1979; Copple, Cocking, & Waxman, 1980; Golomb, 1974). Children often perceive a discrepancy between what they are trying to represent and what they are able to achieve (in the case of their own creations) or select (in the case of object choices). In these instances, investigators have found children are not satisfied. Alongside their imaginative abilities, the children clearly manifest their active use of standards or criteria of representation.

Despite the narrow age range in the current study, an overall increase was found with age in the extent to which children showed a reflectiveness about choosing objects for the play scenarios. There were also marked individual differences. Some children verbalized what they were thinking on every occasion, whereas other children rarely commented.

The unelicited comments of the children not only tell us that they had representational criteria but also indicate the nature of these criteria. The children's comments reveal what sorts of features of the objects mattered to them and which did not. With respect to the issue of object features, we can make a few generalizations, based on the study:

1. *Physical features versus functional features in object choices:* Physical features not related to function were rarely mentioned.

For example, children never commented on a discrepancy of color or substance (e.g., that the phone should be black, the spoon made of metal, or the shoe of leather). On the whole, children did not mention characteristics that might be desirable for the *real* object but not necessary for pretend play purposes. For example, the durability of the shoe, which was made of cardboard, was never criticized.

2. *Essential versus nonessential functional features in object choices:* The features needed to perform the function called for in the scenario were more often commented on than were other functions of the object.

Children often commented about what made the object suitable for the function called for by the make-believe scenario. This finding parallels the object choice results (i.e., the children tended to choose the item with the feature linked to the object's function in the dramatic play episode).

3. *"Disjunct features" in object choices:* The more "disjunct" the feature, the more important it seemed to the child.

Children more often tended to comment on the absence of features that were disjunct or separable, that is, parts that could be *detached* visually or even manipulated separately. For example, children frequently noted the absence of the laces for the shoe, the dial or the receiver for the telephone. In contrast, less disjunct features such as the long, straight portion of the spoon and its concave part were not so often commented on. This may be partly a matter of the ease of describing or demonstrating what was missing for the more disjunct features or parts, but it is probably no harder to say, for example, "the round thing" than "receiver" or "the part that you talk on." A more important reason for this difference seems to be the separateness of the actions one would perform in using the object.

When pretending to pour, one can perform the action without actually having a spout on the pitcher. In contrast, suppose you are pretending to make a phone call. There are two separate parts of telephones that are involved in making a call, holding the receiver and dialing, and each has a separate action associated with it. In such cases, children seemed to see both parts as necessary. Supplementations through action, verbalization, and combining objects were most common on the telephone and the shoe. Incidentally, this appears to be linked to the large number of children choosing a nontarget object on the telephone item. They wanted features for filling *both* functions of a telephone, so they chose either item—the "dial" or the "receiver"—and then supplied the rest through gestures.

## DEVELOPMENTAL PROGRESSIONS IN CHILDREN'S SYMBOLIC PLAY

One additional aspect of the data involves the development of children's representation of objects. The data from the spoon item are particularly suggestive; we will return to these data momentarily, but first we would like to describe some earlier research on the development of object representation.

Werner and Kaplan (1963) proposed a developmental progression for gestural representations: imitation of the actions of other persons and movements of inanimate objects, followed by gestural representation of static objects. According to this theoretical analysis, children's gestures in representing static objects would be increasingly distinct in form from the objects that are represented.

Empirical support for this proposed progression was found by Overton and Jackson (1973). When 8-year-old subjects were pretending to brush their teeth they usually did so by gripping an imaginary toothbrush, whereas younger children more often extended the index finger to represent the brush itself. That is, the younger children typically used a body part to represent the static object—the more literal sort of representation that Werner and Kaplan suggested. The children in the present study were in the age group that commonly made such responses on the Overton and Jackson task. Our results with objects provide additional information about this point in the developmental progression.

There is a characteristic of children's object choices in our data that seems to parallel what children do in their gestural representations. To examine it we need to look at a central criterion for choosing objects to use in carrying out actions. When an individual chooses an object for use in an action sequence, it is natural for him/her to choose one that will allow performing the appropriate action with relative ease. If one wants to pretend to be hammering, a good choice is a grippable, inflexible object, as opposed to a rope or a basketball. An infant will choose good hammering objects through functional assimilation; an adult actor will choose similarly because he or she can show the movements of hammering readily. However, our results indicate that there is a point in development when children are grappling with representation of static objects during which they may make choices of a different kind. The children's actions on the spoon item shed light on this behavior.

Whether one is going to use a spoon for stirring or for scooping, one grips the end of the spoon and performs the appropriate action. From the viewpoint of gestural representation of scooping, it would make sense to select the stick and use it in a scooping motion. Some subjects did this, but on the whole children chose the plastic eggshell with no handle. They appeared to be opting for depicting the hollow portion of a spoon that is important in actual scooping. As in the Overton and Jackson study, they represented a static object in a way that was less "distant" from the actual object. Verification of the developmental progression would require a longitudinal or an expanded cross-sectional investigation. However, looking at our data in the context of Werner and Kaplan (1963) and Overton and Jackson (1973), the following developmental progression in object choices can be suggested: (1) the child chooses any object which can be employed in the action sequence without concern with representing the static object (functional assimilation); (2) the child chooses an object substitute that has the property the static object would need in the pretend action sequence even though it may not be well-suited for manipulation in the requisite way (literal representation); and (3) the child chooses an object that allows him or her to perform the action sequence even though it doesn't resemble the static object (symbolic representation). The numbers and ages of children in the current study were not sufficient for testing such a developmental progression. However, the verbalizations of the children again shed light on what is happening. Two children started to choose the "scoop" for the ice cream scooping episode and then they changed their minds, commenting that they would be able to use the stick more easily. One even said that she would just "pretend one of these (the scoop) is on the end." This seems to be a clear instance of the transition from literal, direct representation to more symbolic types of representation.

## CONCLUSIONS

The objective of the research was to examine the nature of the representation or prototypes underlying children's make-believe object uses, the types of mental activities through which objects are allowed to substitute for real objects, and the awareness children have of the processes involved in the choosing and the pretending.

The results lend support to the view of symbolic object use that Golomb (1977) has put forth, in contrast with the Piagetian view that preschool children do not have representational criteria and standards. Beyond this, the children's choices show attention to the feature or features important for the functions the objects will serve in make-believe episodes. Other features of the objects are relatively less important to the child in comparison to the features linked to the actions she/he anticipates pretending to enact. The child does not operate with a single, unitary prototype of what a given object should be like. What children seek in an object shifts according to its anticipated make-believe use. These results can be added to those of Fein and Apfel (1979) in showing children's selectivity among objects on the basis of how the object will be used.

The data from the spoon item illustrate the particular developmental level of the subjects with respect to the representation of static objects. These results, we suggest, parallel the level of gestural representation posited by Werner and Kaplan and found by Overton and Jackson. The children are still showing a tendency toward "literalness" in representing an object, although our results indicate that they are far more insistent on the presence of function-related features than other features. Rather than choosing a spoon that would allow them to imitate the *action* of scooping, the children typically opted for the item that actually *was* a scoop.

Many of the children showed a considerable degree of reflectiveness in their object choices. They hesitated, and sometimes they spontaneously talked about the difficulty of their choices, particularly with respect to weighing what was good about an object-substitute, or about discrepancies they noticed between the substitute and their notions of the real thing. The children's verbalizations reflected an awareness of their own processes of evaluating and pretending. This awareness appears to be akin to what is termed and studied as metacognition. Our investigation indicates that the use of objects in make-believe play is not only a mentally initiated activity, as emphasized by Golomb, Fein, Cocking and de Lacey, Tambourinni, and others, but one in which the children's awareness of their own mental processes and representational criteria is increasingly explicit.

## ACKNOWLEDGMENTS

The work reported here describes, in part, a collaborative project conducted by the first two authors at Educational Testing Service in the Center for Child Care Research. Funds were made available from a DHEW Biomedical Research Support Grant, No. 1-S07-RR05729-02. We would like to thank Sheila Kraft for her assistance in gathering and analyzing the data, and Irving E. Sigel who was Director of the Center for Child Care Research.

This article was written in the authors' private capacities. No official support or endorsement by the National Institute of Education, U.S. Department of Education or by the College of Medicine and Dentistry of New Jersey is intended or should be inferred.

## REFERENCES

Brown, R. *Word from the language acquisition front.* Paper presented at the meeting of the Eastern Psychological Association, Boston, April 1977.

Cocking, R. R., & Copple, C. E. Change through exposure to others: A study of children's verbalizations as they draw. In *Proceedings of the 8th annual conference on Piagetian theory and the helping professions.* Los Angeles, Cal.: The University of Southern California, 1979.

Copple, C. E., Cocking, R. R., & Waxman, B. *The emergence of representational awareness: An examination of children's comments as they draw.* Paper presented at the Southeastern Conference on Human Development, Alexandria, Va., April 1980.

Elder, J. L., & Peterson, D. R. Preschool children's use of objects in symbolic play. *Child Development,* 1978, *49,* 500–504.

Fein, G. G. A transformational analysis of pretending. *Developmental Psychology,* 1975, *11,* 291–296.

Fein, G. G., & Apfel, N. Some preliminary observations on knowing and pretending. In N. Smith, & M. Franklin (Eds.), *Symbolic functioning in childhood.* Hillsdale, N.J.: Lawrence Erlbaum Associates, 1979.

Field, T. M., DeStefano, L., & Koewler, J. H. Fantasy play in toddlers and preschoolers, *Developmental Psychology,* 1982, *18,* 503–508.

Golomb, C. *Young children's sculpture and drawing.* Cambridge, Mass.: Harvard University Press, 1974.

Golomb, C. Symbolic play: The role of substitutions in pretence and puzzle games. *British Journal of Educational Psychology,* 1977, *47,* 175–186.

Jackowitz, E. R., & Watson, M. W. The development of object transformations in early pretend play. *Developmental Psychology,* 1980, *16,* 543–549.

Matthews, W. S. Modes of transformation in the initiation of fantasy play. *Developmental Psychology,* 1977, *13,* 212–216.

Matthews, W. S. *The notion of equivalence in children's representation activity.* Unpublished manuscript, Harvard University, 1978.

Overton, W. F., & Jackson, J. P. The representation of imagined objects in action sequences: A developmental study. *Child Development,* 1973, *44,* 309–314.

Rosch, E. On the internal structure of perceptual and semantic categories. In T. E. Moore (Ed.), *Cognitive development and the acquisition of language.* New York: Academic Press, 1973.

Rosch, E. Cognitive representations of semantic categories. *Journal of Experimental Psychology: General,* 1975, *104*(3), 192–233.

Ungerer, J. A., Zelazo, P. R., Kearsley, R. B., & O'Leary, K. Developmental changes in the representation of objects in symbolic play from 18 to 34 months of age. *Child Development,* 1981, *52,* 186–195.

Werner, H., & Kaplan, B. *Symbol formation.* New York: Wiley, 1963.

# 8 The Self-Building Potential of Pretend Play or "I Got A Fish, All by Myself"

Greta G. Fein
*University of Maryland*

Pretend play has offered much grist for the mills of developmental theories. One is hard pressed to find a major theoretical framework—especially of the grand genre—that has not offered an account of where pretense fits within its larger perspective. And so, from the perspective of Piagetian theory, we become oriented to the cognitive (or, more exactly, the counter-cognitive) aspects of pretense and, from psychoanalytic theory, we become oriented to the affective-emotional aspects of this behavior. Vygotsky brings us to words or gestures in relation to meaning and Bateson calls our attention to the paradoxical nature of communications about communications (See Fein [1979, 1981b] and Sutton-Smith [1982] for additional discussion of these theoretical variations).

Pretense has provided so rich an arena for theorists interested in diverse issues that often it has seemed deprived of a theoretical framework uniquely its own. However, recent research suggests that this concern may be premature (Fein, 1981a,b). Actually, the grand theories often provide little more than a beginning way of framing an interesting question. For example, in the work of Vygotsky (1967) and Piaget (1962) the notion of object transformation was rather general, illustrated either in anecdote or observational record. In pursuing this interesting question, investigators have gone considerably beyond this beginning by formulating specific statements about the behavioral forms and features of objects that support transformational activity at different ages (Elder & Pederson, 1978; Fein, 1975; Jackowitz & Watson, 1980; Ungerer, Zelazo, Kearsley, & O'Leary, 1981; Watson & Fischer, 1977). Bateson's notion (1956) of "metacommunication" has also fostered research aimed at illuminating how children use language to convey the idea that in play the playful nip connotes the bite without connoting what a bite connotes. In these examples, grand theories give rise to "mini theories'' that, with carefully operationalized constructs, are able to generate testable hypotheses.

However, the work of one grand theorist—George Herbert Mead—who speculated about the significance of pretense has been largely neglected (Rubin & Pepler, 1979; Fein & Kohlberg, in press). Mead's theory is important generally because it draws attention to the elusive question of the development of self during the early years. It is important particularly because Mead views the ''play stage'' as concerned primarily with the child's organization of particular attitudes of others toward himself and toward one another in the specific social acts in which he participates or observes. In Mead's (1934) words:

> When a child does assume a role, he has in himself the stimuli which call out that particular response . . . (when playing Indian), the responses that they would call out in others, and which answer to an Indian. In the play period, the child utilizes his own responses to these stimuli which he makes use of in building a self. The responses which he has a tendency to make to these stimuli organize them [p. 213].

According to Mead, role playing constitutes a form of ''being another to one's self'': ''The child says something in one character and responds in another character, and then his responding in another character is a stimulus to himself in the first character, and so the conversation goes on. A certain organized structure arises in him and in his other which replies to it, and these carry on the conversation of gestures between themselves [p. 213].

## ROLE PLAYING AND ROLE TAKING

Two processes contribute to the self building potential of play. One is overt role *playing* (i.e., the behavioral responses and the stimuli they provide to the player). In a sense, the child observes himself in the role of another. The other process is the covert role *taking* that accompanies the overt behavior. Psychologically, the role-playing child is organizing the attitudes and perspectives of the others whose role responses are being produced. However, the self is always at the center of the encounters, interpreting the social meaning of the relationships being enacted.

For all the potential importance of Mead's ideas, they have yet to be cast in a form amenable to systematic empirical study. Mead himself made no effort to investigate the development of role playing. Therefore, the scheme outlined later in Fig. 8.1 goes beyond what Mead actually proposed but attempts, nonetheless, to be faithful to what he meant.

In this scheme, role playing and its concomitant role taking develop through four levels. At each level, role playing acquires a new refinement and each new refinement implies an added complication in the child's perspective taking. In

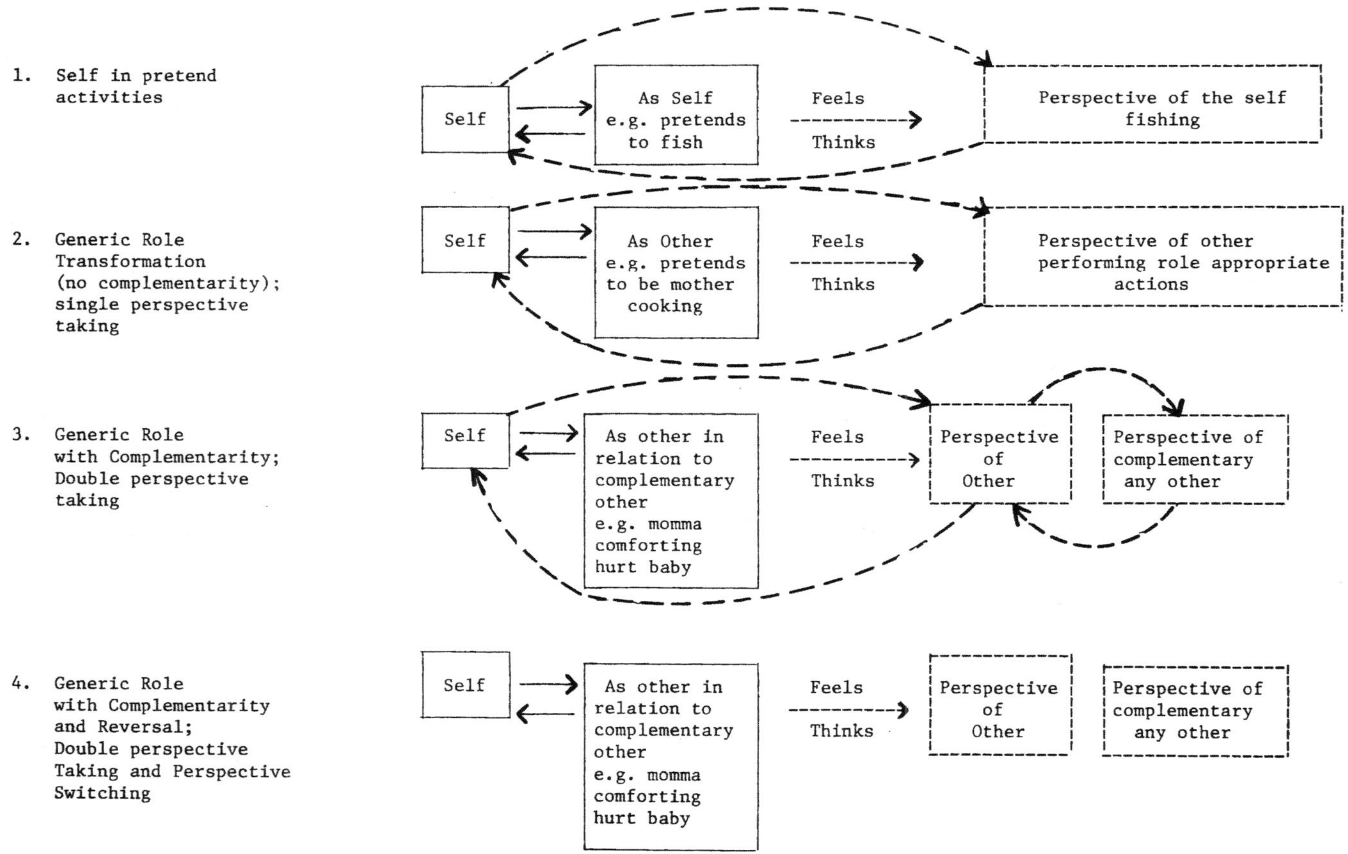


FIG. 8.1 Basic Structures in Mead's Model of Role Playing and Role Taking.

level 1 the child pretends to do something as himself/herself with no evidence that a generic role (i.e., of fisherman, mother, father) is intended. The perspective is simply that of the self doing something difficult, exciting, or even painful. In level 2, the child plays a generic role (e.g., a mother, but not necessarily a particular mother) by pretending to carry out an activity typical of the role, in a manner characteristic of persons who perform this activity. A generic role with complementarity marks level 3. Now the child as "other" interacts with a complementary other (e.g., as mother comforting her hurt baby). In level 2, the child takes the other's perspective in relation to role-appropriate actions minus those actions that involve personal relationships. When these personal relations are added, the child must feel and think as the "other" feels and thinks when feeling and thinking about the complementary other in the relationship. The pretending child therefore takes the attitude of the mother consoling a baby and acknowledging the baby's hurt. Level 4 represents the role reversal that so intrigued Mead. Here the child first plays the role of consoling mother and then switches to the role of crying baby. Again, for Mead, the important point is that the "self" is producing these responses and thus the stimuli that feed back to the self. The solid lines in the figure indicate the *external* response–stimulus configuration, whereas the dotted lines indicate the *internal,* imaginal response–stimulus configuration. As these imagined encounters continue, the child's grasp of "others" becomes organized internally (as well as externally) and as these others become organized, they come differentiated from the "self" while the "self" organizes its relation to these others. This progressive organizational effort, represents the construction of a social self—distinct from, but deeply tied to persons in the child's social world. Taken as a whole, Mead's model implies something like decentration in Piaget's theory—but only insofar as the "self" becomes progressively more fluent in moving through different perspectives.

Because the content of role play is drawn from the real world of people, role playing–role taking is inherently social, even though the child might be playing alone. However, role play with a partner adds measurably to the complexity of the play. Figure 8.2 indicates what happens in level 3 when a partner plays the role of complementary other. When the levels of role playing–taking in a social mode are added to those in a solitary mode, the result is an eight-level developmental progression.

## ILLUSTRATIONS OF THE MODEL

When actual play sequences are examined with respect to the model, it becomes clear that a major milestone occurs when children are able to play roles with a partner as a complementary other. The following episodes are taken from a study in which children were videotaped in four 15-minute play sessions with four different partners.

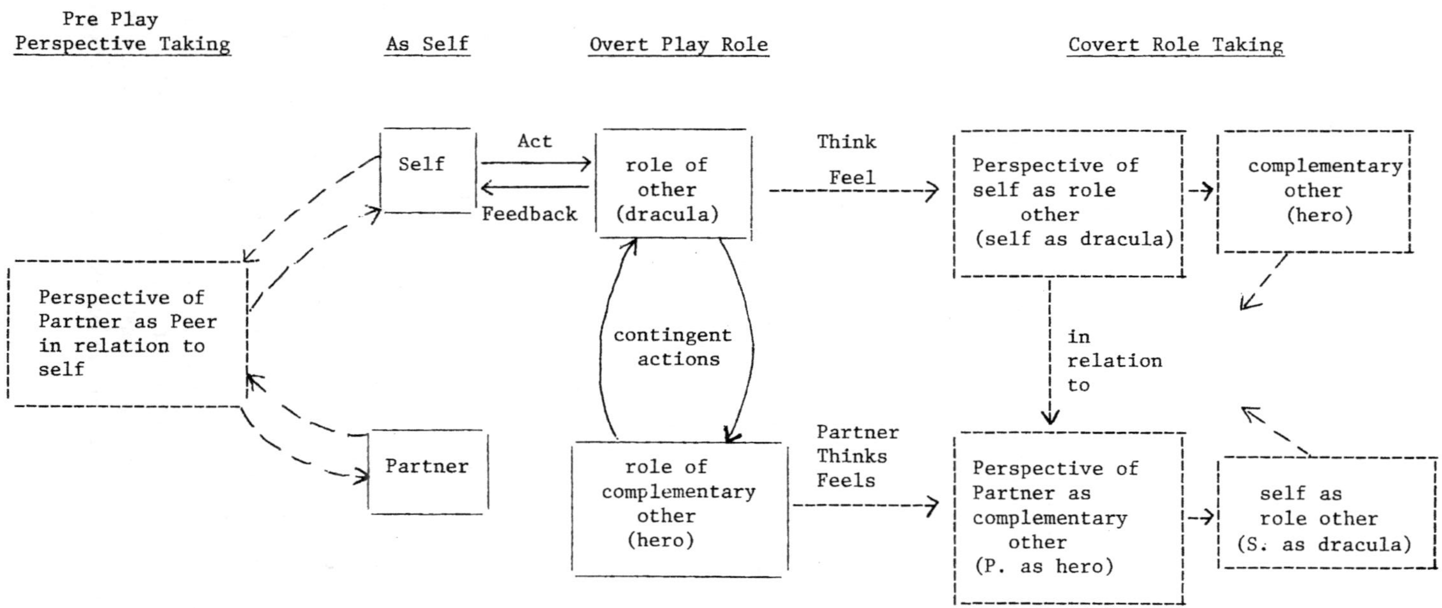


FIG. 8.2 Social Pretense: Role Complementarity and the Perspective of Others.

Consider the first transcript in which Alan, a 2½-year-old child pretends to fish. Note that Richard, a peer, though present during the entire session, neither enters the play nor interacts with Alan aside from a few stray glances.

Transcript 1
*Alan and Richard: 2½ years*

Alan is sitting on a chair near the caregiver, swinging a mop in the air. Richard is sitting on the floor, looking at a book.

A: "I'm gonna get a fish." (Dips end of mop onto floor, brings it up, turns to caregiver)
R: (Looks at A, then resumes looking at book)
A: "He got a fish, he got a fish, all by myself." (Turns toward R) "I got me wet . . . move . . . in the hair."
A. "That's nice sea water." (Leaves with mop) "I want to row."
A: (Crosses mop and broom over head) "I got my boat, over here."
A: (Moves back to chair, extends mop and broom onto floor)
A: "Eee, ooh! I'm in my boat. . . ."
A: "I'm gonna get two fish, fish." (Extends mop and broom over corner of table) "A fish!"
R: (Closes book, looks up at A)
A: (Turns towards caregiver) "This . . . this is your fishing pole." (Gives broom to caregiver)
A: Caregiver: "Okay, set it down here." (Leans broom against Table)
A: "I don't want . . . it." (Throws broom so it leans against buggy) "You have it, you can take mine."
R: (Puts book down, grunts, picks up rake, slides it along rug, glances at A)
A: (Dips mop over table onto rug, brings it back up, turns to caregiver) "Give you a fish."
A: (Turns back around, fiddles with end of mop) "One here." (Fiddles with end of mop) "I don't want your fishing pole." (Hits end of mop against buggy, turns mop around) "I don't want your fishing pole."

Except for a brief moment, when "He got a fish," Alan's perspective is pretty consistently "all by myself." His play is rich in object and substance transformations in a material mode (e.g., mop and broom for fishing pole and oars) and in an ideational mode (e.g., fish, sea water, row boat). However, his effort to engage the caregiver in the play is poorly formed, and the care giver misunderstands the overture.

The next transcript comes from Barb and Sandy, also 2½-years-old. Barb is far more sophisticated than Alan in her orientation to her partner. However, Sandy has little grasp of what is being asked of him. Even though Barb turns didactic when instructing Sandy how to bed down a baby, Sandy seems not to comprehend.

Transcript 2

*Barb and Sandy: 2½ years*

Barb is sitting in chair with doll and blanket on her lap. Sandy is raking floor near Barb.

B. "You brushing?"
S: (Glances at B, continues to rake)
B: (Watches S, turns in chair, whispers) "He's, he's brushing. Yeah."
B: "There's dad, working."
B: (Places doll on floor, whispers to it, stands)
S: (Picks up truck, puts it in buggy, looks at B)
B: "Cover you up." (Covers doll with blanket)
B: "Night-night, night-night. Don't cry . . . will you children go to sleep." (Walks to toy shelf)
S: (Takes truck from buggy, places another truck in buggy)
B: "Dad, do you want to stay with . . ."
S: (Looks at B)
B: "Cover her up, all right Dad?"
S: (Pokes at truck in buggy)
B: (Gets broom and rake, drops rake, carries broom) "I have my brush." (Sweeps floor briefly, drops broom, picks up rake)
B: "Get that one, that one." (Rakes floor) "I'm brushing." (Rakes rug)
S: (Watches B, follows B as she rakes)
B: ". . . your brush, Sandy. Will you watch my baby?" (Falls next to doll) "Uuh! Will you watch my baby so she's not gonna cry?"
S: (Sits next to doll, looks at it)
B: (Stands, rakes rug) "All right, Dad? I'm brushing."
S: (Feeds doll with bottle)
B: (Rakes floor, puts rake back, approaches S) "Thank you Dad, thank you, get up now."
S: (Looks at B, continues to sit and feed doll)
B: (Stoops near doll as if listening) "Let me see . . . I hear what you're saying."
B: (Stands, gets blanket) "The ba-by, da, ah, the ba-by." (Approaches S and doll)
S: (Stops feeding doll, looks at B)
B: (Places doll and blanket in front of S) "Wrap her up, right there." (Spreads blanket onto floor)
B: "Sheet on, put her right there, 'kay?"
S: (Fiddles with bottle, looks at B)
B: (Gets doll, puts it on sheet) "Right there." (Covers with blanket)
B: "Good-night, baby." (Turns to caregiver) "You stay with her, Jane. Stay with her . . . she'll . . . so she'll f . . . she'll."
B: (Complaining to caregiver) "Sandy won't sit on the baby, but over here's a baby" (Picks up doll from corner, walks with it, singing) "Rock, rock my baby."

S: (Feeds doll with bottle)
B: (Aproaches S) "Give me my blank-ey. Get up, give it, Sandy"
S: (Stops feeding doll, B lifts blanket from under his leg. Resumes feeding doll)
B: (Takes blanket and doll across room)
B: (Covers doll with blanket on floor, whispers to it)
B: "See Sandy?"
S: (Looks at B, stops feeding doll)
B: "She want her bottle. Go get the bottle, Sandy, you get my bottle." (Takes truck from buggy)

Barb easily reaches level 3 on the scale shown in Fig. 8.1. She whispers to the baby and even listens to the response. Actually, Barb is a bit more advanced. As "mother" she relates to the doll as "baby," but she also tries to relate to Sandy as "dad" and, in her conversations with her daughter, refers to this fatherly "other." Barb is able to project more than one complementary other, but her vision of the second is much thinner than her vision of the first.

The third transcript describes Alan with Harry, a more sophisticated 2½-year-old partner. Even though the boys interact with one another, the play is essentially parallel play with Harry taking the lead as innovator.

Transcript 3
*Harry and Alan: 2½ years*

H feeding doll with bottle. A feeding self with bottle, watching H.

H. "Oh, don't cry." (Watches A, walks with doll cradled in arms)
A. "Gonna get my baby . . . baby." (Gets baby from buggy) "Baby, don't cry." (Watches H, cradles doll)
H: "Your arm is broken . . . Momma sees it." (Walks toward A)
"Hey teacher . . ."
(Sits down, feeds doll at table)
A: (Sits down, feeds doll at table)
H: (Gets up from table, feeds doll in his arms, looks at A)
A: (Watches H)
H: "Uh, oh . . . it's . . . it's."
H: (Kneels on floor) "I got baby bottles." (Drops doll, picks up bottle)
A: "I got, I got my bottle."
H: "I got . . . I'm gonna drink it all up" (Drinks, steps on doll, picks doll up, feeds it with bottle) "Come on baby, don't cry."
A: (Watches H, holds doll and bottle)
H: "Don't cry baby, don't cry, don't cry."
A: "Don't cry, don't, don't cry."
H: "Don't cry . . . come on Alan. You won't get a cough."
A: "All right." (Approaches shelf) "Get cough?"
H: (Gets spoon and feeds doll) "Won't get cough."

A: (Approaches H, feeds doll with bottle) ''I want to put some on there.''
H: (Leaves) ''No, no. Here's your spoon.''
A: (Gets spoon from shelf)
H: (Still holding doll) ''All finished.''
H: ''The doll is broken, we tell the doctor.''
A: (Watches H)
H: (Approaches door, moves to center of room, faces wall)
A: (Feeds doll with spoon)
H: ''Doctor, he got hurt . . . yep, he got hurt.''
H: (Approaches A) ''Will you go tell the doctor?''
A: ''Yeah.'' (Moves to center of room, feeds doll as he approaches wall)
H: ''He got hurt?''
A: ''Mine got hurt . . . doctor? . . . tell that doctor.''
H: (Approaches wall) ''Doctor, he . . . whacked.''
A: (Watches H) ''Doctor . . . whack.''
H: ''He got a cough, got a cough, here.'' (Gestures with spoon, holds doll out to wall, then hugs doll) ''Oh, you . . . doctor.''
H: (Knocks on wall with spoon)
H: ''He's not home, he's not home.'' (Steps back from wall)
A: ''Let's see.'' (Taps wall with spoon, looks at H)
H: (Steps forward, taps wall with spoon) ''Doctor.'' (Continues to tap)
A: ''Doctor, he's not home.'' (looks at H)
H: ''He's not home, he's on vacation.''
H: (Turns with back to wall, then turns around again, bangs wall with spoon) ''Doctor.'' (Looks at A)
A: ''Doctor.'' (Bangs spoon on wall)
H: ''He's gonna go on vacation. He's not home.'' (Walks away)
A: (Bangs on wall) ''Doctor, he's not home.''
H: (Approaches wall, bangs wall with spoon) ''Hey, Doctor!''
A: ''Doctor.'' (Bangs, looks at H)
H: ''He's not home. Let's go.'' (Leaves wall)
A: (Follows H) ''He's not home.''
H: ''Here he is, he's on vacation.'' (Faces corner) ''Are you on vacation?''
H: (Turns, moves to wall) ''You gonna go home? . . . He go home.''
A: (Watches H, then approaches him) ''Doctor's home.''
H: (Throws doll against wall)
H: ''Doctor's home. He got hurt.''
H: (Picks up doll, cuddles it)
A: (Watches H)
H: ''Oh, baby.''
A: ''Who hurt her? . . . Who hurt her?'' (Drops doll near wall) ''Here doctor, here, doctor, here it is.'' (Looks down at doll)
H: ''Hey doctor.'' (Bangs on wall with spoon)
A: (Bangs on wall)
H: ''Hey doctor . . . He's not home, he's on vacation.'' (Leaves wall)
A: (Follows Harry) ''He's on vacation.''

In this episode Harry plays the role of 'momma'' comforting the hurt baby, but he also switches to the role of ''parent–patient'' interacting with an imaginary doctor. In this exchange, we receive additional glimpses of Mead's ''conversation of gestures between themselves.'' Harry talks to someone at the doctor's house, and listens to what he is told, making sure that Alan also gets the message that ''He's not at home. He's on vacation.'' Harry then invents the doctor himself, ''Are you on vacation? . . . You gonna go home?''

Harry's play involves at least three complementary others, along with recognition of Alan's need to follow the plot. Yet, Harry never suggests that Alan play the role of doctor, as if he had not yet thought of the possibility that a play companion might become a constituent part of the play.

In the next scene, Harry and Sara (2½) produce the first example of social reciprocity in our series. Note, however, that the ''roles'' are as ''giver'' and ''taker'' of medicine, not the generic complementary roles of parent–child or doctor–patient, even though we know that Harry can conceptualize these roles.

Transcript 4

*Harry and Sarah: 2½ years*

Harry is placing objects in buggy, changing nonsense syllables in process. Sarah is combing stuffed animal's hair, talking to it.

H: ''Did-ja-ja-ya-ya-ja.'' (gets spoon and bottle from table, stoops on floor with it) ''get some medicine, okay?''
S: (Continues to talk to animal)
H: (Shakes bottle) ''Take this, okay? . . . okay?'' (Feeds self with bottle, then stands, feeds doll on table with bottle) ''Hello, baby.'' (Kneels with doll, throws it down)
S: (Looks at H, resumes animal play)
H: (Picks up comb from table, combs hair, then combs hair with bottle, puts comb down)
S: (Screams, stoops, picks up comb) ''That was my comb, my comb.''
H: (gets up) ''It's my comb.''
S: ''Here.'' (hands comb to H, screams)
H: (Giggles, combs S's hair)
S: ''I'm gonna comb mine.'' (Pushes H's hand away)
H: (Attempts to comb S's hair)
S: ''I will comb mine.'' (Combs hair)
H: (Leaves, gets spoon and bottle) ''Take this for medicine in, okay?''
S: ''Okay, put my spoon.''
H: (Approaches S, tips bottle into spoon, feeds her with spoon)
S: ''You don't have that in.''
H: ''It's goop. It's for your nose. Take more?''
S: ''Yea, put it in my mouth.'' (Stops combing hair as H feeds her)
H: (Feeds S) (Leaves) ''This is for your mouth, okay?''
S: ''Okay.'' (Combs hair)

H: ''Broke . . .'' (Approaches S) ''Drink, drink some lemonade.'' (Puts object up to S's face)
S: ''Thanks, I'm not hungry.''
H: (Feeds S with spoon, puts bottle and spoon on table) ''Give me it, okay?''
S: ''Okay.'' (Picks up bottle and spoon, feeds H with spoon) ''It's medicine, it's medicine, look.''
H: (Attempts to take spoon and bottle)
S: (Resists) ''I'll!'' (Feeds H)
H: (Attempts to take spoon and bottle) ''It's mine!''
S: ''It's medicine! Okay.'' (Gives H spoon, not bottle) ''Where's my bottle?''
H: (Points to floor, reaches for S's bottle) ''You, your bottle is down there.''
S: (Gives up bottle) ''Okay, thank you.''
H: (Takes objects from S's buggy)
S: ''Don't!''
H: ''Let me, let me show you.'' (Shakes bottle)
S: ''Give me my doll back.'' (Gets doll from floor)
H: (Takes toys out of S's buggy) ''I'll show you, okay, okay? Here it is, here it is . . . your spoon, here's your spoon.'' (Drops spoon on table)
S: ''No! Put 'em back.'' (Puts spoon back in buggy, leaves)
H: ''This is for your nose, okay?'' (Approaches S, dips bottle onto spoon)
S: (Places toys from floor into buggy) ''Put 'em back, in there.''
H: ''This is for your nose, okay?'' (Dips bottle onto spoon)
S: (Sits) ''Thanks.''
H: ''You gonna be all right.''
S: (Leaves)
H: (Puts bottle in mouth, places spoon on table, leaves)
S: ''I will? I will be alright?'' (Puts toy in buggy)
H: ''Uh-huh. Come.''
S: ''Thanks.'' (Puts toys in buggy)
H: ''You're welcome. I'm going for a . . . okay?''
S: ''Come here and give me your medicine. I will feed you, okay? Want me to feed you?''
H: (Picks up spoon) ''Want me to feed you?''
S: ''No, I will feed you.''
H: ''Uh-uh!''
S: ''Uh-uh!''
H: (Puts spoon on table) ''You want to drink it this way?''
S: ''No, I got, I got my bottle.'' (Reaches into buggy for bottle)
H: (Attempts to take S's bottle) ''Ahh! . . . Uh-uh!'' (Leaves)
S: (Dips bottle onto spoon) ''It's medicine . . . You won't be okay. Come here.''
H: ''Uh-uh.'' (Holds bottle, looks at S)
S: (Holds out spoon) ''You will be okay . . . I'll drink from it.'' (Drinks from bottle) ''It's Kool-aid, it's Kool-aid.''
H: (Approaches S)
S: ''Want some Kool-aid?''

H: (Nods head "yes")
S: "Okay, here, Kool-aid." (Feeds H with spoon) "Oh, it's good?"
H: (Puts bottle in mouth, leaves)

For a brief moment, Sara almost plays a seducing adult as she drinks from the bottle and announces: "It's Kool-aid, it's Kool-aid. Want some Kool-aid?" But for the most part, the children pretend to give and take medicines as they are (i.e., level 1 in the model). However, at the level of sensorimotor action roles, there is role reversal and social pretense in the sense of collective symbols. In this episode there is progress in the social interactive aspects of play, but regression in the conceptual social aspects of play (see Fein, Moorin & Enslein [1982] for a discussion of microdevelopmental progressions accompanied by apparent regressions to lower levels of functioning).

The last transcript leaps ahead to two 4-year-olds pretending to be the "dracula monster" and the monster-vanquishing hero. Here at last we have social pretense with generic roles, complementarity, and role reversals.

Transcript 5
*Peter and Michael: 3½ years*

M: (Points block at center of room) "Pow!"
P: "Pow!" (Points block at center of room)
M: "Pow!" (Falls down)
P: (Swings hat in air, approaches M) "You be dracula."
M: "Okay" (Gets up, extends arms in front of him) "Grrow!"
P: (Points block at M) "Pow!"
M: (Falls down)
P: (Approaches, points block at M) "Pow!"
M: (Stirs slightly while lying down)
P: (Starts to put block in pocket)
M: (Starts to get up)
P: (Points block at M) "Pow!"
M: (Falls down)
P: (Puts block in pocket)
M: (Gets up) "Now you be dracula."
P: "Wait . . . I gotta put my cowboy hat on first." (Puts hat on, approaches M)
M: (Points block at P) "Pow!"
P: (Falls down)
M: (Points block at P) "Pow, pow, pow, pow!" (Puts block in pocket) "You're dead." (leaves)
P: Hey, aahh!" (Gets up) "Ahh, ahh!"
M: (Points block at P)
P: (Approaches M)
M: "Prsh, prsh, prsh, prsh, prsh!"
M: (Pushes P down, places block in pocket)

P: (Falls down) (Gets up) "Now you be dracula."
M: (Gets toy from shelf) "No, I . . . pow, pow, pow!" (Points toy at P)
P: "You be dracula."
M: (Pushes P)
P: "Be you like you?"
M: "No, you be dracula, and you say wow, and I push you down and I shoot you." (Approaches P with block extended in front of him)
P: "The hell you shoot me. No" (Pushes M's arm) "You . . ."
M: "All right" (lies down)
P: (Points block at M) "Pow!"
M: (Stirs slightly)
P: (Puts block in pocket, puts hat on head)
M: (Gets up, points block at P) "Pow, pow, pow!"
P: (Points block at M) "Pow!" (Pushes M with block and arms extended in front of him)
M: (Pushes P with arms and block extended in front of him)
P: "Pow, pow!"
M: (Falls down)
P: (Puts block in pocket)

This episode was diagramed in Fig. 8.2 in an attempt to represent fully its psychological implications from Mead's perspective. Peter and Michael are enormously conscious of one another and of the obligations and destiny attendant upon their play roles in relation to their real selves. At one point, Michael becomes rambunctious, ignoring Peter's signal "You be dracula." Peter then queries, "Be you like you?" checking to determine whether Michael's push was in play or for real. The role play of these children thus involves perspective taking at different levels, that is, with respect to their real selves becoming play selves and then with respect to the perspectives of the complementary roles that are enacted and reversed.

Peter and Michael have acquired a firm command of communications about play (i.e., the metacommunicative structures of Bateson's theory [1956]). For Mead, these structures indicate that a new layer of perspective taking (see Fig. 8.2) has been added to those of earlier phases. Now the child acknowledges the perspective of his partner, whose intentions and understanding are so crucial to the collective symbols of sociodramatic play. Egocentric metacommunicative gestures seem present in Alan's fishing episode as he announces to no one in particular what is happening in the play. Barb tries unsuccessfully to talk to Sandy about his role as dad, whereas Harry does much better in keeping Alan informed about the unfolding doctor scenario. For a moment, Harry and Sara step out of the medicine-giving pretense to negotiate who will give and who will take. But it is only Peter and Michael who mark their communications about play with at least three synchronized elements: (1) a standard linguistic form (e.g., "You be - - -"); (2) communication directed to the partner with insistance on a response; and (3) termination of the pretend activity until satisfactory terms have been negotiated.

## FROM STRUCTURE TO CONTENT

Mead offers a structural analysis of the role-playing child who steps outside himself to view the self from another perspective. Play, by allowing the child to imagine himself as an other, clarifies or consolidates a vision of aspects of the self that are either similar or different from others in the child's social world. In the process, the self gains coherence and the child gains a sense of his own identity as a distinct and distinctive human being. The model described in the previous section was inspired by the Meadian viewpoint, adding to this viewpoint the idea that the child's progress can be monitored as changes in the play itself.

Missing in Mead and in the discussion thus far is an analysis of the content of play, even though this content most certainly has a bearing on the self-building process. Several major developmental issues are expressed in the first five transcripts. For Alan, the issue is mastery, for Harry it is bodily injury and physical health. For Barb, the theme is nurturance and separation, whereas for Paul and Michael it is dominance and aggression. These themes are of great interest to psychoanalytic theorists (Erikson, 1963, 1977; Mahler, 1975; Peller, 1954). Importantly, these themes identify those affective aspects of being that become organized between 2 and 6 years of age: a view of one's body, its strength and fragility; a view of one's affectional ties to significant others; and, a view of one's anger and hostility toward others.

In conclusion, consider a final transcript of play between two 5-year-olds, Lil and Jim. Note first that structurally Lil can contemplate a set of alternative role structures—mother–father, sister–brother, and, within the play, herself as "sister" in relation to brother; daughter in relation to parents, and "sister-as-baby sitter" in relation to younger siblings. However, it is in the content of the play that we find clues to those attributes of self and others that constitute gripping issues at this age.

Transcript 6
*Lil and Jim: 5 years*

L: "Are you the father or the son?"
J: "I'm the big brother."
L: "OKay, then I'll be the big sister."
J: "'Cause fathers don't even play with toys."
L: "Well, I'm the big girl, I'm the big sister. Anyway, Mom told me to take care of the two babies, our little brother and sister and you better not touch them or I'm gonna tell Mom on you."

J: ''You're not gonna tell anybody on me.''
L: ''Huh! I'm gonna tell someone on you, don't you think I'm not. So brother, if you want to say something, keep it to your own self.''
J: ''You know I'm bigger than you.''
L: ''Huh, you're not bigger than anybody.''
J: ''Hey, I'm bigger than you—you're just nine. So you better watch it!''
L: ''You're the biggest 'cause you're just 12 years old. You're even bigger than me.''
J: ''You're just . . .''
L: ''If you want to fight just go fight yourself.
J: ''You think I'm bigger than you 'cause I'm 12 years old. You, you're just nine. Hey, hey, you better watch it 'cause I'm babysitting for you all.''
L: ''You mean us three?''
J: ''Yeah.''
L: ''One, two three.''
J: ''There, just . . .''
L: ''One, two three, four, and your own self. You're a baby; your own self.''
J: ''Hey, I ain't no baby girl, what goes and tattles on you.'' (Jim and Lil begin to whisper)
L: ''You better watch it 'cause they're waking, brother.''
J: ''Shut up.''
L: ''Well, make me.''
J: ''Shut up before you make me wake the babies up.''
L: ''Then I'll really tell Mom on you.
J: ''Hey you can't, you cannot tell Mom on me. I'll . . .''
L: ''Then I'll tell Dad on you. Let me tell you; you be the dad and . . .''
J: ''Uh-uh, I ain't playing no dad and I'm certain not no daddy.''
L: ''And I'm certain not no mommy.''
J: ''If you wanna find a daddy, if you wanna find a daddy, ask John.'' (the children's teacher)

Jim vigorously refuses to play father (''Cause fathers don't even play with toys''), and yet he must find a basis for holding his own in relation to a dominating, provocative pretend sister. Jim's solution—to be 12 years old—is a marvelous compromise. Jim thereby deals with the vulnerability of being a 5-year-old male without taking on the burdens of adulthood, the complications of fatherhood, and the dangers of marital involvement. One must applaud the psychological brilliance of Jim's symbolic solution to the threat inherent in the Oedipal triangle and the tensions of sibling rivalry. The ''self'' Jim projects is safe, enjoyable, developmentally sensible, and in touch with social reality.

Lil, as a female, confronts strikingly different issues: she is eager to play mother–wife, but the role of sister will do. Note that Lil sees herself consistently on the side of parental authority, as a properly delegated carrier of this authority in the parents' absence. However, note also her expectation that this delegated authority will be challenged and her preventive maneuvers designed to protect it. Wonderfully, she takes advantage of Jim's guilty discomfort, in response to which Jim finally protests: "Shut up before you make me wake the babies up."

In the play, both children practice responses adapted to the exigencies of family relationships. Mead's theory tells us that these responses are cast to permit the playing child to penetrate the multiple viewpoints of significant others in relation to the child's self concept as it is and as it might become. The content insights of psychoanalytic theory fit nicely with the structural insights of symbolic interactionist theory. Together these insights provide a preliminary framework for investigating the child's vision of a changing self in a world of comprehensible others.

## ACKNOWLEDGMENT

This research was supported by a grant from the Spencer Foundation.

## REFERENCES

Bateson, G. The message "This is play." In B. Schaffner (Ed.), *Group processes: Transactions of the second conference*. New York: Josiah Macy Foundation, 1956.

Elder, J. L., & Pederson, D. R. Preschool children's use of objects in symbolic play. *Child Development*, 1978, *49*, 500–504.

Erikson, E. H. *Childhood and society*. New York: Norton, 1963.

Erikson, E. H. *Toys and reasons*. New York: Norton, 1977.

Fein, G. G. A transformational analysis of pretending. *Developmental Psychology*, 1975, *11*, 291–296.

Fein, G. G. Echoes from the nursery: Piaget, Vygotsky and the relation between language and play. *New Directions in Child Development*, 1979, *6*, 1–14.

Fein, G. G. The physical environment: Stimulation or evocation. In R. M. Lerner & N. A. Busch-Rossnagel (Eds.), *Individuals as producers of their development*. New York: Academic Press, 1981. (a)

Fein, G. G. Pretend play: An integrative review. *Child Development*, 1981, *52*, 1095–1118. (b)

Fein, G. G., & Kohlberg, L. Play and constructive work as contributors to development. In L. Kohlberg & R. DeVries (Eds.), *Developmental psychology and early education*. New York: Longman, in press.

Fein, G. G., Moorin, E. R., & Enslein, J. Pretense and peer behavior: An intersectoral analysis. *Human Development*, 1982, *25*, 392–406.

Jackowitz, E. R., & Watson, M. W. The development of object transformations in early pretend play. *Developmental Psychology*, 1980, *16*, 543–549.

Mahler, M. *The psychological birth of the infant*. New York: Basic Books, 1975.

Mead, G. H. *Mind, self, and society*. Chicago: University of Chicago Press, 1934.

Peller, L. Libidinal phases, ego development, and play. *Psychoanalytic study of the child*, 1954, *9*, 178–198.

Piaget, J. *Play, dreams and imitation in childhood*. New York: Norton, 1962 (originally 1945, English translation, 1951).

Rubin, K. H., & Pepler, D. J. The relationship of child's play to social-cognitive growth and development. In H. Foot, J. Smith, & T. Chapman (Eds.), *Friendship and childhood relationships*. New York: Wiley, 1979.

Sutton-Smith, B. Piaget, play and cognition revisited. In W. Overton (Ed.), *The relationship between social and cognitive development*. Hillsdale, N.J.: Lawrence Erlbaum Associates, 1982.

Ungerer, J. A., Zelazo, P. R., Kearsley, R. B., & O'Leary, K. Developmental changes in the representation of objects in symbolic play from 18 to 34 months of age. *Child Development*, 1981, *52*, 186–195.

Vygotsky, L. S. Play and its role in the mental development of the child. *Soviet Psychology*, 1967, *5*, 6–18.

Watson, M. W., & Fischer, K. W. A developmental sequence of agent use in late infancy. *Child Development*, 1977, *48*, 828–836.

# 9 Relationships Between Exploration and Play

Joachim F. Wohlwill
*The Pennsylvania State University*

Exploratory activity and play are generally linked together as similar if not identical phenomena, based it seems on the fact that both share a similar motivational basis. Exploratory behavior, as well as play, are forms of intrinsically motivated behavior that are not directed at the achievement of some externally imposed goal, or even the satisfaction of some internal drive or need (though exploration has in some instances—Fowler, 1965—been considered to conform to the characteristics of drive-mediated behavior). There is an additional reason why these two forms of child behavior are often found lumped together, and why there is diffidence in some quarters (Weisler & McCall, 1976) about drawing a sharp distinction between them. That is the undeniable fact that play in its early or most primitive forms, such as encountered in infants or animals, is indeed difficult to differentiate from exploration.

Yet, as we shall see documented in diverse ways, the two really do represent different forms of behavior. It is important to try to arrive at a consistent distinction between them, not only in order to arrive at a full understanding of each, but to appreciate the interrelationships between them. That, in short, is the aim of this chapter.

## DIFFERENTIATING BETWEEN EXPLORATION AND PLAY

Let us start with Weisler and McCall's (1976) eminently useful definition of exploration: "*Exploratory behavior consists of a relatively stereotyped perceptual-motor examination of an object situation, or event the function of which is to reduce subjective uncertainty* (i.e., *acquire information*) [p. 493].'' One might quarrel with the inclusion of the stereotypy criterion in this definition: While it turns out empirically to be true that this type of behavior tends to be relatively invariant over situations, and to a degree even over species, there does not seem to be any reason for considering that to be a defining characteristic. Otherwise, however, the definition serves admirably both to bring out the essence of exploration and to establish a sound basis for differentiating it from play.

The definition of play is admittedly rather more problematical, and a long and eminent list of writers on the subject have come to grief over it, to the point that some (Berlyne, 1969) have arrived at the not unreasonable conclusion that the term is not sufficiently useful to be worth retaining. Certainly Weisler and McCall (1976) are of little help here, with their definition of play as consisting of: ''behaviors and behavioral sequences that are organism dominated, behaviors that appear intrinsically motivated, and apparently performed 'for their own sake' and that are conducted with relative relaxation and positive affect p. 494].'' The references to ''organism dominated'' and ''intrinsically motivated'' are hardly calculated to facilitate a differentiation of play from exploration; further, the specification of relaxation and positive affect are questionable as a priori criteria for play, just as much as is the inclusion of spontaneity as a criterion for exploration.

The problem is of course that play encompasses such a large variety of forms of behavior, from activity on a jungle gym to playing house to building a castle from blocks, to acting out a trip into space or similar make-believe activity. It is indeed difficult to come up with a serviceable definition. For our present purposes, however, interested as we are in comparing play with exploration, and more particularly tracing their interrelationship, it will be helpful to confine ourselves to one category of play, namely that of object play, because exploration likewise typically involves a set of objects (or else discrete visual, kinesthetic, or auditory stimuli presented for examination). Thus, the proposed restriction to object play will put us in a favorable position for comparing the two. Let us then define *object play* as *spontaneous activity, not directed at some externally imposed goal or serving some ulterior purpose, which involves manipulation of or other actions directed at an object or set of objects, resulting in some transformation of their location, arrangement, shape, etc., or of their meaning for the child (pretend play).*

We can agree that the preceding definition is far from airtight, yet it appears to encompass the major forms of what we generally call play with objects, whether in the form of block play, role play, or make-believe play. It points directly, furthermore, to a specific criterion to help us differentiate play from exploration: Whereas the latter is directed at information extraction, the former is directed at the transformation of an object, whether at the level of reality or of fantasy. Admittedly, for certain kinds of objects or materials this difference in the direction of the activity may be difficult to determine, but at least it provides a basis for devising materials calculated to contrast the two activities.

## Some Correlates of the Exploration–Play Distinction

Various behavioral indices have been suggested as bases for differentiating between these two activities. Rather than considering them as *criteria* for such a differentiation, as some authors have been disposed to do (Hutt, 1966), I suggest that they be given the status of behavioral attributes with respect to which the two types of activities may typically—though not invariably—differ. Of these, let us consider three in particular: the degree of stereotypy of behavior, the deployment of attention focused on the stimulus object, and the affective state of the child.

*Behavioral Stereotypy.* According to Hutt (1970), exploratory activity tends to be highly stereotyped, that is, unvarying across a given situation, whereas play may take on a great variety of specific forms. More specifically, Hutt postulated that exploration in contrast to play consists of highly stereotyped sequences of behavioral elements. This notion led Hughes (1978) to devise a direct test of this hypothesis in terms of the amount of uncertainty contained in any sequence of a child's actions performed with the "exploration box" (to be described later) that Hutt had originally devised to study exploration and play. Hughes devised a classification scheme including 14 separate categories of behavior that children engaged in when confronted with this box (e.g., visual inspection, different varieties of manipulation, movement of the levers that were the box's major manipulanda). Hughes then categorized the children as involved in exploration or play, following Hutt's criterion (i.e., according to whether their attention was focused on what they were doing [exploration], or whether they were failing to monitor their own actions [play]). We return to the appropriateness of this criterion later. For the moment, suffice it to note that Hughes not only found a very much higher diversity of actions during play as compared to exploration ($H = 3.65$ vs. 2.76)[1], but similarly a much more restricted set of dyadic and triadic sequences of behaviors during exploration, compared to play. For instance, less than one-fourth of the possible dyadic combinations of events were actually observed during exploration, whereas during play the fraction was close to two-thirds.

Hughes' procedure might be criticized on two grounds. The first is the lack of complete independence of the various categories, because a number involved manipulation of the box along with some other activity (e.g., gesturing, physical activity, talk). A second possible objection concerns the bias contained in the

[1]Hughes uses the symbol $U$ to index uncertainty, though it is most commonly represented as $H$.

definition of play employed (i.e., behavior that is not fully self-monitored). This definition is problematical, because several categories involved a juxtaposition of two or more activities (e.g., manipulating the box while engaging in physical activity or talking), which could by definition have occurred only during play using this nonself-monitored criterion. On the other hand, both Hutt's postulate and Hughes' attempted empirical verification of it appear plausible enough, if we define exploration as directed at information extraction, and play as defined not in terms of its goals but in terms of some real or imaginary transformation of the material. It is virtually inevitable then that the number of differentiable forms of behavior should be greater for play than for exploration. The different ways in which information can be extracted are quite limited (e.g., visual inspection, tactual exploration, manipulation, and investigation from different sides), whereas play can, again by definition, take on a virtually limitless variety of different forms.

Stereotypy in a somewhat different sense is considered by both Hutt (1970) and Weisler and McCall (1976) with reference to the sequence of phases of behavior involved in exploration. Weisler and McCall point out that exploration typically involves a predictable series of discrete steps, from an initial alerting or orienting response to a final phase of active interaction with an object. This phase would generally drop out where the object being explored is either insubstantial (e.g., a picture, an auditory stimulus) or inaccessible to the exploring organism. They do not consider any equivalent series of steps that might apply to play—for the simple and sufficient reason that play is not sequentially structured in terms of any comparable invariant series of steps. Very much the same point was made by Hutt (1970), who compared response sequences for exploration and play in terms of the schemata represented in Fig. 9.1.

One might well amplify this comparison between exploration and play in terms of stereotypy by noting that the former is also much more *invariant* than the latter across different stimulus situations, age levels, and species. Presumably it reflects the more evident functional value of extracting information about an object or situation in comparison with whatever purpose may be served by object play. However, the primary significance of the stereotypy criterion lies perhaps in its coherence with the other two differentiating characteristics cited previously. Let us turn next, then, to that of the deployment of attention.

*Deployment of Attention.* Let us recall that Hughes used the organism's attentional focus as the criterion on the basis of which exploration was to be differentiated from play, based on Hutt's (1966) earlier observation that the child's attentional state appeared to differ markedly during what might impressionistically be termed exploration, as compared to play. Hutt (1966) had expressed this difference as follows: "During investigation all receptors were oriented toward the object, the general expression being one of 'concentration' . . . in play for much of the time the receptors were desynchronized (i.e.,

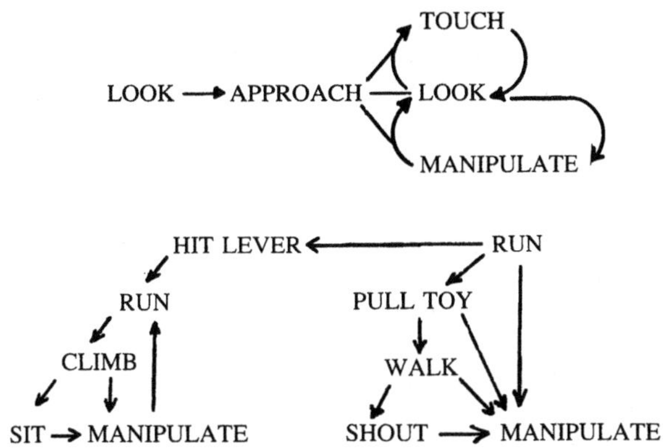


FIG. 9.1 Schematic representation of sequential response patterns involved in investigatory activity (top) and in play (bottom). From Hutt (1970). (Reprinted by permission of Academic Press.)

vision and manipulation were no longer simultaneously directed toward the object) and the behavior towards the object might also be described as 'non-chalant' [p. 71].'' Hutt did not provide any concrete data bearing on this differentiation. Because Hughes used this as the criterion to distinguish exploration from play, no independent verification of this as a *correlate* of the distinction could emerge from her study. In a further study, however, Hughes and Hutt (1979) provided more direct empirical support for their hypothesis. They demonstrated that when 2-year-old children were presented with a set of familiar toys, thus favoring play over exploration, their heartrate variability was significantly higher than it was in a subsequent period in which one of the familiar toys was replaced by a novel one, so as to elicit exploration. (Independent ratings of the child's actual behavior confirmed the fact that the dominant type of behavior during the first phase was play, and during the second exploration.) This physiological index had previously been demonstrated to be highly sensitive to changes in attentional state, fluctuation in heartrate being inhibited during periods of concentrated attention to a particular stimulus or event (Porges, Arnold, & Forbes, 1973; Porges & Raskin, 1969). Accordingly, the conclusion that play involves a less highly focused attentional state than does exploration appears reasonable. It is consistent, furthermore, with the difference in stereotypy of behavior (i.e., it would seem that during a period in which attention is concentrated on a particular stimulus the diversity of behaviors that a child engages in would be reduced, relative to one in which attention is more fleeting, or more widely distributed over different objects or locations).

A further observation by Hughes and Hutt serves to warn us, however, against generalizing this principle in too unqualified a fashion. Their study also included the presentation of a problem involving the placement of six wooden cut-out pieces into a formboard. Heartrate variability during the course of working on this task was the lowest of all of the three situations—clearly reflecting the high degree of concentration demanded by such a task. The question arises, however, whether play may not, in some situations, involve similar problem-solving activity and thus a state of heightened attention. Consider constructive play with blocks, in which a child essentially sets a problem to solve (i.e., the building of a particular structure such as a tall tower). Surely, one would anticipate a degree of focused attention elicited by such a situation that would be at least comparable to that involved in exploration. Thus the assumption that exploration and play will invarably be differentiated in terms of the degree of focusing of attention involved in each should probably be rejected, unless the type of play is more narrowly defined. Yet, as we shall see, it is precisely constructive play with blocks that may provide the play situation best suited for a direct comparison with exploration.

*Affective State.* Related to the preceding correlate of the differentiation between exploration and play is the individual's state of affective arousal characterizing these two forms of behavior. Exploration is generally considered to be marked by either neutral or mildly negative affect. The absence of positive affect reflects the state of tension created by the focusing of attention, and perhaps the state of uncertainty in which an exploring organism generally finds itself. Indeed, in some accounts of exploration based on a drive reduction model of motivation, the reduction of this state of tension is thought to be the aim of exploratory activity. Play, on the other hand, tends to be marked by expressions of positive affect—smiling, even laughter and similar manifestations of pleasure consonant with the greater degree of relaxation thought to be characteristic of play.

However intuitively obvious and plausible, the assumption that play entails a state of positive affect is supported more by incidental observation (Hutt, 1966, 1970) than systematic evidence. The matter merits more systematic investigation, for it is by no means certain that play is invariably accompanied by this type of affective state. The example of play directed at problem solving noted previously is surely relevant in this same context, for here the smile or laughter may not occur until the goal is achieved—that is, the tower of blocks stands completed—or, for that matter, deliberately nullified by the child, causing the tower to collapse with a loud thud. In a very different context we find that play may be very serious business indeed, as in the case of doll play of the type used as a projective device by clinicians, where a considerable amount of tension may be manifested and released.

Part of the problem may derive from the tendency in some quarters—notably in the writings of Hutt (1970: 118–180; 1981: 251–298)—to identify play with *diverse* exploration, in contrast to specific exploration. Berlyne (1960) introduced this distinction on the basis of the level of arousal involved in different types of exploratory activity. Specific exploration is directed at information extraction (which involves a high degree of uncertainty, and thus high arousal), whereas diversive exploration is directed at achieving an optimal level of arousal experienced as pleasurable, the individual seeking out stimulation to dispel boredom (e.g., by going window-shopping, or sightseeing). As the author has noted elsewhere (Wohlwill, 1981), diversive exploration in this sense is best reserved for such generalized (i.e., nonspecific) stimulus-*search* behavior. Thus it is of uncertain relevance for behavior in the face of a particular object, let alone the particular type of behavior we are designating as play, which we are by definition differentiating from exploration. In the same paper I suggested a further differentiation between inspective exploration and affective exploration. Both occur as kinds of exploratory activities in the face of a particular stimulus, but the former is aimed at information extraction whereas the latter is directed at affective gratification (as in a child's manipulation of a kaleidoscope). This analysis further throws into question the use of an affective state as a reliable differentiator between exploration and play, because it recognizes that stimulus exploration may well have an affective component (or phase), whereas play, as already noted, may occur without any marked positive affect.[2]

## APPROACHES TO RESEARCH ON THE RELATIONSHIP BETWEEN EXPLORATION AND PLAY

In this section we consider briefly the major types of materials utilized in research on this topic. In addition we will explore the methodological approaches for obtaining information on the relationship between exploration and object play as studied in animals, infants, and young children, and examine their suitability as well as their limitations for this purpose.

*Animals.* Although a considerable literature exists on both exploratory activity and play in animals, no attempt has been made to study their interrelationship. At the animal level the major part of research on play has concentrated on forms of behavior clearly different from and unrelated to exploration, for example, general motor activity, social play, and playlike forms of behavior associ-

---

[2]It is interesting to note that in his own comprehensive survey of the field of play Berlyne (1969) refrained from interpreting play as diversive exploration; indeed, the latter term does not seem to appear in his chapter. He was inclined in fact to question the identification of play with pleasure, or positive arousal, emphasizing the frequent role of tension and conflict in various play activities, although his major conclusion was that "play" was far too diversified and heterogeneous a behavioral category to be susceptible to interpretation in terms of any single process. But it is clear that Hutt's borrowing of the diversive-exploration concept in her account of play is her own, and as shown in the text, represents a questionable application of this concept.

ated with maternal behavior, reproduction, and feeding (Millar, 1968, chap. 3), as contrasted to object play. As regards the latter, its study has been largely limited to incidental observations of one variety of animal or another responding to a familiar object in what appeared to be playful fashion, such as a bear making and tossing a snowball, or dolphins tossing an object out of their compound repeatedly. Cats' play with balls of yarn would presumably come under the same heading, representing behavior closely akin to that which Piaget has described as "circular reactions" in his observations of human infants. Apart from being at best nonsystematic, these observations do not link up this behavior with exploration. Those, on the other hand, who have studied exploration experimentally in animals (see Welker [1961] for a review), have generally been reluctant to set up a separate behavioral category of play, preferring to consider the latter as a more vigorous, motirically intense form of manipulatory exploration. One of Welker's studies (Welker, 1956) is of some interest, however, in demonstrating a roughly inverse relationship between time spent in passive observation of an object initially unfamiliar and that spent in active manipulation of it. This relationship held both ontogenetically (i.e., in terms of a progressive shift from exploration without contact to active manipulation with age) and at a given age over the course of a session. In Welker's terms this amounts to a transition from exploration to play, but there is clearly a question here as to whether the manipulation phase served merely to reduce uncertainty about the object further (in which case the change from passive inspection to manipulation presumably reflects principally the dissipation of the inhibition of approach to a novel object over time, or with age), or whether the manipulation entailed a functionally separate kind of behavior (such as is generally understood under the concept of play).

*Infants.* In the case of human infants, one finds diverse studies in which separate results are reported for exploration and for play, without much significance being attached to the difference between them. Furthermore, few attempts were made to trace the functional relationship between them. For example, Fenson, Sapper, and Minner (1974) report data on visual exploration of a set of simple pictorial stimuli in 1-year-olds, along with further data on the amount of time spent manipulating a set of three-dimensional objects (such as discs, a chain, a brush) ostensibly chosen to elicit play. Necessarily this procedure does not permit a differentiation between exploration and play considered as alternative forms of response to a single set of objects, although the authors did report correlations between the amounts of time spent in visual exploration to the first set of stimuli and in play with the second set. (Interestingly enough, for a number of different indices of the visual exploration phase, the correlations with the play data are substantial in magnitude for the girls, but negligible for the boys.)

A similar but considerably more extensive investigation is that of McCall (1974) of 10-month-old infants. Like Fenson et al. (1974), the latter used different stimuli for exploration and for play, although in his case all were three-dimensional objects as McCall's interest was in *manipulative* exploration. The primary objects used were of five types: a set of sheets of paper, a set of arrows, geometric figures, square alphabet blocks, and small pots. These objects were chosen to provide evidence on the role of plasticity, configural complexity, and sound potential. For the play study, on the other hand, commercial toys were employed. Again, the use of a different set of stimuli precludes an analysis of possible relationships between the two forms of behavior. (Intraindividual relationships, in the form of correlations similar to those reported by Fenson et al., could have been obtained, but none are reported.) McCall did, however, elaborate his analysis of play considerably beyond that carried out by Fenson et al. by differentiating play into a number of separable types of behaviors, chosen in part with Piaget's formulation of early sensorimotor development in mind. These included not only time spent in different kinds of holding, mouthing, and manipulatory responses, but also frequencies of secondary and tertiary circular responses, specific toy-appropriate behaviors, and parallel as well as integrative play with two different objects. The implicit separation of play from exploration is apparent here, but no attempt is made to compare or contrast the two kinds of activities.

Some exceptions to the tendency for researchers at the infant level to ignore the relationship between exploration and play may be noted, however. Thus, Collard (1979) reports observations of infants of average age 46 weeks, in regard to their response to a single toy: a bracelet consisting of four wooden beads on a keychain also containing a bell. These responses were differentiated into 25 categories, of which 10 fell under the heading of exploration and 9 under play; the remaining 6 made up a class of social–play behaviors. An interesting feature of Collard's data is the differential patterns for exploration and play over the course of the 6-minute session: whereas exploration remained well above play throughout, it tended to decrease in frequency with time, whereas play increased—foreshadowing the similar findings from early childhood to be reported later.

A further study dealing very explicitly with a differentiation between exploratory and play responses to a constant set of objects (mostly familiar toys) is that of Belsky and Most (1981). In contrast to Collard's study, which was confined to a single age level (approximately 11 months), Belsky and Most traced the changes in these responses over the course of the first 2 years, with the specific aim of delineating a shift from exploration to play. This study is thus of particular significance in regard to the developmental side of the exploration–play relationship and shall be discussed more fully in a subsequent section of this paper devoted to that issue.

*Young Children.* The bulk of the work that has dealt specifically with the differentiation between exploration and play and with their functional interrelationship has been carried out at the preschool level. First and foremost among these studies is the work of Hutt and Huges (Hughes, 1978, 1979; Hughes & Hutt, 1979; Hutt, 1966, 1967). This work has relied heavily on the use of the "exploration box"—a red metal box mounted on four brass legs, featuring a lever mounted on its top at one end that could be shifted into four different positions. Both visual and auditory feedback from the lever movements was provided for in the form of four counters that responded selectively to each type of movement, and a bell and a buzzer activated by movements in two of the four directions. Hutt's original interest appears to have been in the manifestation of exploratory behavior to such a novel object, as a function of the different types of feedback that a child was able to obtain from it, and the habituation of exploration over time. In fact, under two experimental conditions involving either no or only visual feedback, there was apparently little evidence of any but purely exploratory activity (i.e., repeated movements of the lever), which dropped sharply over a series of six sessions. In the other two conditions, however, involving auditory feedback with or without visual feedback, there was little evidence of habituation of the lever-manipulation response over time. Rather, there was some increase, at least up to the fifth session, as well as a marked qualitative change in the form of the child's response to the box. To use Hutt's (1966) own words to describe what she found:

> As investigation of the object decreased other activities involving it increased. When analyzed these consisted of repetitive motor movements, manipulations of long duration accompanied by visual inspection of other objects, and a sequence of activities incorporating both the novel object and other toys—in other words a game. Examples of these were respectively: patting the lever repeatedly, leaning on the lever making the bell ring continuously while looking around the room, and running round with the truck ringing the bell each time the object was passed. There is another group of responses which can be termed transposition-of-function—those responses which resulted in the object explicitly fulfilling another function, e.g., something to climb, a bridge, or a seat. All these activities . . . are those which an observer would recognize and label as *play* [p. 70].

Hutt was impressed not only with the changes in these forms of behavior observed on the part of the child but with accompanying changes in the child's state, from one of concentrated attention and tenseness to one of more relaxed facial expression and a nonchalant attitude toward the box (i.e., lack of specific visual attention to it, even while retaining manual contact with it). In subsequent studies with this same box, Huges devised more systematic ways of documenting the difference between the two forms of behavior, notably in regard to their relative degree of sterotypy, as noted previously. That is, exploration was characterized both by a considerably narrower range of behaviors and behavioral chains (Hughes, 1978) and by a more rigidly structured hierarchy of elements (Hughes, 1979) in comparison to play.

The major limitation of Hutt and Hughes' work, considered as an approach to studying the interrelationship between exploration and play, relates to the shortcomings of the apparatus used, which was designed to reveal exploratory and manipulatory behavior rather than play as such. The box is in fact much too rigid, as well as bulky, to allow for much manifestation of object play, at least in the sense that we have defined it here (i.e., as involving some *transformation* of an object, at either a physical or imaginal level). An examination of Hughes' data reveals that the most frequent type of behavior exhibited during what was considered to be play did not in fact involve the exploration box at all. Rather, it involved manipulation of other toys. This category accounted for 14% of the behavioral acts observed by the total group of children. Another 9% took the form of manipulating the box while holding (and possibly playing with?) a toy. The only two response categories (out of a total of 14) that involved playing with the box *per se* were lever manipulation accompanied by some motor behavior directed at the box (e.g., sitting, standing, or climbing on it), and unconventional manipulation of the lever (e.g., other than with the hands). These two categories accounted for 8% and 7%, respectively. That leaves a total of 62% of the responses taking diverse forms not specifically indicative of play per se, such as manipulation of the lever (the primary category exhibited during exploration), manipulation while talking, watching "something else" in the room, and gross locomotor activity not associated with the box.

A rather different approach, and specifically a very different kind of material, was utilized by Switzky and his associates (Switzky, Haywood, & Isett, 1974; Switzky, Ludwig, & Haywood, 1979) in their research on exploration and play in young children. In part because of these investigators' particular interest in the role of stimulus complexity, they resorted to a set of three-dimensional black objects in the form of random polygons, constructed of vinyl, approximately 50 × 50 × 20 cm. in size. They defined play as either sensorimotor activities such as bouncing, bending, rolling, throwing, or jumping on these objects, or symbolic use of the object to represent something else. The potential for play to occur is clearly greater with such materials than with Hutt's exploration box. Yet even here the potential for true play is limited by the rigidity of the materials, and their presentation to the child one at a time (a procedure dictated by the interest in the functions relating the complexity variable to the behavioral indices). It is thus not surprising to find that the amount of time spent in exploring the stimulus exceeded that spent in play by far in both of their studies, and at all age levels.

Two other studies may be cited more briefly. Hughes (1981) employed a set of objects in two different versions: one (Set A) consisted of three colored sticks and a set of strips shaped so that by use of the latter several of the sticks could be joined to one another; the other (Set B) involved three sticks shaped as persons, and strips shaped as meaningful objects. The primary interest was in the effectiveness of a familiarization period with either of these sets of objects in facilitating subsequent problem solving, (i.e., joining the sticks together). As expected, during the familiarization phase children exhibited considerably more exploratory behavior (i.e., inspection, manipulation, as well as spontaneous problem-solving activity) with the materials of Set A compared to those of Set B, whereas play (i.e., "ludic" behavior, not otherwise specified) was more common with Set B. Differences between the two groups in the problem-solving phase were, however, negligible.

Finally, a study by Vliestra (1978) compared exploration and play via a preferential choice procedure. Preschool children, as well as a comparison group of college adults, were presented with a set of "bristle blocks" for potential constructive play, along with a set of picture boxes, each of which featured three doors that when opened revealed a picture of a novel, incongruous looking animal. The children were simply told that they might "look in the houses and play with the blocks as they wished," and left to themselves. In this situation, amount of time spent in play with the blocks exceeded by far that spent in exploration of the picture boxes, and to an extent even greater for the adults than for the children. The use of *different* materials to compare the two types of behavior leaves the significance of this finding uncertain, however—it would be easy to think of pairings of materials that would yield an opposite result.

## EXPLORATION AND PLAY IN DEVELOPMENTAL PERSPECTIVE

It would be a mistake to look for any general principle that might express the changes in the relationships between exploration and play over the course of the development of the child—for example, in terms of a systematic shift from one to the other with age—for at least two reasons. First, exploration can be expected to occur at any age, depending on the potential of a given stimulus to elicit activity directed at information extraction, which is a function of the degree of uncertainty it contains, in terms of its complexity, novelty, incongruity, etc. (Berlyne, 1960). This uncertainty level in turn is determined by a combination of stimulus characteristics, previous experience of the individual with the object, and schemata or expectations developed relating to it. Thus, a toy dog is apt to elicit less exploration on the part of a 5-year-old as compared to a 3-year-old, because of the former's greater familiarity with it. On the other hand an object that was a combination dog and locomotive might show the reverse trend, on the assumption that the schemata of these two types of objects would be more strongly developed at age 5, thus providing a stronger incongruity response. For many objects no very clear developmental pattern may emerge, and this is indeed reflected in the inconsistent results obtained with respect to amount of exploration at different ages with respect to stimuli varying in complexity, for instance.

For somewhat different reasons, developmental trends concerning amount of play at different ages are likewise difficult to determine because they are greatly affected by the nature of the materials, the context (e.g., how facilitative of play it is), and quite likely such individual difference factors as the "playfulness" (Lieberman, 1977) of the child. In general one might expect play to decrease with age, at least beyond the early childhood years. This is due in part to socialization pressures and opprobrium placed on such nonserious kinds of activity. The finding of Vliestra (1978), indicating that college adults spend a *greater* amount of time playing with blocks than do preschool children should caution us against too ready a generalization in this regard—if any were needed, in view of the popularity of such devices as video games and card games at all ages.

Undoubtedly, in any event, the major developmental process that takes place concerns the qualitative forms taken by play at different ages. Once we consider these it soon develops that we may be able to place different forms of exploratory activity *and* play on a continuum, so as to arrive at a developmental sequence moving from pure exploration to pure play, characterizing the course of development at least over the first years of life. This possibility is indeed borne out by empirical results, as Belsky and Most (1981) have demonstrated most convincingly in their study of infants over the period from 7½ to 21 months.

These investigators started with a hypothesized 13-step sequence, based in part on observations of exploration and play in previous studies, which they believed could be used to describe the developmental progression in the qualitative modes of infants' response to common objects. Accordingly, they selected two sets of toys (e.g., baby dolls, teacups, and saucers, a wooden rattle, a seashell, a Fisher-Price telephone), the first consisting of 16 items, the second of 10. They presented these to 40 infants in the presence of their mothers, one set at a time, and observed the type of behavior engaged in with these toys for periods of up to 15 minutes for each set. These observations were then coded into the terms of the predefined sequence, each child being "credited" with scoring at each level on the basis of at least one observation coded to fit that level. Table 9.1 presents a detailed description of each of these levels, along with the median age of all infants exhibiting the behavior, and that of the youngest infant doing so. Belsky and Most found that the sequence does in fact correspond to a Guttman scalogram pattern, with children observed to engage in a response at any level also (with only few exceptions) exhibiting the behaviors at all levels preceding it in their scale.

Although the total number of subjects in this investigation (40) is rather small as a basis on which to establish such a developmental sequence, the broad outlines of the sequence are confirmed by the findings of other investigations, such as those of McCall (1974), Fenson, Kagan, Kearsley, and Zelazo (1976), Lowe (1975), and Zelazo and Kearsley (1980), although some of these covered a much shorter age range. Nevertheless this body of research certainly serves to confirm in the aggregate the transition that Belsky and Most note, from behavior marked by undifferentiated exploration (Levels A and B) through transitional

TABLE 9.1
Developmental Sequence of Exploratory and Play Behavior Observed during the First 2 Years of Life, with Median Age of Children Exhibiting each Behavior Type, and Youngest Age at which It Was Observed[a]

| | *Median Age* (*in months*) | *Youngest Age* |
|---|---|---|
| 1. Mouthing—indiscriminate mouthing of materials. | 14.5 | 7.5 |
| 2. Simple manipulation—visually guided manipulation (excluding indiscriminate banging and shaking) at least 5 sec in duration. | 14 | 7.5 |
| 3. Functional—visually guided manipulation that is particularly appropriate for a certain object and involves the intential extraction of some unique piece of information (e.g., turn dial on toy phone, squeeze piece of foam rubber). | 14 | 7.5 |
| 4. Relational—bringing together and integrating two or more materials in an inappropriate manner, that is, a manner not initially intended by the manufacturer (e.g., set cradle on phone, touch spoon to stick). | 14 | 7.5 |
| 5. Functional-relational—bringing together and integrating two objects in an appropriate manner (e.g., set cup on saucer, place peg in hole of pegboard, mount spool on shaft of cart). | 15 | 9 |
| 6. Enactive naming—approximate pretense activity but without confirming evidence of actual pretense behavior (e.g., raise phone receiver in proximity of ear without making talking sounds). | 15 | 9 |
| 7. Pretend self—pretense behavior directed toward self in which pretense is apparent (e.g., stroke own hair with miniature brush; raise phone receiver to ear and vocalize). | 16.5 | 12 |
| 8. Pretend other—pretense behavior directed away from child | 18 | 13.5 |

play (Levels C through F), and culminating in pretense play (Levels G through L). The developmental significance of these three broad phases of infants' behavior in dealing with this type of material is enhanced, furthermore, in Belsky and Most's finding that the relative amount of time spent in these three categories of activity decreases steadily with age for the first (undifferentiated exploration), increases in direct complementarity to the first in the case of the last (pretend play), and first increases, then decreases slightly for the middle category (transitional).[3]

[3]This pattern might seem to contradict the cumulative Guttman-type scalogram pattern to which the steps in Belsky and Most's sequences were shown to confirm. The discrepancy is more apparent than real: the scalogram pattern was based on any type of behavior manifested by each child, regardless of its frequency; thus the lower-level forms of behavior, exhibited by all children to some degree, fit into this scalogram pattern, even though the relative amount of time that they accounted for decreased steadily with age.

TABLE 9.1 (*Continued*)

| | *Median Age* (in months) | *Youngest Age* |
|---|---|---|
| toward other (e.g., feed doll with spoon, bottle, or cup; brush doll's hair; push car on floor and make car noise). | | |
| 9. Substitution—using a "meaningless" object in a creative or imaginative manner (e.g., drink from seashell; feed baby with stick as "bottle") or using an object in a pretense act in a way that differs from how it was previously used by the child (e.g., use hairbrush to brush teeth after already using it as a hairbrush on self or other). | 18 | 13.5 |
| 10. Sequence pretend—repetition of a single pretense act with minor variation (e.g., drink from bottle, give doll drink) or linking together different pretense schemes (e.g., put doll in cradle, then kiss goodnight). | 18 | 13.5 |
| 11. Sequence pretend substitution—same as sequence pretend except using an object substitution within sequence (e.g., put doll in cradle, cover with green felt piece as "blanket"). | 18.5 | 15 |
| 12. Double substitution—pretense play in which two materials are transformed, within a single act, into something they are not in reality (e.g., treat stick as person and seashell as cup, and give stick a drink). | 18 | 16.5 |

[a]From Belsky and Most (1981). Abbreviated from Table 1. Values for Median and Youngest Ages based on data for individual children in Table 2. (Reprinted by permission of American Psychological Association).

At the descriptive level, then, we can regard the transition from exploration to play over the course of the first 2 or 3 years of life as well established. What remains to be determined, however, is the developmental significance of this finding. From a Piagetian framework, or perhaps a neo-Piagetian (Gardner, 1982), one might see it as a reflection of the transition from the sensorimotor stage of early intellectual functioning (e.g., mouthing objects, banging them on a table or against one another, bouncing them off the floor), to the early phases of symbolic functioning, in terms of which Piaget (1946) analyzes play. Yet there are some important caveats to be noted in interpreting this shift. Probably the one of greatest moment concerns the role of familiarity. The objects that the oldest children in Belsky and Most's study used in elaborate forms of play were at the same time for the most part quite familiar to them—cups and saucers, baby dolls, rattles, hair-brush, etc. Because of their familiarity, these objects hardly left room for much exploration at the older age levels. Conversely, if mouthing and simple manipulation was observed in all subjects regardless of age, this is plausibly attributed to the fact that the two sets of toys included a few that were probably not very familiar to even the oldest children—such as a seashell, a foam rubber cube, a pegboard, and two Fisher-Price toys. By the same token, given a highly familiar toy such as a well-loved teddybear, even a very young child will probably engage in little if any exploratory activity, but instead exhibit rudimentary forms of play, such as those Belsky and Most labeled "transitional."

More generally, it may be questioned whether the developmental transition is in fact one moving from exploration to play at all. Given the functionally different character served by these two forms of activity, perhaps they develop rather in parallel, in terms of the qualitative forms characterizing either type at a given developmental level, as well as certain quantitative parameters, such as degree of thoroughness and systematic character in the case of exploration, and degree of elaboration of fantasy or imaginativeness in the case of play. As just suggested, exploration and play serve different purposes, the one being directed at extraction of information about a stimulus that, by virtue of its complexity, novelty, etc. generates uncertainty, whereas the other is directed at the elaboration of an already familiar stimulus or object to create a new reality, as it were. Each of these is clearly subject to developmental change. It may well be—as Belsky and Most do indeed demonstrate as the child grows older—that a progressively higher proportion of the child's time is accounted for by forms of play, but surely in part because of progressively greater familiarity with standard play objects. On the other hand, where there is information to be extracted, or uncertainty to be resolved, one may presume that exploratory activity will take precedence over play, if not in the sense of preempting the latter, then at least in the sense of preceding it temporally. We thus come to the next section of this paper, in which the temporal structuring of exploration and play is examined.

## THE TEMPORAL RELATIONSHIP BETWEEN EXPLORATION AND PLAY

A major reason why a number of investigators have considered it important to differentiate between exploration and play is that there are theoretical as well as empirical grounds for postulating that over the course of a period of time spent with any given set of play materials, exploration will change to play as the dominant mode of activity. The assumption is that exploration is the preferred response initially, at least where the materials are not as yet fully familiar to the child, so that some degree of uncertainty remains to be resolved. Once the child has been able to reduce such uncertainty to some satisfactory minimum level, a play phase can ensue, provided of course the materials provide the opportunity for it. The transition between the two phases need of course not be abrupt; rather, the possibility of an intermediary phase in which the child will oscillate between the two needs to be considered.

The temporal succession from exploration to play is at least strongly implied in Hutt's (1970) formulation of specific and diversive exploration. Specific exploration declines over time as a result of stimulus satiation, whereas play, which Hutt considers a particular form of diversive exploration, first increases in strength, and declines subsequently, as a result of response inhibition. There is no clearly articulated progression through a series of phases in Hutt's account of this process, however. Just such a phase progression scheme has been proposed by Nunnally and Lemond (1973). These writers consider specific exploration as the initial activity elicited by an encounter with a stimulus. It progresses from there to an intermediary phase of manipulative investigatory activity, which is still directed at information extraction, but at information relating to the structural as well as functional properties of the object—a phase that Nunnally and Lemond consider to entail ''transformational thinking,'' though the reasons for doing so are not entirely clear. Play represents a third phase, following the cessation of manipulatory exploration; it is identified with autistic thinking on the grounds that it involves elaboration of the object in thought in the form of fantasy, directed primarily at pleasure—or possibly a cessation of thought about the object entirely. One might well entertain strong reservations about this conception of play, thus stripped of any cognitive significance. The case of block play would seem to be difficult to subsume under such a view of play, to name but one example. For our purposes, the important point relating to Nunnally and Lemond's scheme is that it conceives of play as clearly following upon exploration. A final phase, following the cessation of play, is of further interest in relation to Hutt's formulation. For Nunnally and Lemond, the total cycle terminates with a diversive exploration phase, characterized by a search for some new object or source of stimulation, to ward off the boredom engendered by the completion of the earlier phases. Diversive exploration is not, in other words, considered to be a generic activity under which play may be subsumed, as Hutt would have it, but rather an activity directed at search for stimulation—a view that this writer finds most persuasive, and indeed in conformance with Berlyne's original definition of this elusive concept (Wohlwill, 1981: 341–364).

Nunnally and Lemond do not, however, back up their schema with any data, either original or based on the work of others. Hutt did so, both in incidental fashion in her original investigation (Hutt, 1966) and more systematically in a succeeding one (Hutt, 1967), in which different temporal schedules for exposure to the exploration box were compared. The results from that study are shown in Fig. 9.2.

The results of Hutt and Hughes are both confirmed and extended in important ways in more recent research by Schneider, Moch, Sandfort, Auerswald, and Walther-Weckmann (1981). These researchers utilized Hutt's exploration box but adapted her set of behavior categories, arriving at a set of 12. Eight of these were selected for detailed analysis (the other four represented forms of behavior unrelated to the exploration box), and reduced to a set of four by combining three into a broader category termed *perceptual investigation* and three more into a category termed *play*. The frequency of occurrence of behaviors in these two composite categories was plotted as a function of time in the session, along with

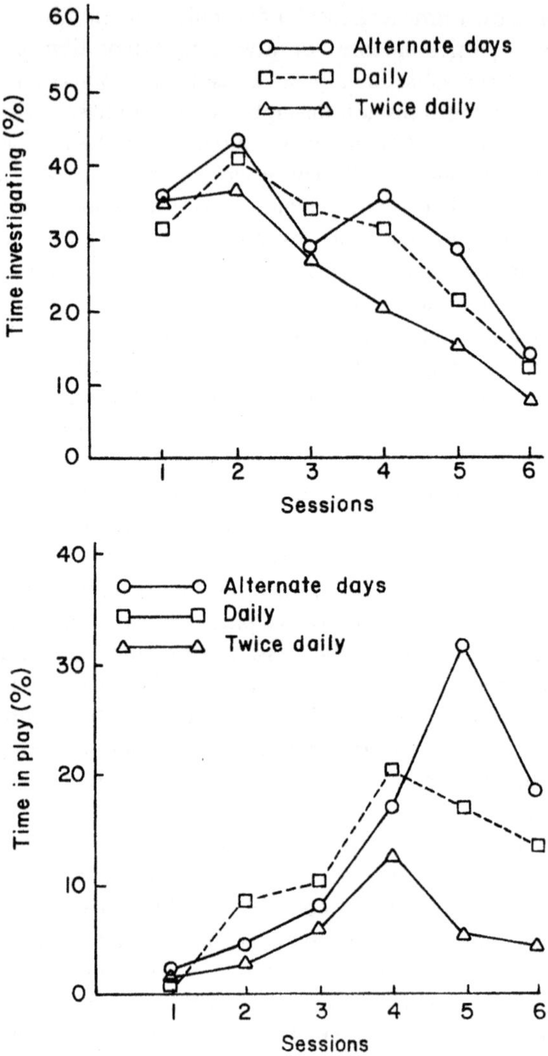


FIG. 9.2 Temporal course of change in investigatory responses (left) and play (right) to the "Exploration Box," in children studied under three different schedules. From Hutt (1970). (Reprinted by permission of Academic Press.)

those falling into the categories of manipulation and looking behavior (i.e., visual orientation to the box, from a distance).

Schneider et al.'s data are of particular interest because their children were divided into three age groups (3-, 4-, and 5-year-olds), thus permitting age changes in the relative dominance of the various forms of response to the object to reveal themselves. Looking behavior and perceptual investigation steadily increased over the course of the experimental session (which lasted 10 minutes in the first study and 15 mintues in a subsequent replication). In neither case were there appreciable age differences. The same was true for behavior in the category of play, which increased with time in the session. Thus far the results have done little more than confirm the data of Hutt and Hughes and others. But the inclusion of manipulation as a separate category showed that this type of behavior represents a phase intermediary between perceptual investigation and play, in that it increases over the first half of the session and then decreases. There were, furthermore, significant age differences in this regard, the oldest children engaging in considerable more manipulation than the younger ones, and (in the second study, using the 15 minute sessions) reaching the peak of manipulation earlier. Schneider et al.'s findings thus provide support, not only for the broad transition from exploration to play hypothesized by Hutt, but for the more specific differentiation between inspection and manipulation as successive phases of exploration that Nunnally and Lemond (1973) postulated in their model.

Schneider et al.'s data, as well as Hutt's, are subject to an important limitation, which was already noted earlier. The primary object—the exploration box—would seem to be deficient in terms of its suitability for eliciting play, because of its bulk and lack of modifiability, though the movements of the lever and the feedback obtained from them could be incorporated into some forms of play and apparently were to some extent. Yet even at its height the time spent in play did not come close to matching that spent earlier in exploration, as Fig. 9.2 shows. It should be remembered also that some of the child's play activity (apparently not reflected in these graphs) was directed at other familiar toys available to the child.

A somewhat similar picture of the temporal patterns for exploration and play comes from a study by Switzky et al. (1979). It involved responses to a set of nonsense shapes (see previous discussion) given to children at ages 30 and 43 months, of whom half were normal, the other half retarded. The relevant data are reported for both groups combined (no group differences are mentioned with respect to the trends over time). The data showed a marked increase in play over time when the total session is divided into thirds, while exploration decreased. The actual mean changes (in seconds) are from approximately 8.6 to 7.0 for exploration, and from 1.8 to 3.0 for play; thus—contrary to Hutt's findings—a very clear majority of the time was occupied with exploration even during the final third of the session. Switzky et al.'s exposure time functions look in fact surprisingly similar to those reported by Collard (1979) in the study of 11-month-old infants' response to a bracelet toy cited earlier. One suspects that the rather innocuous nature of the stimuli may be implicated in Switzky et al.'s results, at least in part, both as regards the overall low values of these means, whether for exploration or play, and as regards the fact that play remained at a relatively low level throughout.

Vliestra's (1978) study, also cited earlier, likewise provides some evidence of a shift from exploration to play, but mainly in a precipitous drop in amount of exploration of the picture boxes from the first to the second half; amount of activity with the bristle blocks was almost the same in both halves, and bristle-block play exceeded by far the visual exploration of the picture boxes in both the nursery school and the adult group. Recall that Vliestra's procedure entailed the use of two different sets of materials to elicit the two types of activities. The considerable drop in exploration of the incongruous pictures from the first to the second half (of 5-minute length each in both groups) suggests that even the children did not need much time to satisfy their curiosity about the pictures (of which there were 12 in all): the blocks, with their great potential for constructive play, usurped the very large share of the time. (Given the nature of the bristle blocks, little if any exploratory activity directed at them was to be expected, and in fact 92% of adults' responses to the blocks, and 79% of that of the children, took the form of constructive play.)

A major limitation, in my view, of the work conducted to date on the temporal interrelationships between exploration and play is the choice of materials. They have not been chosen so as to elicit a potentially balanced amount of both forms of behavior. This situation is reflected in the grossly dominant role that exploration took in Hutt's and Hughes' studies, and in the research of Switzky et al., as well as in the reverse pattern found in the results of Vliestra's study. What suggests itself instead is the use of materials that on the one hand are sufficiently laden with perceptual information to evoke exploration, while at the same time being structurally and materially suited for the elicitation of play activity.

One such type of material that appears well suited for this purpose is a set of ordinary wooden blocks of the kind favored by children for block play. These blocks, considerably smaller than the bristle blocks employed by Vliestra, may be decorated with stimuli for visual and tactual exploration. This was the material chosen for a pilot study of the transition from exploration to play at the nursery school level, which shall be briefly described here.[4]

Subjects were children between the ages of three and five, enrolled in a university nursery school. A set of 12 blocks was laid out in front of the child—generally in a relatively secluded space, in some cases a separate room, free from distraction from or interference by other children—and the child was simply asked to do whatever it liked with the blocks.

The blocks—adapted from a set originally constructed for the study of spontaneous classification behavior in early grade school children—contained pictures of familiar objects on three of their faces (e.g., birds, objects of furniture, ice cream cones, faces of girls). A fourth face contained simply a patch of a solid color, and the last two faces featured, respectively, a patch of sandpaper, and a

[4]The author is pleased to acknowledge the assistance of Judy Burgess, and the staff of the Child Development/Child Services Laboratory of the College of Human Development, The Pennsylvania State University, for their assistance and cooperation in the conduct of this pilot study, as well as of Nancy Galambos, Thomas Miller, Erica Sade, and Francis Schuster, who participated in the conduct of the study.

patch of a fabric. These materials thus provided an opportunity for the child to engage in both visual and tactual exploration by simple examination and manipulation of the blocks. The blocks at the same time invited constructive play, through tower building and construction of other simple structures such as houses. Each child was observed for up to 10 minutes, each 15-second segment of the session being scored with respect to the degree of dominance of exploration or play during that segment via a 5-point rating scale (from "exclusive exploration" to "exclusive play"). Behavior involving manipulation or inspection of any of the blocks was considered exploratory; play required the manipulation of several blocks in some way that transcended a focus on the content of the faces of the blocks (e.g., to produce some structure such as a tower) or a purely horizontal arrangement of the blocks (e.g., to form a square) or some purely motoric action, such as rubbing one block against another.

A total of 21 children between the ages of 3-0 and 5-10 have been observed at play with these materials. (Four others were discarded for failing to engage the materials for at least 3 minutes, which was considered the minimum time necessary to reveal temporal changes in behavior in a meaningful fashion.) The instructions simply encouraged the child to "play with the blocks; do anything you like with them." In sheer quantitative terms a shift from exploration to play could again be documented in terms of the average amount of time spent with each activity as the dominant activity over the course of a child's session with the materials, as shown in Fig. 9.3.

The more impressive finding is the diversity of patterns observed among the different children, in terms of the order in which the major dominant forms of behavior occurred: pure exploration, pure play, and mixed (e.g., a child examining each block as it was added to the stack of blocks already placed during the course of the construction of a tower). Of the 21 children, five showed a clear shift from exploration to play, although for one of these there was an intermediary mixed phase. Just as many children (five) exhibited play exclusively, whereas four others moved from exploration to mixed and two from mixed to play. Three moved in reverse, as it were, from play to mixed (i.e., they continued playing, but started to respond to the individual blocks while engaged in their constructive play), while one each exhibited exploration and mixed behavior exclusively.

Clearly these results are at best tentative and may well be in part a function of the stimulus materials, which, except for the textures, were fairly innocuous and probably uninteresting to some of the older children (though obvious age changes could not be discerned in this small sample). However, we should take note of the frequent occurrence of mixed play, in which attention to individual features of the block faces was combined with the use of the blocks in constructive play (though frequently only in two-dimensional arrangements of the blocks on the surface). This suggests that the kind of sharp differentiation drawn by Hutt and Hughes between investigative behavior (marked by heightened attention and

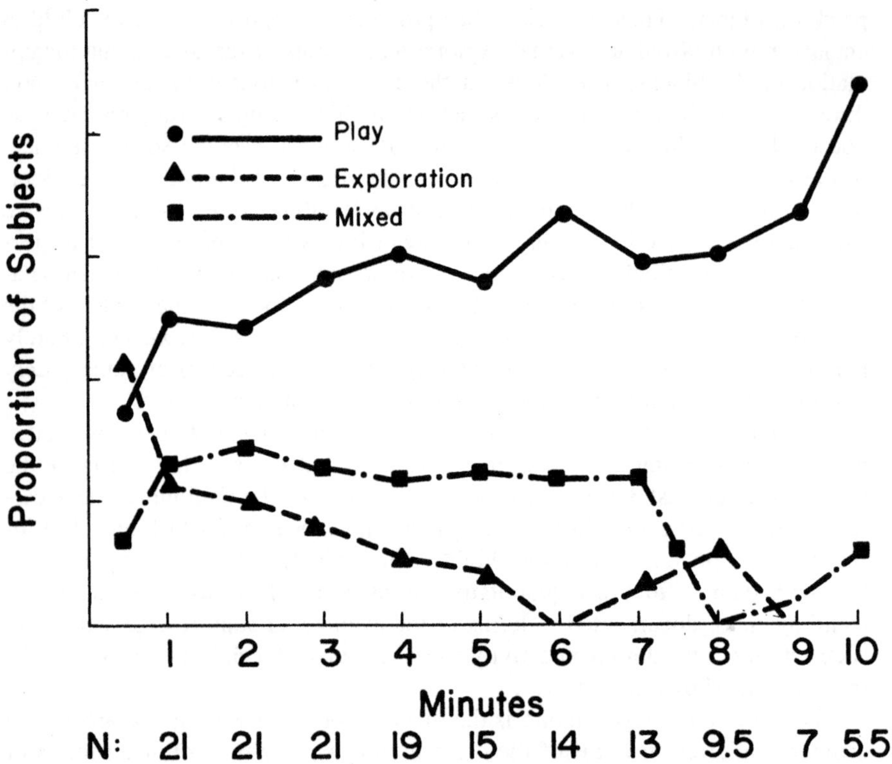


FIG. 9.3 Proportion of subjects engaged in play, exploration, and mixture of both, as a function of time. Values are averaged over four 15-sec periods (except for first two values plotted, which are based on first two and last two 15-sec periods of initial minute).

tenseness) and play (marked by relaxation, smiling, etc.) may not be generalizable to these kinds of materials, and possibly not beyond the box and manipulanda used by Hutt. It might be noted that in our observations exploration of the blocks frequently was accompanied by expressions of surprise, pleasure, smiling, and laughter as a child recognized a particular object or felt the textures (notably the soft ones; the sandpaper evoked rather expressions of mild aversion). Thus, it seems that inspective exploration may itself have an affective component, or at least be followed by such affective reactions—a point to which we shall return presently.

## CONCLUSION

Our brief foray into the exploration–play relationship has provided reasonably conclusive evidence not only of the value to be derived from attempts to differentiate them systematically and operationally, but of the onto- and microgenetic relationship to be expected between these forms of activity. From a developmental standpoint, it is apparent that the kinds of elaboration of reality that qualify as play, such as the transformation of objects for constructive purposes, or for the creation of an imaginary or pretend world, appear after exploration, ontogenetically. That is, they demand the formation of cognitive structures that are not as yet in evidence at the ages at which exploration of the stimulus environment through locomotion, manipulation, and diverse investigatory responses becomes initially manifest (i.e., by the middle of the first year, if not earlier). Also, in a different sense, exploration generally precedes play microgenetically, at least to the extent that play is not apt to be exhibited with a set of materials until some initial familiarization with these materials through exploratory activity has occurred, so that uncertainty concerning their nature and characteristics has been reduced to a minimum. However, if the results of our pilot research are to be trusted, the possibility needs to be seriously considered that such an overall shift from exploration to play may be only an abstraction from quite diverse patterns of individual behavior and that there may be important individual differences in the propensity of children to engage in one activity or the other and even perhaps in the temporal sequence in which they are undertaken.

Quite apart, furthermore, from this issue of the temporal relationships between investigatory response and play, this dichotomy may fail to do justice to the complexities and diversity of children's response to objects. Let us return to the schema of Nunnally and Lemond (1973: 89–109) cited earlier. As was noted, these writers differentiate between two kinds of exploratory activity, one involving (predominantly visual) inspection of an object, and a subsequent phase involving active manipulation of and perhaps experimentation with it (assuming it permits it). Direct evidence for this proposed differentiation between perceptual investigation and manipulation and for their postulated temporal ordering was found in the results of the research by Schneider et al. (1981), cited previously. Rather than invoking a process of transformational thinking to apply to the manipulation phase, as Nunnally and Lemond do, a different concept suggests itself, one that does better justice to the curiosity-based nature of such exploratory activity. This is J. Gibson's concept of *affordances,* which he developed in his last book (Gibson, 1979) in an attempt to provide a more functionally oriented view of perception than that which characterized his earlier writings. It appears to lend itself ideally to behavior of the kind Nunnally and Lemond describe, as well as to the kind of motor exploration of object stimuli that Belsky and Most (1981), among others, found characteristic of exploration during the first year of life.

Affordances, as Gibson formulated this concept, represent properties of stimuli, and of objects in particular, that are isomorphically related to particular behaviors or functional actions. It is a view of perception curiously close to the kind of functionally based definitions of objects that characterize answers to vocabulary tests at an early age: "A cup is to drink; a shovel is to dig." For Gibson, a cup, because of its structural–morphological properties, "affords" drinking, whereas a shovel "affords" digging. The concept is not limited to objects: a floor affords standing, whereas water affords swimming (or floating). For Gibson, writing as a perception psychologist, the essential point was that affordances represent isomorphic relationships between specifiable stimulus characteristics and particular forms of action—much as Lewin, for instance, spoke of objects having certain "demand characteristics." The relational nature of the concept notwithstanding, Gibson insisted—in contrast to Lewin—that these characteristics are independent of the organism's intention or internal state and can in fact be systematically formulated in terms of given stimulus properties that are subject to systematic description and study.

Just such an attempt has been made in a recent paper by E. Gibson (1982: 55–81), who has brought to bear a variety of evidence from perception and behavior in infancy to buttress the relevance of the affordance concept for early behavioral functioning. Neither she nor her late husband, however, concerned themselves much with the motivational side of this concept, i.e., the fact that infants and young children are particularly prone to engage in activity—especially manipulative activity—that serves the purpose of informing them about the functional properties of their object world: the fact that balls afford bouncing, whereas plates do not, that chairs afford sitting, whereas picket fences do not, that pencils afford writing, whereas needles do not. This behavior, then, is a very close cousin, at the least, of the visual, auditory, or even tactual inspection of an object to size it up perceptually and from a motivational standpoint serves presumably a very similar purpose (i.e., to reduce uncertainty about an object, and extract information about it). The information, in the case of affordance-directed activity, is extracted via manipulative actions aimed at uncovering the makeup, consistency, and other properties of the object that are generally not revealed by direct inspection. This activity thus entails a direct interaction with the object, and a possible transformation of it, that clearly is of a different kind than that which takes place in pure visual examination of a two-dimensional stimulus, for instance. This may be what Nunnally and Lemond (1973) meant in designating this kind of manipulative exploration as transformational thinking, though transformation does not appear to occur invariably as a necessary aspect of such activity, and when it does take place it does so at the physical rather than the cognitive or imaginal level.

Nevertheless, precisely because of the potential for this type of activity to result in some transformation of an object, whether in the sense of a change in shape (e.g., the breaking of a plate, the stretching of a rubber band) or a change merely in position (e.g., the throwing of a ball), it may well play a core role in the transition from inspective exploration to play, both microgenetically and above all ontogenetically. That is, what may start as mainpulation of an object directed at discovering its properties may lead to interaction with it entailing ideational elaboration, as in block play or even doll play (which itself may include a fair amount of such motor activity, e.g., in the form of sticking the doll down the toilet bowl). There are clearly possibilities here for an exciting convergence between Piagetian views of early sensorimotor development (e.g., the secondary and tertiary circular reactions), Gibsonian affordance theory directed at the establishment of a veridical sense of the physical environment, and formulations of the ideational and transformational nature of play such as we find in the accounts of Piaget (1946), Singer (1973), and others.

There is still another form of exploration that deserves consideration as an integral part of the exploration–play relationship. Consider, once more, Nunnally and Lemond's formulation, which saw play as following upon exploration and as serving an autistic gratification function. Although it is true that play generally is marked by expressions of positive affect (e.g., smiling) and of relaxation, it would seem to go a bit far to dub it as autistic in the wishful thinking or loss-of-reality-contact sense. Also, as noted earlier, this formulation completely fails to fit the case of some forms of play, such as constructive play, that are strongly goal directed and may be very serious business indeed.

Conversely, we may ask whether there are forms of exploratory activity that may serve a primarily affective role, not in the sense of true autistic behavior, but rather in the sense of being primarily directed at the generation of affect. The child gazing for a long while at a picture (e.g., of its favorite cat [and thus a highly familiar object]) or at a pattern created in a kaleidoscope or listening entranced to a tune repeated ad infinitum on a record player or musical toy—all these indicate the potentially affect-laden character of children's response to stimuli, and particularly to stimuli that have become familiar and whose uncertainty has thus been dispelled. Perhaps the term exploration will sound like a misnomer for this kind of behavior; indeed, the activity entailed may be assumed to differ from that involved in information extraction (e.g., in being less active, mobile, and thus less truly exploratory). At the same time some motor activity may well play an important part in such exploration, as in the case of a child passing its hand over a soft fur, or clapping its hand in rhythm to a tune. It may be rather a difference in kind, in the form the activity takes, than in amount of exploration that occurs. In any event, this form of activity—whatever we may call it—clearly deserves a central place in a comprehensive account of children's exploration, as this writer has argued at greater length elsewhere (Wohlwill, 1981). It may be, furthermore, that affective exploration in this sense represents an alternative to play, following upon the completion of inspective (i.e., information extraction directed) exploration. Perhaps it is primarily the characteristics of an object in providing an opportunity for either of these to occur that determines which of these will become predominant, or in what kind of balance they are maintained relative to each other. Clearly an answer to such a question presupposes in the first instance greater attention to the positive affect that may result from a child's interaction with a stimulus—attention that with rare exceptions (Schachtel, 1959) has been absent from the thinking and even more from the research of child psychologists.

Finally, the findings from our previously cited pilot study, along with a considerable body of literature on individual differences in both curiosity (Maw & Maw, 1978) and play (Lieberman, 1977), point to the need for attention to the *differential* expression of these two kinds of activities in different children. It may be that there are children who engage predominantly in exploration and others in play, possibly reflecting two modes of orientation towards the world, one based on seeking out and obtaining information and knowledge, the other on transforming reality and elaborating on it at the level of imagination and fantasy. If such types do in fact exist, it would be of obvious consequence for conceptualizing the long-term correlates of these forms of behavior: towards epistemic curiosity on the one hand, and towards creativity on the other. Past theorizing has not kept these two facets separate: On the one hand, curiosity has been thought to play an intrinsic part in creative activity (Torrance, 1963), or at least to be closely correlated with it (Houston & Mednick, 1963). Furthermore, Hutt and Bhavnani's (1972) findings of a moderate correlation between response to novelty at the preschool level and subsequent creative behavior might seem to provide support for such a link in a developmental continuity sense, even though the relationship in this particular study held up only for boys (and the number of children involved was quite small). On the other hand, play has not only been frequently tied to cognitive development generally, but more specifically to learning and obtaining information about the environment (Smilansky, 1968). Perhaps Day's (1981) differentiation between exploratory and creative play is pertinent in this regard, especially because he considers the former to be equivalent to Berlyne's specific exploration. Similarly relevant is the work of Voss and Keller (1977; Keller & Voss, 1976, pp. 120–129) questioning the assumed relationship between exploration and creativity. This suggests the desirability for differentiating more rather than less sharply between exploration and play, and to attempt to chart systematically the developmental transformations of each, both for children in general, and as an important aspect of differences in children's mode of orienting to their environment.

## ACKNOWLEDGMENT

The author wishes to acknowledge the helpful comments and criticisms of an earlier draft of this paper made by Jay Belsky.

## REFERENCES

Belsky, J., & Most, R. From exploration to play: A cross-sectional study of infant free-play behavior. *Developmental Psychology*, 1981, *17*, 630–639.

Berlyne, D. E. *Conflict, arousal and curiosity*. New York: McGraw–Hill, 1960.

Berlyne, D. E. Laughter, humor, and play. In G. Lindzey & E. Aronson (Eds.), *The handbook of social psychology*. (Vol. 3, 2nd ed.). Reading, Mass.: Addison–Wesley, 1969.

Collard, R. R. Exploration and play. In B. Sutton-Smith (Ed.), *Play and learning*. New York: Gardner Press, 1979.

Day, H. I. Play: A ludic behavior. In H. I. Day (Ed.), *Advances in intrinsic motivation and aesthetics*. New York: Plenum, 1981.

Fenson, L., Sapper, V., & Minner, D. G. Attention and manipulative play in the one-year-old child. *Child Development*, 1974, *45*, 757–764.

Fenson, L., Kagan, J., Kearsley, R. B., & Zelazo, P. R. The developmental progression of manipulative play in the first two years. *Child Development*, 1976, *47*, 232–236.

Fowler, H. *Curiosity and exploratory behavior*. New York: Macmillan, 1965.

Gardner, H. *Developmental psychology* (2nd ed.). Boston: Little, Brown, 1982.

Gibson, E. J. The concept of affordances in development: The renascence of functionalism. In W. A. Collins (Ed.), *Minnesota symposia on child psychology*, Vol. 15: *The concept of development*. Hillsdale, N.J.: Lawrence Erlbaum Associates, 1982.

Gibson, J. J. *The ecological approach to visual perception*. Boston: Houghton Mifflin, 1979.

Houston, J. P., & Mednick, S. A. Creativity and the need for novelty. *Journal of Abnormal and Social Psychology*, 1963, *66*, 137–141.

Hughes, M. Sequential analysis of exploration and play. *International Journal of Behavioral Development*, 1978, *1*, 83–97.

Hughes, M. M. Exploration and play re-visited: A hierarchical analysis. *International Journal of Behavioral Development*, 1979, *2*, 215–224.

Hughes, M. M. The relationship between symbolic and manipulative play. Paper presented at Conference on Curiosity, Imagination and Play, Technical University of Berlin, Berlin, September, 1981.

Hughes, M., & Hutt, C. Heart-rate correlates of childhood activities: Play, exploration, problem-solving and day-dreaming. *Biological Psychology*, 1979, *8*, 253–263.

Hutt, C. Exploration and play in children. *Symposia of the Zoological Society*, London, 1966, *18*, 61–81.

Hutt, C. Temporal effects on response decrement and stimulus satiation in exploration. *British Journal of Psychology*, 1967, *58*, 365–373.

Hutt, C. Specific and diverse exploration. In H. W. Reese & L. P. Lippsitt (Eds.), *Advances in child development and behavior* (Vol. 5). New York: Academic Press, 1970.

Hutt, C., & Bhavnani, R. Predictions from play. *Nature*, 1972, *237*, 171–172.

Hutt, C. Toward a taxonomy and conceptual model of play. In H. I. Day (Ed.), *Advances in intrinsic motivation and aesthetics*. New York: Plenum, 1981.

Keller, H., & Voss, H. G. *Neugier und exploration: Theorien und ergebnisse*. Stuttgart: Kohlhammer, 1976.

Lieberman, J. N. *Playfulness: Its relationship to imagination and creativity*. New York: Academic Press, 1977.

Lowe, M. Trends in the development of representational play in infants from one to three years: An observational study. *Journal of Child Psychology and Psychiatry*, 1975, *16*, 33–47.

Maw, W. H., & Maw, E. W. Nature and assessment of human curiosity. In P. McReynolds (Ed.), *Advances in psychological assessment* (Vol. 4). San Francisco: Jossey–Bass, 1978.

McCall, R. B. Exploratory mainpulation and play in the human infant. *Monographs of the Society for Research in Child Development*, 1974, *39*, (2, Whole No. 155).

Millar, S. *The psychology of play*. London: Penguin, 1968.

Nunnally, J. C., & Lemond, L. C. Exploratory behavior and human development. In H. Reese (Ed.), *Advances in child development and behavior* (Vol. 8). New York: Academic Press, 1973.

Piaget, J. *La formation du symbole chez l'enfant*. Neuchatel: Dalachaux & Niestle, 1946. (English version: *Play, dreams and imitation in childhood*. New York: Norton, 1962.)

Porges, S. W., Arnold, W. R., & Forbes, E. J. Heart-rate variability: An index of attentional responsivity in human newborns. *Developmental Psychology,* 1973, *8,* 85–92.

Porges, S. W., & Raskin, D. C. Respiratory and heart rate components of attention. *Journal of Experimental Psychology,* 1969, *81,* 497–503.

Schachtel, E. G. *Metamorphosis: On the development of affect, perception, attention, and memory.* New York: Basic Books, 1959.

Schneider, K., Moch, M., Sandfort, R., Auerswald, M., & Walther-Weckmann, H. Exploring a novel object by preschool children: A sequential analysis. Unpublished manuscript, 1981.

Singer, J. L. (Ed.). *The child's world of make-believe: Experimental studies of imaginative play.* New York: Academic Press, 1973.

Smilansky, S. *The effects of sociodramatic play on disadvantaged preschool children.* New York: Wiley, 1968.

Switzky, H. N., Haywood, C. H., & Isett, R. Exploration, curiosity, and play in young children: Effects of stimulus complexity. *Developmental Psychology,* 1974, *10,* 321–329.

Switzky, H. N., Ludwig, L., & Haywood, H. C. Exploration and play in retarded and nonretarded preschool children: Effects of object complexity and age. *American Journal of Mental Deficiency,* 1979, *83,* 637–644.

Torrance, E. P. *Education and the creative potential.* Minneapolis: University of Minnesota Press, 1963.

Vliestra, A. G. Exploration and play in preschool children and young adults. *Child Development,* 1978, *49,* 235–238.

Voss, H. G., & Keller, H. Critical evaluation of the obscure figures test as an instrument for measuring cognitive innovation. *Perceptual and Motor Skills,* 1977, *45,* 495–502.

Weisler, A., & McCall, R. B. Exploration and play: Resume and redirection. *American Psychologist,* 1976, *31,* 492–508.

Welker, W. I. Effects of age and experience on play and exploration of young chimpanzees. *Journal of Comparative and Physiological Psychology,* 1956, *49,* 223–226.

Welker, W. I. An analysis of exploratory and play behavior in animals. In D. W. Fiske & S. Maddi (Eds.), *Functions of varied experience.* Homewood, Ill.: Dorsey, 1961.

Wohlwill, J. F. A conceptual analysis of exploratory behavior: The specific-diversive distinction revisited. In H. I. Day (Ed.), *Advances in intrinsic motivation and aesthetics.* New York: Plenum, 1981.

Zelazo, P. R., & Kearsley, R. B. The emergence of functional play in infants: Evidence for a major cognitive transition. *Journal of Applied Developmental Psychology,* 1980, *1,* 95–117.

# 10 The Social Context of Exploratory Play

Bruce B. Henderson
*Western Carolina University*

In the more than 2 decades since the publication of Berlyne's (1960) seminal *Conflict, Arousal, and Curiosity,* developmental psychologists have shown an increasing interest in the constructs of curiosity and exploratory play. This interest is most obvious in the number and variety of reviews of various aspects of the research literature available, including treatments of the effects of stimulus variables on perceptual exploration (Cantor, 1963; Nunnally & Lemond, 1973), the relationship between exploration and play (Hutt, 1970; Wohlwill, 1981), and the educational implications of curiosity and exploration (Vidler, 1977). Exploration seems to have engaged developmental psychologists, in part, because of the theoretical import of its epistemic functions and, in part, because it is a common behavior in many contexts. Lorenz (1971) has argued that the most important feature of man, "the specialist in nonspecialization," is "his persistent, inquisitive and exploratory interaction with the world of concrete objects [pp. 173–174]."

The major emphasis in the reviews just listed has been the examination of the stimulus variables of inanimate objects, particularly novelty, that elicit or maintain curiosity and exploration. What has not been emphasized, however, is that the child's exploration of novel objects, novel people, and novel environments frequently occurs in the presence of parents, peers, teachers, or strangers. The social situation may have a telling effect on what is explored and how it is explored. There are sources of encouragement, cooperation, and competition in contexts of scarce novel resources. A father may reinforce or discourage his child's manipulation of items on the grocery shelf. A mother's intervention in a young child's exploration of a new toy may facilitate or inhibit further interaction with the toy and/or the mother. In the preschool, a peer's modeling of exploration of a novel object may change the probability of a child's later exploration of that same object. Throughout development, social factors may have important effects on the frequency, duration, and forms of children's exploration.

The purpose of this chapter is to provide a review of the empirical literature on the social context of exploration. Coverage includes studies of children under the age of 8 or so, though studies of older children are mentioned when they are directly related to a particular theoretical issue. The first section outlines some assumptions about the nature of exploration that will provide a foundation for the discussions of: (1) the factors in the social environment that influence exploration; and (2) social exploration. The final section is an attempt to draw some of the implications of the research reviewed.

## BASIC ASSUMPTIONS: VARIETIES OF EXPLORATION

Before examining the social influences on exploration and the social functions, something must be said about what exploration is. In this section, exploration is described in terms of its objects, its structure, and its function. Patterns of individual differences in exploration are also described.

### The Object of Exploration

The stimulus attributes that consistently elicit exploratory behavior include surprise, incongruity, complexity, responsitivity, and unfamiliarity (Berlyne, 1960; Charlesworth, 1964; Nunnally & Lemond, 1973). A common thread in these attributes is novelty. Exploration is elicited by objects, people, places, and events that represent stimulus change, those that are somehow different relative to the child's past experience. Presumably, unusual or unfamiliar stimuli produce a motivational state of curiosity or subjective uncertainty (Berlyne, 1960). The behavior that follows from this state of curiosity is called *exploration.*

Two distinctions about types of novelty seem particularly useful for avoiding confusion about the effects of social influences. First, Hutt (1970) has suggested three types of novelty: object novelty, environment novelty, and conspecific novelty. Object novelty occurs in both two-dimensional and three-dimensional forms. Studies of perceptual investigation usually use the former, whereas studies of manipulative exploration and questioning generally use the latter. Environment novelty has received little attention except for some studies with infants (Rheingold & Eckerman, 1970; Ross, Rheingold, & Eckerman, 1972). Conspecific novelty as an elicitor of both exploration and fear has been studied as "stranger anxiety" or "wariness" in infants (Bronson, 1972; Rheingold & Eckerman, 1973; Sroufe, 1977). Although Hutt's distinctions seem to be clear conceptually, studies of exploration frequently confound the effects of these different types of novelty.

A second useful distinction about types of novelty is Berlyne's (1960) differentiation between absolute novelty and relative novelty. According to Berlyne, an absolutely novel stimulus is one the child has never encountered before. A relative novel stimulus represents an unfamiliar combination of familiar elements. These categories might best be thought of in terms of a continuum. The first concerns degree of novelty, familiar to unfamiliar. The second concerns degree of incongruity, congruous to incongruous. As will be seen, most studies of social influence on exploration involve exploration of objects on the unfamiliar end of the novelty dimension, though the actual degree of novelty is seldom specified.

## The Structure of Exploration

A number of theorists have represented exploratory behavior as a sequence of relatively discrete behaviors or behavioral categories (Hall & Smith, 1903; Livson, 1967; Nunnally & Lemond, 1973). A modification of the sequence suggested by Nunnally and Lemond (1973) is presented in Fig. 10.1. Orienting and perceptual investigation and manipulation appear to be what Hutt (1970) has called "specific exploration" and play and search appear to be what she called "diversive exploration." Specific exploration, according to Hutt, is a consummatory response directed at novel stimulation. Diversive exploration, on the other hand, is an instrumental response that occurs in the absence of novelty and that is directed at creating stimulus change. The child may play with the previously novel stimulus or search for additional stimulation. Hutt indicated that

| | | | | | |
|---|---|---|---|---|---|
| *Observed behavior:* | Encounter novel Stimulus X | Orienting | Perceptual Investigation and Manipulation (if possible) | Play or Search | Encounter Stimulus Y |
| *Covert Events:* | | Heightened attention/ arousal | Focused attention & encoding of information | Variable: From fantasy to boredom | |
| *Novelty:* | Stimulus novelty present to a high degree | | Decreasing stimulus novelty | Stimulus novelty absent, response novelty increases | |
| *Time period* | Generally very brief | | Variable, depending on degree of stimulus novelty, social influences, availability of other sources of novel or familiar stimulation. | | |

FIG. 10.1 The sequential nature of exploration (adapted from Nunnally & Lemond, 1973).

specific exploration is distinguished by response stereotyping and a superordinate position in the motivational hierarchy. Diversive exploration, on the other hand, is characterized by response variability and a low position in the motivational hierarchy. Wohlwill reviews the conceptual and empirical status of this distinction in Chapter 9, this volume. The available research on the sequencing of the various components described previously indicates that the structure of exploratory behavior is not rigid, even under relatively controlled laboratory conditions (Hughes, 1978; Schneider, 1981). However, because research on exploratory behavior has tended to involve one aspect of the sequence to the exclusion of the others, it seems worthwhile to take a brief look at each.

*Orienting and Perceptual Investigation.* This is probably the single largest category of studies on exploration. Research in this area focuses on the effects of stimulus variables such as novelty, complexity, and incongruity on visual attention. Common measures include direction of gross head movements, duration of visual fixation, frequency of viewing, latency to first contact of an object, and stated choice or preference.

*Manipulation.* Conceptually, this category of exploration could be considered a subcategory or sequel to perceptual investigation (Weisler & McCall, 1976). However, most studies of perceptual exploration methodologically preclude the opportunity for children to interact tactually with the stimulus object and studies of manipulative exploration do not always include standard measures of visual exploration separate from manipulation. The measures used in this category include frequency of manipulations, number of different manipulanda made to function, and time spent with the stimulus objects. One other possible measure that does not have any clear place in Nunnally and Lemond's (1973) sequence is question asking. However, it is often measured during manipulation of novel objects.

*Play.* The exploration sequence shifts from manipulation to play and from specific to diversive exploration as the objective of the child shifts from determining what the stimulus is and what it will do to the variety of responses that can be performed using the object. This shift is assumed to occur as a result of declining novelty of the stimulus as it is explored (Hughes, 1978).

*Search.* Once a child has thoroughly explored an object's characteristics and what can be done with it, boredom presumably sets in and he or she begins to search the environment for additional stimulation. This component of exploration has often been studied as a dimension of individual differences in older children with the use of self-report questionnaires or ratings (Maw & Maw, 1977). The most common behavioral measure of search in young children is locomotion. One other behavioral measure that has been used (Harter & Zigler,

1974; Smock & Holt, 1962) provides the child with the choice of playing with or looking at an unknown or known toy or picture.

## The Function of Exploration

Curiosity behavior is generally assumed to be adaptive (Hutt, 1970; Lorenz, 1971; Weisler & McCall, 1976). Phylogenetically, selective pressures such as need for new food sources and new habitats in general have apparently acted on man and his ancestors so as to favor individuals with the greatest predispositions to explore novel aspects of the environment (Hughes, 1978; Hutt, 1970). Ontogenetically, it makes good sense that more curious children would be more likely to explore new stimuli actively, thus learning more and more quickly. To date, however, there is little direct empirical evidence that exploratory behaviors function this way, though there is some support for the adaptive function of play in several recent studies (Herman, 1980; Smith & Dutton, 1979; Sylva, Bruner, & Genova, 1976; Vandenberg, 1981).

## Individual Differences in Exploratory Behavior

If exploratory responses to novel stimuli are, in fact, highly adaptive, then a narrow range of individual differences in exploratory tendencies might be expected. On the other hand, all human behaviors show some variability. It also seems likely that there are differences in preferred styles of exploring. Some children may be "watchers;" others, "touchers;" and still others, "questioners." Thus, children may differ both in the level of exploration they typically exhibit in response to novelty and in the particular mode or modes in which they express it.

A small body of data supportive of some of these speculations exists. Kreitler, Zigler, and Kreitler (1975) obtained data on six measures from first-graders: observation of simple and complex stimuli, stated preference for simple or complex stimuli, preference for unknown stimuli, a structure of meaning assessment (i.e., eliciting different descriptions of four ordinary objects), object manipulation, and teacher ratings of curiosity. Their factor analysis yielded five factors: manipulatory curiosity, perceptual curiosity, structure of meaning, preference for complexity, and common uses. In a similar factor-analytic study, Henderson and Moore (1979) administered four tasks to preschool boys and girls and first- and second-grade girls: stated preference for complexity, preference for unknown, investigation of novelty toys contained in a drawer box, and exploration of an unusual box. Factor analyses of these data yielded two modes of exploration factors, manipulation and question asking, and two styles of exploration factors, breadth and depth, for both preschool and school-age children. Preference for complexity scores, preference for unknown scores, and teacher ratings did not load on any of the mode or style factors.

Further evidence for the multidimensional nature of individual differences in exploration is provided in several correlational studies of infants, toddlers, and preschoolers. Keller (1981), in a longitudinal study of the exploration of infants in the first postnatal year, found no correlations between visual, auditory, and manipulatory measures of exploration. Moore and Pancake (1982) administered a battery of tasks similar to those of Henderson and Moore (1979) to 2-year-olds. The correlations between their various measures revealed patterns of interrelationships indicative of both mode and style components of individual difference like those reported for preschoolers (Henderson & Moore, 1979). Finally, Schneider (1981) found only low correlations between perceptual exploration and manipulations and questions and between manipulations and questions in preschoolers' responses to Hutt's (1970) manipulandum (a box with a movable lever).

The existence of several dimensions of individual differences in exploration of novel objects, then, seems well established from infancy through the early school years. It is less clear, however, how stable these differences are within children, across time and situations. Of particular interest for the purpose of the present chapter is the relationship between dimensions of individual differences in exploration and social context. Studies relevant to this issue are considered below.

## Summary: Three Traditions in the Assessment of Exploration

The measurement of children's exploratory behavior has generally followed one of three approaches. One is the laboratory study of perceptual exploration, usually visual exploration of two-dimensional stimuli. A second tradition is the study of what might be called "exploratory play." The focus in this tradition has been on the child's manipulation of and questions about novel toys in more or less naturalistic conditions in homes, schools, or laboratories. Finally, there are studies that assume an underlying exploratory predisposition or curiosity trait in the child as indicated by teacher or peer ratings or responses to questionnaires.

Most of the research on social influences on exploration involves the exploratory play approach. There are methodological and conceptual reasons for this emphasis. For example, perceptual exploration may be difficult to measure reliably in a situation where more than one person is present and where the child is free to move about. Locomotion is frequently used as an indicator of exploration. However, in the absence of other measures it is difficult to distinguish exploratory locomotion from other forms of general activity. In addition, it seems children's questions and manipulations are more likely to be influenced by other people than perceptual investigation. The types of novel objects used in studies of exploratory play also have the advantage of being interesting to children. Young children are probably not generally very curious about random polygons or two-dimensional figures even if these are unfamiliar, complex, or incongruous. A much greater emphasis on perceptual exploration (looking) is apparent, however, in the study of social exploration. There the objects of exploration are persons rather than artificial stimuli.

There are two serious problems in using the predisposition/trait approach with young children. The more obvious one is the difficulty in developing a questionnaire for children under 10 years of age. The second problem is the inadequate reliability and validity of teacher ratings. Teacher ratings tend to be correlated with intelligence (Coie, 1974; Maw & Maw, 1975) and uncorrelated with behavioral measures of exploration (Henderson & Moore, 1979; Kreitler et al., 1975) and another teacher's rating of the same child (Henderson & Moore, 1979). A different approach to the assessment of individual differences in the tendency to explore is the use of a battery of behavioral measures, combining the predisposition/trait approach with the exploratory play approach. The few studies of social influence that have used this type of assessment are reviewed following.

The definition of exploration used here, then, is what Hutt has called "specific exploration." It includes the child's locomotor, inspective, manipulative, and questioning responses to object, environment, and conspecific novelty. The function of exploratory play is assumed to be the acquisition of information.

## SOCIAL INFLUENCES ON EXPLORATION

There are no naturalistic, descriptive studies available to indicate the frequency or duration of exploration of novel objects or environments under social versus individual conditions (Henderson, Charlesworth, & Gamradt, 1982). Certainly much of the exploration of infants and toddlers must occur in the presence of at least parents or caretakers. Likewise, much of the exploration of preschoolers and school-age children must occur in the presence of teachers and peers. In this section studies documenting influences of parents, other adults, and peers on exploration are examined.

### Parents

*Stimulation and Interaction.* Parents can influence the frequency, duration, and quality of their child's exploration in positive and negative ways. These influences can be indirect or direct. Parents influence exploration indirectly through the provision or lack of provision of novel objects and opportunities to explore. They influence exploration more directly during interactions involving novel objects. Of course, for the newborn, everything is novel. This fact may account for Rheingold's (1969) finding of no differences in the exploration of institutionalized and noninstitutionalized infants at 3 months of age. In contrast, Collard (1971) did find differences in the exploratory behavior of infants from institutions and lower-class and upper-middle-class homes. Home-reared infants exhibited a wider variety of exploratory responses to a novel object than did the infants from the institutionalized setting. Informal observations of the institutionalized infants and interviews with the mothers of the home-reared children led Collard to suggest that the presence of restrictions on movement and the absence of interesting materials in the institution were responsible for the more stereotyped exploratory behavior of the infants there.

An obvious weakness in the Collard study is the presence of sample differences and the confounds they represent. According to Rubenstein (1967), Collard's results might have been due to the emotional trauma experienced by the institutionalized infants through separation from their mothers. Rubenstein tried to avoid this problem by relating maternal stimulation and exploration in normal infants. Mothers were prescreened as being high, medium, or low in attentiveness (looking at, touching, holding, talking) toward their infants. Variety of stimulation provided by the mother when the infant was 5 months of age, as measured by play opportunities provided and toys within reach of the infant, and the exploration of a novel object and preference for playing with novel objects when the infant was 6 months of age were assessed. Mothers in the high-attentive group did not provide more toys for their infants than mothers in the other groups. They did, however, provide a greater variety of toys and more play opportunities than did low-attentive mothers. Infants of high-attentive mothers explored a novel object and preferred novel objects to a greater extent than did infants from the low-attentiveness group.

Additional evidence for the importance of the variety of stimulation provided in the home to the development of infant exploratory behavior is provided in a study by Yarrow, Rubenstein, and Pederson (1975). They correlated four measures of 5- and 6-month-old infants' exploration based on responses to novel toys with frequency of various modes of maternal social stimulation. One measure of exploration, manipulation of novel toys, was correlated with frequencies of the mothers' contingent response to positive verbalization or to distress. Otherwise, no correlation was obtained between infant exploration and tactile, kinesthetic, visual, or auditory modes of maternal stimulation. Variety of available social stimulation was, however, moderately correlated with manipulation of a toy. Ratings of the responsiveness, complexity, and variety of the available inanimate stimulation in the home was related more substantially to infant exploration. These results might suggest the relative importance of the inanimate over the social environment in the development of infant exploratory behavior. However, Jennings, Harmon, Morgan, Gaiter, and Yarrow (1979) failed to replicate the relationship between measures of inanimate stimulation and exploratory play at 6 or 12 months of age.

So far, each of the studies described has been correlational in nature. The importance of the provision of a variety of inanimate stimulation, and to possibly a lesser extent, social stimulation, for infant exploration is suggested in several of the studies. However, no strong conclusions about cause and effect relationships can be made from these investigations. Recently, Belsky, Goode, and Most (1980) provided stronger evidence for a causal role for maternal stimulation in the development of exploration. They hypothesized a close relationship between maternal verbal and physical efforts to focus the infant on objects and events and the infant's ability to control his or her own attention in exploration. In a correlational/observational study of infants 9 to 18 months of age in homes, Belsky et al. found moderate correlations between mothers' physical strategies of focusing the child's attention (e.g., pointing, demonstrating, manual prompts) and the level of exploration displayed by the infant. The total stimulation provided by the mother was also correlated with level of exploratory response, but verbal strategies for focusing infant attention were not. An unobtrusive, short-term, experimental intervention was then instituted with 12-month-olds. During a series of three observation sessions, one of the observers verbally pointed out each mother's attention-focusing activities to her at frequent intervals. No attempt was made to make mothers in the control group conscious of their stimulating activity. Experimental mothers showed significantly more attention-focusing activity than control mothers. In a semistructured play session with novel toys 2 months later, experimental infants exhibited higher levels of exploratory competence, less unfocused exploration, fewer simple manipulations, and more functional play.

Although the Belsky et al. (1980) intervention was conducted with a small number of infants (8 in each group) and at only one age, it is important for several reasons. First, it shows a causal relationship between maternal stimulation and infant exploratory behavior. Second, it shows a theoretically important relationship between a particular type of maternal stimulation, attention focusing, and exploration. Finally, it shows that intervention of a relatively unobtrusive and low-key kind can influence the course of infant exploration.

It seems likely that other kinds of parental behavior may also positively influence exploration (see the section ''Attachment'' following). It is also possible, however, that there are parental behaviors that have negative effects on infant exploration. Gray, Tracy, and Lindberg (1979) examined the effects of one possible negative influence: maternal interference with the child's play with novel objects. Mothers in an interference condition repeatedly interrupted the play of 1-year-old infants during the first 10 minutes of a 20-minute session. Despite this interference, there were no significant differences between infants in the interference condition and those in a control condition on touching of novel objects or vocalizations to play materials during the second 10 minutes of play. Although these results suggest a common parental behavior like interference in play does not have clear negative effects, it may be that a high level of exploratory behavior attenuated condition differences. The lack of a decrement in exploration over time (i.e., first 5 minutes versus second 5 minutes) indicates the objects remained novel over this short period of time. Also, as Gray et al. noted, interference occurring over a much more extended period in natural situations may have stronger negative effects. This would certainly be the case if exploration at one age is involved in the development of exploration at later ages, because repeated interference obviously precludes the opportunity to explore.

Infancy may be the developmental period when parental influences are greatest because of the nature of sensorimotor interactions with the environment and the sheer amount of time the child spends with parents. Parents, however, continue to be involved in their children's exploratory behavior throughout the preschool and early school years. Parents are often present when children encounter objects in backyards, parks, museums, shopping trips, etc. For example, Henderson et al. (1982) observed the exploratory behavior of preschool (3- to 5-years-old) and school-age children (6- to 8-years-old) in the "Touch and See" room of a museum of natural history. Half the children in each age group were accompanied by 6 to 12 classmates and an adult, and half were accompanied by one or two parents. The exploratory behavior of the children in the two accompaniment groups differed in many ways. Children with their parents stayed longer in the room, moved from area to area and object to object more slowly, paid more attention to and manipulated objects more, and verbalized about objects more frequently. Henderson et al. suggested that this more focused exploration resulted from the ability of parents to structure the child's behavior actively by pointing out novel objects and their features and by responding to the child's questions and comments.

The museum study highlights the potential role of parents in influencing children's exploration. The design of the study did not, however, allow Henderson et al. (1982) to determine the precise parent behaviors which facilitated investigation of novel objects. Three laboratory studies of parent–child interaction provide a clearer picture of those parent behaviors that affect exploration. Saxe and Stollak (1971) observed first-grade boys' play with novel and familiar objects in the presence of their mothers. They found no positive correlation between maternal punitiveness or parental nonattention and the child's exploration. Children's exploration of novel objects was, however, highly correlated with maternal exploration of novel objects. Endsley, Hutcherson, Garner, and Martin (1979) conducted a partial replication and extension of the Saxe and Stollack study with 5-year-old boys and girls. Maternal general positive interaction and contingent negative interaction were not substantially related to children's visual and manipulative exploration and question asking. On the other hand, the mother's own exploratory behavior, contingent positive interaction, question answering, and behaviors that oriented the child to novel objects were all highly correlated with each other and with the children's exploration. Johns and Endsley (1977) also showed the positive effects of maternal modeling on preschoolers in an experimental study in which children were shown to imitate directly their mothers' tactual exploration.

The studies reviewed in this section all have weaknesses. As is usually the case, the correlational, naturalistic studies reveal a number of parental behaviors that have the potential to affect the child's explorations but do not establish the existence of cause–effect relations. The one available experimental study with infants (Belsky et al., 1980) indicates the sufficiency of maternal focusing behaviors in increasing child exploration but cannot show that they are necessary in the development of exploration. The studies used time sampling or one/zero sampling during data collection and therefore do not provide information on sequences in mother–child interaction. Possibly the most glaring deficiency is the paucity of data on father–child interaction. Despite these problems, three aspects of parent–child interaction emerge as being particularly facilitative of exploration. First, the variety of novel stimulation provided in the infant's environment is related to the child's tendency to explore. It is hardly surprising that children who have had more opportunity to practice exploration are better at it. Second, the mother's attempts to focus or to orient the infant or child to novel features in the environment increases the child's exploratory involvement. Mothers appear to be sensitive to novelty and its attraction for young children (Corter & Jamieson, 1977). Finally, the expression of curiosity by the mother results in exploration in the child. This modeling effect may be mediated by disinhibition or through the tendency of modeling to orient the child to novel features.

These generalizations about parental influences on exploration are based on studies designed to assess active behavior directly on the part of the parent. In the next section, studies that were conducted to document a different aspect of parent–child interaction, attachment, are examined because of their implications for exploration.

*Attachment.* That infants, about as soon as they are able to move around, leave their mothers in order to explore novel objects, environments, and people is a well-documented finding (Rheingold & Eckerman, 1970; Ross, 1974). The distance infants will spontaneously move from mother in natural situations increases with age (Anderson, 1972; Rheingold & Eckerman, 1970). In these cases, infants are the ones who initiate the movement away from the mother who is still present. If, however, the mother (or father) is absent from or leaves a novel environment, the child's exploration occurs at depressed levels (Ainsworth, Blehar, Waters, & Wall, 1978; Willemsen, Flaherty, Heaton, & Ritchey, 1974). This negative influence on the child's exploration becomes attenuated with age but is apparent to a lesser degree in at least some children until age 2 or 3 (Marvin, 1977).

One explanation for these findings comes from the ethological/organizational theory of attachment (Ainsworth et al., 1978; Bowlby, 1969; Sroufe & Waters, 1977). According to this perspective, attachment and exploration are separate, but related behavioral systems. When the infant's mother is present and available, the attachment system is activated at a relatively low level. The infant is then free to initiate exploration using the attachment figure as a "secure base" for his or her exploratory sorties. Exploration continues until the child feels threatened (e.g., by the appearance of an unfamiliar adult) or until the attachment figure leaves. If either of these events occurs, the "balance" between the attachment and exploration systems shifts. Attachment behaviors aimed at maintaining close contact with the attachment figure (e.g., physical contact, proximity seeking) then preclude the possibility of exploration.

The evidence for this explanation consists mainly of data collected in the Ainsworth "strange situation" (Ainsworth et al., 1978). The "strange situation" is a standardized series of eight episodes involving the presence or absence of the mother and a stranger with the child in various combinations in a novel environment. Exploration is operationalized in terms of locomotion toward toys and around the room, manipulation of toys, and visual exploration of the toys and environment. A general finding in studies employing the strange situation (Ainsworth et al., 1978) is that exploratory locomotion and manipulation of novel objects declines when the stranger enters. Visual exploration continues, but more time is spent looking at the stranger than at the toys. All three types of exploration tend to decline when the baby is left alone or with the stranger.

Overall, these results appear to support the notion of a secure base and a balance between attachment and exploration. However, an alternative explanation for depressed levels of exploratory behavior in the absence of a caretaker that does not involve an emotional attachment has been suggested. Hutt (1970) argued that children are most likely to explore when an environment is neither too familiar nor too novel. Highly novel situations are likely to produce anxiety that interferes with exploration. When the mother is present, however, the overall level of novelty in the situation is reduced into the child's range of "optimal" stimulation. Gershaw and Schwarz (1971) tested this hypothesis with two groups of boys 50- to 29-months-old and 31- to 42-months-old. Children left a room where they had been playing with a set of novel toys in the presence of their mothers with an experimenter. When the children returned, their mother was still there, one of their favorite toys from home was on the chair where their mother had been, or a novel toy was on the chair. Gershaw and Schwarz hypothesized that the presence of the familiar toy would, like the presence of the mother, reduce the level of novelty in the situation, thus resulting in more exploratory behavior than in the novel toy condition. Actually, the younger children spent more time touching the set of novel toys and exhibited fewer attachment behaviors (crying and staying close to the door) in the novel toy condition than in the familiar toy condition. The absence of the mother had little effect on the exploration of the older children in either the familiar toy or novel toy condition.

The Gershaw and Schwarz (1971) findings can be interpreted as supporting the concept of an attachment–exploration balance. Ainsworth et al. (1978) have argued that in the presence of a very high degree of novelty the exploratory system could be activated at a level where separation from the attachment figure would be tolerated for some time. It is still possible, however, that it is unnecessary to postulate an emotionally based attachment system to explain higher levels of exploration in the presence of the mothers. Mothers may simply act as discriminative stimuli signaling the appropriateness of exploratory responses. If so, there may be stimuli other than the mother herself to which these responses have generalized. Passman and his colleagues have conducted several studies designed to determine the stimulus factors that facilitate exploration. In one study (Passman & Weisberg, 1975), blanket-attached 3-year-olds explored novel objects more in the presence of their blankets than in their absence. In a second study, Passman and Erck (1978) compard 3- and 4-year-olds' exploration in the presence of their mothers, a film of their mothers, a film of a stranger, or a formless control film. Locomotion and frequency of play was greatest in the mother-present condition. Duration of play was greatest in the mother-present and filmed-mother conditions. The locomotion and frequency measures did not discriminate the filmed-mother and filmed-stranger conditions. However, post hoc analyses based on the fact that almost half the children in the filmed-stranger condition thought the stranger was their mother led Passman and Erck to conclude that a two-dimensional representation of the mother was sufficient to facilitate exploration. A similar study (Adams & Passman, 1979) was conducted to determine if only visual or auditory representation of the mother would facilitate exploration. Children between the ages of 2 years-8 months and 4 years explored in the presence of their mothers or strangers or in the presence of visual or auditory representations of mothers or strangers. Children explored less in the presence of strangers, but the mode of presentation of the mother had no differential effect on exploration.

The Passman studies suggest that actual maternal presence, and therefore mother–child interaction, may not be critical to exploration. However, these studies were conducted with preschool children. It is not clear that the attachment construct means the same thing before and after 2 years of age (Ainsworth et al., 1978; Marvin, 1977). A recent study by Sorce and Emde (1981) raises a question about whether even the mere presence of a real mother is sufficient to facilitate the exploration of toddlers. Fifteen-month-olds played in a situation with a stranger present and with their mothers either available for intervention or present but "unavailable" because they were unresponsive while reading a newspaper. Visual exploration of the stranger, locomotor exploration, and exploration of a novel toy (a remotely controlled robot) were each inhibited in the "unavailable" condition. Corter (1976) also reported that infants explored objects more when their mothers were visible (in an adjoining room), although whether the infant had initiated the separation or not had little influence on exploration.

According to attachment theory, important components of the attachment relationship include the attachment figure's sensitivity to the infant's signals, accurate interpretation of those signals, and a willingness to provide an appropriate response quickly. The results of the Sorce and Emde (1981) study and the other attachment studies reviewed above clearly indicate that the ability of the attachment figure to be responsive to the infant affects the nature of the infant's exploration in particular situations. Recently, evidence has been provided that suggests a broader, long-term role of the attachment relationship in the development of the tendency to explore. In attachment theory, caretaker–infant relationships are presumed to vary in quality. Securely attached infants are those who are able to use the attachment figure more effectively as a ''secure base'' for exploration. Arend, Gove, and Sroufe (1979) have argued that security of attachment can be used as an index of competent adaptation to the environment. They have also hypothesized continuity between success in adaptation at infancy and success in adaptation at 4 or 5 years of age in the form of exploratory behavior. To test this, they assessed 4- and 5-year-olds who had been classified as securely or insecurely attached at 18 months of age on a battery of tasks, including a measure of exploration. Children who had been securely attached at 18 months showed higher levels of manipulatory exploration of a novel object as preschoolers. Thus, the early caretaker–child relationship is implicated in the quality of both infant and preschool exploration.

## Nonparental Adult Influences

As children get older, there are increasingly frequent opportunities for them to be influenced by adults other than their parents. Studies involving the influence of experimenters, teachers, and educational programs in general are reviewed in this section. These studies do not represent an interrelated set of concepts that have received research attention. Instead, they represent relatively narrow investigations of particular influences on exploration or broader studies of program effects where a measure or measures of exploration or curiosity were included in an assessment battery.

*Question Answering.* An obvious social influence on exploration is the availability of someone who is able and willing to answer questions. Although some questions may be asked as a means of eliciting and maintaining social interaction (Endsley & Clarey, 1975; Isaacs, 1930; Lewis, 1939) or of ignoring an adult's command (Blank & Allen, 1976), many questions appear to be asked as a means of satisfying curiosity in novel situations. Both theory (Berlyne, 1960) and common sense would attribute a reinforcing function to answers. Surprisingly, Berlyne and Frommer (1966) did not find a positive effect of answers on frequency of questions about novel pictures and stories in groups of children in kindergarten, first grade, or fifth grade. Third-graders did ask more questions when answers were provided. Ross & Balzer (1975) suggested that Berlyne and Frommer's failure to find a positive effect from answers may have been due to an insensitive test (insufficiently novel stimuli) or due to a delay until the end of the session in answering questions. Ross and Balzer, using novel pictures and immediate answers for the children who received answers, found a positive effect of answers at grades 1, 3, and 5. Endsley and Clarey (1975) obtained a similar result with preschool children in a within subjects design. It seems likely that in natural situations children would soon stop asking questions out loud if they did not receive answers. Henderson and Moore (1980) found a very low level of questions by both high- and low-curiosity preschoolers in a series of six sessions with novel toys when the experimenter was unresponsive to the child's questions. In a generalization session, however, the frequency of questions by high-curiosity children immediately returned to a high level when responses were given to questions.

*Modeling and Teaching Styles.* A number of investigations have provided evidence for a modeling effect on exploratory behavior. The Saxe and Stollak (1971), Endsley et al. (1979), and Johns and Endsley (1977) studies described previously all showed a relationship between maternal modeling and child exploration. The influence of other adults as models for question asking has been demonstrated in several experiments by Zimmerman and his colleagues. Henderson, Swanson, and Zimmerman (1975) reported a higher number of questions among preschool children following exposure to a televised model who asked questions in a series of sessions than among those in a control group. Zimmerman and Pike (1972) compared the effects of praise on question asking with the effects of a combination of modeling and praise. Seven-year-olds from the combination condition asked more questions and were better able to generalize question asking to novel tasks. A follow-up to this study suggests, however, that simple modeling may actually be a relatively weak influence on question asking. Rosenthal and Zimmerman (1972) had 9-year-olds watch models asking various types of questions (e.g., nominal, causal, functional). Some children just watched, some imitated the model's questions, some had to imitate and decide how the questions were similar to each other, and some had to imitate, abstract the pattern (e.g., nominal, causal, function), and generate new examples of the questions having the same categorical properties. During a generalization session, the children who had generated examples asked more questions than did abstractors or imitators (who asked an equivalent number of questions). The fewest number of questions was produced by those who just watched the model.

None of the modeling studies described thus far took into account individual differences in the child's baseline tendency to explore. Henderson and Moore (1980) attempted to do so in a study of the effects of three teaching styles, including a demonstration or modeling condition, on the exploration of preschoolers. Based on their responses on a curiosity assessment battery (Henderson & Moore, 1979), children were identified as high-curiosity (approximately one-third of assessed children) or low-curiosity (also approximately one-third of assessed children). Each child then was involved in six play sessions with novel toys and an adult who demonstrated exploratory behaviors at the start of each session, simply was responsive to the child's initiations, or was totally unresponsive. Observations of the exploratory behavior of the children in the six sessions and a generalization session revealed no effects of the adult behavior. High-curiosity children explored at a high level, and low-curiosity children explored at a low level regardless of the behavior of the adult. These results suggest that the child's general predisposition to explore may be as important a determinant of his or her exploration as the behavior of an accompanying adult, at least for children at the extremes.

*Negative Influences.* Under certain conditions, then, it appears that an adult may facilitate children's exploration through answering questions and modeling exploratory behavior. Some adult influences may, however, be negative rather than positive. The effects of a general atmosphere of adult criticalness have been studied by Moore and Bulbulian (1976). Preschool children participate in two tasks with an adult who was either aloof and critical of the child's behavior or was friendly and accepting of the child's involvement. They were then given the opportunity to explore novel objects. Children who had been criticized by the aloof adult explored less and began exploration less quickly than children who had been with the friendly adult. Another negative effect, the sex typing of toys, was examined by Bradbard and Endsley (in press). Five- and six-year-olds were told that novel objects were for boys, for girls, or for both boys and girls. Same-sex-typed toys were tactually explored more than toys that had been labeled as for both sexes, which in turn were explored more than opposite-sex-typed toys.

A third possible negative influence is reinforcement. The studies of answers to questions reviewed above (Endsley & Clarey, 1975; Ross & Balzer, 1975) indicated a reinforcing effect of answers. The correlation between maternal contingent positive interaction and child exploration obtained in the previously described Endsley et al. (1979) investigation also suggests a relationship between reinforcement and exploration. A very different view of the role of reinforcement has been provided recently by social and developmental psychologists who have reported a negative or undermining influence of rewards on intrinsic motivation. Space is not available here to present the many complex theoretical and empirical issues involved in this literature (recent reviews include Bates, 1979; Condry, 1977; Deci & Ryan, 1980; and Williams, 1980). Basically, the contention is that children lose interest in tasks that were previously interesting to them when an opportunity for a salient reward becomes contingent upon performance on the task. In other words, intrinsically motivated play becomes extrinsically motivated work.

Intrinsic motivation in this research is rather broadly defined as any behavior that is motivated by a need for competence and self-determination (Deci & Ryan, 1980). Presumably, this definition includes exploratory behavior. In fact, some researchers have quite explicitly tied the undermining effect of reward to exploration (Condry, 1977). There are, however, reasons for questioning the applicability of this literature to exploration. First, intrinsic motivation is usually operationally defined as amount of time spent with a rewarded task or object after the removal of the reward. The tasks that have been used include drawing, puzzle solving, and play with conventional toys (Condry, 1977; Deci & Ryan, 1980). No study to date has used free exploration of objects clearly unfamiliar to the child with questions or manipulations as dependent variables (rather than measures of nonexploratory play).

A second problem arises if reward or reinforcement is defined as something that increases the probability of a behavior (Williams, 1980). Suppose a child is rewarded for manipulating or asking questions about novel object A. What kind of behavior would be predicted when the object A is presented a second time (as required by the undermining effects of reward paradigm)? If the reinforcement "worked" by increasing exploration or increasing attentiveness during the original task session, then the child should be less likely to explore that same object later, because the novelty of the object will already have been reduced. However, this could hardly be interpreted as an "undermining" of intrinsic motivation. More important than observing the child's responses to novel object A would be observation of his or her response to a different novel object to determine the effects of reinforcement on the generalization of exploratory behavior in like situations.

Finally, there is the question of how frequently reinforcement of the type that undermines intrinsic motivation is given contingent upon exploratory behavior in natural situations. In a recent review of the literature in this area, Deci and Ryan (1980) suggested two separate effects of reinforcement or reward: informational (feedback about competence) and controlling. When the controlling component of reinforcement is salient, intrinsic motivation decreases. When the informational component is salient, on the other hand, intrinsic motivation increases. The types of rewards that tend to make the controlling component salient are those that are expected, contingent, tangible, and dispensed by an authoritarian (controlling) person (Deci & Ryan, 1980). Unlike structured play and learning in schools, exploration is often incidental and unplanned (e.g., examining the anthill in the backyard or the coffee grinder in the attic). Reinforcement for exploration is not likely to be expected, contingent, or tangible. Instead, it is likely to be spontaneous, noncontingent, and verbal.

Thus, the literature on the effects of reward on intrinsic motivation does not include data bearing directly on exploratory behavior. Research directed at discovering links between reward and exploration will have to be guided by careful considerations of the nature of reinforcement and the nature of exploratory behavior.

*Day-Care and Educational Programs.* Because mothers can positively influence the exploratory behavior of young children (see previous review), the exploration of the child who is separated from his or her mother through experience in day care may be affected unless substitute caregivers compensate. The limited evidence on the effects of day care on exploration provides mixed results. Rubenstein, Pederson, and Yarrow (1977) compared infants who spent substantial portions of their time with substitute caregivers with home-reared infants on 17 measures of various behaviors. The two groups differed on only one measure. Home-reared infants showed more focused exploration at home. Blehar (1974) found that 3-year-olds who had spent 5 months in day care explored less in the Ainsworth strange situation than home-reared children. Niether Moskowitz, Schwarz, and Corsini (1977) nor Portnoy and Simmons (1978) were, however, able to replicate Blehar's findings. Moskowitz et al. reported that day-care males exhibited more exploratory manipulation of objects than home-reared males but that there were no differences for females. Portnoy and Simmons (1978) found no differences in exploration between rearing groups. Thus, if day-care experience does influence exploratory behavior, the effects are neither consistent nor robust.

School's provide a setting in which children have many opportunities for interaction with an adult, the teacher. Although not necessarily a social influence on exploration in itself, the school curriculum provides a framework for determining the degree to which social interaction during exploration occurs. Less direct effects may also occur in areas such as the child's style of interacting with objects and attitude about asking questions. Horowitz (1979), in a review of the effects of open and traditional classrooms on child characteristics, concluded that children from open classrooms show more curiosity. Only two of the studies he reviewed dealt with young children. Rothschild (cited in Horowitz, 1979) found higher scores on a measure of interest in novel stimuli among first-graders from an open class in comparison to those from a traditional classroom. However, because the two types of classrooms did not differ on measures of theoretical dimensions of openness, the source of the differences is not clear. An open-traditional difference in exploration was also reported by Stallings (1975) in her study of follow-through classrooms. More questions were asked in open, interdisciplinary classrooms where students had a wide variety of activities and materials to choose from than in more academically oriented classrooms where drill, practice, and the use of praise by teachers were emphasized.

Findings similar to those of Rothschild and Stallings were obtained by Miller and Dyer (1975) in their comparison of the short- and long-term outcomes of various Head Start programs. A basic skills/reinforcement model (Bereiter–Engelman), a parent-oriented model aimed at remediating linguistic and conceptual deficiencies (DARCEE), a Montessori model, and a traditional free-play model were all compared to a control group on a host of cognitive and motivational measures, including a measure of curiosity about an unusual box. After 1 year, curiosity scores for the children in the control group had declined whereas the scores for the children in the four preschool programs had not.

Follow-ups 1, 2, and 3 years after the preschool experience indicated that curiosity had increased from preschool entrance to grade 2 for all children in the model programs except those in the basic skills/reinforcement model.

A more experimental approach to the question of the effects of adult structuring was taken by Vliestra (1980). She randomly assigned preschool children from existing structured, teacher-led and child-centered, free-choice classrooms to explore common objects in containers by free choice or with adult direction. Children from the adult-direction condition spent more time manipulating the objects from containers and less time playing with a set of conventional toys than did children from the free-choice condition. Vlietstra interpreted these results as indicating more exploration under lower levels of adult direction. However, because the objects (paper clips, crayons, balls, pots and pans) were probably not very novel, it is not clear whether the effects were on exploration or play.

Only one explicit attempt to train children to explore has been reported. Dansky (1980) investigated the relative effects of exploration training with those of sociodramatic experiences and free play on preschool children. The exploration training consisted of a guessing game in small groups with the trainer emphasizing the discussion of physical properties of objects and modeling of exploration through naming of properties overlooked by the children. Children who received exploration training did not, in a posttest, display more exploratory play with an interesting box than children from the other two groups. They did, however, outscore children from both the other groups on recall of properties of the box and outscored the free-play group on being able to describe attributes of four simple objects. It appears that the exploration training may have influenced attention and information extraction rather than the ability or disposition to explore.

## Peers

Children spend a great deal of time with peers in our culture. They encounter siblings, classmates, playmates, and other fellow travelers in homes, day cares, schools, play areas, and many other settings. Interactions with peers are believed to facilitate socialization and cognitive development. However, the means by which peers influence cognitive development have not been well documented (Hartup, 1976). A logical candidate for such effects would seem to be peer influence on what information children do or do not obtain from their animate and inanimate environments through exploration and play. These influences could occur in several ways. Models might call a child's attention to novel aspects of the environment or disinhibit the child who was hesitant to manipulate an object or ask a question. Peers, especially friends, might, like mothers of infants, provide a secure base for exploration or reduce the novelty of the environment into a more "optimal" range for the child. Peers could also interfere with exploration in competition for scarce novel resources or by extracting the novel information available in an object, rendering it uninteresting, or by simply distracting the child from attending to novelty.

The data base for peer influences on exploration is very thin. For example, there is no direct evidence about conditions under which children will imitate the exploration of a peer. There are no data to indicate how frequently children encounter novel objects alone or in the presence of peers. A few studies do, however, provide some information on how peers influence exploration.

In a study that parallels an earlier one on children's exploration in the presence of their mothers (Rheingold & Eckerman, 1970), Samuels (1980) watched 2-year-olds explore a novel backyard with their mothers or with their mothers and an older sibling. Children moved farther away from their mothers and explored more of the yard when accompanied by an older sibling. They not only followed the siblings around but showed more independent behavior unrelated to the siblings' actions. Samuels suggested that older siblings provided a model for exploratory behavior.

Samuels' study indicates higher levels of locomotor exploration of a novel environment in the presence of a sibling. Are other types of exploration, such as manipulations of and questions about objects also increased by the presence of a companion? Does the companion have to be someone the child knows or knows well? Schwarz (1972) addressed these issues in a study of the exploration of 4-year-olds who played alone, in the presence of a friend, or with an unfamiliar peer. Children were given the opportunity to explore two novel toys (i.e., a large toy helicopter and a toy dashboard) and two toys from their classroom (i.e., a flannel board and a steering wheel), all of which could be played with by two children at the same time. The dependent variable relevant to exploration was time spent with novel versus familiar toys. Schwarz hypothesized that the presence of a friend would reduce novelty (and arousal), which would lead children with friends to spend relatively more time with the novel (arousing) objects. Children in the other conditions were expected to avoid the novel objects because they would tend to increase already high levels of arousal to aversive levels. The results did not support the hypothesis. Children in all three conditions spent more than 90% of their time with the novel objects.

A similar study with preschoolers was reported by Rabinowitz, Moely, Finkel, and McClinton (1975). A large paperboard clown figure with obvious levers and hidden buttons that lighted lights and generated sounds was presented along with four familiar toys. Children who played with these toys in two sessions with a peer spent relatively more time with the clown than children who played alone. Pairs of children were also more likely to discover the hidden buttons. The discrepancy between the Schwarz and Rabinowitz et al. studies may be due to differences in the amount of time allowed for exploration (i.e., 5 minutes versus a total of 30 minutes, respectively). Also, the exploratory possibilities of the toys used in the Schwarz investigation may have been more obvious.

Neither the Schwarz (1972) study nor the Rabinowitz et al. (1975) study took into account individual differences in children's predispositions to explore. Children who are generally low in curiosity may be more susceptible to the influence of a peer than children who are high in curiosity and who are likely to explore under most any condition. Henderson (1981) examined this possibility by identifying high- and low-exploratory preschoolers on the basis of their responses to novel objects, then observing their exploration when with high-exploratory peers, low-exploratory peers, or when alone. Manipulations of and questions about novel objects by low-exploratory children were unaffected by the presence of a peer. Their exploration remained at a low level with a peer present. High-exploratory children, on the other hand, asked fewer questions and performed fewer manipulations when with either high- or low-exploratory companions. This interference effect of the presence of peers has also been reported in a study of the relation between group size and question asking. Endsley and Gupta (1978) found that children asked more questions about novel objects when alone than when with one or two others. This effect may be important because children remember answers to their own questions better than answers to a peer's questions (Ross & Killey, 1977).

In summary, the evidence on the effects of peer presence on exploration is mixed. Only Rabinowitz et al. (1975) have reported positive effects of peer presence. The other available evidence suggests that the influence of the objects of exploration may be more powerful or that the presence of a companion may interfere with exploration. Further research will have to elucidate how factors such as age, type and availability of novel toys provided, time allowed for exploration, and quality of relationship between companions affect exploration.

## SOCIAL EXPLORATION: CHILDREN'S RESPONSES TO NOVEL PEOPLE

### Adults

Do children respond to novel people in the same ways as they respond to novel objects? That is, do they show interest in novel people by approaching, touching, looking, and asking questions? Hutt (1970) suggested a qualitative difference between responses to novel inanimate objects and to novel people. She indicated that, in contrast to novel objects, novel people tend to elicit fear and decreases in exploration rather than exploratory behavior. On the other hand, it seems just as important for the child to acquire information about unfamiliar aspects of the social world as to discover new aspects of the physical world.

Most of the research on children's responses to novel adults has been limited to the study of "stranger anxiety" during infancy (see Sroufe, 1977, for a review). Little is known about the response of older children to unfamiliar adults.

The nature of the infant's response to unfamiliar adults is complexly determined. Wary responses (e.g., gaze aversion, frowns, crying) are most likely between 8 and 12 months of age (Greenberg, Hillman, & Grice, 1973; Skarin, 1977; Sroufe, 1977). They are more likely in the laboratory than at home (Skarin, 1977), when mother is absent or separation is anticipated (Harmon, Morgan, & Klein, 1977; Skarin, 1977) and when the infant is not in mother's arms (Bronson, 1972). Taller (Weinraub & Putney, 1978), less familiar (Levitt, 1980), and male (Greenberg et al., 1973) strangers tend to elicit more negative responses. Finally, wariness is more likely to be exhibited by irritable infants (Harmon et al., 1977) and insecurely attached infants (Main & Weston, 1981).

These studies indicate that, under some circumstances, wariness rather than exploration characterizes infant responses to strangers. However, there is ample support for the contention that wariness or fear is not the most common infant reaction to unfamiliar adults. Riccuiti (1974), for example, found sustained, sober visual regard with interest to be the modal response of 10- and 12-month-olds to strangers. Rheingold and Eckerman (1973) have gone even further, arguing that positive rather than negative reactions are the typical response to strangers among infants of any age. Although they did not find infants engaging strangers in play or conversation, Bretherton, Stolberg, and Kreye (1981) did find infants at 12, 18, and 24 months of age approaching, smiling and looking at, vocalizing to, and sharing toys with strangers. Responses to novel adults appear to be especially positive when the stranger is active (Bretherton, 1978; Ross & Goldman, 1977). After 2 years of age, even mild forms of wariness decrease in frequency and social or affiliative responses to strangers tend to occur very quickly after first encounters with strangers (Greenberg & Marvin, 1982).

Whether positive or negative responses to strangers occur, then, is a function of many factors. It is not clear that the positive responses that do occur can always be considered exploratory. Certainly the visual examination of a stranger at a distance could be considered exploratory. Bretherton and Ainsworth (1974) have argued, however, that the positive responses to strangers serve affiliative rather than exploratory functions. By its nature, looking, unaccompanied by manipulation, question asking, or other exploratory behavior is ambiguous as to function and meaning. Perhaps a useful strategy would be to compare responses directly to novel objects and people. In one attempt to do so, Eckerman and Rheingold (1974) allowed 10-month-olds to explore a room containing novel toys and/or a room containing an attentive but passive adult. Infants approached toys more often and more quickly and maintained contact with toys longer. However, twice as many visual regards were directed at the adult than at the toys. Eckerman and Rheingold concluded that infants direct different kinds of exploration at social and nonsocial objects (distal and proximal exploration, respectively) but that through exploration infants learn about the world of people as well as the world of things.

Children clearly explore novel inanimate objects more than familiar objects. Exploration of a novel object also decreases over time. To determine if these patterns apply to responses to novel and familiar adults, Eckerman and Whately (1975) compared 9- and 10-month-old infants' responses to novel and familiar adults and charted responses to the novel adult over time. Infants exhibited more looking, smiling, and vocalizations and gestures toward the novel adult, and these behaviors toward the novel adult declined in frequency with continued exposure. These results show commonalities with exploration of objects. In contrast, Brooks-Gunn and Lewis (1981) found that infants 9 through 24 months of age looked longer at pictures of their parents than at pictures of strangers. These latter results, however, may be due to the overriding of exploration by attachment behaviors.

## Peers

Little in the way of behavioral detail is available on children's exploratory reactions to novel peers. Infants tend to show more interest in toys than in novel peers (Jacobson, 1981; Mueller, 1979). Looking is, however, a common response directed at novel peers (Eckerman, Whately, & Kutz, 1975; Jacobson, 1980; Lewis, Young, Brooks, & Michalson, 1975). It is not clear whether looking behavior is indicative of exploration or wariness, although the absence of frank expressions of negative affect seems to favor the former. At least one study has shown a strong positive influence of peer novelty on social interaction. Jacobson (1981) reported longer and more frequent interactions between unacquainted peers than between peers who were familiar with each other. A more typical finding is that more social interaction and higher levels of social interaction occur between infants (Lewis et al., 1975; Young & Lewis, 1979) and preschoolers (Doyle, Connolly, & Rivest, 1980; Perrin, 1979) who know each other. If the child's initial reactions to novel peers are exploratory in function, it seems that the period of exploration is very short in most instances. Affiliative and other more negative social behaviors seem to take over very quickly, probably somewhat more quickly for preschoolers (Greenberg & Marvin, 1982; Perrin, 1979) than for infants (Lewis et al., 1975).

## Social Exploration and Object Exploration

The relationship between exploration of novel people and exploration of novel inanimate objects has been examined in only a few investigations. Mueller and his associates (Mueller, 1979; Mueller & Lucas, 1975) have suggested that much of early peer interaction occurs in the context of play with objects. Eckerman, Whatley, and McGehee (1979) have also shown that objects may facilitate social interaction with an adult stranger. Perhaps novel objects would provide a particularly strong attraction that would lead to frequent social interaction (positive or negative). Haskett (1977) has reported more interaction of preschoolers with an unfamiliar adult when that adult has a novel toy. However, it could also be argued that a focus on novel objects inhibits rather than facilitates social interaction. Young children are apparently more likely to interact and interact in more sophisticated ways in the absence of objects (Vandell, Wilson, & Buchanan, 1980), at least over short periods of time.

There do seem to be some similarities in the exploration of objects and people, particularly adult strangers (see previous material). Just as exploration tends to precede play, it may precede affiliative involvement with unfamiliar adults and peers. Exploration of social objects appears, however, to be distal rather than proximal. One type of evidence for a common exploratory construct underlying responses to novel objects and novel people would be a relationship between individual differences in the tendency to explore objects and individual differences in the tendency to explore novel people. Support for such a relationship has recently been reported by Moore and Leiman (1982). Preschoolers who were high on a battery of measures of object curiosity spent relatively more of their time looking at an unfamiliar rather than at a familiar peer than children low on the battery. They also were more likely than lows to approach the novel peer and ask him or her questions. Further research along these lines could go a long way in clarifying the nature of exploratory responses to people.

## PROBLEMS AND CONCLUSIONS

The evidence pertaining to the relationship between exploration and its social context comes from a variety of sources. To date, there is no conceptual or theoretical framework capable of organizing these findings. One major reason for the absence of such a framework is the failure of investigators to study the influences on exploration in the complexity in which they occur in natural settings. Three generalizations about children's exploration are well established. First, novelty normally arouses curiosity in young children. Second, the degree to which children express their curiosity through exploratory behavior differs to a considerable extent in amount and kind from child to child. Finally, the expression of curiosity is influenced by the presence or absence and behavior of other people in the environment. Much less well established is how the types of novelty available in the environment, individual differences in the tendency to explore, and social influences on exploration interact. As a result, it is difficult to predict how an individual child will respond in a particular novel setting or how to judge the general importance of exploratory behavior in the child's developing competence in dealing with the physical and social world.

Many of the problems in the research on the social context of exploration were alluded to briefly in the previous review. They include problems concerning the object of exploration, the nature of exploratory behavior, and individual differences in styles and modes of exploration. It is frequently impossible to discern the novel aspect of an experiment to which a child was responding. The effects of novel environments, objects, and people are often confounded. At times, the child may be responding to the unfamiliarity of objects, to the incongruity of the behavior of another person (e.g., the experimenter or the mother) in that setting. It is not always clear just how novel the objects employed really are. They may range from interesting, but conventional, toys to objects of a type not likely to have been encountered in past experience. Researchers need to be more careful about isolating the effects of different degrees and kinds of novelty. More attention also needs to be given to the variety of exploratory behaviors exhibited by children, to developmental and individual differences in the styles and modes of the expression of those behaviors, and to the possibility of their differential sensitivity to social influences.

Despite these problems, some speculative conclusions about the social context of exploratory play can be made based on or extrapolated from the available evidence:

1. Children cannot explore when novelty is absent from their environments. Parents and teachers vary in their sensitivity to the need for making a wide variety of novel objects available for exploration and for allowing the child the freedom to explore the rich sources of novelty in the natural world.
2. A secure attachment to a caretaker provides the young child a base from which to explore. It seems likely that the presence of a secure base allows the child to enter a developmental cycle in which he or she becomes increasingly competent in dealing with the environment and increasingly aware of and capable of assimilating new experiences.
3. Adults, and sometimes peers, may facilitate play by focusing the child on novel objects and their features. The basic exploratory behaviors (visual examination, manipulation, questioning) probably are not taught directly. Modeling, however, may disinhibit exploration and behaviors such as the asking of leading questions, pointing or prompts, or casual comments may make the child more aware of novel features.
4. Parents and teachers act as consultants for the child. Questioning increases when questions are answered and encouraged. Adults provide information or help the child find out things on their own.
5. The behavior of another may interfere with the child's exploration. The exploration of children who are predisposed to explore at a high level is probably especially susceptible to interference. Peers are less likely than adults to be sensitive to or concerned about behaviors that interfere with another child's exploration.
6. Object exploration and social exploration are different in form if not in function. Individual differences in curiosity about novel people and things may

be correlated. It would appear that in most situations, and even at early ages, exploratory interest in conspecifics quickly gives way to interactive play.

Some of these generalizations are supported by more evidence than others. The past decade of research has provided a growing body of knowledge about the contexts of children's exploratory play. Perhaps the research of the next decade will allow us to make much more specific statements and to make them more confidently.

## REFERENCES

Adams, R. E., & Passman, R. H. Effects of visual and auditory aspects of mothers and strangers on the play and exploration of children. *Developmental Psychology,* 1979, *15,* 269–274.

Ainsworth, M. D. S., Blehar, M. C., Waters, E., & Wall, S. *Patterns of attachment.* Hillsdale, N.J.: Lawrence Erlbaum Associates, 1978.

Anderson, J. W. Attachment behaviour out of doors. In N. Blurton-Jones (Ed.), *Ethological studies of child behavior.* Cambridge: Cambridge University Press, 1972.

Arend, R., Gove, F. L., & Sroufe, L. A. Continuity of individual adaptation from infancy to kindergarten: A predictive study of ego-resiliency and curiosity in preschoolers. *Child Development,* 1979, *50,* 950–959.

Bates, J. A. Extrinsic reward and intrinsic motivation: A review with implications for the classroom. *Review of Educational Research,* 1979, *49,* 557–576.

Belsky, J., Goode, M. K., & Most, R. K. Maternal stimulation and infant exploratory competence: Cross-sectional, correlational, and experimental analyses. *Child Development,* 1980, *51,* 1163–1178.

Berlyne, D. E. *Conflict, arousal, and curiosity.* New York: McGraw-Hill, 1960.

Berlyne, D. E., & Frommer, F. D. Some determinants of the incidence and content of children's questions. *Child Development,* 1966, *37,* 177–189.

Blank, M., & Allen, D. A. Understanding "why." In M. Lewis (Ed.), *Origins of intelligence.* New York: Plenum, 1976.

Blehar, M. C. Anxious attachment and defensive reactions associated with daycare. *Child Development,* 1974, *45,* 683–692.

Bowlby, J. *Attachment and loss: Attachment* (Vol. 1). New York: Basic Books, 1969.

Bradbard, M. R., & Endsley, R. C. The effects of sex-typed labeling on preschool children's information-seeking and retention. *Sex Roles: A Journal of Research,* in press.

Bretherton, I. Making friends with one-year-olds: An experimental study of infant-stranger interaction. *Merrill-Palmer Quarterly,* 1978, *24,* 29–51.

Bretherton, I., & Ainsworth, M. D. S. The responses of one-year-olds to a stranger in a strange situation. In M. Lewis & L. A. Rosenblum (Eds.), *The origins of fear.* New York: Wiley, 1974.

Bretherton, I., Stolberg, A., & Kreye, M. Engaging strangers in proximal interaction: Infants' social initiative. *Developmental Psychology,* 1981, *17,* 746–755.

Bronson, G. W. Infants' reactions to unfamiliar persons and novel objects. *Monographs of the Society for Research in Child Development,* 1972, *37* (3, Serial No. 148).

Brooks-Gunn, J., & Lewis, M. Infant social perception: Responses to pictures of parents and strangers. *Developmental Psychology,* 1981, *17,* 647–649.

Cantor, G. N. Responses of infants and children to complex and novel stimulation. *Advances in Child Development and Behavior,* 1963, *1,* 1–29.

Charlesworth, W. R. Instigation and maintenance of curiosity behavior as a function of surprise versus novel and familiar stimuli. *Child Development*, 1964, *35*, 1169–1186.

Coie, J. D. An evaluation of the cross-situational stability of children's curiosity. *Journal of Personality*, 1974, *42*, 93–116.

Collard, R. R. Exploratory behavior in institutionalized and non-institutionalized children. *Child Development*, 1971, *42*, 1003–1015.

Condry, J. Enemies of exploration: Self-initiated versus other-initiated learning. *Journal of Personality and Social Psychology*, 1977, *35*, 459–477.

Corter, C. The nature of the mother's absence and the infant's response to brief separations. *Developmental Psychology*, 1976, *12*, 428–434.

Corter, C., & Jamieson, N. Infants' toy preferences and mothers' predictions. *Developmental Psychology*, 1977, *13*, 413–414.

Dansky, J. L. Cognitive consequences of sociodramatic play and exploration training for economically disadvantaged preschoolers. *Journal of Child Psychology and Psychiatry*, 1980, *20*, 47–58.

Deci, E. L., & Ryan, R. M. The empirical exploration of intrinsic motivational processes. *Advances in Experimental Social Psychology*, 1980, *13*, 39–80.

Doyle, A. B., Connolly, J., & Rivest, L. P. The effect of playmate familiarity on the social interactions of young children. *Child Development*, 1980, *51*, 217–223.

Eckerman, C. O., & Rheingold, H. L. Infants' exploratory responses to toys and people. *Developmental Psychology*, 1974, *10*, 255–259.

Eckerman, C. O., & Whately, J. Infants' reactions to unfamiliar adults varying in novelty. *Developmental Psychology*, 1975, *11*, 562–566.

Eckerman, C. O., Whately, J. L., & Kutz, S. L. Growth of social play with peers during the second year of life. *Developmental Psychology*, 1975, *11*, 42–49.

Eckerman, C. O., Whately, J. L., & McGehee, L. J. Approaching and contacting the object another manipulates: A social skill of the 1-year-old. *Developmental Psychology*, 1979, *15*, 585–593.

Endsley, R. C., & Clarey, S. A. Answering young children's questions as a determinant of their subsequent question-asking behavior. *Developmental Psychology*, 1975, *11*, 863.

Endsley, R. C., & Gupta, S. Group size as a determinant of preschool children's frequency of asking questions. *Journal of Genetic Psychology*, 1978, *132*, 317–318.

Endsley, R. C., Hutcherson, M. A., Garner, A. P., & Martin, M. J. Interrelationships among selected maternal behaviors, authoritarianism, and preschool children's verbal and nonverbal curiosity. *Child Development*, 1979, *50*, 331–339.

Gershaw, N. J., & Schwarz, J. C. The effects of a familiar toy and mother's presence on exploratory and attachment behaviors in young children. *Child Development*, 1971, *42*, 1662–1666.

Gray, M. D., Tracy, R. L., & Lindberg, C. L. Effects of maternal interference on the attachment and exploratory behavior of one-year-olds. *Child Development*, 1979, *50*, 1211–1214.

Greenberg, D. J., Hillman, D., & Grice, D. Infant and stranger variables related to stranger anxiety in the first year of life. *Developmental Psychology*, 1973, *9*, 207–212.

Greenberg, M. T., & Marvin, R. S. Reactions of preschool children to an adult stranger: A behavioral systems approach. *Child Development*, 1982, *53*, 481–490.

Hall, G. S., & Smith, T. L. Curiosity and interest. *Pedagogical Seminary*, 1903, *10*, 315–358.

Harmon, R. J., Morgan, G. A., & Klein, R. P. Determinants of normal variation in infants' negative reactions to unfamiliar adults. *Journal of Child Psychiatry*, 1977, *16*, 670–683.

Harter, S., & Zigler, E. The assessment of effectance motivation in normal and retarded children. *Developmental Psychology*, 1974, *10*, 169–180.

Hartup, W. W. Peer interaction and the behavioral development of the individual child. In E. Schopler & R. J. Reichler (Eds.), *Psychopathology and Child Development*. New York: Plenum, 1976.

Haskett, G. J. The exploratory nature of children's social relations. *Merrill-Palmer Quarterly*, 1977, *23*, 101–113.

Henderson, B. B. Exploration by preschool children: Peer interaction and individual differences. *Merrill-Palmer Quarterly*, 1981, *27*, 241–255.

Henderson, B. B., Charlesworth, W. R., & Gamradt, J. Children's exploratory behavior in a novel field setting. *Ethology and Sociobiology*, 1982, *3*, 93–99.

Henderson, B. B., & Moore, S. G. Measuring exploratory behavior in young children: A factor-analytic study. *Developmental Psychology*, 1979, *15*, 113–119.

Henderson, B., & Moore, S. G. Children's responses to objects differing in novelty in relation to level of curiosity and adult behavior. *Child Development*, 1980, *51*, 457–65.

Henderson, R. W., Swanson, R., & Zimmerman, B. J. Inquiry response induction in preschool children through televised modeling. *Developmental Psychology*, 1975, *11*, 523–524.

Herman, J. F. Children's cognitive maps of large-scale spaces: Effects of exploration, direction, and repeated experience. *Journal of Experimental Child Psychology*, 1980, *29*, 126–143.

Horowitz, R. A. Psychological effects of the "open classroom." *Review of Educational Research*, 1979, *49*, 71–86.

Hughes, M. Sequential analysis of exploration and play. *International Journal of Behavioral Development*, 1978, *1*, 83–97.

Hutt, C. Specific and diversive explorations. *Advances in Child Development and Behavior*, 1970, *5*, 119–180.

Isaacs, S. Children's "why" questions. In S. Isaacs, *Intellectual growth in young children*. New York: Harcourt, 1930.

Jacobson, J. L. Cognitive determinants of wariness toward unfamiliar peers. *Developmental Psychology*, 1980, *16*, 347–354.

Jacobson, J. L. The role of inanimate objects in early peer interaction. *Child Development*, 1981, *52*, 618–626.

Jennings, K. D., Harmon, R. T., Morgan, G. A., Gaiter, J. L., & Yarrow, L. J. Exploratory play as an index of mastery motivation: Relationships to persistence, cognitive functioning, and environmental measures. *Developmental Psychology*, 1979, *15*, 386–394.

Johns, C., & Endsley, R. C. The effects of a maternal model on young children's tactual curiosity. *Journal of Genetic Psychology*, 1977, *131*, 21–28.

Keller, H. *The development of exploratory behavior in the first year of life*. Paper presented at the meeting of the International Society for the Study of Behavioral Development, Toronto, August 1981.

Kreitler, S., Zigler, E., & Kreitler, H. The nature of curiosity in children. *Journal of School Psychology*, 1975, *13*, 185–200.

Levitt, M. J. Contingent feedback, familiarization, and infant affect: How a stranger becomes a friend. *Developmental Psychology*, 1980, *16*, 425–632.

Lewis, M., Young, G., Brooks, J., & Michaelson, L. The beginning of friendship. In M. Lewis & L. A. Rosenblum (Eds.), *Friendship and peer relations*. New York: Wiley, 1975.

Lewis, M. M. The beginning and early functions of questions in a child's speech. *British Journal of Educational Psychology*, 1939, *8*, 150–171.

Livson, N. Towards a differentiated construct of curiosity. *Journal of Genetic Psychology*, 1967, *111*, 73–84.

Lorenz, K. *Studies in animal and human behavior* (Vol. 2). Cambridge, Mass.: Harvard, 1971.

Main, M., & Weston, D. R. The quality of the toddler's relationship to mother and father: Related to conflict behavior and the readiness to establish new relationships. *Child Development*, 1981, *52*, 932–940.

Marvin, R. S. An ethological-cognitive model for the attenuation of mother–child attachment behavior. In T. Alloway, P. Pliner, & L. Krames (Eds.), *Advances in the study of communication and affect* (Vol. 3): *Attachment behavior*. New York: Plenum, 1977.

Maw, W. H., & Maw, E. W. Note on curiosity and intelligence of school children. *Psychological Reports,* 1975, *36,* 782.

Maw, W. H., & Maw, E. W. Nature and assessment of human curiosity. In P. McReynolds (Ed.), *Advances in psychological assessment* (Vol. 4). San Francisco: Jossey-Bass, 1977.

Miller, L. B., & Dyer, J. L. Four preschool programs: Their dimensions and effects. *Monographs of the Society for Research in Child Development,* 1975, *40*(5–6, Serial No. 162).

Moore, S. G., & Bulbulian, K. N. The effects of contrasting styles of adult–child interaction on children's curiosity. *Developmental Psychology,* 1976, *12,* 171.

Moore, S. G., & Leiman, B. *Object exploration and peer exploration.* Unpublished manuscript, University of Minnesota, 1982.

Moore, S. G., & Pancake, V. R. *Individual differences in the exploratory tendencies of toddlers.* Unpublished manuscript, University of Minnesota, 1982.

Moskowitz, D. S., Schwarz, J. C., & Corsini, D. A. Initiating day care at three years of age: Effects on attachment. *Child Development,* 1977, *48,* 1271–1276.

Mueller, E. Toddlers + toys = an autonomous social system. In M. Lewis & L. A. Rosenblum (Eds.), *The child and its family.* New York: Plenum, 1979.

Mueller, E., & Lucas, T. A developmental analysis of peer interaction among toddlers. In M. Lewis & L. A. Rosenblum (Eds.), *Friendship and peer relations.* New York: Wiley, 1975.

Nunnally, J. C., & Lemond, L. C. Exploratory behavior and human development. *Advances in child development and behaviors,* 1973, *8,* 59–109.

Passman, R. H., & Erck, T. W. Permitting maternal contact through vision alone: Films of mothers for promoting play and locomotion. *Developmental Psychology,* 1978, *14,* 512–516.

Passman, R. H., & Weisberg, P. Mothers and blankets as agents for promoting play and exploration by young children in a novel environment: The effect of social and non-social attachment objects. *Developmental Psychology,* 1975, *11,* 170–177.

Perrin, J. E. *Reciprocal social influences on play in four-year-olds: Friends and strangers.* Paper presented at the meeting of the Society for Research in Child Development, San Francisco, March 1979.

Portnoy, F. C., & Simmons, C. H. Day care and attachment. *Child Development,* 1978, *49,* 239–242.

Rabinowitz, F. M., Moely, B. E., Finkel, N., & McClinton, S. The effects of toy novelty and social interaction on the exploratory behavior of preschool children. *Child Development,* 1975, *46,* 286–289.

Rheingold, H. L. The effect of a strange environment on the behavior of infants. In B. M. Foss (Ed.), *Determinants of infants behavior* (Vol. 4). London: Methuen, 1969.

Rheingold, H. L., & Eckerman, C. O. The infant separates himself from his mother. *Science,* 1970, *168,* 78–83.

Rheingold, H. L., & Eckerman, C. O. Fear of the stranger: A critical examination. *Advances in Child Development and Behavior,* 1973, *8,* 185–222.

Riccuiti, H. N. Fear and the development of social attachments in the first year of life. In M. Lewis & L. A. Rosenblum (Eds.), *The origins of fear.* New York: Wiley, 1974.

Rosenthal, T. C., & Zimmerman, B. J. Instructional specificity and outcome expectation in observationally induced question formation. *Journal of Educational Psychology,* 1972, *63,* 500–504.

Ross, H. S. The influence of novelty and complexity on exploratory behavior in 12-month-old infants. *Journal of Experimental Child Psychology,* 1974, *17,* 436–451.

Ross, H. S., & Balzer, R. H. Determinants and consequences of children's questions. *Child Development,* 1975, *46,* 536–539.

Ross, H. S., & Goldman, B. D. Infants' sociability toward strangers. *Child Development,* 1977, *48,* 638–642.

Ross, H. S., & Killey, J. C. The effect of questioning on retention. *Child Development,* 1977, *48,* 312–314.

Ross, H. S., Rheingold, H. L., & Eckerman, C. O. Approach and exploration of a novel alternative by 12-month-old infants. *Journal of Experimental Child Psychology,* 1972, *13,* 85–93.
Rubenstein, J. Maternal attentiveness and subsequent exploratory behavior in the infant. *Child Development,* 1967, *38,* 1089–1100.
Rubenstein, J. L., Pederson, F. A., & Yarrow, L. J. What happens when mother is away: A comparison of mothers and substitute caregivers. *Developmental Psychology,* 1977, *13,* 529–530.
Samuels, H. R. The effect of an older sibling on infant locomotor exploration of a new environment. *Child Development,* 1980, *51,* 607–609.
Saxe, R. M., & Stollak, G. Curiosity and the parent–child relationship. *Child Development,* 1971, *42,* 373–384.
Schneider, K. *Subjective uncertainty and exploratory behavior in preschool children.* Paper presented at the Curiosity, Imaginative, and Play Activity Conference, Berlin, September 1981.
Schwarz, J. C. Effects of peer familiarity on the behavior of preschoolers in a novel situation. *Journal of Personality and Social Psychology,* 1972, *24,* 276–284.
Skarin, K. Cognitive and contextual determinants of stranger fear in six- and eleven-month-old infants. *Child Development,* 1977, *48,* 537–544.
Smith, P. K., & Dutton, S. Play and training in direct and innovative problem solving. *Child Development,* 1979, *50,* 830–836.
Smock, C. D., & Holt, B. G. Children's reaction to novelty: An experimental study of curiosity motivation. *Child Development,* 1962, *33,* 631–642.
Sorce, J. F., & Emde, R. N. Mother's presence is not enough: Effect of emotional availability on infant exploration. *Developmental Psychology,* 1981, *17,* 737–745.
Sroufe, L. A. Wariness of strangers and the study of infant development. *Child Development,* 1977, *48,* 731–746.
Sroufe, L. A., & Waters, E. Attachment as an organizational construct. *Child Development,* 1977, *48,* 1184–1199.
Stallings, J. Implementation and child effects of teaching practices in follow-through classrooms. *Monograph of the Society for Research in Child Development,* 1975, *40*(7–8, Serial No. 163).
Sylva, K., Bruner, J., & Genova, P. The role of play in the problem solving of children 3–5 years of age. In J. Bruner, A. Jolly, & K. Sylva (Eds.), *Play: Its role in development and evolution.* New York: Basic Books, 1976.
Vandell, D. L., Wilson, K. S., & Buchanan, N. R. Peer interaction in the first year of life: An examination of its structure, content, and sensitivity to toys. *Child Development,* 1980, *51,* 481–488.
Vandenberg, B. The role of play in the development of insightful tool-using strategies. *Merrill-Palmer Quarterly,* 1981, *27,* 97–109.
Vidler, D. C. Curiosity. In S. Ball (Ed.), *Motivation in education.* New York: Academic Press, 1977.
Vliestra, A. G. Effects of adult-directed activity, number of toys, and sex of child on social and exploratory behavior in young children. *Merrill-Palmer Quarterly,* 1980, *26,* 231–238.
Weinraub, M., & Putney, E. The effects of height on infants' social responses to unfamiliar persons. *Child Development,* 1978, *49,* 598–603.
Weisler, A., & McCall, R. B. Exploration and play. *American Psychologist,* 1976, *31,* 492–508.
Willemsen, E., Flaherty, D., Heaton, C., & Ritchey, G. Attachment behavior of one-year-olds as a function of mother vs. father, sex of child, session, and toys. *Genetic Psychology Monographs,* 1974, *90,* 305–324.
Williams, R. B. Reinforcement, behavior constraint, and the overjustification effect. *Journal of Personality and Social Psychology,* 1980, *39,* 599–614.
Wohlwill, J. F. A conceptual analysis of exploratory behavior: The "specific-diversive" distinction

revisited. In H. Day (Ed.), *Advances in intrinsic motivation and aesthetics*. New York: Plenum, 1981.

Yarrow, L. J., Rubenstein, J. L., & Pederson, F. A. *Infant and environment*. New York: Halsted, 1975.

Young, G., & Lewis, M. Effects of familiarity and maternal attention on infant peer relations. *Merrill-Palmer Quarterly*, 1979, *25*, 105–119.

Zimmerman, B. J., & Pike, E. O. Effects of modeling and reinforcement on the acquisition and generalization of question-asking behavior. *Child Development*, 1972, *43*, 892–907.

# 11 Play, Novelty, and Stimulus Seeking

Michael J. Ellis
*University of Oregon*

## INTRODUCTION

Customarily, play behavior has been studied in the light of systems of interpretation generated to explain other functional behaviors. Thus, behavioristic, psychoanalytic, and learning theories were expanded to encompass the phenomena of play and playfulness. The result was often awkward but the process was useful in that it pointed up the limits of the theories. In the last few years, according to Csikszentmihalyi (1976), a theoretical system derived largely from attempts to theorize about play have sent ideas moving in the opposite direction, and this chapter attempts to continue that process.

This chapter is about intrinsically motivated behavior that is not directly maintained by the contingent rewards involving the transfer of materials or energy, or the promise of such in the future. It involves behaviors that do not seem tied to food, tokens, or smiles. Even though it is not easy to see the consummatory act in others, we must be willing to accept the notion that this behavior is motivated and lawful.

## STIMULUS SEEKING

Explanations for intrinsically motivated behavior have led to theories of information seeking and salience of reward that have much to say about the maintenance of socially appropriate behaviors, hyperactivity, creativity, and attention. Some have gone further and argued in a circular fashion that such intrinsically motivated behavior, being disconnected from extrinsic rewards, is play because play is the behavior conducted for its own sake. The only way out of this circular trap, while honoring the requirement for a motivational system that impels and guides behavior, is to examine in greater detail the nature of the rewards presumed to accrue inside the player.

One of the systems propounded to explain and order playful behavior is that it produces information (Ellis, 1973). The possession of information conveys a biological advantage to individuals wresting their survival from changing and changeable habitats. Thus, playful individuals survive and the trait is exaggerated or stabilized by natural selection. To play, an organism must possess an internal system that can remember, recognize, and process new configurations and be rewarded by the information contained in them. The explanations involving this chain argue that exposure to novelty and the resolution of uncertainties lead to arousal and that attaining moderate levels of arousal are rewarding. This work has recently been reviewed by Hurwitz (1975) and Wood (1977).

The work on this notion harks back to the early work of Hebb (1949) on sensory restriction, Mackworth (1948) on vigilance, and then Berlyne (1960) on arousal and the properties of stimuli. Berlyne, however, is responsible for the important notion that stimuli can be described in terms of their collative properties of novelty, complexity, and surprisingness, which depend not on the configuration of the stimulus itself but on the relation of a stimulus to the train of stimuli in which it is embedded. Novelty, of course, refers to the fact that the stimulus has not been perceived before. Complex objects of stimulus fields contain more elements or relations between stimuli that capture attention. Surprisingness stems from the dissonance generated by an expectation not being realized in a way that is not threatening, as in the punch line of a joke.

Thus, relations between stimuli are important, and those relationships are either salient or not. The salient stimuli are those signaling a contingency to be acted on and carry the reward inherent in their response. Nonsalient stimuli are rewarding at first but with repetition cease to be so. When these stimuli become familiar, simple, and redundant, they do not capture attention nor do they provide the reward of being arousing. Thus, the collative properties can be thought of as those properties of stimuli that carry information by resolving uncertainties and that unless they signal extrinsic rewards soon cease to be rewarding.

The research dependent on Berlyne's (1960) original work with the collative properties of novelty, complexity, and surprisingness (incongruity) has maintained the list of collative properties largely as they were. However, recently, first Dember (1960) and more recently Barnett (1976) have argued that they all boil down in essence to novelty. A novel stimulus field is unfamiliar in some respect and when a difference is identified, it is attended to, often generating its incorporation into the perceiver's cognitive scheme of things. If after awhile its probabilities and relations to the field in which it is embedded become well known and familiar, it ceases to generate the treatment reserved for novel stimuli.

Complexity is not really a different property of stimuli. That which is complex is merely the combination of novelties that require the perceiver to deal with first one juxtaposition of stimuli and then another, so that it is not possible to make a simple encompassing unit response or decision about it. The complex array of stimuli contains more information, but at root it still is merely the felting together of novel elements.

Thus it is argued that humans, and other mammals, are wired to struggle to reduce the bewildering buzzing confusion of stimulus arrays surrounding them to order, to find in them the "causal context" that links parts with others in a way that produces predictability (Gibson, 1969). The process of searching for the causal context simplifies matters by reducing uncertainty or, obversely, by gaining information. This process of decoding linkages and likelihoods has clear biological utility, and as a result mechanisms that produce the search have been stabilized in the genotype.

The mechanism seems best described by curiosity and playfulness. In a broad sense the propensity to play, to expand behavior divergently, pushes individuals to the limits of what is currently known to them and beyond, thus improving each individual's preparedness for dealing with the changing circumstances of the individual's habitat.

So to summarize this point, it seems reasonable to consider that there is really only one collative property: novelty. Novelty represents the unexpected that arouses or alerts the organism. To the extent that the arousal process is rewarding, then novelty is an intrinsically sought-for stimulus pattern and this explains much behavior. "Stimulus seeking" is the general term used to describe the propensity to seek out information; yet it is clearly not any stimulus that is sought. Information bearing, or novel, stimuli are sought, not redundant and familiar stimuli (Hurwitz, 1975). So this chapter uses the terms *novelty seeking* to describe the behavior itself and *stimulation seeking* to connect the behavior to the reward presumed to maintain it.

The question for developmentalists devolves into whether this propensity to be rewarded by novelty develops or comes fully developed as a fundamental characteristic of the genotype. If the former, then what is the true course and path whereby humans acquire their highly developed capacity to generate information and be rewarded by its processing?

The study of the impact of the collative properties of novelty, and its obverse, familiarity, on very young children has inadvertently been accelerated by the use of novel stimuli in research on memory. Typically, researchers interested in the development of memory in preverbal children have had to rely on differential responding to recurrent or, in our context, familiar compared with new stimuli. Thus memory researchers have argued that if the very young child behaves differently to one or other of a pair of stimuli, one of which is familiar, then that is evidence that the child must have remembered the familiar stimulus.

Sophian (1980) identifies a flaw in the recognition paradigm. It is as convincing to argue that changes across development in behavior that differentiates between novel and familiar stimuli—regard, or fixation, diffuse behavior, heart-rate, etc.—result from changes in preference for novel/familiar stimuli. Sophian goes further by citing several authors that assert that recognition is a primitive memory form that is invariant over development and that it is the emergence of a preference for novelty that accounts for the differentiation of the infant's behavior. Thus the memory work leaves a rich tailing of data with which to study preference for collative properties of stimuli over the course of development.

The earlier assumptions that memory for stimuli gradually develops allowing older children to habituate more rapidly, to recognize familiar stimuli more rapidly, and to require fewer dimensional differences to discriminate recurring stimuli can be reinterpreted. It seems appropriate to assert that what is developing in children is not their capacity to recognize but *either* their emergent capacity to extract information from a display *or* to be rewarded by it *or* both. Thus, as children accumulate experience, they could just as well be said to increase their capacity either to extract information or to habituate, to reject familiar stimuli more quickly, or to extract finer grain information from the display.

Research on habituation/preference suggests that prior to 8 weeks the infant prefers or fixates longer on familiar stimuli (Fantz, 1964; Weizmann, Cohen, & Pratt, 1971; Wetherford & Cohen, 1973). However, at about 8 weeks of age the preference shifts in favor of novelty. This suggests that by this time infants have developed both of the ingredients necessary for information seeking—capacity to recognize previously presented patterns/stimuli and the propensity to select elements that are different.

The propensity to attend to novel elements or, to stretch a point, the incongruous requires that there be some motivational system that either rewards the infant for exposure to the novel or the incongruous per se or indirectly rewards the individual for organizing the data on the display and bringing it into a "cognitive schema." When the display is correctly classified and juxtaposed coherently with the memories of other events, it becomes familiar and its contingencies predictable. If it is salient for survival, then it may hold attention or induce action but, if not, then its capacity to generate attention wanes with repeated exposure. This is simply an extension of the orienting reaction in which changes in an array of stimuli require a memory and an attention-directing function rather than merely a threshold.

Thus, at 8 weeks the additional cognitive structures necessary to be rewarded by novelty rather than familiarity seem to be in place. Although it can be said of adults that there is a positive affect associated with intermediate levels of information that identifies preference, in the sense "to like," we cannot yet claim that infants like intermediate levels of information. However, it is plausible to assume that there is positive affect, a sense of reward, that comes from removing inconsistency, or incongruity from the total environmental display, because it patterns so much of the behavior of all humans older than 8 weeks. Getting to know about the environment influences survival and this biologically critical capacity is exhibited very early in development.

Given that infants start to exhibit preferences for novel stimuli as early as 8 weeks, the preferred stimuli seem to escalate in complexity thereafter. Karmel (1969) reviewed the literature and plotted the mean fixation times, the index of preference, with the amounts of contour for six studies in which methods were comparable and which represented different groups of children from "birth" through "20 weeks" and "older." The modal value for preferred complexity as measured by "contour" increased as children aged. Similar findings but with different stimuli are reported by Martin (1975), and Bradbury (1975). Such observations were formalized by Coopersmith (1976) who asserted that as the complexity of the object increased logarithmically, the exploration time increased linearly. If fixation time is considered a functional index of exploration, then all these findings are in accord with the early theoretical predictions of Dember and Earl (1957) that the cognitive processes of the developing young would rapidly become more complex in response to the processed information garnered from the environment. They are also clearly in accord with our experience.

Dember and Earl (1957) also noted that for the upward spiral in cognitive complexity to take place, then there had to be a concomitant upward spiral in the complexity of the stimuli leading the developing child (or person for that matter). This would explain the "preference" data. Further, Dember and Earl claim there is an optimal disparity beyond which the person could no longer organize the information—it became mere noise. It is this notion that leads us to try to order and structure the stimuli presented to/received by the child to facilitate the process of development through education (Bruner, 1972; Hunt, 1961).

The body of research reviewed customarily analyzed data by sex in addition to the other independent variables, and there were repeated hints that the process of development of stimulus preference was different for boys and girls. There seemed to be two threads to the findings reviewed. One school of research found that males habituated to stimuli faster than females, arguing that in some way males processed information faster (Pancratz & Cohen, 1970; Weizmann, Cohen, & Pratt, 1971). Others, Franks and Berg (1975), Greenberg & Weizmann (1971), and Caron and Caron (1969) found the opposite.

This must remain an open question at this time. The eventual resolution of the question whether males and females grow along different developmental paths will have to take into account the propensity for males to be more active and for females to develop faster. These aspects of the developmental process, and probably many others, will need to be brought together to explain differences in age-related change in stimulus seeking across males and females.

Ignoring sex differences, the evidence seems clearly to support the notion that increased complexity is preferred with increased age, if it is accepted that fixation time measures preference. However, at around 2 years of age there is evidence that indicates that although there is a relationship between visual fixation time and complexity, there is no consistent relationship between fixation time and preference (Wood, 1977). Thus, it may be that mere duration of regard does not measure the cognitive processes underpinning the preference, at least in those 2-years-old or older. It is most likely that as children age, they become more skilled at determining salience of stimuli and are more able to interact with stimulus objects. They will also have greater stores of representations of past events so that "preference" has more dimensions. This notion is in accord with Hunt's (1963) theoretical position:

> Once children have been exposed to a given pattern of stimulation enough times to make it familiar, the emerging recognition of the pattern brings pleasure that motivates an effort to retain or re-elicit the pattern. I have further attempted to elaborate this explanation with the notion that, after a pattern has continued to be familiar for a time, it is variation in that pattern that brings pleasure and the effort to find that variation in either the child's own activities or in external stimulation. One can consider none of these suggestions established, but they constitute hypotheses for investigation [p. 273].

Hunt's ideas are borne out by a body of research conducted on children of about 3–5½ years of age at Illinois. The research that is summarized later in the chapter used more global indicators of preference in which aspects of the whole and naturalistic interplay of the child, peers, and environment were studied by Gramza (Ellis & Scholtz, 1978). He did not restrict the observed variables to regard or expressed preference but made the assumption that total behavior represented the final expression of the interaction of stimulus input from objects and peers and the reverberations of past experiences. When this was done, it was clear that more complex stimuli attracted greater interaction with these children.

The literature on the topic of novelty/complexity preference thins rapidly further up the time course of development. It is as if after a few months the cognitive complexity of the developing child and hence the complexity of the preferred interactions has exceeded the capacity of the researchers to quantify and control the stimuli.

For example Caron, Caron, Minichiello, Weiss, and Friedman (1977) recently have criticized the two fundamental methods used to observe the effect of reduced novelty or increased familiarity in infants. They argue that the method of presentation of paired displays with familiar and novel displays alternating can as well be considered serially alternating displays if the infant adopts a strategy of observing just one side of the display. They further argue that more complex displays take more scanning time to extract information so fixation time is merely an index of the processing of the information added into the display and not necessarily preference.

Wood (1977) found that 2- to 4-year-old children exhibited no age-related preference for stimuli that she asserted exhibited varying information. Wood created arrays of flashing lights. She arranged for some to flash randomly, some to repeat a random pattern, and a third set to alternate red and green. The first array it was claimed provided information, the second complexity, and the third alternation. Not surprising to me was the fact that no differences emerged in the 66 four-year-old subjects. It seems clear that the randomness of the displays carefully eliminated information—the visual equivalent of white noise, and the complex displays, if they were recognized as repeated displays, contained very little information. Red and green flashes would become redundant very quickly. Yet Wood claimed that children had not yet acquired the quest for information that characterizes adults.

In sum, it is clear that the recognition paradigm that once looked so clear is now muddied methodologically on several counts. The concept of information and the time it takes to extract it from a display raises questions concerning the assumption that visual fixation in the very young indicates preference. Because it is difficult to obtain expressions of preference from infant subjects, without perhaps invading their central nervous system or discovering a noninvasive indicator of pleasure, the question may have to remain moot. However it is clear that infants are complex in themselves; they learn quickly and are responsive to information in their environments. Their capacity to extract information rises rapidly with experience, which presents difficulties in simplifying the process to allow research.

Hutt and McGrew (1969) raise an important issue in which they clearly separate "interestingness" from "pleasingness." They argued that for us to make inferences concerning what is pleasing we must present the child with choices and have the child display it. They designed a study that went beyond the classical experimenter-paced familiarity display studies and allowed the children themselves to step through a series of displays that varied in complexity. The children studied were old compared to the infants on the majority of studies considered previously. Using 5-, 8-, and 11-year-old children, they found that voluntary viewing time decreased with age. Thus, extracting the information was done more efficiently by older children. They also found that children of 5 years preferred simpler displays whereas 11-year-olds preferred the complex. Eight-year-olds were undecided. Hutt and McGrew argue then that not until age 11 can it be demonstrated that the people will choose more complex rather than simpler displays. This raises serious questions, yet seems to be dissonant with other work presented later. However, it is entered here to introduce the notion that "pleasingness" is best studied when children can overtly signal their pleasure behaviorally. This approach to preference uses children rather than infants and is summarized in the following.

The manipulation of stimulus displays by altering the grain of the checkerboard, the width of stripes, or number of turns in random polygon produces the kind of display containing little meaningful information. Even very young will only select them for attention when they are presented, suddenly triggering an orienting reaction, or when a meaningful and salient contingency is attached to the stimulus, or when a state of perceptual deprivation exists. Thus the difficulties of conducting research with completely quantified complexity has cramped the development of the time course of preferred complexity started by Karmel (1969).

The next data set bearing on the problem concerns preferences expressed by children for toys and play objects. This was the thread running through the work conducted by Gramza on children 3 through 5 years. Clearly Gramza was not able to measure the dimensions of the information contained in ''real'' play objects. They presented stimuli varying in many ways most of which were beyond direct measurement. This is in direct contrast to the undimensional displays of the work cited so far. Further, Gramza extended this work to include large and playful behaviors rather than restrict respondents to the pressing of buttons or measuring their fixations. The behavior of concern was the naturalistic responding of children to careful manipulations of features of a large natural play setting.

The upshot of a long series of studies (reviewed by Ellis & Scholtz, 1978) can be summarized by saying that, whereas it is possible to manipulate various characteristics of play objects, the only way to influence the interaction consistently of children with the objects is to manipulate what Gramza called their ''functional complexity.''

Functional complexity is defined as the ''number, variety, and quality of responses the objects are capable of eliciting and sustaining.'' Thus it was not a characteristic inherent in the display per se that generated preference by the opportunities for interaction that garnered sustained attention but its capacity for interaction. This work paralleled the work of Hutt (1966) who also showed that it was the interactional capacity of a play object that generated play behavior.

For example, Gramza and Scholtz (1974) created 3-feet high cubes that were identical in every way except that one was painted in a 9-inch blue and red checkerboard pattern, whereas the other had one large block of blue with a red border on each side. There was the same area devoted to each color, yet their stimulus complexity was markedly different. The cubes did not generate any differences in their play usage. It was concluded that they were equally complex (or simple). However, simply cutting a few footholds in the boxes presented opportunities for climbing, feeling, poking, peeking, and so on, and the preference change was dramatic (Gramza & Scholtz, 1974).

To summarize, it seems that up to 8 weeks infants seem to prefer familiar stimuli. They can differentiate the stimuli before then, but only thereafter do they express a tendency to seek novelty. Their preference thereafter rises rapidly with experiences until the point may be where their cognitive complexity soon exceeds the capacity of the researcher to quantify the stimuli. When three or a little older, preference for objects with ''functional complexity'' manifests itself in realistic settings. Finally, in late childhood Hutt produces data that argue for separating "interestingness" (i.e., an object's or display's information load) from its "pleasingness" (i.e., its relative capacity to engender positive affect).

## SOCIAL DEVELOPMENT

Frequently researchers, educators, and designers, in attempting to provide information to sustain play and learning ignore a major source of information and functional complexity in an environment—other people. It is clear that we acquire social skills over the course of development. We customarily organize our thinking around the notion of social competence and its instrumentality for the world of work. It is equally clear that social competence is instrumental in involving others in the search for information. Others are a rich source of information and social competence is also critical for the play process.

Social competence requires first an ability to separate the self from others and the environment and then the ability to read the intentions of others with a reasonable probability and to integrate them and their ensuing actions into a personal stream of behavior (Whiteside, Busch, & Horner, 1976). It requires the individual to initiate their own acts in appropriate relations to those of others, to time those acts, and to communicate about them. It also requires a capacity to negotiate, lead, and follow. Without these capacities, it is not possible to integrate peers, objects, and self within a setting to maintain a rewarding stream of behavior. Thus, it can be seen that cooperative behavior necessary to accomplish a known or given task is difficult and cooperating to define a goal as well as achieve it is still more so.

These competencies require an accurate map of the social and objective contingencies in an environment. However, the network is not fixed but probablistic. Multiple exposures, probes, responses are needed to establish the network of likelihoods. Given the nature of the social setting with all its complexity and the propensity of children (people) to seek novelty, it is clear that very considerable learning is accomplished in situations where the children are placed together. Whiteside et al. (1976) show work that children make the journey to cooperative play in 4 to 5 years, and there is much evidence of a developmental path along which children play. This next section attempts to review and organize some of the work completed on social relations in maturing children and the role others play in the ongoing search for information.

### Social Relations

There seems to be a clear thread of evidence running through our own experiences and research data that people themselves are a potent source of information and that social interactions are sought for the stimulation that results.

Woodworth in 1958 (cited by Haskett, 1974) identified that children were a source of information for other children. More recently there have been some papers addressing this topic empirically. The first of which I am aware was conducted by Wuellner in 1969 at Illinois (see Ellis & Scholtz, 1978) who added a piece of novel apparatus to the free-play period in a child development program. Baseline line data on a large variety of elements of the children's free-ranging behavior was established over six sessions. On the introduction of the novel piece of apparatus for the seventh through ninth session, the behavior of the group was dramatically changed. The behavior during the baseline period was diffuse with the children ranging across the space, the possibilities, and the partners and with boys more active than the girls. After introduction the children's behavior was focused, crowded with intense interpersonal interaction as the object was explored together. The normal high level of activity emitted by boys was reduced to that of girls as they clustered with them around the novel object.

This finding was mirrored more recently in a study reported by Haskett (1974). Here social interaction was explored directly. Again the baseline rate of interpersonal social interaction, this time with adults, was so dramatically changed by the introduction of novel toys that Haskett argued ''that novelty elicits social play.'' The following year Eckerman, Whatley, and Kutz (1975) reported that by 2 years of age young children exhibited a strong tendency to integrate novel playthings with outgoing ''positive social interaction'' in preference to interaction with their mothers.

A more detailed analysis of slightly older children was conducted by Scholtz and Ellis (1975) who deliberately manipulated novelty and complexity of a play setting and then observed the relative incidence of interactions with objects and peers.

To study novelty and complexity conjointly, Scholtz and Ellis (1975) implemented an interesting design with groups of 3- to 5-year-old children playing in three play settings. One simple and one complex setting were maintained unchanged for 3 weeks. This allowed the observation of the interactive effect of novelty or complexity to be observed. Preference for interaction with the play objects was less in the simple setting than the complex and declined in both during the study. Children's preference for interaction with peers had the opposite trend. The third group experienced a complexification of the setting such that in the first week the setting was simple, in the second intermediate, and the third complex. Thus in each week there were novel elements and the overall complexity of the setting rose. Preference for objects oscillated predictably, and preference for peers was intermediate when summed across the sessions.

To summarize, the children soon habituated to the objects in the setting and with increasing exposure introduced social play.

All these results can be simplified by arguing that the available stimulus/information potential of the setting is a powerful influence on behavior. The children will interact with whatever aspect of the setting has the greatest probability of generating information. In Wuellner's study (Ellis and Scholtz, 1978), the new object required social interaction to permit exploration. Formerly diffuse activity was concentrated on the new object. In Haskett's study, the presence of a single new toy in a setting with two participants stimulated this mutual play. The people cooperated to mine the information available.

The evanescence of novelty was identified by Haskett and Scholtz. The interaction waned as familiarity grew. In Scholtz' study the only way to maintain interaction with objects was to escalate their complexity. Scholtz concluded that *peers* are a rich source of information and that with passage of time (or the accumulation of exposure) peers, being dynamic and complex, were the best source of information and were thus preferred over objects in a play setting.

Wade and Ellis (1971) also found effects of social interactions on behavior. In studies designed to measure the impact of peers on activity of 4- and 5-year-olds, they systematically varied both complexity of the setting and the numbers of children using the setting. They found the strongest effects when dyads used the setting. They argued that when only two children were playing, it was required for them to intermesh their activities to include each other. The input from each serves to enrich the activity of the other and maintain higher levels of behavior than when playing alone or as a member of a group of four. Wade and Ellis found no effect due to varied complexity of the setting, again suggesting the power of peers to maintain and direct behavior.

This finding among 5- to 6-year-olds seems to be a logical extension of the turn taking social play with words and objects described by Garvey (1977). Here very young children learn the benefits of interacting systemtically with others, often the caregiver, but also with equally young peers. The peekaboo, alternate clapping, or verbal signals and the alternation of complementary acts with objects (e.g., rolling a ball back and forth) all indicate that the child has learned to traffic with others. The costs of honoring the rule are repaid with a series of ongoing events that generate sharp stimuli, tests of the environment, and/or tests of self.

This set of data supports the idea that others and their social interactions lead to the generation of rewarding information. This is in accord also with our private experience as adults. We as social beings value highly social interaction for probably many reasons. The informational content of that process manifests itself in extremely complex interpersonal exchange of information. We call it conversation, gossiping, joshing, joking, "playing the dozens," visiting (Kochman, 1969). The central feature seems to be the playing with the contents of our own thoughts and that of others. The possibilities are very extensive, and it is recognized as a highly rewarding activity among adults. It has been indicated that "visiting with family and friends" ranks highly on surveys of leisure activity and is also reported as activity that the respondents most desire to do more (Ellis & Hood, 1975).

At the adult level of the social interaction continuum then it is clear the verbal interplay is common and rewarding. How does this manifest itself among children?

The answer to the question was first advanced by Parten in 1932 when she showed a propensity for children to escalate the social complexity of their play as they aged. Thus she proposed the stages of play as beginning with solitary play and developing through parallel and associative play to cooperative play.

Iwanaga (1973) and Whiteside et al. (1976) confirmed Parten's (1932) findings recently. A similar pattern of increasing time spent in more socially complex behavior with increased age was found in young Chinese American children. Iwanaga categorized social play continuum into independent, parallel, complementary, and integrative behaviors. Boys and girls followed the same path, but Iwanaga found a sudden burst of integrative social behavior in the play of boys of 5 years of age.

This fits well with our conceptions of escalating complexity to the point where we as adults can cooperate to generate and trade verbal information and the necessity for physical interaction with the environment to generation information drops away. Thus as knowledge of the matrix of social contingencies expands, capacity to sustain complex social interactions that generate information also expands. This concept led to the notion that the mode of choice was integrative/cooperative social interaction and that solitary/independent play was immature.

Moore, Evertson, & Brophy (1974) questioned the notion that solitary play is necessarily immature. They point out that solitary/independent play has a structure in and of itself, from passive watching through to becoming involved in a challenging problem solving activity. The solitary player may well be engaged in complex problem solving and independent play may be as functional as integrative play albeit less common. Thus solitary play is not necessarily an indicant of immaturity.

Garvey (1977) devotes a whole chapter to a fine-grained analysis of what she called "ritualistic play." The rituals or turn takings involved a paradigm in that a complex of elements was repeated and could involve simple pairings of utterances to multiple elements involving movement and utterances.

The content of the paradigm could be shifted by including new elements from the same class as the interplayers proceeded through the rounds as turns. Further, some rituals involved snytactically correct connections between one person's utterance and the others. Garvey (1977) found that these ritualistic interplays grew more complex with age.

I suspect these rituals become so complex that they eventually merge with our conventions for conversation that create the structure within which the introduction of variances is interesting, irritating or humorous.

Garvey (1977) concludes the analysis with the following:

> A ritual is unmistakably play. It exhibits all the descriptive characteristics by which instances of play are recognized. It is apparently enjoyable, performed for *its own sake rather than for a goal such as information exchange or the resolution of a*

> *disagreement* (my emphasis). It is quite spontaneous and engages both partners in precision performances, rituals are generally based on some other behavior that *could be performed* as nonplay, like peeking out of the doors, exchanging greetings, asking and answering questions, and so on. Finally, rituals are very clearly marked as nonliteral by their repetition and by their highly controlled rhythmic execution.
>
> The message, "This is play," is emblazoned on the ritual.

There is an inconsistency here between Garvey's (1977) conclusion that in ritual information exchange is not the goal and the inclusion of this material in a chapter on information seeking. It points up the difficulty in accounting for repeated and presumably redundant acts during complexes of behavior that have all the other characteristics of play. The notion that information seeking is the goal of play is not convincing at first glance when the unitary acts observed are redundant. This problem presents itself not only in interpersonal play but in solitary repetition and in the stereotyped acts of animals and people.

The only way the information-seeking motive can be sustained without having to plead an expensive exception is to argue that the inconsistency arises from miscalculating the level at which the behavioral complex as ritual is analyzed. If the complex of acts is considered as the unit of interaction, then it as a whole can carry information or the answer to a question.

In her analysis, Garvey (1977) not only timed all the elements of a ritual but also noted intensity and tone of the utterances as well as other "qualities" of the acts comprising the rounds. The children were capable of creating and following multidimensional paradigm shifts in which timing, tone, intensity were all varied systematically. Thus, in subtle ways there are new answers in passing to each new round.

A series of questions that could sustain a ritualistic interplay could be:

Will the other recognize the invitation to follow a paradigm?

Will the other comprehend and follow a syntactical modification to the paradigm?

What modifications can I introduce?

How long can this ritual be kept going?

. . . and so forth.

All these questions require multiple rounds to establish the answer and generate the information.

Adopting a similar explanation for other repeated events that are similar and apparently redundant, it can be argued that the question refers to the set of repetitions not the unit acts. Where there are probabilistic responses or outcomes, the lawfulness of the interaction will require, by definition, many repeated responses to answer questions like:

Does it always do that?

What are the limits of my capacity?

Can I always do this?

Thus, I argue that even in apparently repetitious acts, a player can be generating information. When that information flow drops below a rewarding level or the question is answered, then the repetition can only be maintained by extrinsic rewards.

## SUMMARY

In the course of development it is clear that children interact selectively with peers and objects in their environment. Their behavior includes peers in their search for rewarding interactions. As they accumulate experience the complexity of the information, generating rewards increases. Usually, the most potent source of information in the child's environments are other children. Thus as their experience mounts and their capacity to communicate expands increasingly integrative and cooperative behavior is evinced. As children mature, they move through progressive stages of social playful interaction till at maturity (this point is probably at adolescence) they reach a stage where cognitive/verbal interaction is highly developed and preferred.

This chapter identifies that there is a progression to the way in which young humans mine their physical and social environment for rewarding stimuli. The data starts firmly and simply but soon fades as the children rapidly gain complexity, thus often thwarting the researchers' need to simplify the situation.

The notion of the interaction between the cumulative effects of being rewarded for processing information and the selection of increasingly complex social and physical stimuli is in accord with the data and our experience. Thus, information seeking seems a profitable framework for viewing the process of development.

## ACKNOWLEDGMENT

The author acknowledges the benefit of critical reading and comments by R. Shewchuk.

## REFERENCES

Barnett, L. A. Play and intrinsic rewards. *Journal of Humanistic Psychology,* 1976, *16,* 83–87.

Berlyne, D. E. *Conflict, arousal, and curiosity.* New York: McGraw-Hill, 1960.

Bradbury, H. Consistency of children's inconsistent performances attributable to novelty. *Developmental Psychology,* 1975, *11,* 79–86.

Bruner, J. The nature and uses of immaturity. *American Psychologist,* 1972, *20,* 163–180.

Caron, A. J., Caron, R. F., Minichiello, M. D., Weiss, S. J., & Friedman, S. L. Constraints on the

use of the novelty familiarity method in the assessment of infant discrimination. *Child Development,* 1977, *48,* 747–762.
Caron, R. F., & Caron, A. J. Degree of stimulus complexity and habituation of visual fixation in infants. *Psychonomic Science,* 1969, *14,* 78–79.
Coopersmith, P. F. The effects of preceding event upon subsequent object exploration, stimulus seeking, and novelty preference of kindergarten children. *Dissertation Abstracts International,* 1976, (7-B) 3570.
Csikszentmihalyi, M. What play says about behaviour. *Ontario Psychologist,* 1976, *8,* 5–11.
Dember, W. N. *Psychology of perception.* New York: Henry Holt, 1960.
Dember, W. N., & Earl, R. W. Analysis of exploratory, manipulatory and curiosity behaviors. *Psychological Review,* 1957, *64,* 91–96.
Eckerman, C. O., Whatley, J. L., & Kutz, S. L. Growth of social play with peers during the second year of life. *Developmental Psychology,* 1975, *11,* 42–49.
Ellis, M. J. *Why people play.* Englewood Cliffs, N.J.: Prentice-Hall, 1973.
Ellis, M. J., & Hood, C. C. Leisure in Halifax, Nova Scotia. *Behavioral Attitude and Opinion Study: Report to the City Council,* 1975.
Ellis, M. J., & Scholtz, G. J. L. *Activity and play of children.* Englewood Cliffs, N.J.: Prentice-Hall, 1978.
Fantz, R. L. Visual experience in infants: Decreased attention to familiar patterns relative to novel ones. *Science,* 1964, *146,* 668–670.
Franks, A., & Berg, W. K. Effects of visual complexity and sex of infant in the conjugate reinforcement paradigm. *Developmental Psychology,* 1975, *11,* 388–389.
Garvey, C. *Play.* Cambridge, Mass.: Harvard University Press, 1977.
Gibson, E. J. *Principles of perceptual learning and development.* New York: Appleton-Century-Crofts, 1969.
Gramza, A. F., & Scholtz, G. J. L. Children's responses to visual complexity in a play setting. *Psychological Reports,* 1974, *35,* 895–899.
Greenberg, D. J., & Weizmann, F. The measurement of visual attention in infants: A comparison of two methodologies. *Journal of Experimental Child Psychology,* 1971, *11,* 234–243.
Haskett, G. J. The exploratory nature of children's social relations. *Paper presented at Biennial Southeastern Conference The Society for Research in Child Development, Chapel Hill,* 1974, *ED 101827.*
Hebb, D. O. *The organization of behavior.* New York: Wiley, 1949.
Hunt, J. McV. *Intelligence and experience.* New York: Ronald, 1961.
Hunt, J. McV. Motivation inherent in information processing and action. In O. J. Harvey (Ed.), *Motivation and social organization: Cognitive determinants.* New York: Ronald Press, 1963.
Hurwitz, R. *Autonomic arousal, sensory deprivation and response for visual information.* Unpublished M.A. thesis. Arizona State University, 1975.
Hutt, C. Exploration and play in children. In P. A. Jewell & C. Loizos (Eds.), *Play exploration and territory in mammals, Symposium of the Royal Zoological Society of London, # 18.* London: Academic Press, 1966.
Hutt, C., & McGrew, P. C. Do children really prefer complexity? *Psychonomic Science,* 1969, *17,* 113–114.
Iwanaga, M. Development of interpersonal play structure in three, four and five year old children. *Journal of Research and Development in Education,* 1973, *6,* 71–82.
Karmel, B. The effect of age complexity and amount of contour on pattern preferences in human infants. *Journal of Experimental Child Psychology,* 1969, *7,* 339–354.
Kochman, T. Rapping in the Black ghetto. *Trans-Action,* 1969, *6,* 26–34.
Mackworth, N. H. The breakdown of vigilance during prolonged visual search. *Journal of Experimental Psychology,* 1948, 6–21.

Martin, R. M. Effects of familiar and complex stimuli on infant attention. *Developmental Quarterly,* 1975, *11,* 178–185.
Moore, N., Evertson, C., & Brophy, J. Solitary play: Some functional reconsiderations. *Developmental Psychology,* 1974, *10,* 830–834.
Pancratz, C. N., & Cohen, L. B. Recovery of habituation in infants. *Journal of Experimental Child Psychology,* 1970, *9,* 208–216.
Parten, M. B. Social participation among pre-school children. *Journal of Abnormal Psychology,* 1932, *27,* 243–269.
Scholtz, G. J. L., & Ellis, M. J. Repeated exposure to objects and peers in a play setting. *Journal of Experimental Child Psychology,* 1975, *19,* 448–455.
Sophian, C. Habituation is not enough: Novelty prefences search and memory in infancy. *Merill Palmer Quarterly,* 1980, *26,* 239–58.
Wade, M. G. & Ellis, M. J. Measurement of free range activity in children as modified by social and environmental complexity. *The American Journal of Clinical Nutrition,* 1971, *24,* 1457–60.
Weizmann, F., Cohen, L. B., & Pratt, J. Novelty, familiarity and the development of infant attention. *Developmental Psychology,* 1971, *4,* 149–154.
Wetherford, M. J., & Cohen, L. B. Developmental changes in infant visual preferences for novelty and familiarity. *Child Development,* 1973, *44,* 416–424.
Whiteside, M. F., Busch, F., & Horner, T. From egocentric to cooperative play in young children: A normative study. *Journal of American Academy of Child Psychiatry,* 1976, *15,* 294–313.
Wood, R. L. *Drive and incentive properties of stimulus variability in young children.* Unpublished Ph.D. Dissertation, Arizona State 1977.

# 12 Play, Incongruity, and Humor

Paul E. McGhee
*Texas Tech University*

The inclusion of a chapter on humor in a book dealing with children's play suggests that humor and play must be closely related. It is proposed here that humor can best be viewed as a subset of the broader category of play. More specifically, humor is considered a form of intellectual play; that is, play with ideas. Incongruous ideas (i.e., ideas whose elements are in some way inconsistent with the child's knowledge or understanding of familiar objects or events) are considered here to be a necessary condition for humor, but not a sufficient one.

Conceptualizing humor in this way implies that humor should share many of the properties of make-believe play that are discussed in this book, because make-believe play also consists of play with ideas. Make-believe play does not necessarily lead to the production of incongruous fantasy, but when fantasy incongruities are produced, they should be structurally similar to those experienced as humorous. It is suggested in the following that the child's information-processing frame of mind plays the key role in determining whether humor or some other form of enjoyment is experienced when incongruous relationships are entertained in fantasy play. In the context of ongoing play activities, children shift back and forth between a more serious frame of mind and a playful one. Although great joy and excitement may be experienced in either case, only in the latter case can it take the form of humor.

## WHAT IS HUMOR?

Achieving agreement upon a definition has proved just as difficult for humor as it has for play. Numerous definitions have been offered for both concepts, with each definition capturing certain essential properties of the phenomenon but failing to capture others. Space limitations do not permit a complete review of general or developmental theories of humor here (see Keith-Spiegel, 1972, McGhee, 1979, or McGhee & Goldstein, 1983, for a review), so attention is restricted here to theories, issues, and research that focus on the cognitive aspects of humor development and on the role of incongruity in humor.

I have argued elsewhere (McGhee, 1979) that some form of incongruous or nonfitting relationship is a necessary prerequisite for humor in children, but it is not a sufficient condition for humor. Among adults and older children, much everyday humor contains elements of sex, aggression, or other emotionally salient themes. The humor associated with sex and aggression is not due to the sexual or aggressive themes alone; sex and aggression presented in a straightforward manner may produce a wide range of emotions, but humor does not occur unless these themes are presented in an incongruous way or linked in some way to an independent incongruous event. This may appear not to be the case in very young children, who often laugh uproariously at the mere mention of such words as "pee-pee," "ka-ka," or "doo-doo." The incongruity in this case, however, may be the mere verbalizing of words that are not generally said.

The main effect of increasing the emotional salience of humor material appears to be an increased display of affect (laughter). However, humor cannot be equated with laughter because both adults and children exhibit nonhumorous as well as humorous forms of laughter (see McGhee, 1979, for a discussion of this issue). Because children learn very early that cartoons, jokes, and other clearly defined "funny events" are things that you laugh at, they commonly laugh at humor stimuli that they do not really understand (McGhee, 1974). When genuine humorous laughter does occur, it is a result of certain cognitive insights—the perception of relationships between ideas or events that are in some way at odds with the child's prior knowledge. The laughter produced reflects the pleasure experienced from considering in fantasy an idea or relationship that is *known to be at odds with reality* (as the child sees it).

Regardless of the position taken on the issue of whether all humor relies at some level on incongruity, theorists and investigators studying humor appear to agree that incongruous events *can* be humorous. However, the fact that other kinds of reaction can occur in response to perceived incongruity (namely, interest and curiosity or wariness/fear) suggests that cognitive factors should play central roles in defining humor—not the stimulus situation alone. Distinctive modes of processing information related to incongruities are described in the following. These modes differ in terms of whether the incongruous elements stimulate accomodation and cognitive change. It is suggested here that humor will not be experienced unless the child is in a playful frame of mind, leading to a focus of attention on the absurdity of the incongruous relationships themselves rather than on the modification of existing cognitive structures to fit the novel elements of the incongruous relationship. Incongruous relationships may also be produced in nonhumorous make-believe play. Although basic similarities exist here (e.g., an emphasis on assimilation in the absence of accommodation, as suggested by Piaget, 1962), it is proposed later that humor results from the playful production of fantasy incongruities when relatively greater attention is given to the impossibility or (at later ages) the improbability or inappropriateness of the imagined event.

## ONSET OF THE CAPACITY FOR HUMOR

Research on infant attention and perception has demonstrated that attention is drawn to stimulus events that contain novel elements. This attention tends to be maximized in response to moderate degrees of novelty (McCall & McGhee, 1977). The occurrence of smiling (McCall & McGhee, 1977) and laughter (Sroufe & Wunsch, 1972) by infants in response to novel or incongruous events suggests that infants derive pleasure from making sense out of events that pose some cognitive challenge for comprehension. The key issue here, however, is the point in development at which the enjoyment of incongruous or novel events begins to be associated with the mental experience of humor rather than mere pleasure in successful assimilation of new events following some accommodatory effort.

Little agreement has been reached upon the age at which infants become capable of experiencing incongruous or other events as humorous. Both Shultz (1976) and McGhee (1977, 1979) argued that the perception of incongruities as humorous depends on the development of symbolic capacities that emerge early in the second year. Whereas McGhee proposed that symbolic capacities are necessary for any form of humor, however, Shultz concluded that other more primitive forms of humor occur in the first year. He noted that pleasure in cognitive mastery (i.e., assimilating initially unassimilable events) and certain infant games (e.g., peekaboo) share the characteristic arousal fluctuations associated with humor and should accordingly also be viewed as humor. McGhee (1979) has criticized this view, arguing that other explanations for infant smiling or laughter are available in such cases, eliminating the need to use humor as the explanation for the laughter.

Pien and Rothbart (1980) proposed that the only prerequisites for humor are the capacity for play and the ability to detect incongruity. Because each of these has been observed in infants as young as 4 months of age, they conclude that this is when humor experiences are first possible. McGhee and Chapman (1980) also criticized this view, noting that other explanations offered for infant laughter are sufficient to explain the behavior observed. Rothbart (1973, 1976) herself has noted that an infant's evaluation of the overall context in which an incongruous or arousing event occurs determines whether laughter or crying results (see Sroufe, Waters, & Matas, 1974, for related evidence). Thus, if the situation in which the incongruity occurs is familiar or is perceived as safe or nonthreatening, laughter or smiling should occur. If the situation is perceived as threatening in some way, crying or wariness should occur. Sroufe and Waters (1976) have similarly argued that the infant's interpretation of an incongruous event as safe or threatening determines the quality of the resulting affect and note that the degree of affect (e.g., smiling versus laughter) hinges on the amount of arousal or tension induced. Thus, it is possible to explain laughter in early infancy without consideration of early experiences of humor.

These views indicate that to a great extent definitional issues are at the center of any determination of when infants first begin to experience humor and that it is not strictly an empirical question. The one thing that has been agreed upon, however, is that children's play activities begin to take on new characteristics during the second year. Several chapters in this book draw attention to the fact that early in the second year children begin to treat objects *as if* they were other objects. This new play activity reflects the child's new symbolic capacity that initially consists of mere manipulation of images of objects in the absence of those objects and constitutes the beginning of imaginative or make-believe play. Because this is the first form of play that has generated consistent agreement as being potentially related to humor, further discussion is restricted to developmental changes and cognitive activities associated with children possessing representational capacities.

## Reality Assimilation and Fantasy Assimilation

McGhee (1972, 1979) distinguished between two separate means that symbolic organisms have of making sense out of incongruous events: reality assimilation and fantasy assimilation. Reality assimilation refers to the standard equilibration mechanism described by Piaget (1952). That is, when children encounter stimulus events that are inconsistent with previously stored information about those events, they stretch or accommodate existing schematas or concepts to incorporate the new information. This reality assimilation/accommodation sequence, of course, is how cognitive development occurs. McGhee (1979) argued that until early in the second year this is the only means the infant has for understanding new information. With the onset of representational capacities in the second year, however, the child can disengage the accommodatory half of this cycle and assimilate incongruous or discrepant information *as if* no accommodation were necessary. McGhee has argued that this fantasy assimilation process is central to the young child's experience of humor in connection with incongruity. This position is similar to Piaget's (1962) general explanation of play as a predominance of assimilation over accommodation. This similarity points to the present writer's view that play or playfulness is the basic foundation on which the capacity for humor evolved phylogenetically and develops in children ontogenetically.

*Playful Fantasy and Humor.* If play and fantasy activities are central to young childrens' humor, how then does humor differ from the kind of make-believe play that is a focus of much of this book? An answer to this question requires consideration of the nature of early imaginative play activities. As noted earlier, Piaget (1952) and others (e.g., in this volume, see Chapter 11) have emphasized that humans are novelty-seeking and stimulation-seeking organisms. This leads them to seek out moderately new forms of stimulation long before imaginative capacities have begun to appear. This need to explore appears to be an inherent property of our nervous system. Given this basic tendency in humans, it follows that as new cognitive capacities develop, these should also be used in the service of exploration and maintenance of an optimal level of stimulation. Ellis (1973), Singer (1973), and McGhee (1979) have all viewed young children's early fascination with fantasy activity in terms of the child's tendency to use newly developed cognitive capacities to maintain a varied and interesting environment. Imaginative play offers an ideal means of doing this because the child has complete control over the nature of the stimulation produced. As a pattern of make-believe play grows repetitive and boring, the child can modify it by simply reconceptualizing the play situation.

The important point for the concerns of the present book is that this kind of make-believe play can occur within either of two different frames of mind; that is, within two mental sets or attitudes toward dealing with incongruities, regardless of whether they are self-generated or externally provided. One mental set is similar to that described previously in connection with reality assimilation, even though we are now referring to fantasy or imaginative activity. That is, even though the child is engaged in the production of incongruous or other events at the fantasy level, he or she is in a more serious frame of mind. In this serious frame of mind, exploration occurs just as it does in connection with external events in the "real" world. The main orientation of the child here is toward learning what happens when inappropriate objects or events are assimilated into various schematas. The production of fantasy incongruities in this manner is experienced as interesting, not as funny. Children become endlessly fascinated with the outcome of bringing various nonfitting ideas and events together and may show considerable positive affect in the process.

This kind of behavior is best referred to as exploratory play, even though it is occurring at a strictly fantasy level. One of the major unresolved issues in the field of play research is the question of whether exploratory activity can really be referred to as play. The term *playful play* may be the best way to refer to the kind of play most investigators universally agree upon as being play. In the case of make-believe play and the production of fantasy incongruities, McGhee (1979) has argued that the fantasy production of incongruities is associated with humor *only when the child is in a playful frame of mind* (also see Lieberman, 1977) *and focuses attention on how the incongruous event deviates from known reality.*

> The child who is in a playful frame of mind when attending to incongruous events at the fantasy level is not concerned with exploring the world of fantasy; rather the prime focus is on acknowledging (to oneself or to others) the impossibility or absurdity of the events imagined. The events are humorous precisely because they are known to be at odds with reality [p. 61].

In any particular situation, it is impossible to be certain whether a given fantasy incongruity has been experienced as humorous by a child. Because the experience of humor is private, we can only guess whether the event was seen as humorous by relying on available cues in the child's behavior. For example, because elevated laughter and characteristic facial expressions usually accompany playful forms of play, we might assume that an incongruous production was funny instead of just interesting if the child laughed or showed these expressions. McGhee (1979, 1983) has cautioned, however, that social or other forms of laughter make it difficult to determine when a genuine humor experience has occurred.

## THE MASTERY-PLAY CYCLE

Hutt (1966) and others have shown that a close relationship exists between the degree of novelty of an object and the amount of play behavior shown in connection with it. Garvey (1977), Hutt (1966), and Piaget (1962) all noted that heightened curiosity and exploration generally precede play with novel or incongruous objects. Children typically visually examine and manipulate strange objects in order to become familiar with them or to understand them. There is no play in this initial phase, unless the exploratory activity itself is viewed as exploratory play. Because the child's main interest at this point is in understanding the object, there is a serious frame of mind rather than a playful one. Play with the object is likely to begin only after the child has satisfied his/her curiosity about it. Hutt (1966) has noted that characteristic mood changes accompany this sequence of intellectually mastering an object before playing with it:

> Investigative, inquisitive, or specific exploration is directional, that is, it is elicited by or oriented towards certain environmental changes . . . Play, on the other hand, occurs only in a known environment, and when the animal or child feels that he knows the properties of the object in that environment; this is apparent in the gradual relaxation of mood, evidenced not only by changes in facial expression, but in greater diversity and variability of activities. In play the emphasis changes from the question of "what does this object do?" to "what can I do with this object [cited from Bruner, Jolly, & Sylva, 1976, p. 211]."

Hutt's description of the mastery-play cycle is clearly demonstrated in the following example offered by Garvey (1977):

> A three-year-old boy saw a large wooden car in our playroom for the first time. (a) He paused, inspected it, and touched it. (b) He then tried to find out what it could do. He turned the steering wheel, felt the license plate, looked for a horn, and tried to get on the car. (c) Having figured out what the object was and what it could do, he got to work on what he could do with it. He put telephones on it, took them off, next put cups and dishes on it. These activities were a form of trying out ideas to see how they work. Finally, the car was understood, its properties and immediate usefulness reasonably clear. (d) He then climbed on it and drove it furiously back and forth with suitable motor and horn noises. We can readily accept the last activity as play [p. 47].

The initial phases of this activity should be viewed as exploration or exploratory play. That is, all the early activity with the car can be described as reality assimilation/accommodation processes. Only with the onset of (d) did the child begin fantasy assimilation of the now familiar and well-understood object. As long as playful fantasy assimilation does not advance beyond activities or functions known to be associated with cars, the child's play will remain in the realm of make-believe or pretend. Laughter may occur in the context of this play as a reflection of enjoyment of the activity, but it will not be humorous laughter. *Only as the child begins to introduce incongruous elements into his play does humor emerge as a component of pretend.* For example, the child may have the horn make the mooing sound of a cow instead of the normal horn sound. Knowledge of the absurdity or inappropriateness of this sound in this context adds a sense of funniness or humor to the ongoing experience of having fun.

McGhee (1979) argued that humorous as well as nonhumorous forms of imaginative play activity change during development in a manner that reflects both the mastery of new cognitive capacities as well as the mastery (i.e., understanding) of familiar aspects of the environment. Thus, humorous and nonhumorous forms of make-believe play activity should follow similar developmental sequences. Humor differs from other make-believe activities in the preschool child not in terms of cognitive prerequisites or ideational content. Rather it differs in terms of what the child does with the content (e.g., imagining congruous or incongruous events), the information processing focus at the time (reality assimilation or fantasy assimilation), and the presence of a playful or serious frame of mind. *The combination that leads to humor is the fantasy assimilation of incongruous events when in a playful frame of mind.* Incongruous events that are fantasy assimilated while in a serious frame of mind constitute another form of curiosity/exploration at the fantasy level and do not lead to humor.

## THEORIES OF INCONGRUITY HUMOR DEVELOPMENT

Only two theoretical models have been advanced in connection with developmental changes in children's incongruity humor. In each case, cognitive development is assumed to account for progress from one level of humor perceptions to the next.

## Shultz: Transition from Pure Incongruity to Resolvable Incongruity

Shultz (1972, 1976) and Suls (1972, 1983) distinguished between two distinct stages in the appreciation of cartoons or jokes based on incongruity.

> In the first stage, the perceiver finds his expectations about the text disconformed by the ending of the joke, or in the case of a cartoon, his expectations about the picture disconfirmed by the caption. In other words, the recipient encounters an incongruity—the punch line. In the second stage, the perceiver engages in a form of problem solving to find a cognitive rule which makes the punch line follow from the main part of the joke and reconciles the incongruous parts. A cognitive rule is defined as a logical proposition, a definition, or a fact of experience. The retrieval of such information makes it possible to reconcile the incongruous parts of the joke [Suls, 1972, p. 82].

Consider the following joke offered by Suls:

> One prostitute said to another, ''Can you lend me ten dollars until I get back on my back?''

The incongruity here results from the substitution of *back* for *feet*. We resolve the incongruity and appreciate the subsequent humorous insight when we realize that a prostitute earns her living by working on her back.

Shultz (1972, 1974) and Shultz and Horibe (1974) completed several studies that led him to conclude that children below 6 or 7 years of age are unable to resolve incongruities and so must be responding to ''pure incongruity'' alone. In his view, even if the resolution information is available young children are cognitively unable to detect it: This view leads to the conclusion that although adults and older children find incongruity humor funny because it makes sense in some unexpected or improbable way, preschoolers find it funny because it *makes no sense*.

Shultz (1972, 1974) and Shultz and Horibe (1974) claimed support for a transition (at about age 7) from appreciation of incongruity alone to resolvable incongruity humor on the basis of studies which present a riddle-type question and two possible answers: the original joking answer and a resolution-removed answer. The following examples demonstrate the humor stimuli used by Shultz (1974):

> Why did the farmer name his hog Ink? (Question)
> Because he kept running out of the pen. (Original answer)
> Because he kept getting away. (Resolution-removed answer)

Why did the cookie cry? (Question)
Because its mother had been a wafer so long. (Original answer)
Because its mother was a wafer. (Resolution-removed answer)

Shultz's findings indicated that children older than 7 or 8 years of age find the answer which contains the resolution-information funnier, whereas younger children find the two answers equally funny. McGhee (1974) and Shultz and Pilon (1973) have similarly demonstrated that this age marks the onset of the ability to understand the double meanings or linguistic ambiguity common to most verbal humor. Shultz and Bloom (1974) and Whitt and Prentice (1977) have demonstrated that the acquisition of concrete operational thinking enables children to appreciate the resolution aspects of such verbal humor.

Pien and Rothbart (1976) and Rothbart and Pien (1977) criticized Shultz's conclusions that preschool children's incongruity humor appreciation was based on awareness of the incongruity alone, arguing that this simply appeared to be true because of the humor stimuli used by Shultz. That is, because children below about 7 years generally cannot keep two alternate meanings of a word in mind simultaneously, they could not possibly appreciate the resolution information. Pien and Rothbart (1976) found that even 4- and 5-year-olds can appreciate the resolution information in a cartoon or joke if it is simplified, especially if visual incongruities are substituted for verbal ones.

Because no other research has been completed on this issue, it can only be concluded that concrete operational thinking does not appear to be necessary for appreciation of the resolution aspects of incongruity humor unless the ambiguity or incongruity that provides the basis for humor requires operational thinking for the mere detection of the presence of some incongruity. It remains to be determined whether there is a transition age before which no form of resolution information contributes to humor appreciation. McGhee (1979) concluded that "it is questionable whether children ever pass through a 'stage' in which they are capable of appreciating only the fact that an incongruity exists [pp. 37–38]." If prior cognitive mastery or understanding of an event is a prerequisite for seeing any distorted or incongruous depiction of that event as humorous as early as the second year, it may be more fruitful to investigate developmental changes in the kinds of resolution information appreciated by children than to attempt to determine the point at which resolution information is first appreciated. It may be that the earliest form of resolution consists of nothing more than retrieval from memory of the "correct" or "normal" composition of a stimulus event, in contrast to the present distortion of that typical and expected state.

Rothbart (1977) suggested that it may also be inappropriate to view all incongruity humor as allowing for complete resolution. In many cases, the punch line only appears to provide resolution information; it may actually create new incongruities rather than resolve existing ones. Rothbart used the following joke to demonstrate this:

"What is grey, has four legs, and a trunk?"
"A mouse on vacation."

Whereas "an elephant" is clearly understood to be the nonjoking answer, the incongruous answer of a "mouse" makes sense when the word "vacation" leads us to switch to an alternate meaning of "trunk." Rothbart correctly points out, however, that even after this resolution leads to appreciation of the intended humor, we are still left with the incongruous notion of a mouse taking a vacation (including luggage). This example may simply indicate that as children grow older (rather, as they develop more sophisticated cognitive skills), they become capable of appreciation of humor with multiple levels of incongruity—not all of which need achieve some ultimate resolution.

### McGhee: Cognitively Based Stages of Humor Development

Whereas Shultz's model draws attention to a form of developmental change that may occur as a function of the acquisition of concrete operational thought capacities, McGhee (1977, 1979) distinguished between four stages of humor development that were based on specific cognitive acquisitions. If humor is conceptualized as depending on cognitive insight into relationships that are in some way inconsistent with the child's prior knowledge or experience with the elements composing those relationships, then developmental changes in the child's cognitive abilities should be closely reflected in the kinds of humor the child is capable of either initiating or understanding. To some extent, then, stages in humor development should parallel stages in cognitive development. Moreover, because make-believe play does not begin until the same point at which humor begins (i.e., early in the second year), developmental trends in imaginative play should also correspond closely to developmental trends in humor initiation and comprehension. It is the same set of cognitive capacities that serve both of these forms of play, as well as nonplayful forms of interaction with the environment.

*Stage 1: Incongruous Actions Toward Objects.* The first stage of humor described by McGhee (1977, 1979) appears in the context of pretend play with objects. The earliest form of pretend appears to take the form of mentally substituting one object for another. Initially this occurs in connection objects bearing a high degree of physical similarity to the "intended" object; with increasing age, however, pretend may occur with decreasingly similar objects (Elder & Pederson, 1978; Fein, 1975; Piaget, 1962). The child is, in effect, assimilating an object into a schema that does not really match that schema; and yet no attempt is made to accommodate the schema to fit the discrepant object. As noted earlier, this kind of activity can occur either in a more serious information processing frame of mind or a more playful one. In the original Piagetian sense, both activities should be referred to as play because the activity consists of an emphasis on assimilation with no attempt at accommodation where accommodation seems called for. If both are viewed as play, then they might be best distinguished as exploratory (or serious) play and playful play. It is the latter form of play that provides for the child's earliest humor: "Given a playful set, it is this incongruous juxtaposition of object, image, and action that is at the heart of the child's first experience of humor [McGhee, 1979, p. 66]."

It should be noted that most of the examples of early pretend play involving substitute objects described by Piaget (1962) include observations of laughter occurring immediately after the action on the substitute object occurred. Assuming that this early laughter is a genuine reflection of specific underlying cognitive activity and not social laughter, it is likely that these pretend substitutions were experienced as humorous. The general importance of prior cognitive mastery (of the stimulus elements composing the humor event) for incongruity humor also applies here: "It is the very knowledge of the inappropriateness of the action toward an object that leads to humor and its accompanying laughter when the child is in a playful frame of mind . . . *laughter reflects the pleasure derived from creating in fantasy play a set of conditions known to be at odds with reality* [McGhee, 1979, p. 67]."

*Stage 2: Incongruous Labeling of Objects and Events.* Later in the second year, children's newly acquired language capacity is extended to the production of humor. This initially takes the form of simply calling objects, body parts, etc., by some name other than the one the child knows to belong to it. Every parent has probably witnessed the enjoyment 2-year-olds derive from calling their nose an ear, calling a truck an airplane, etc. This form of humor is similar to that of Stage 1 in that it requires assimilation of an object or event into a schema appropriate to some other object or event. It differs from Stage 1 humor, however, in that it does not necessarily involve any accompanying action. The language symbol here takes the place of action, even though an image of the comparison object or event is similarly experienced in both cases.

Most of the humor of 2- to 3-year-olds probably involves some combination of Stages 1 and 2 humor. That is, in the context of ongoing fantasy play, incongruous actions and verbal statements tend to occur together or in close alternation with one another. Especially as play behavior becomes more social, verbal statements increasingly reflect what is essentially Stage 1 humor.

*Stage 3: Conceptual Incongruity.* Although the kinds of humor characteristic of Stages 1 and 2 continue throughout the preschool years, a new form of humor emerges with the onset of conceptual thought capacities at about 3 years of age. Language at this point begins to be used to refer to classes of objects with certain common defining characteristics. Once conceptual thought capacities have been achieved, perceptions of humor may result when any one or more of the defining features of the concept are altered in some way. Thus, instead of simply imagining a dog to be a cow (or any other object or animal) or calling it a cow, the Stage 3 child may find humor in some reference to milking a dog, putting it out to pasture, having it make a "moo" sound, etc. The fact that any number of constituent elements composing a concept may be altered simultaneously means that the Stage 3 child's humor is more complex and abstract than that of younger children.

Although language is often associated with preschoolers' humor, it is not central to conceptual forms of humor. Research and theory in the Piagetian tradition long ago established the strong perceptual orientation to preschool children's thinking. It is not surprising, then, that much of children's humor at this point is based on violations of perceptual appearances of things (McGhee, 1979). Distortion of familiar sights and sounds (e.g., rhyming or nonsense words) are popular sources of humor at this point.

*Stage 4: Humor in Multiple Meanings.* The first major step toward adult forms of incongruity humor occurs when children start to realize that words often have ambiguous meaning. They may know both meanings of a word as preschoolers but are unable to keep both meanings in mind at the same time (a prerequisite for this level of humor) until about 7 years of age. Because children below this age cannot detect linguistic ambiguity (Shultz & Pilon, 1973), it is not surprising that they do not appreciate humor based on double meanings (McGhee, 1974; Shultz, 1974; Shultz & Horibe, 1974). As already noted, the transition to appreciation of this kind of humor appears to be mediated by the acquisition of concrete operational thinking.

## Fantasy Versus Real Incongruities

It has been suggested that playful (as opposed to serious) fantasy assimilation of incongruities is necessary in order for young children to find humor in incongruity. Although most early incongruity humor appears to be based on the imagination of events "known" to be impossible, or at least inconsistent with the child's prior experience, preschoolers' humor is not restricted to the world of fantasy. Real everyday events that deviate sharply from the child's prior experience may also lead to humor. For example, seeing a person with a large or oddly shaped nose, watching a clown or other adult show ineptness at things that even children can do, or seeing someone make a distorted face may trigger hilarious laughter in young children. No fantasy element is involved here; the event is really happening right in front of the child.

The important distinction to be made between early humor in real versus fantasy in congruities may lie in the question of whether an event is merely improbable or impossible. A big nose, a distorted face, and inept adult behavior are all possible, although they are not often seen. The events that are humorous to young children are most likely to be incongruities that the child believes to be at odds with his or her understanding of the real world. The child knows that you don't shave with a toothbrush, that one object cannot really have the name of another, that a dog cannot really talk, etc. It is this knowledge that makes imagining such an alternation funny when in a playful mood. If, instead of a big nose, a person had an ear or a small light bulb in the normal nose position (one that looked real and the child believed to be real), humor should be replaced by puzzled curiosity or wariness. Piaget (1952) observed that preoperational children do not show a high level of confidence or stability in their knowledge of familiar events. Their perceptual orientation in thinking and making judgments leads them to change their mind readily about what can and cannot happen, depending on what appears to be happening or not happening. This reliance on appearances may lead the young child to assimilate playfully even incongruities that really occur, thereby producing humor either from the fantasy assimilation or reality assimilation of incongruities. At this point, only one study has been completed in an attempt to determine the importance of the reality versus fantasy status of incongruities for children's humor.

*Effect of Manipulation of Reality and Fantasy Cues.* McGhee (1972, 1979) argued that the degree of certainty a child feels concerning the possible real occurrence of an incongruous event should interact with the presence of reality or fantasy cues to determine the probability of humor in connection with that event. If a child is confident about the impossibility of a given outcome, experiencing it in the presence of fantasy cues should support humor (given a playful frame of mind) whereas experiencing it in a realistic context should interfere with humor. Children lacking such confidence in the impossibility of the incongruous event should find comparable levels of humor in either a fantasy or reality context. McGhee and Johnson (1975) manipulated the extent of reality and fantasy cues in a study in which the incongruity providing the potential basis for humor consisted of a violation of conservation of weight. In a reality-cue-only condition, children saw conservation violated using a two-pan balance. For example, a thinly sliced loaf of bread was shown to weigh less than a thickly sliced loaf of bread—even though both loaves weighed the same before they were sliced (one of the thin slices was surrepetitiously removed). A reality-cue plus fantasy-cue condition also used the balance to demonstrate the lack of conservation, but a short story was read that paralleled the events with the balance. One story, for example, was as follows: "Mary is six years old and went to the bakery one day to get five one pound loaves of bread for her mother's party. When she saw that the bread was cut into very thick slices, she said, 'Oh, you'd better slice it thin! I could never carry them home cut that thick.'" A fantasy-cue group of children heard only the story and did not see the violation using the balance. Finally, a fantasy-joke group also heard the story in the absence of the balance but was told in advance that the stories were jokes. This condition was expected to provide the most optimal conditions for humor, whereas the first condition was expected to provide the greatest interference with humor.

Preliminary testing was completed to obtain groups of third-grade conservers and nonconservers of weight. Children from each group (along with a fifth-grade group of conservers who had presumably been conservers for a longer period of time; these children should have been more confident in their beliefs about conservation) were included in all four conditions. Although conservers of weight were more surprised by the conservation violation and were more confident that "it couldn't really happen," both conservers and nonconservers found the violation funnier as fantasy cues became relatively more predominant than reality cues. The highest funniness ratings were obtained for the fantasy-joke condition, followed by the fantasy cues, reality-plus-fantasy cues, and reality-cues-only conditions. These findings support the position that the occurrence of incongruities in a fantasy context is important for humor, whereas the same incongruities in a reality context interfere with humor.

## The Role of Optimal Cognitive Challenge

Piaget (1962) suggested that infants and young children derive pleasure from the process of gaining a sense of intellectual mastery over an event. That is, successful assimilation following some accommodatory effort should be more enjoyable than assimilation following minimal need for accommodation. It was noted earlier that studies of infant attention have supported this view, indicating that attention and smiling (presumably indicative of pleasure in information processing) are both related in an inverted-U fashion to amount of discrepancy between the present stimulus and some familiar standard (see McCall & McGhee, 1977, for a review of these data). These findings suggest that making sense out of new stimulus events is most enjoyable if neither too little nor too much effort is required in the process. These infant studies also indicate that events that are initially interesting (and lead to smiling) to infants become less interesting as they are repeatedly presented. Presumably, they become less interesting because they are too easily recognized and understood as they become better remembered.

These findings and related findings for older children (Harter, 1977), relate only to the form of cognitive processing that has been referred to here as serious reality assimilation. That is, infants and young children who are processing new or discrepant information that requires some optimal moderate amount of accommodatory effort for comprehension. This same pattern should hold when young children are engaged in serious forms of fantasy assimilation as well, although no pertinent data have been obtained along these lines. Given the concerns of the present chapter, the key question is whether maximal pleasure in the exertion of intellectual capacities also occurs at moderate levels of cognitive challenge in connection with playful fantasy assimilation. Specifically, is the amount of effort required to make sense out of a joke or some other humor event related to the enjoyment derived from the joke? In the case of serious reality assimilation, the pleasure derived from effortful assimilation stems from the formation of new knowledge. In playful fantasy assimilation, however, this pleasure would stem from the comparison of existing schemata or knowledge with information known to be at odds with that knowledge. This comparison process can also be conceptualized along a continuum of difficulty, with some comparisons being very easy and others very difficult. If humor appreciation were found to be greatest when moderate levels of cognitive effort are required to understand the basis for humor, this would point to the general importance of cognitive challenge for pleasure across the full range of serious and playful cognitive activity.

McGhee (1976) developed jokes based on the violation of conservation and class inclusion to determine whether degree of cognitive challenge offered for comprehension of the humor depicted contributed to the level of humor appreciation experienced. The following examples are typical of the jokes used:

> Mr. Jones went into a restaurant and ordered a whole pizza for dinner. When the waiter asked if he wanted it cut into six or eight pieces, he said: "Oh, you'd better make it 6! I could never eat 8!"
>
> Mr. Barley teaches first grade. One day his class was talking about religion; so he asked how many of the children were Catholic. When Bobby didn't raise his hand, the teacher said: "Why, Bobby, "I thought you were Catholic too!" "Oh no," said Bobby, "I'm not Catholic; I'm American."

Jokes violating these two Piagetian concepts were presented to two groups of first-graders (children who had acquired both concepts and children who had acquired neither concept), and to second- and fifth-graders who possessed both concepts. As expected, first-graders who possessed the concepts found the jokes funnier than both first-graders who had not acquired them and older children who had presumably possessed the concepts for a longer time period than the first-graders. The first-graders who lacked the concepts did not have the intellectual capacity to understand the humor resulting from the incongruity depicted. Second- and fifth-graders, on the other hand, had been conservers for some time, so the jokes did not require much effort for comprehension. The jokes presumably still offered some challenge to comprehension among the first-graders who had only recently acquired conservation and class inclusion. Other investigators have also obtained findings consistent with the view that an optimal moderate amount of cognitive effort maximizes funniness, although these studies did not utilize jokes requiring the use of specific cognitive skills determined to be present or absent in subjects (Whitt & Prentice, 1977; Zigler, Levine, & Gould, 1966, 1967).

One study has been completed that suggests that optimal moderate levels of cognitive challenge may contribute to humor appreciation across the life span.

Schaier and Cicirelli (1976) argued that because cognitive capacities tend to be lost during aging in the reverse manner that they were acquired, conservation (or other Piagetian) jokes like those just described should once again begin to show increased funniness with increasing age as cognitive regression reaches the point that comprehension again becomes challenging. This is exactly what they found. Comprehension of conservation jokes progressively deteriorated with age among 50- to 80-year-olds, whereas appreciation increased with age.

*The General Role of Cognitive Challenge in Intellectual Play.* The data reviewed here point toward the conclusion that the moderately effortful exertion of cognitive capacities in any form of intellectual activity may be experienced as pleasurable. The degree of effort experienced as most pleasurable may vary across individuals, as well as within individuals in different contexts, but it appears that there will always be a level of cognitive exertion above and below which pleasure in cognitive activity will be reduced. Enjoyment of challenging intellectual activity extends to both reality and fantasy modes of assimilation and may occur when the child is in either a playful or a serious frame of mind. Developmental trends in pretend play reviewed elsewhere in this book may also be explained on this basis. In pretend play with objects, for example, initial object substitutions are highly realistic or bear a high degree of similarity to the original object; as children grow older, however, they are more likely to pretend with dissimilar objects or completely imaginary objects (Elder & Pederson, 1978; Fein, 1975).

Thus, the mastery-play cycle referred to previously appears to apply to both a particular new object or idea and to newly acquired cognitive capacities. As new cognitive capacities emerge, they are first used in the service of a progressively higher order and more differentiated understanding of the real or imaginary world. As the child gradually comes to feel more confident in the use of these new skills, they begin to be extended to playful forms of activity, as in make-believe or humor. Although playful forms of enjoyment of incongruities follow more serious forms of pleasure in making sense out of incongruities, both clearly occur. Similarly, pleasure in each case appears to be maximized when moderate amounts of cognitive effort are involved. In a child who has stabilized at a level of functioning with a particular set of cognitive abilities (e.g., concrete operational capacities), any particular new situation or idea will similarly initially generate more serious efforts at assimilation. Once a sense of understanding is achieved, however, this new content may then be incorporated into either a humorous or a nonhumorous form of intellectual play.

## REFERENCES

Bruner, J. S., Jolly, A., & Sylva, K. (Eds.). *Play: Its role in development and evolution.* New York: Basic Books, 1976.

Elder, J. L., & Pederson, D. R. Preschool children's use of objects in symbolic play. *Child Development,* 1978, *49,* 500–504.

Ellis, M. J. *Why people play.* Englewood Cliffs, N.J.: Prentice-Hall, 1973.

Fein, G. G. A transformational analysis of pretending. *Developmental Psychology,* 1975, *11,* 291–296.

Garvey, C. *Play.* Cambridge: Harvard University Press, 1977.

Harter, S. *Pleasure derived from optimal challenge and the effects of extrinsic rewards on children's difficulty level choices.* Unpublished manuscript, University of Denver, 1977. (Cited by S. Harter, Effectance motivation reconsidered: Toward a developmental model. *Human Development,* 1978, *21,* 34–64.)

Hutt, C. Exploration and play in children. *Symposia of the Zoological Society of London,* No. 18, 1966.

Keith-Spiegel, P. Early conceptions of humor: Varieties and issues. In J. H. Goldstein & P. E. McGhee (Eds.), *The psychology of humor: Theoretical perspectives and empirical issues.* New York: Academic Press, 1972.

Lieberman, J. N. *Playfulness: Its relationship to imagination and creativity.* New York: Academic Press, 1977.

McCall, R. B., & McGhee, P. E. The discrepancy hypothesis of attention and affect in children. In I. C. Uzgiris & F. Weizman (Eds.), *The structuring of experience.* New York: Plenum, 1977.

McGhee, P. E. On the cognitive origins of incongruity humor: Fantasy assimilation versus reality assimilation. In J. H. Goldstein & P. E. McGhee (Eds.), *The psychology of humor: Theoretical perspectives and empirical issues.* New York: Academic Press, 1972.

McGhee, P. E. Development of children's ability to create the joking relationship. *Child Development,* 1974, *45,* 552–556.

McGhee, P. E. Children's appreciation of humor: A test of the cognitive congruency principle. *Child Development,* 1976, *47,* 420–426.

McGhee, P. E. A model of the origins and early development of incongruity-based humor. In A. J. Chapman & H. C. Foot (Eds.), *It's a funny thing, humour.* Oxford, England: Pergamon Press, 1977.

McGhee, P. E. *Humor: Its origin and development.* San Francisco: Freeman, 1979.

McGhee, P. E. Humor development: Toward a life span approach. In P. E. McGhee & J. H. Goldstein (Eds.), *Handbook of humor research: Basic issues.* (Vol. I). New York: Springer-Verlag, 1983.

McGhee, P. E., & Chapman, A. J. (Eds.) *Children's humour.* Chichester, England: Wiley, 1980.

McGhee, P. E., & Goldstein, J. H. (Eds.) *Handbook of humor research: Basic issues.* (Vol. I). New York: Springer-Verlag, 1983.

McGhee, P. E., & Johnson, S. F. The role of fantasy and reality cues in children's appreciation of incongruity humor. *Merrill–Palmer Quarterly,* 1975, *21,* 19–30.

Piaget, J. *The origins of intelligence in children.* New York: International Universities Press, 1952.

Piaget, J. *Play, dreams, and imitation in childhood.* New York: Norton, 1962.

Pien, D., & Rothbart, M. K. Incongruity and resolution in children's humor: A reexamination. *Child Development,* 1976, *47,* 966–971.

Pien, D., & Rothbart, M. K. Incongruity, humour, play, and self-regulation of arousal in young children. In P. E. McGhee & A. J. Chapman (Eds.), *Children's humour.* Chichester, England: Wiley, 1980.

Rothbart, M. K. Laughter in young children. *Psychological Bulletin,* 1973, *80,* 247–256.

Rothbart, M. K. Incongruity, problem-solving and laughter. In A. J. Chapman & H. C. Foot (Eds.), *Humour and Laughter: Theory, research and applications.* Chichester, England: Wiley, 1976.

Rothbart, M. K. Psychological approaches to the study of humour. In A. J. Chapman & H. C. Foot (Eds.), *It's a funny thing, humour.* Oxford, England: Pergamon, 1977.

Rothbart, M. K., & Pien, D. Elephants and marshmallows: A theoretical synthesis of incongruity-resolution and arousal theories of humour. In A. J. Chapman & H. C. Foot (Eds.), *It's a funny thing, humour*. Oxford, England: Pergamon Press, 1977.

Schaier, A. H., & Cicirelli, V. C. Age changes in humor comprehension and appreciation. *Journal of Gerontology*, 1976, *31*, 577–582.

Shultz, T. R. The role of incongruity and resolution in children's appreciation of cartoon humor. *Journal of Experimental Child Psychology*, 1972, *13*, 456–477.

Shultz, T. R. Development of the appreciation of riddles. *Child Development*, 1974, *45*, 100–105.

Shultz, T. R. A cognitive-developmental analysis of humour. In A. J. Chapman & H. C. Foot (Eds.), *Humour and laughter: Theory, research and applications*. Chichester, England: Wiley, 1976.

Shultz, T. R., & Bloom, L. *Concrete operational thought and the appreciation of verbal jokes*. Unpublished manuscript, McGill, University, 1974.

Shultz, T. R., & Horibe, F. Development of the appreciation of verbal jokes. *Developmental Psychology*, 1974, *10*, 13–20.

Shultz, T. R., & Pilon, R. Development of the ability to detect linguistic ambiguity. *Child Development*, 1973, *44*, 728–733.

Singer, J. L. (Ed.). *The child's world of make-believe: Experimental studies of imaginative play*. New York: Academic Press, 1973.

Sroufe, L. A., & Waters, E. The ontogenesis of smiling and laughter: A perspective on the organization of development in infancy. *Psychological Review*, 1976, *83*, 173–189.

Sroufe, L. A., Waters, E., & Matas, L. Contextual determinants of infant affective responses. In M. Lewis & L. A. Rosenblum (Eds.), *The origins of fear*. New York: Wiley, 1974.

Sroufe, L. A., & Wunsch, J. P. The development of laughter in the first year of life. *Child Development*, 1972, *43*, 1326–1344.

Suls, J. A two-stage model for the appreciation of jokes and cartoons: An information-processing analysis. In J. H. Goldstein & P. E. McGhee (Eds.), *The psychology of humor: Theoretical perspectives and empirical issues*. New York: Academic Press, 1972.

Suls, J. Cognitive processes in humor appreciation. In P. E. McGhee & J. H. Goldstein (Eds.), *Handbook of humor research: Basic issues*. (Vol. I). New York: Springer-Verlag, 1983.

Whitt, J. K., & Prentice, N. M. Cognitive processes in the development of children's enjoyment and comprehension of joking riddles. *Developmental Psychology*, 1977, *13*, 129–136.

Zigler, E., Levine, J., & Gould, L. Cognitive processes in the development of children's appreciation of humor. *Child Development*, 1966, *37*, 507–518.

Zigler, E., Levine, J., & Gould, L. Cognitive challenge as a factor in children's humor appreciation. *Journal of Personality and Social Psychology*, 1967, *6*, 332–336.

# 13 The Effects of Exploration and Play on Young Children's Associative Fluency: A Review and Extension of Training Studies

Anthony D. Pellegrini
*University of Georgia*

## Introduction

This chapter summarizes, critiques, and extends experimental studies attempting to facilitate young children's associative fluency. The earliest studies had children playing with or exploring objects as a treatment for their generating creative uses for objects. This research suggests that play enables children to establish a playful disposition towards objects that results in their increased associative fluency. The review, which differentiates play from exploration, suggests that children in these earlier studies may have been trained in exploration, not play. The review then discusses studies that trained children to explore objects actively by engaging them in an exploration–open question dialogue with an adult about the objects. The review concludes that the exploration questioning technique is a more effective facilitator of associative fluency than a free play treatment because the former has children actively exploring more object attributes in a relatively short period of time.

## A REVIEW AND EXTENSION

The effects of play on different aspects of young children's development have been documented by many researchers (see Bruner, Jolly, & Sylva, 1976, for a compendium). This body of research, as a whole, suggests that play is related development. In the area of problem-solving, Sylva, Bruner, and Genova (1976) suggested that children's play with objects facilitated their ability to use the same objects in problem-solving situations. Cazden (1974) and others (C. Chomsky,

1979; Kirschenblatt-Gimblet, 1976; Pellegrini, 1980, 1981b) noted positive relations between children's play with language and their subsequent metalinguistic awareness. In the area of social development, Rubin (1980) posits that the social interaction characteristic of young children's peer interactions relates to their improved social perspective training. The effect of play on children's creativity has been subjected to less analyses. In this chapter the literature outlining the effects of play and its precursor, exploration, on children's ability to generate creative uses for conventional objects, associative fluency, will be reviewed and extended. First, associative fluency will be defined as *a subset of creativity*. Second, the differences between exploration and play will be articulated. Third, studies that used play and/or exploration to facilitate associative fluency will be reviewed. Finally, directions for future research will be suggested.

## ASSOCIATIVE FLUENCY AND CREATIVITY

Associative fluency is a subset of creativity. According to Wallach (1970), associative fluency is: "The ability to rapidly generate words that meet particular requirements for meaning, such as providing a word which has the meaning as each of a pair of words that differ in meaning themselves [p. 1213]."

Associative fluency has been typically measured by the alternate uses test (Dansky, 1980; Pellegrini, 1981a, 1982; Pellegrini & Greene, 1980; Wallach, 1970). With the alternate uses test children are presented with a conventional object (e.g., a paper clip) and asked to give as many standard and novel uses for the object as they can. Children's performance on this measure has been shown to be independent of intelligence but positively and significantly correlated with other measures of creativity (Wallach, 1970). Wallach (1970) stated that the alternate uses test measures children's ability to form new associations for elements of objects. That is, it measures the ability to form associations for specific aspects of objects. For example, an association for a triangular block of wood may be a slice of pie. The association, a piece of pie, is related to an attribute of the block, its triangular shape. Children are most fluent on this measure when they are encouraged to be playful and when no time limit is imposed on their generating uses. Wallach (1970) concluded that children's ability to form associations for objects' contents and playful attitudes towards the objects are the bases of children's associative fluency.

## EXPLORATION AND PLAY

Children's ability to give creative uses for conventional objects, based on Wallach's hypothesis, may vary according to their familiarity with the objects' attributes and the children's playful attitude toward the objects. The behaviors characteristic of children familiarizing themselves with objects has been labelled *exploration* (Hutt, 1966; Hutt & Bhavnani, 1972; Vandenberg, 1980; Weisler & McCall, 1976). Children's exploration behaviors are said to be dominated by attitudes of "What is it?" and "What can it do?". Children exhibit exploration behavior toward objects when they are unfamiliar with the objects. During exploration children familiarize themselves with objects' properties and functions by visual and tactile inspection (Hutt, 1966). The function of exploration, then, is to familiarize oneself with the attributes of objects and objects' functions. Hutt (1966) has shown that preschoolers' exploration behavior of unfamiliar objects is very deliberate; that is, their gaze towards the objects seldom deviates from the objects, their attention to the object is sustained, and they have an increased heart rate during exploration. Exploration behaviors are elicited by objects until children become familiar with the objects' attributes and functions. Hutt and Bhavnani (1972) state that exploration is a montonic function of time; that is, exploration decreases with the amount of time that children explore the object.

As children's exploration of an object wanes, they exhibit playful behaviors toward that object. Hutt (1966) characterized playful behavior as using the object in repetitious and fantastic ways: An example is repeatedly bouncing a ball and using the ball as an apple, respectively. Children's playful behaviors toward objects are said to be dominated by a "What can I do with it?" attitude. Preschoolers' play with an object is less deliberate than their prior exploration of the same object. That is, in play with objects, children's attention toward the object can be easily interrupted, their heart rate decreases, and their gaze often wanders from the object.

Hutt (1966) and Hutt and Bhavnani (1972) suggest that children must explore objects before they can play with them; exploration is a necessary, but not sufficient, condition for play. This conclusion seems to correspond with Wallach's (1970) bases for associative fluency. The "What is it?", or exploration attitude corresponds to Wallach's familiarity with objects' content principle; the "What can I do with it?", or playful attitude, corresponds to his playful attitude principle. Before children can generate novel uses for objects (i.e., "What can I do with it?") they must become familiar with (or explore) the objects' contents, "What is it?". The contents of objects become explicit during exploration. During play with the object children generate associations for these contents. These associations, according to Wallach, are the bases for the novel uses given for objects.

## EFFORTS TO FACILITATE PRESCHOOLERS' ASSOCIATIVE FLUENCY

The studies reviewed in this section should provide some insight into the effects of children's exploration and play with objects on their associative fluency. In addition, this review will raise a number of questions about the procedures most facilitative of preschoolers' associative fluency.

Sutton-Smith (1967) was one of the first researchers to examine the effects of preschoolers' play with objects on their ability to give creative uses for those same objects. He hypothesized that children became familiar with objects by engaging in free play with them. Further, Sutton-Smith stated that in free play, which he did not differentiate from exploration, children not only familiarized themselves with objects' attributes but they also formed associations for these attributes. The associations formed in play were said to be the bases for children's ability to give novel uses for the objects with which they played. Based on this thesis he stated that children should generate most creative uses for objects they most often played with. Play with specific objects, then, served a function of helping children generate associations for those objects.

In testing this hypothesis, Sutton-Smith chose nine boys and nine girls in kindergarten as subjects. He then chose sex-stereotyped toys; that is, toys that he determined were frequently played with by boys (e.g., blocks, trucks), and toys frequently played with by girls (e.g., dolls, dishes). Even though children of both sexes were familiar with the opposite sex toys, he argued that their play with opposite sex toys was limited; that is, children did not play with opposite sex toys as frequently as with sex-stereotyped toys. He blindfolded each child and gave him/her each of the toys to manipulate while the child answered descriptive and function questions about each object. There was not a significant difference by sex for the number of descriptors generated by children for any of the toys. Based on this measure, Sutton-Smith stated that children's familiarity with opposite sex toys was equal to their familiarity with same sex toys. There were significant differences, however, by sex, on the number of creative uses children gave for sex specific toys; boys gave more creative uses for the masculine toys and girls gave more creative uses for the feminine toys. According to Sutton-Smith, the children played most often with sex stereotyped toys. Sutton-Smith argued that it was *play* with the toys that accounted for the sex differences in the number of creative uses given for the toys. He did not, however, experimentally manipulate children's previous play or familiarity with the objects.

Based on the methodological weakness of the Sutton-Smith study, (i.e., play with objects confounded with familiarity of objects) Dansky and Silverman (1973, 1975) designed experiments that attempted to manipulate these factors systematically so as to determine the specific effect of play on children's associative fluency. In the first Dansky and Silverman study (1973), groups of preschoolers were exposed to conventional objects through either free play with the objects, imitating an adult's actions on the objects, or observing an adult act upon the objects. All sessions lasted 10 minutes. Children were then given an alternate uses test for one of the two objects with which they interacted. Those in the play condition gave significantly more creative uses for the object than those in the other groups. Dansky and Silverman did not venture an explanation for the effectiveness of the play condition, though they did notice that the creative uses for the objects given by children were related to the objects' physical attributes. Play may have helped children explore objects' attributes and generate associations for these attributes.

In a follow-up study, Dansky and Silverman (1975) utilized the same procedure but gave children the alternate uses test on objects they had not interacted with previously. In the transfer, players gave significantly more standard and creative uses for the new object than children in either of the other groups. Dansky and Silverman noted that children transferred the play set or a playful predisposition towards objects from the treatment to the new stimuli in the criterion phase of the experiment. That is, children's playful mode of interacting with the objects during the training sessions was transferred to a new object; the specific associations for specific objects gained through play were not transferred. In terms of Wallach's (1970) two factors to associatve fluency (i.e., contributing associations for specific objects and a playful attitude towards objects), Dansky and Silverman (1975) suggest that the latter may make the more important contribution to preschoolers' associative fluency.

One should question the extent to which children in the Dansky and Silverman studies had an opportunity to establish a "playful set" in light of the instructions they were given (i.e., "Do what ever you would like to do with them") and the limited time constraint of 10 minutes of the play treatment. In light of these limitations an alternate hypotheses for the Dansky and Silverman (1975) results shall be posed. It may be that these children were not playing with the objects in the play condition. They may have been exploring the objects; that is, discovering the objects' attributes. In 10 minutes preschoolers may not have had time to play with them. The alternate hypothesis states that children transferred an exploration not a play set to the new stimulus object. That is, when they were presented with the new objects they explored the objects' attributes, and their creative uses for the new objects were based on their ability to explore objects and then generate associations for the attributes they discovered through exploration.

Pellegrini, in a recent series of studies (Pellegrini, 1981a, 1982; Pellegrini & Greene, 1980), examined the extent to which preschoolers could be trained to explore objects and subsequently give novel uses for explored and previously unexplored objects. His exploration training model engaged individual children in an exploration questioning dialogue with an adult. Children handled the objects as they answered the questions. The form and content of the questions, taken from Sigel (1979), were designed specifically to stimulate children's exploration of various aspects of objects.

In terms of form, the exploration questions were open-ended to the extent that there was no one right answer (e.g., "What do you see here?"). The open form necessitated exploration of objects and generation of responses to questions. The open form is easily contrasted with convergent questions such as yes/no questions, "Is it hard?", and forced choice questions, "Is it hard or soft?" With convergent questions certain attributes of the object are identified. In turn, children attend to the attribute they are directed to and then choose one answer from a list of adult-provided alternatives. Open-ended exploration questions are sufficiently vague. To answer them children must actively explore the objects by searching the contents of objects. Here children also verbally encode an answer in their own words. Thus, the form of open-ended questions stimulates children's active exploration of objects to the extent that they search the attributes of objects themselves and answer the questions in their own words.

The content of the open questioning exploration paradigm also has specific effects on children's exploration of objects. First, children are asked descriptive exploration questions about objects (e.g., "What do you see here?"). By answering descriptive exploration questions children can thoroughly explore and verbally encode attributes of objects in a relatively short period of time. Children answer descriptive explorative questions about two objects before they are asked difference exploration questions (e.g., "How are they different?") and similarity exploration questions about the objects (e.g., "How are they the same?"). Children's ability to note differences and similarities between objects may be based on the attributes of the objects explored while answering the descriptive exploration questions. The function of difference and similarity exploration questions enables children to put the objects into categories. For example, a spool and a cork belong to the same class (i.e., cylindrical objects) and to different classes (i.e., classes of brown objects and the class of objects that are both white and brown).

It was argued by Pellegrini that the content of this series of questions facilitated associative fluency because it enabled children to explore attributes of objects and class membership traits of objects. First, by exploring and verbally encoding objects' attributes, children could use associations for these attributes as bases for creative uses. For example, the round shape of a spool might result in a child using it as a wheel. Second, by noting similarities and differences between objects, class identifies are formed. Children could draw upon other objects belonging to those assigned classes for possible alternate uses. For example, because a thread spool belongs to the class of wooden objects, along with trees, a novel use for a spool is that it can be a tree.

The adult's role in this model is to pose questions that motivate children to explore objects. Children describe attributes, articulate similarities and differences between the objects, and verbally encode their explorations in their own words. The adult's role is to pose questions that enable children to explore objects' contents in a relatively short period of time.

The effects of this exploration questioning paradigm on preschoolers' associative fluency was compared to play and control groups in two Pellegrini studies. The children in the play conditions in both studies were given instructions following the directions given to the play groups in the Dansky and Silverman (1973, 1975) studies. In the first Pellegrini study (Pellegrini & Greene, 1980), children in the exploration questioning condition generated significantly more, compared to children in both play and control groups, creative uses for an object they had examined previously; players gave more uses than control children. The effects in this experiment may have been due to the thorough exploration of objects' attributes in a relatively short period of time (10 minutes) by children exposed to the questions. Children in the play group may have centered their explorations on a limited number of object attributes. If associative fluency is based on children's ability to generate associations for attributes of objects, children in the exploration questioning condition probably explored more of the objects' attributes than did the players.

Another reason for the effectiveness of the exploration questioning condition may have been that the children in this condition verbally encoded descriptors for objects and similarities and differences between the objects. The verbalizations may have helped children recall objects' characteristics during the criterion phase of the experiment. Much research (e.g., Rohwer, 1970, for a review) has shown that verbally encoding items facilitates children's remembering the encoded items. They may have used these verbally encoded characteristics as bases for their creative responses.

The transfer of the exploration questioning paradigm to a previously unexplored object was tested in a second Pellegrini (1981a) experiment. The research question asked in this experiment was: Did children use specific associations for the objects they explored as bases for creative uses or did they transfer an exploration set to that object? The sample, objects, and conditions in this study were similar to the Pellegrini and Greene (1980) study. The criterion phase of the later study was designed to test the transfer effect of the exploration questioning strategy; that is, were children able to transfer the exploration set from the training objects to a previously unexplored object. Children were asked to give alternate uses for an object they did not interact with during their treatments. Results indicated that preschoolers were able to transfer the exploration questioning strategy more effectively than children in the play and control conditions. Specifically, children in the exploration questioning group gave significantly more creative uses for previously unexplored objects than children in either the play or control groups. Players generated more uses than control children.

The results of this experiment were explained in terms of the children transferring the exploration set on which they were trained. Children were trained to explore attributes of objects by describing attributes and noting similarities and differences between the objects. When they were presented with the unexamined objects they probably explored the objects' attributes covertly and used associations for these attributes for alternate uses for the objects. It was also hypothesized that these children were able to transfer the exploration strategy because they were trained on a *process* of exploring objects.

In Pellegrini (1982), the specific effects of children's active exploration of objects were compared with adult direction of children's exploration. The different conditions in this study varied to the extent that they required children to explore actively the stimulus objects. In the most active condition, children explored objects by way of the exploration questioning paradigm used in earlier Pellegrini studies. As stated earlier, open exploration questions had children identifying objects' attributes and subsequently encoding these attributes in their own words. In the convergent questioning exploration condition, children responded to adults' yes/no and forced choice questions about objects. *What color is it?* Is an example of a forced-choice question. The least active condition was the declarative exploration condition. This condition had children repeating, verbatim, adult descriptions for objects and similarities and differences between objects. The declarative exploration condition had children in the least active role in exploring the objects because adults centered children's attention on the objects' attributes, and adults provided the labels. Children in this condition were not analyzing the objects, they were encoding the adults' concept of the objects.

In each of these exploration conditions children verbally encoded responses to questions or descriptors relating to the same number of object descriptors and similarities and differences between objects. The exploration conditions were different in two ways. First, conditions differed to the extent that they required children's active involvement in the exploration process. The two exploration questioning conditions required more activity on the part of children than did the declarative exploration condition; in order to answer the questions they had to explore objects and then verbally encode an answer. The open exploration questioning condition required more activity than the convergent exploration questioning condition for reasons stated previously. The second difference among the exploration conditions was in terms of the number of descriptions, similarities, and differences between objects the children actually verbally encoded. Children in the declarative exploration condition encoded 12 attributes for the two stimulus objects whereas children in the convergent questioning condition actually encoded only two attributes; the remaining 10 convergent questions elicited yes/no responses, not actual object descriptors. Children in the open exploration questioning condition encoded a total of 12 descriptors, similarities, and differences.

In the criterion phase of this experiment children were asked to give alternative uses for two objects: for an object they previously explored in their respective treatments and for an object they had not previously explored. For the objects previously explored, children in the open questioning exploration condition generated the most creative uses. Children in the declarative condition gave more creative uses than children in both the convergent questioning exploration and control conditions. For the previously unexamined objects, the open questioning exploration group, again, gave significantly more uses than all other conditions. There were no significant differences among the other conditions for the member of creative uses given for unfamiliar objects.

The differential effects of the exploration conditions on children's ability to give alternative uses for previously examined objects might be explained in terms of the image (Pavio, 1978), on representation (Sigel, 1979), of the examined objects. More specifically, when children verbally encoded object attributes they constructed a mental image of that object (Pavio, 1978) that they stored in their long-term memory. In the criterion phase of the experiment children drew upon these images and generated associations for them. Children in the declarative exploration condition constructed object images based on their verbally encoding 12 descriptors for two objects. The object images constructed by children in the convergent exploration questioning condition were based on their encoding only two object attributes and attributes were actually encoded. The relative richness of the images constructed by children in the declarative exploration condition, in terms of the number of descriptors verbally encoded, may have been responsible for their generation of more creative uses for examined objects than children in convergent questioning and control conditions.

The open exploration questioning paradigm was the most effective facilitator of associative fluency on previously examined objects because children's mental images of objects may have been analogic (Cocking & Sigel, 1979; Rumelhart & Abrahamson, 1973), not homologic. Children's images of the examined objects may have been based on the objects' form and structure, (i.e., interrelations among attributes) not specific object content. As a result of inferring similarities and differences between objects, children probably transformed objects from concrete entities to images based on the interrelations among object attributes. Consequently, analogic concepts of the objects may have been constructed (Rumelhart & Abramson, 1973). Children probably used these more abstract object concepts as bases for novel responses. As a result, they were not limited to drawing from an object image of one object, as were the children in the declarative exploration condition. Children in the declarative exploration condition probably constructed representations based on the specific content of one object (homologic concepts). Children with an image for one object were limited to drawing for novel uses from the attributes of that one perceptually present object. Their novel uses were probably based on associations for only the attributes of that one object. Children with an analogic object concept of an object probably realized that the object belonged to many conceptual categories. Thus, they may have been able to draw upon all the objects and their respective attributes, from these analogic categories, for potential novel uses.

The children exposed to the open exploration questioning model transferred their training to previously unexamined objects most effectively. Indeed, the data indicated that children in the declarative exploration and convergent exploration questioning condition did not transfer their previous training; they generated as many uses for previously unexamined objects as did the control group. Children in the open exploration questioning group may have transferred their training because they were trained in the process of exploring objects. They were not directed to specific aspects of stimuli to explore. They themselves identified those aspects of the stimuli to explore. Such an active involvement in the exploration process seems necessary if children are to transfer the exploration set to unfamiliar stimuli.

## FUTURE RESEARCH

Vandenberg (1980) suggested that children's associative fluency may be improved by training them in exploration, play, or divergent thinking. Based on Pepler and Ross' (1981) research he suggests that training children in divergent thinking may be related to associative fluency, a measure of divergent thinking. Pepler and Ross found that training preschoolers to think divergently improved their performance on a divergent problem-solving task; convergent training did not improve performance on a divergent task.

These results provide an interesting use with Pellegrini's open exploration questioning paradigm. If divergent training facilitates performance on a divergent task, then asking children divergent questions, such as exploration difference questions alone, may facilitiate associative fluency. More specifically, Vandenberg's suggestion that associative fluency may be facilitated by divergent thinking training could be tested by asking separate groups of children descriptive, differences, or similarity questions. If children exposed to difference questions alone outperformed children exposed to descriptive questions alone then improved associative fluency might be a function of divergent thinking, not the ability to extract object attributes and generate associations for them. It should also follow that asking similarity questions, a convergent task, should interfere with the associative fluency.

## EXPERIMENT 1

The separate conditions in Experiment 1 were designed to determine the effects on associative fluency of specific aspects of the exploration questioning model. Condition 1 in Experiment 1, the descriptive exploration condition, had an adult engaging children in dialogue with descriptive exploration questions (i.e., "What do you see/feel? *Tell me about this.*"). This condition trained children to explore and verbally encode attributes of objects. Condition 2 in this study was a descriptive exploration plus memory condition. Children in this condition answered the same descriptive exploration questions as children in the descriptive condition. After they answered descriptive questions about two objects, the experimenter asked children to tell him/her what they remembered about the first object they described. The memory condition served the function of being able to determine the effect of remembering about attributes on associative fluency.

Condition 3 had an adult asking children similarity exploration questions about two objects (i.e., "How are they the same?"). In Condition 4 children were asked to answer difference exploration questions about two objects (i.e., "How are they different?"). Conditions 3 and 4 were designed to provide insight into the extent to which training children to explore either differences or similarities between objects affected children's associative fluency.

In Condition 5 children were exposed to all of the previously outlined questions in a set sequence of descriptive, similarity, and difference exploration questions. This condition should help determine the additive effect of the questions on children's associative fluency. In this study, unlike previous Pellegrini studies (Pellegrini, 1981a, 1982; Pellegrini & Greene, 1980) children exposed to the total exploration questioning paradigm were asked similarity exploration questions before difference exploration questions. We did not want to place convergent questions, noting similarities, before the divergent associative fluency task.

In summary, the intent of Experiment 1 was to examine the extent to which different types of exploration training effected children's associative fluency. The specific questions posed were: Are descriptive exploration questions more effective in facilitating associative fluency than asking either similarities or differences exploration questions? What is the effect of asking children to remember objects' attributes? What is the additive effect of the exploration questioning model?

## Method

*Subjects.* The 60 children involved in Experiment 1 were drawn from a public kindergarten in the vicinity of Athens, Georgia. The sample was randomly drawn from a population of 100 children. The sample of 30 boys and 30 girls ranged in age from 63 to 72 months ($\bar{x}$ = 68.083; SD = 3.618). From this sample children were randomly assigned to one of six experimental groups: descriptive questions; descriptive questions and recall of attributes; similarily questions; difference questions; descriptive, similarity, and differences questions; or control.

*Materials and Procedure.* The materials consisted of a wooden thread spool, a pipe cleaner, a wooden clothes pin, and a wine bottle cork. In all questioning conditions children were questioned about two of these objects. During the criterion phase they interacted with one familiar object (i.e., an object on which they were previously questioned).

All children were exposed to their respective treatments twice within a 3-day period. In all exploration questioning conditions children were questioned on two stimulus objects. They were told they could handle the objects as they answered questions. Each treatment lasted about 10 minutes.

In the descriptive exploration question treatment, Condition 1, individual children were given two objects one object at a time and asked: "Tell me something about this. What does it feel/look like?'' In the descriptive exploration and recall condition, Condition 2, individual children were asked the same series of descriptive exploration questions about two objects. After they answered these questions they were asked ''Tell me all you remember about the (*the first object described*).''

In the similarity exploration question condition, Condition 3, children were presented with two objects simultaneously and asked ''How are these two things the same? How else are they the same?'' In the difference exploration question condition, Condition 4, children were presented with two objects simultaneously and asked: ''How are these two things different? How else are they different?''

In the descriptive, similarity, and difference exploration condition, Condition 4, children were asked each type of question, as previously outlined, in a specific order: descriptive, similarity, and difference exploration questions. Children in the control condition engaged in conversation about their favorite school activities with the experimenter.

Children were questioned individually in a vacant room in their school by an experimenter. Experimenters, two female and one male, were randomly assigned to each of the treatments.

*The Dependent Measure.* Immediately following each of the treatment and control conditions, each subject was given an alternate uses test by the same experimenter with whom they interacted in their assigned condition. Children were asked to give alternate uses for one of the two objects with which they interacted in their respective conditions. Children in the control condition were given an alternate uses test on one stimulus object randomly selected from the total array of four stimulus objects.

In presenting each student with a stimulus object the experimenter said: ''You can use this in lots of ways. Tell me how you can use it?. What can you make with it?. How can you play with it?'' No time limit was imposed on this part of the session. All subjects' utterances were audiotaped during the experimental sessions. Tapes were coded by the author on the same day on which they were recorded. Uses were coded as conventional when children suggested using the stimulus object in the following way(s): the cork to plug bottles, the clothes pin to hand things, the pipe cleaner to clean pipes, the thread spool for sewing. All other uses (i.e., alternate uses) were coded as creative. No differentiation was made within the class of creative responses. A second coder reexamined all alternate uses given. She also coded uses as creative or conventional.

## Results and Discussion

Children in the total exploration questioning paradigm generated the greatest number of creative responses to familiar objects (i.e., 79). Children exposed to the descriptive exploration questions (i.e., 49) generated more creative uses than children in each of the following groups: difference exploration (i.e., 44); descriptive exploration and recall exploration (i.e., 28); and the control (i.e., 28).

A one-way ANOVA was used to determine the effect of condition on the number of creative uses for familiar objects. Condition had a significant effect, $F$ (5, 54) = 4.15, $p < .003$ ($R^2 = .277$). The results of Newman-Keuls post hoc, preset at .10, indicated that children in the total exploration questioning group ($\bar{x}$ = 7.90) generated significantly more creative uses than children in all other groups. Children in the descriptive exploration questions group ($\bar{x}$ = 4.9) gave significantly more uses than children in the descriptive exploration and recall group ($\bar{x}$ = 2.8), the similarity exploration group ($\bar{x}$ = 3.7), and the control group ($\bar{x}$ = 2.8). Children in the difference exploration questions group ($\bar{x}$ = 4.4) generated significantly more creative uses than children in control and descriptive exploration and recall groups.

These results support the interpretation set forth earlier by Pellegrini and Greene (1980) that children's ability to generate novel uses for objects seems to be a result of their answering descriptive and contrastive explorative questions about the objects and generating associations for these explored attributes. The described attributes became the bases for these creative associations. In addition, when children answered similarity and difference exploration questions they categorized the objects. Subsequently they can use the other objects in those categories for possible creative uses.

Answering descriptive exploration questions about objects seems to be more important in the facilitation of associative fluency than answering only differences exploration questions about objects. Children may need to describe objects thoroughly before answering difference exploration questions about them. Answering difference exploration questions, does, though, seem to be an effective facilitator of associative fluency. Similarity exploration questions alone and descriptive exploration and recall, seem to be no more effective than control treatment. These data seem to indicate that both descriptive exploration and difference exploration questions are both effective facilitators of associative fluency. In order to further describe the effects of the forms on exploration on associative fluency a second experiment was conducted.

## EXPERIMENT 2

Experiment 1 indicated that answering descriptive exploration and difference exploration questions both contribute to children's improved associative fluency. In Experiment 2 we attempted to identify the effect of these forms of questions separately and in combination with each other on a transfer task. That is, in addition to the descriptive exploration questions alone conditon, the difference exploration questions alone condition, and descriptive, difference, and similarity exploration questions condition, another group was asked, both descriptive and difference exploration questions. The first research question posed in Experiment 2 was: To what extent was answering descriptive exploration questions and difference exploration questions together more effective than answering either of these types of questions alone? The second research question posed in Experiment 2 was: Do children exposed to descriptive, similarity, and difference exploration questions perform better than children exposed to descriptive and difference exploration questions?

## Method

*Subjects.* The 50 children in Experiement 2 were drawn from two kindergarteners in and around Athens, Georgia. The sample of 25 boys and 25 girls ranged in age from 62 to 74 months ($\bar{x}$ = 68.428; SD = 3.655). Ten children were randomly assigned to one of five experimental conditions: descriptive exploration questions; difference exploration questions; descriptive and difference exploration questions; descriptive, similarity, and difference exploration questions; or control.

*Materials and Procedure.* The materials were the same as described in Experiment 1. The procedure was the same as in Experiment 1 to the extent that children were exposed to two 10-minute training sessions. The contents of each condition (the difference exploration questions alone, descriptive exploration questions alone; and descriptive, similarity, and difference exploration questions conditions) were identical to the content outlined for those conditions in Experiment 1. A new condition was added to Experiment 2, a descriptive and difference exploration questions together condition. Thus, there were four treatment groups and a control group. The control group talked with the experimenter about their favorite school activities for 10 minutes. There were two experimenters in Experiment 2, one male and one female. They were randomly assigned to condition.

*The Dependent Measure.* Immediately following each treatment children were given the alternate uses test for one object on which they had not been questioned—an unfamiliar object. The criterion phase of Experiment 2 followed the procedure outlined in Experiment 1. Criterion phase objects were randomly chosen from the total array of four objects. The same crtieria as outlined in Experiment 1 for creative uses for each of the objects was followed.

*Results and Discussion.* The results of Experiement 2 indicate that the children exposed to the total array of exploration questions generated 64 creative uses for unfamiliar objects. Children exposed to descriptive exploration questions alone gave 41 creative uses, and children exposed to descriptive and difference exploration questions gave 55 uses. Children exposed to difference exploration questions alone gave 31 creative uses, and control children gave 13 creative uses.

A one-way ANOVA was used to determine the effect of condition on the ability to generate novel uses for unfamiliar objects. A significant effect for condition was detected, $F$ (6, 42) = 5.81, $p < .002$ ($R^2 = .453$). Newman-Keuls post hoc, preset at .10, indicated that the total exploration questioning paradigm ($\bar{x} = 6.4$) was significantly more effective than the descriptive and difference exploration ($\bar{x} = 5.5$) condition which was, in turn, significantly more effective than the descriptive exploration condition ($\bar{x} = 4.1$). The latter condition was significantly more effective than the difference exploration alone condition ($\bar{x} = 3.1$) which was, in turn, significantly more effective than the control group ($\bar{x} = 1.3$).

These results replicate previous work by Pellegrini (1981a, 1982) indicating that children exposed to the total exploration questioning paradigm are able to transfer the strategy to an unfamiliar object. The results from Experiment 2 further indicate that posing both descriptive and difference exploration questions to children is more successful than either of these strategies alone. The effectiveness of the condition was due to its additive structure. That is, it combines two factors that by themselves are facilitative of young children's associative fluency.

## GENERAL DISCUSSION

The two experiments reported here provide insight into the methods of exploration training most responsible for facilitating one aspect of children's creative behavior, associative fluency. In the first study, children were asked to generate creative uses for objects they had previously examined in their respective training conditions. Two important individual methods facilitative of associative fluency were identified in Experiment 1: answering descriptive exploration questions and answering difference exploration questions. Descriptive exploration questions allowed children to explore objects' attributes and generate associations for the attributes; for example, cylindrical shape can be associated with a barrel. Difference exploration questions allowed children to put objects into many different categories; for example, a pipe cleaner is a member of the class of white objects and of soft objects. Children in this condition could draw upon objects from these new classes for possible creative uses. For example, a pipe cleaner could be used for a cigarette, because they are both members of the class of white objects.

Results from Experiment 2 showed that children could transfer both the descriptive and difference exploration strategies to objects not examined during treatments. These two conditions had an additive effect on the transfer task in

Experiment 2: the combination of descriptive and difference exploration questions was more effective than either of the questioning strategies alone that were, by themselves, effective.

The most effective facilitator of associative fluency for both unfamiliar and familiar objects was the condition where children explored objects first by answering descriptive exploration questions then answered similarity and difference exploration questions about the objects. The similarity exploration questions probably enabled children to explore further each objects' attributes. For example, noting that a spool and a cork are both cyclindrical may have enabled children to describe attributes not described while answering the descriptive exploration question. The similarity exploration questions placed before the difference exploration questions, then, may have functioned as additional training in exploring objects' attributes.

In summary, the results of the two experiments indicate that young children's associative fluency can be facilitiated by training two skills. The first skill is exploration of objects attributes by answering descriptive exploration questions and then similarity and difference exploration questions. The second skill relates to the ability to answer difference exploration questions.

## ACKNOWLEDGMENTS

I would like to acknowledge Bill Owens and the Institute for Behavioral Research for their support of this project. I dedicate this chapter to Charles Smock, friend and colleague.

## REFERENCES

Bruner, J., Jolly, A., & Sylva, K. (Eds.) *Play.* New York: Basic Books, 1976.

Cazden, C. Play with language and metalinguistic awareness: One dimension of language experience. *The Urban Review,* 1974, *1,* 23–29.

Chomsky, C. *Consciousness is relevant to linguistic awareness.* Paper presented at International Reading Association seminar on Linguistic Awareness and Learning to Read, June 1979, Victoria, British Columbia.

Cocking, R., & Sigel, I. The concept of decalage as it applies to representational thinking. In N. Smith & M. Franklin (Eds.), *Symbolic functioning in childhood.* Hillsdale, N.J.: Lawrence Erlbaum, 1979.

Dansky, J. L. Cognitive consequences of sociodramatic play and exploration training for economically disadvantaged preschoolers. *Journal of Child Psychology and Psychiatry,* 1980, *20,* 47–58.

Dansky, J. L., & Silverman, I. W. Effects of play on associative fluency in preschool-age children. *Developmental Psychology,* 1973, *9,* 38–43.

Dansky, J. L., & Silverman, I. W. Play: A general facilitator of associative fluency. *Developmental Psychology,* 1975, *11,* 104.

Hutt, C. Exploration and play in children. *Symposia of the Zoological Society of London,* 1966, *18,* 61–81.

Hutt, C., & Bhavnani, R. Predictions from play. *Nature,* 1972, *237,* 216–219.

Kirschenblatt-Gimblet, B. (Ed.). *Speech play.* Philadelphia: University of Pennsylvania, 1976.

Pavio, A. Dual coding: Theoretical issues and empirical evidence. In J. Scandura & C. Brainerd (Eds.), *Structural models of complex behavior.* Alphen and denRijn, The Netherlands: Sijthoff & Noorhoff, 1978.

Pellegrini, A. The relationship between kindergartners' play and achievement in pre reading, language, and writing. *Psychology in the Schools,* 1980, *17,* 530–535.

Pellegrini, A. A sequenced questioning paradigm as a general facilitator of preschoolers' associative fluency. *Perceptual and Motor Skills,* 1981, *52,* 649–650. (a)

Pellegrini, A. Speech play and language development in young children. *Journal of Research and Development in Education,* 1981, *14,* 73–80. (b)

Pellegrini, A. Learning through verbal interaction: The effects of three conceptual conflict strategies of preschoolers' associative fluency. *Journal of Applied Developmental Psychology,* 1982, *3,* 39–46.

Pellegrini, A., & Greene, H. The use of a sequenced questioning paradigm to facilitate associative fluency in preschoolers. *Journal of Applied Developmental Psychology,* 1980, *1,* 189–200.

Pepler, D., & Ross, H. The effects of play on convergent and divergent problem solving. *Child Development,* 1981, *52,* 1202–1210.

Rohwer, W. Implications of cognitive development for education. In P. H. Mussen (Ed.), *Carmichael's manual of child psychology* (Vol. 1). New York: Wiley, 1970.

Rubin, K. Fantasy play: Its role in the development of social skills and social cognitive. In K. Rubin (Ed.), *Children's play.* San Francisco: Jossey–Bass, 1980.

Rumelhart, D., & Abramson, A. A model of analogical reasoning. *Cognitive Psychology,* 1973, *5,* 1–28.

Sigel, I. On becoming a thinker: A psycho-educational model. *Educational Psychologist,* 1979, *14,* 70–78.

Sutton-Smith, B. The role of play in cognitive development. *Young Children,* 1967, *22,* 364–369.

Sylva, K., Bruner, J., & Genova, P. The role of play in the problem solving of children 3–5 years old. In J. Bruner, A. Jolly, K. Sylva (Eds.), *Children's play.* New York: Basic Books, 1976.

Vandenberg, B. Play, problem solving, and creativity. In K. Rubin (Ed.), *Children's play.* San Francisco: Jossey–Bass, 1980.

Wallach, M. Creativity. In P. H. Mussen (Ed.), *Carmichael's manual of child psychology* (Vol. 1). New York: Wiley, 1970.

Weisler, A., & McCall, R. Exploration and play: Resume and redirection, *American Psychologist,* 1976, *31,* 492–508.

# 14 Play in Public School Settings: A Philosophical Question

Carl D. Glickman
*University of Georgia*

## Introduction

> The play school is a school organization with its programme of activities and methods based on the central idea of uniting the spontaneous play-life of the child, who needs and desires leadership, with society's demand that he be instructed. It is an effort to solve the problems of elementary education by harmonizing the child's extra-home educational experiences through combining in one institution, the functions of the schools; hence, the term "play school" [Hetherington, 1914, p. 1].

So began the description of the first experimental play school in elementary education at the University of California. In the summer of 1913 the school, located in an eucalyptus grove in Berkeley, California, was under the directorship of Clark W. Hetherington, a former student of G. Stanley Hall. Other educators had incorporated play as a methodology for learning into their elementary school curriculums in such diverse places as Greenwich Village, New York, in 1912 and Fairhope, Alabama, in 1914. The early 1910s were a unique time for the use of play in school settings. Yet there were others who saw the solution to educational problems in a far different light and the play movement eventually died, not to reappear again until the 1960s and then only to fade again.

In the 1980s the response to educational problems might be typified by the work of researcher Rosenshine (1979) who has found "direct instruction" to be the most successful methodology in assuring student achievement. Direct instruction, he admits, can appear to be "something grim . . . large groups, decision making by the teacher, limited choice of materials and activities by students, orderliness, factual questions, limited exploration of ideas, drill, and high percentages of correct answers [p. 48].'' Rosenshine's conclusions are based on results of over a dozen studies of teaching effectiveness.

The two methodologies for learning—play and direct instruction—are two views of education that have been in conflict since the appearance of the play school movement in the early 1900s. The choice between these methodologies cannot be empirically solved as they revolve around the changing purposes of public education. By looking at the span of preindustrial to contemporary times and focusing on historical and social issues, we might better understand why play in school settings has been always a philosophical decision. The chapters in this book present research on the results of play. The outcomes can be used to justify play in the school curriculum only if the public is willing to reconsider the purposes of education. To what extent this will occur and to what extent play will make greater inroads into public school curriculum will become apparent as the historical and philosophical voyage is undertaken.

This chapter focuses on public schools and primarily elementary schools. Preschool curriculum and methodology have paralleled elementary schools in limited ways. Much of the preschool movement originated apart from public funding and traditionally has been immune to public concern. Early childhood education until recent times has been mainly a private affair provided by the wealthy for the wealthy or by the wealthy for the poor (Braun & Edwards, 1972). Preschool, in being apart from public or government purpose has been largely allowed to operate as the head teacher or director wished. The director would determine the ''what'' and the ''how'' of curriculum and instruction. For that reason, play has been more evident in preschools. Parents either chose to send their children to a certain preschool or not. The element of choice, or ''if you don't like it, leave'' mentality allowed for greater autonomy of the early education curriculum planners. Ironically, when such preschool settings become important to government purpose and therefore were supported by public funds did preschool curriculums become more susceptible to pressures placed on public elementary schools. The preschool curriculum and elementary school curriculum are now closer intertwined and subjected to the same influences, pressures, expectations, and limitations.

The preschool and elementary curriculum, however, never will be identical because of the strong tradition of play as essential for the learning of the very young. Such a tradition goes back to the first formal preschool settings developed by the pioneers of play—Rousseau, Froebel, and Pestalozzi. However, where preschool and elementary school meet, at the kindergarten level, the raging controversy of purpose and curriculum as it relates to play is most evident. Is play a frill for kindergarteners? Should kindergarten curriculum consist of direct instruction methods or is play of lasting educational purpose that should be a part of all children's schooling, preschool through adulthood?

In an introduction we must define some terms. Obviously, the most critical word to define would be "play". Yet that is the definition that must remain undefined. The definition of play is tied to educational purpose and each historical setting has had a different purpose and therefore a different definition. A brief example might suffice. Garvey (1977) has a contemporary definition of play as: "(1) pleasurable, enjoyable . . . (2) . . . no extrinsic goals. Its motivations are intrinsic . . . (3) involves some active engagement [p. 4]." To say that play is "pleasurable and enjoyable" is to suggest its purpose is self-satisfaction. To say that "play has no extrinsic goals" is to suggest a lack of conscious purpose. To say that play involves "active engagement" would suggest the purpose of activity. This is a definition written in 1977 and does not reflect how play was viewed in 1777 or 1877. There is danger in interpreting historical events, ideas, and feelings according to terminology of a present era.

The definition of play in preindustrial times was commonly thought of as a child's imitation of adults and the release of surplus energy. The definition in industrial times was that play was a frivolous and nonproductive activity. During the progressive era, play was viewed as active problem solving and socialization. In the post-World War II era, it was again seen as frivolous and nonproductive. During the protest era, play was thought of in Garvey's terms of pleasurable, enjoyable, intrinsic, and the active base for cognitive, social, motor, and language development. In today's era, play again is being defined as unimportant. These are simplified definitions according to periods of times. They don't take into account the changing definitions of one time swirling into later times or the unnoticed definitions of one time becoming dominant later. However, such generalized definitions of play help in understanding what is needed today for play to become an accepted practice in elementary school settings.

The terms educational philosophy, curriculum, methodology, and epistemology, are more stable terms that will be defined for purposes of this chapter. Educational philosophy is the *why* of education; it answers the question "why" should there be education? Curriculum is the *what* of education; it answers the question "what" should be learned by students? Methodology is the *how* of education; it answers the question of "how" should curriculum be taught? Epistemology is the *study of knowledge;* it is a study of the nature and existence of knowledge.

## EDUCATIONAL PHILOSOPHY AND EPISTOMOLOGY OF THE TIMES

Periods of time can be characterized according to educational philosophies of essentialism, experimentalism, and existentialism (Morris, 1961; Pratte, 1971). These characteristics of philosophy and period do not account for all thought about education but they do explain the dominance of thought within particular periods. Essentialism is a philosophy of absolute order, external knowledge, and predetermined regulation of life (Johnson et al., 1973). Experimentalism is a philosophy of interactionalism, knowledge as practical, and life as changeable (Morris, 1961). Existentialism is a philosophy of irrationality, knowledge as individualistic, and life as despair (Johnson, Collins, Dupuis, & Johansen, 1973).

Essentialism is the educational encompassment of the philosophies of idealism and realism. Idealism was a belief in ultimate truths that the human mind could be prepared to glimpse but would never attain on its own. The mind when properly trained could through the act of faith leap the void and be at one with truth. Plato's allegory of the cave is perhaps the best example. The truth could not be seen by human eyes, only its reflection could be observed. Education, therefore, was the practice of instilling the mind with the proper rigor, discipline, and knowledge that would ready a person to observe the reflections of truth and be transformed by it. Realism on the other hand was a belief that knowledge consisted of the natural rhythms and regulations of life. Knowledge was not gained by faith but rather by reason. With proper training in logic and science, one could observe first hand the predetermined cycles of existence. Man was part of that natural order and understanding one's place was of utmost importance. Educational philosophers have placed both of these philosophies under the same title of essentialism because of the similarity of purpose. The aim of education for both idealism and realism was for students to learn the essential and timeless facts of existence. Those facts were taught by a teacher who possessed that superior knowledge and who transmitted it through lecture, recitation, and drill to students. Transmission of an external body of knowledge was critical to students learning and accepting their place in the world. For example, the *New England Primer* in 1848 (Braun & Edwards, 1972) taught students "It is man's duty to accept his place in the social scheme uncomplainingly [p. 86]."

The second educational philosophy was that of experimentalism, often referred to as progressivism. The notions of fixed bodies of knowledge and universal principals of nature unalterable by man were replaced by an optimism that man could change the external order. Knowledge was what worked. Reason and science were the means, not the ends, of education. The purpose of education was for man to be able to assess his environment and then experiment with ways to improve it. Ultimately, man could use knowledge to better his lot in life with increased comfort, consumption, and efficiency. A teacher was one who could facilitate problem solving among students. The teacher was prepared to understand the student as well as the skills of inquiry and then place them together in scientific, experimental ventures.

The third educational philosophy is existentialism. It emerged as a loose body of literature, poetry, and drama that had in common the dismissal of ultimate knowledge, science, and reason as means or ends but instead proclaimed the world as irrational. Existentialism was a philosophy that rejected any truths or any common principles other than the subjectivity of the individual's experience. Chaos existed outside of the human mind and it is only the human mind that puts meanings on that chaos. To learn a body of knowledge was to mislead oneself to think that there is outside reason to existence. Existence was simply itself. Education was thus a process of enabling an individual to free himself from conventional thinking in order to explore his own inner feelings, thoughts, and experience. A teacher was therefore one who removes the obstacles from a student in knowing the self. He helps to open the expressive channels of the person's being.

These educational philosophies can be compared in several ways so that they acquire force when history, play, and school curriculum are explained. Please refer to Fig. 14.1.

According to each educational philosophy, the value and type of play as a methodology becomes distinct. Essentialism as a practicing philosophy would have little use for play in a school setting. Play would be used, if at all, only as pleasurable activities ordered to result in student acquisition of predetermined knowledge. Experimentalism as a practicing philosophy in a school would have greater use for play as a pleasurable, interactive process between the learner and the environment that would result in problem solving. Existentialism would use play as both intrinsic method and content that gives insight to the individual's inner self. The same word "play" interpreted according to a distinct set of educational beliefs makes for very diverse applications in a classroom or school setting. The use and purpose of play in schools has developed throughout American history. It is time to look at that development.

| | *Essentialism* | *Experimentalism* | *Existentialism* |
|---|---|---|---|
| Knowledge: | Absolute, Basic, | Interactional, Relevant, Change Oriented | Subjective, Personal |
| Teacher: | Possessor of knowledge | Guider of scientific inquiry | Agent for liberation |
| Student: | Absence of kowledge | Explorer of outside world | Unaware of existence |
| Method: | Transmittal-lecture, recitation | Laboratory process, problem solving | Self awareness through discussion contemplation |
| Purpose: | Understand the individuals role within the order | Create change of the established order to improve human existence | Understand one's self as the meaning to the world |

FIG. 14.1 Characteristics of educational philosophies.

## THE HISTORICAL AND SOCIAL EVOLUTION OF PLAY[1]

The following section describes the historic development of play within the public school curriculum. A look is taken at the beginnings of play, the preindustrial era, the industrial era, the progressive era, the post-World War II era, and the Protest era.

### History

*The Beginnings of Play.* Play, as an educational enterprise, has its roots in the French revolution. The restricted, constrained society of France in the eighteenth century came under direct challenge by persons who attacked the formality and class privileges of the aristocracy. Rousseau believed that changes in a society were linked intricately with changes in the education of society's youth. The classical schooling of memorization and recitation for children of the aristocracy, according to Rousseau, accounted for the rulers of society being detached and unconcerned with the needs of the people. Rousseau (1762/1911) believed that those who were destined to rule must, so to speak, ''get their hands dirty'' as children and live as children not as affected adults. He wrote in *Emile:*

> What is to be thought, therefore, of that cruel education which sacrifices the present to an uncertain future, that burdens a child with all sorts of restrictions and begins by making him miserable, in order to prepare for some far off happiness which he may never enjoy?. . . . As soon as they are aware of the joy of life, let them rejoice in it; Mankind has its place in the sequence of things; childhood has its place in the sequence of human life; the man must be treated as a man and the child as a child [pp. 42–44].

Rousseau's rather startling idea of treating a child as unique and respecting joyfulness and curiosity within the natural environment was the beginning of the belief that play contributed to later development. He believed that a child needed to be active in a natural environment where a tutor would follow the child and respond to the child's questions and movements.

Rousseau initiated the idea of using a student's own inclinations to question, to act, and to explore as a foundation for learning. His book on pedagogy, *Emile,* was a theoretical discourse about such an ideal education. A few followers of Rousseau put such radical ideas into actual settings. Pestalozzi (1898) first operated a school on a farm for poor children. He later operated an orphanage and wrote two works about his ways of teaching. He applied Rousseau's view of the

---

[1]The following section is a slight adaptation of part of a previous article by the author entitled ''Play and the school curriculum: The historical context,'' *Journal of Research and Development in Education,* 1981, *14* (3).

child as an active explorer of nature, with a prescribed teaching methodology based on "sense impression." He wrote: "I wish always to let sense impression precede the word, and definite knowledge the judgment. I wish to make words and talk unimportant on the human mind and to secure that preponderance due to the actual impressions of physical objects [p. 336]." Pestalozzi stated that a child needed concrete, tactile experiences prior to abstract, symbolic experiences. He believed in a loving, firm teacher who would work with children following guidelines of extending knowledge from sense to abstraction.

Froebel (1887), who read Rousseau's writings and worked with Pestalozzi, went beyond theory and method to create materials for children. He organized a child's activities by developing instructional materials, or "gifts." His natural gardens for young children (i.e., kindergartens) eventually became formalized schools for preschoolers. In such settings, he provided materials such as balls of yarn, cubes, cylinders, and clay. Teaching manuals were developed on how to use each "gift" with a child. He emphasized the teacher's role of providing the materials, organizing the environment, and encouraging the child to discover meaning in the objects. He wrote:

> Do not however tell him in words much more than he could find himself without your words. For it is, of course, easier to hear the answer from another, perhaps to only half hear and understand it, than it is to seek and discover it himself . . . Do not, therefore, always answer your children's questions at once and directly; but as soon as they have gathered sufficient strength and experience, furnish them with the means to find the answers in the sphere of their own knowledge [pp. 85–87].

It might appear that Rousseau's, Pestalozzi's, and Froebel's establishment of a pedagogy of play would gather momentum from that point on. Their pedagogy was a break from the essentialist philosophy of education with Rousseau advocating an existentialist position and Pestalozzi and Froebel taking a more interactional or experimentalist position. However, it was over a century before schools adopted a large scale infusion of play as educational methodologies. Nineteenth century society had little use for such pedagogy in schools.

*The Preindustrial Era.* Ironically, it was because of the common man's subsistence, or "natural living," that Rousseau and others extolled as ideal for a child's learning that kept the role of play restricted in education. In preindustrial America and Europe, the lay citizenry spent their time farming or hunting. As a result, life was a predictable natural process. A man's young son learned to walk with his father, observed how to find or produce food, and as soon as he was sufficiently grown began to participate in this process. The same was true of a woman's daughter; the child learned the home maintenance role of her mother and gradually took a contributing role. Whether it was a boy learning to hoe, or a girl learning to mend, the same process of learning was at work. It consisted of imitation, apprenticeship, and finally, graduation into adulthood. Where communities established common or religious schools, the curriculum of the school was subservient to the curriculum of home. The planting, harvesting, or hunting season took priority over school. School was a place to go when the work at home was done. The subjects of school were religious instruction, reading, writing, and arithmetic. The purpose of school was to exercise the mind through recitation and memorization, as the home exercised the muscles of the body through physical work. Play was therefore viewed as useful in only two respects. First, for the very young child, play at home in the form of pretending to be the father (e.g., farmer or hunter) or the mother (e.g., cook, child care) was acceptable. The young could begin to learn their destined role through imaginary role play. Secondly, play as using surplus energy was seen as necessary at school (before the bell or at lunch time) to keep body energy from interfering with mental energy once the school work began.

The restricted role of play in traditional, stable societies has been illustrated by the research of Ager (1974) who studied a relatively intact Eskimo culture. Eskimo children played at being like their parents until outside influences disrupted the traditional society. Play in the preindustrial age can be characterized as imitative and surplus, rooted in agrarian existence.

Prior to the Industrial Era and the turn of the twentieth century, there were two parallel views of the educative value of play. In one, the Rousseauian vision, carried on by Pestalozzi and Froebel, that viewed concrete, sensory experience with a natural environment as the predecessor for abstract symbolic thinking. The other, and the prevailing cultural view, was that play was used to learn the roles of later life (Lee, 1915). The Rousseauian vision had some impact in the private nursery schools of Europe and later in the burgeoning Montessori movement. But this vision remained out of the mainstream of schools. The impact of the role view of play could be seen in the readings and recitations of the classroom (Huck, 1979). Students learned about the adult position, virtues, and responsibilities that they were to practice as children. In the practice of schooling, student initiated activity had little part in the school curriculum. Work was what life was all about. Play detracted from work and did not fit into this essentialist philosophy of education.

*The Industrial Era.* The cruel results of industrialization (e.g., massive exploitation of immigrants, child labor, and dislocation of families), demanded that children's roles in society be redefined. The question of what a child is and what will he become became critical concerns that emerged from a fragmentation of traditional society. In traditional society, children were viewed as immature adults who had to be taught and molded to be less childlike and less impulsive and active. Children were expected to become what their parents had been. In an industrial society, these views and expectations of children were no longer sufficient. A curious emergence of an experimentalism philosophy under a pervading essentialist point of view began to alter the schools in dramatic ways.

Industrialization became the metaphor for education (Kliebard, 1975). The application of industrial bureaucracy, specialization, and engineering was readily transferred to schools. The curriculum writing of Cubberly was indicative of this emphasis. Cubberly (1916) wrote:

> Our schools are, in a sense, factories in which the raw products (children) are to be shaped and fashioned into products to meet the various demands of life. The specifications for manufacturing come from the demands of twentieth-century civilization, and it is the business of the school to build its pupils according to the specifications laid down. This demands good tools, specialized machinery, continuous measurement of production to see if it is according to specifications, the elimination of waste in manufacture, and a large variety of the output [p. 338].

The turn of the century and the onset of industrialism meshed with the philosophy of realism and the predeterminism of man. All behavior could be viewed through cause and effect in accord with the rhythms of nature. The universe had a specific predetermined order in which every event could be traced to a previous one. In this view, schools should prepare children to find their place in this industrial order and contribute to the existing society.

The most influential spokesman of school engineering was Bobbitt (1918) who derived his principles of curriculum from the industrial management work of Taylor (1911). Teachers were trained according to scientific principles of instruction that standardized objectives, lesson plans, and methods of evaluation.

The study of social behavior through scientific principles was the means for finding more efficient educational practices. Curriculum now included those subjects that made man productive. Industrial subjects and vocational skills were introduced. Because play was not viewed as productive, it was regarded as frivolous and thus not included in schools.

Also at the turn of the century, immigrants came flowing into America, displaced from traditional agricultural societies arriving into a new world of varying cultures, experiences, ideas, and languages. The old use of play as imitation of adult life no longer seemed to fit (Lee, 1915). Immigrant parents no longer wanted their children to assume their adult roles. They had come to the new world so that their children might have a different and better life. The long hours of drudgery in the factory could be endured as long as the immigrants held to the belief of a better life for the next generation. Children were the future and children were a parent's investment in a better tomorrow. To prepare their children, many immigrants consciously abandoned preparing their children in the customs, manners, and speech of the old country. Instead, the schools were given the responsibility for the whole child, to "Americanize" the child culturally, socially, vocationally, and academically. This was the juncture where experimentalism and play made inroads into curriculums that were essentialistic and work oriented.

Schools had the tasks of Americanization. Schools were to be run scientifically, and with the age of science came a scientific curiosity for studying and analyzing new topics. Children's development was such a topic. The movement headed by Hall, and later Terman and Gessell, focused on children and studied the idiosyncrasies of intellectual, social, and physical growth of children as distinct from adults (Cremin, 1964).

The turn of the century was a time of departure and contradiction. On one hand, science was being used to serve schools as the principle for engineering an efficient, stripped-down, bureaucratic curriculum, and, on the other hand, science was being used to study children as distinct from adults, implying that they might not be best served by a factory model of schooling. With this, the incessant waves of immigrants enlarged the schools' responsibilities beyond "exercising the mind" into socialization and acculturation. As with every age, the dominant pattern of schooling (i.e., educational engineering movement) was hiding the emerging pattern of schooling for the next age (i.e., child-centered movement). This heady ocean of crosscurrents of science, child study, industrialization, immigration, and assimilation eventually broke into distinct rivers, and, in the progressive era, conflicting currents of educational thought clarified and clashed.

*The Progressive Era.* The definitive historian of the progressive education era, Cremin (1964) wrote:

> Actually, progressive education began as part of a vast humanitarian effort to apply the promise of American life—The ideal of government by, of, and for the people—to the puzzling new urban industrial civilization that came into being during the latter half of the nineteenth century . . . In effect, (progressivism was) a man-sided effort to use the schools to improve the lives of individuals. [p. viii]

This "many-sided effort" was not a uniform strand of thought and action. Progressivism was experimental philosophy in action. Progressivism manifested itself in alternative schools with different curriculums, diverse from each other but common in their rejection of the traditional schools. According to Cremin (1964): "The movements were marked from the very beginning by a pluralistic, frequently contradictory, character." The crosscurrents of science, production, immigration, assimilation, and child study made intriguing configurations and broke forever a restricted view of the purpose of school. Schools were not limited to training the mind and learning how to adapt. Schools were to be the lever for changing and improving society. The child's own inclination towards play was to be capitalized on as a method for learning social change.

Progressive education became identified with one person, Dewey, who combined his background as an educator, psychologist, and philosopher to develop a new look at children, learning, and teaching. His philosophy was, at least rhetorically, embraced by schools and political leaders. Dewey viewed man as an active agent who was not simply a cog in a machine, but one who could redesign or change the machine. This newly activated emphasis on man, previously expoused by Rousseau and others, opened the gates for the use of exploration, inquiry, problem-solving, and creativity as critical components of a school curriculum. Alternative schools experimented with ways to include student enjoyment and student choice.

Play, as the core methodology of curriculum, perhaps had its greatest implementation in Caroline Pratt's play school, begun in 1914 in Greenwich Village. Play was viewed as the means for artistic expression and the pursuit of a student's own ability, interest, and talent. The organic school in Fairhope, Alabama, headed by Johnson and described by the Deweys in 1915, capitalized on play activity and student initiative to lead to expanded studies. The previously mentioned play school in Berkeley, California in 1913 was another indication of how broad the play movement had become.

The play schools were Rousseauian visions put into a total curriculum. Pratt, Johnson, and Hetherington believed that play was the medium for all meaningful and lasting learning. Such a notion was given added credence by the popularity of Freudian psychology with its emphasis on childhood suppression as a cause of later adult neurosis. Therefore, play, as the expression of inner conflict, was vital for mental health. Play now had many supporters and with the pressure on the schools to assimilate the immigrants, the use of activities that were enjoyable to students such as role playing, socialization games, and field trips became essential components of school. Play became appropriate for the new, expanded role of the schools.

By the 1930s, the activity and child-centered curriculums were solidly established in university laboratory schools, in many school districts, and in traditional school subjects such as science and social studies. Students were encouraged to initiate learning by discussing, questioning, experimenting, and "brainstorming."

Categorizing 50 years of progressivism as the "play era in curriculum reform" might be misleading. Most teachers and schools persisted with lecture, textbooks, and written assignments, but such methods were slipping in adovacy. Active and pleasurable learning became ingrained in popular and professional thinking about what should exist in schools. The social group research of Lewin, Lippit, and White (1939), the perceptual laboratories of Kelley (1947), the child study of Gessell (1928), and the psychology of Freud (1935) supported curriculum being built around the child. It was "in" to be progressive.

The shift in educational purpose from essentialist to experimental had been made. The "tug of war" would go back and forth from this time on. The bureaucratic, factory model of school still held, but pleasure and activity within such a model was encouraged as a better way to learn to read, to write, to cooperate, and to live. However, by the 1950s the momentum towards incorporating more "play" opportunities in the school began to slow.

*The Post World War II Era.* The progressive era, characterized by a tolerance and encouragement for experimentation with all forms of subjects and methods in the curriculum, gradually dissipated in popularity. According to Cremin the movement died quickly due to (1) distortion; (2) negativism; (3) inordinate demands on teachers' time and ability; (4) outdated purpose in a new social order; and (5) a more general swing towards conservativism after World War II. According to Cremin (1964), the citizenry wanted "to keep taxes down . . . demand(ed) that fads and frills be eliminated from the system [p. 348]." Progressive education was attacked for being permissive and lacking intellectual rigor. The "mental discipline" curriculum of traditional subjects and teacher-directed instruction returned. Students were to sit, be quiet, listen, and memorize their textbooks. To allow students to interact, to laugh, and to play was no longer appropriate in a climate of cold war between the United States and the Union of the Soviet Socialist Republics. National security was the priority and McCarthy's purges of "pro-communists" were making the headlines (Manchester, 1973, pp. 636–645). Pressure was put on schools to produce loyal and obedient Americans.

"Playless" curriculum became more restrictive with the first successful Sputnik satellite launch by Russia. Russia's success was interpreted by the American government as a failure of the schools to teach properly mathematics and science. The solution was to provide funds for curriculum laboratories to establish faster-paced learning in the schools. Instead, those hired to construct more efficient curriculum materials turned to the previously ignored cognitive studies of Piaget of the Geneva Institute, Bruner of the Institute for Cognitive Studies at Harvard, and others. These researchers documented the crucial role of early childhood experiences for later learning. Practitioners later would translate such research into programs in which the natural vehicle for learning in early childhood was a child's play. Head Start would be established as a nationally funded compensatory program for preschoolers to insure early educational experiences for poor children (Dittman, 1980). Many of these projects would incorporate all three elements of play (pleasure, intrinsic motivation, and active engagement). Furthermore, the early childhood research implied that learning was developmental and that activity was important for older as well as younger students. School reform based on cognitive research would make inroads into the mental discipline, subject-centered schools of the 1950s. Eventually play as the core of curriculum would reemerge in the informal activity-centered, open schools of the late 1960s and early 1970s. These schools would mirror the laboratory schools of the progressive era.

*The Protest Era.* As the traditional agrarian life of the nineteenth century was shattered by industrialization and immigration, so was life of the 1950s and early 1960s shattered by civil rights, Vietnam, and the antiwar movement. School reform and alternatives became once again ''in,'' and the schools became the lightning rods for changes in society. Integration, attacking poverty, and a new egalitarian morality were to be carried out through the schools. Federal money went into developing activity-based, inquiry-centered curriculums in almost all subjects. Federal monies were used to develop and purchase materials, train teachers, and implement ''new math,'' ''inquiry science,'' ''moral education,'' etc., in the new child-centered schools. Such curriculums consisted of structured activities that were often ''fun'' and engaging for students.

Smilansky, in her classic work published in 1968, documented play as both developmental and related to academic achievement. Her work was built on that of the child study researchers and the child cognitivist researchers, and moved ahead in its clear delineation of play as a field of important study. The ongoing research work of persons such as Mahler (1975), Freud (1971), Sutton-Smith (1967), Singer (1973), Bruner, Cole, and Lloyd (1977) and Piaget (1971) has lent stature to play in schools. The late 1960s was a time of revolutionary ferment, ripe for alternative schools that capitalized on activism in the curriculum. The use of play could be readily defended by respected international authorities. Play was justified as essential for learning, but beyond that as a moral and constitutional right of students to be able to question, to move, to puzzle, and to make choices.

*Today.* After the protest movement had waned, the war was over, and the political scandal of Watergate had abated, societal concerns shifted from reforming government and alternative schools to slowing inflation and reversing the decline in student achievement scores. The conservative ''back to basics'' movement took hold of school and ''play'' was one of its first victims. Direct instruction became the banner of instruction for the late 1970s and early 1980s. More time on direct instruction in reading, writing, and arithmetic replaced the time previously spent on activities such as developing a skit, planning a trip, or brainstorming.

## SCHOOL PURPOSE

Goodlad's (1982) recent study on public schooling has documented that over 80% of classroom time is spent in ''up front'' teaching, the teacher standing in front of the class, lecturing, asking specific recall questions, and giving written seat work assignments. Goodlad mentioned that this preponderence of teacher direction and student passivity is reinforced by the research that ''direct instruction'' produces higher student scores on reading and mathematics instruction. Clearly if the purpose of education is students making immediate gains on achievement tests than play should *not* be part of the curriculum.

Keep in mind that childhood did not become a distinct period of life until the time of Rousseau. The first books for children's amusement were written by Newbery around 1740. Until then children were viewed, dressed, and expected to behave as miniature adults. Only in the last 300 years has there been acknowledgment of childhood as an age unto itself (Greenleaf, 1978, p. 66–67). Furthermore, play as a desirable activity of childhood is very recent. The following is a description by Greenleaf of the first playgrounds in America:

> Only slowly did there develop an appreciation of play and the benefits it could bring to children, especially poor city children. Following the lead of German educators, a woman's charitable organization had heaps of sand dumped at two locations in Boston in 1885. The neighborhood children seemed to enjoy them, so the following year three heaps of sand were set out. Thus was born the American playground [106].

Play as an organized recreational activity and sponsored by adults for children is only about a hundred years old. By 1913, some 28 years from the first heap of sand, some elementary schools were basing their *entire* curriculum around play. Within 30 years play went from obscure importance to the core of education. Why it did not remain and why it has continued to recycle in and out of public school settings since then is the critical issue for those who desire its future use in school curriculum.

The research on play has not demonstrated its value to schools that have essentialist purpose. If the purpose of schools were experimental or existential than a stronger case for its use could be made. Peterson (1979) has shown that in schools in which the educational purpose is problem-solving, creativity, cooperation, and self awareness, the use of play is an appropriate means to those ends.

The times in which we sit are again characterized as essentialist. The political and social climate is one of fiscal austerity and accountability for predetermined ends. Schools have been reduced in budget, staff, and materials. Schools are being asked to limit their purpose and to focus on reversing declining achievement scores. Unless research can show the benefits of play to such goals, it will not find a place in today's schools. Many researchers (including many of the authors of chapters in this book) have attempted to show the relationship of guided play of preschoolers with cognitive and academic gains. For example, both Pellegrini and Yawkey have shown that as symbolic and sociodramatic play is developed by preschool children, the better students perform on reading tests. Yet these studies, as most other play studies, are of preschool or primary children and are used to support an ongoing tradition of play that is a foundation of early childhood education. There are relatively few studies of the relationship of play with upper primary and elementary school achievement. Without such knowledge, the work tradition of public schools will be little altered.

How might play advocates respond to this problem? There are at least three courses of action. First, play advocates can attempt to alter or enlarge the purpose of public schools so that experimental or existential learning is valued. By enlarging purpose, justifications for play as part of curriculum exists. For example, Eisner (1982) has argued that learning must include social and aesthetic activities if society is to have adults who use their full intelligence to process, interpret, and represent information.

Second, play advocates can accept the current purpose of schools and call for more research on play's role in student academic outcomes. For example, there is a possibility that play, although not producing short-term measurable skill achievement, might have an accumulative effect that raises achievement over several years. The longitudinal studies of Head Start students have shown that in secondary schools they academically outperform control groups (Weikart, Epstein, Schweinhart, & Bond, 1978). How many of those students were influenced by early childhood play is not known. Third, play advocates might select and defend only those play interventions that research has shown already to be achievement producing and therefore justifiable to the current essentialist curriculums.

These are three responses that are sure to divide play advocates. The issue is whether to alter current school purpose or accept it as is. A case in point is the friendly rebuttal between two colleagues on the research in play. Silvern (1981) chided Yawkey for defending play as contributing to the essentialist purpose of academic achievement. Silvern argued that play is of larger value than basic skills and, therefore, need not be defended. His reasoning was that Yawkey's defense of play as related to school achievement would restrict the use of play as an activity good unto itself. We have an example of two friends engaged in a serious philosophical debate about the purposes of education.

To possibly resolve this debate, this author would begin by siding with Yawkey but hope to eventually side with Silvern. The view of play as good in itself has had a major contribution to the demise of play today. Cremin (1964) described this demise as: "Taken up as a fad, it eliciated not only first rate art, but every manner of shoddiness and self-deception as well. In too many classrooms license began to pass for liberty, planlessness for spontaneity, recalcitrants for individuality, obfuscation for art, and chaos for education [207].

Cremin was writing of the death of the play and expressionist schools of the progressive era but the same could be said for the play and open classroom movement of the late 1960s and 1970s. There were many fine classrooms and schools where students engaged in play that was purposefully directed toward certain ends whether they be academic, social, or attitudinal. Yet in some classrooms, teachers used play as a reason for not teaching and not guiding. Almost anything could and did occur. Students were often left without guidelines, materials, or organized environments. The teacher could rationalize that because play was good in itself, one need not be concerned with purposeful or developmental sequences or activities, experience, and knowledge.

It was a minority who viewed play in such an irresponsible way but they dragged down an entire movement of a majority of educators who believed in purposeful play. The simple crux of the issue is that *play, to be incorporated into a public school that is an educative institution, must be educative.* Public institutes are organized and supported according to educational purpose. Therefore, play as intrinsic is not enough to justify its use or the expenditure of time, materials, monies, and human energy allocated by the public. Play in schools has to be structured according to purpose, such as reading test scores or self esteem outcomes. Researchers have to provide practitioners with guidance of the type of play, the method of play, the organization of play, and the props of play that will improve the purpose of school. In doing so, they also might suggest some other purposes of education that play could accomplish.

To summarize, what is needed are two levels of play application to public schools. First, researchers must show what type, form, and structure of play will achieve essentialist purposes of academic achievement. Second, researchers must show what other purposes besides academic achievement play can contribute. In doing so, researchers will provide curriculum developers and public school leaders with an information base as to the means for attaining other experimental and existential purposes.

## ACKNOWLEDGMENT

My thanks to Dr. Sylvia Feinburg of Tufts University for helping to extend my thinking about play and purpose.

## REFERENCES

Ager, L. P. Play among Alaskan Eskimos. *Theory into Practice,* 1974, *13* (4), 252–256.

Bobbitt, F. *The curriculum.* Boston: Houghton Mifflin, 1918.

Braun, S. J., & Edwards, E. P. *History and theory of early childhood education.* Belmont, Cal.: Wadsworth, 1972.

Bruner, J., Cole, M., & Lloyd, B. (Eds.). *The developing child.* Cambridge, Mass.: Harvard University Press, 1977.

Cremin, L. A. *The transformation of the school.* New York: Vintage Books, 1964.

Cubberly, E. O. *Public administration.* Boston: Houghton Mifflin, 1916.

Dittman, L. L. Project Head Start becomes a long distance runner. *Young Children,* 1980, *35,* 2–9.

Eisner, E. W. *Cognition and curriculum: A basis for deciding what to teach.* New York: Longman, 1982.

Freud, A. *The ego and the mechanisms of defense.* New York: International Universities Press, 1971.

Freud, S. *A general introduction to psychoanalysis.* New York: Liveright, 1935.

Froebel, F. *The education of man.* Translation by W. N. Hailman. New York: Appleton, 1887.

Garvey, C. *Play.* Cambridge, Mass.: Harvard University Press, 1977.

Gessell, A. L. *Infancy and human growth.* New York: Macmillan, 1928.

Glickman, C. D. Play and the school curriculum: The historical context. *Journal of Research and Development,* 1981, *14*(3), 1–10.

Goodlad, J. A study of schooling. A presentation to the Stanford (Cal.) Teacher Education Project, Jan. 28, 1982.
Greenleaf, B. K. *Children through the ages: A history of childhood.* New York: McGraw–Hill, 1978.
Hetherington, C. W. *The demonstration play school of 1913.* Berkeley, Cal.: University of California Publications, 1914.
Huck, C. S. *Children's literature in the elementary school* (3rd edition). New York: Holt, Rinehart & Winston, 1979.
Johnson, J. A., Collins, H. W., Dupuis, V. L., & Johansen, J. H. *Foundations of American education.* Boston: Allyn & Bacon, 1973.
Kelley, E. C. *Education for what is real.* New York: Harper & Row, 1947.
Kliebard, H. M. Bureaucracy and curriculum theory. In W. Pinar (Ed.), *Curriculum theorizing.* Berkeley, Cal.: McCutchan, 1975.
Lee, J. *Play in education.* New York: Macmillan, 1915.
Lewin, K., Lippit, R., & White, R. Patterns of aggression in experimentally created social climates. *Journal of Social Psychology,* 1939, *10,* 271–299.
Mahler, M. S. *On psychological birth of the human infant.* New York: Basic Books, 1975.
Manchester, W. *The glory and the dream: A narrative history of America 1932–1972.* Boston: Little, Brown, 1973.
Morris, V. C. *Philosophy and the American school.* Boston: Houghton Mifflin, 1961.
Pestalozzi, J. H. *How Gertrude teaches her children and an account of the method.* Translation by L. E. Holland & F. C. Turner. Syracuse, N.Y.: C. W. Bardeen, 1898.
Peterson, P. S. Direct instruction reconsidered. In P. O. Peterson & J. H. Walberg (Eds.), *Research on teaching.* Berkeley, Cal.: McCutchan, 1979.
Piaget, J. *The construction of reality in the child.* New York: Ballantine, 1971.
Pratte, RR. *Contemporary theories in education.* Scranton, Pa.: T. Y. Crowell, 1971.
Rosenshine, B. V. Content, time and direct instruction. In P. L. Peterson & J. J. Walberg (Eds.), *Research on teaching.* Berkeley, Cal.: McCutchan, 1979.
Rousseau, J. J. *Emile* (translation by B. Foxley). New York: Dutton, 1911. (Originally published, 1762).
Silvern, S. B. A Response to Yawkey: Play! Why not? *Educational Research Quarterly.* 1981, *6* (1), 77–79.
Singer, J. L., 19 *The child's world of make believe: Experimental studies of imaginative play.* New York: Academic Press, 1973.
Smilansky, S. *The effects of socio dramatic play on disadvantaged preschool children.* New York: Wiley, 1968.
Sutton-Smith, B. The role of play in cognitive development. *Young children,* 1967, *22,* 361–370.
Taylor, F. W. *The principles of scientific management.* New York: Harper, 1911.
Weikart, D. P., Epstein, A., Schweinhart, L., & Bond, J. T. *The Ypsilanti preschool curriculum demonstration project: Preschool years and longitudinal results.* Ypsilanti, Mich.: High Scope Press, 1978.

# 15 Play in Developmental Preschool Settings

Nancy E. Curry
Sara H. Arnaud
*University of Pittsburgh*

## THE DEVELOPMENTAL PRESCHOOL

Recognizing the yeastiness in the preschool field centering around the controversy over the academic versus the developmental preschool—a controversy that was engendered and enlivened by Head Start and other rapidly expanding programs such as Title XX Day Care for preschool children, we wish to make it clear from the outset that we espouse the developmental approach (as exemplified by Bank Street, Dalton School, Arsenal Family & Children's Center of the University of Pittsburgh, and laboratory schools of Oregon State University and the University of Minnesota).

The ideal of a developmental preschool is to provide a facilitating environment in which children can achieve their potential for optimal social, intellectual, emotional, moral, and physical growth and development. There is a basic philosophy underlying the program for all the children. Each child is seen as an individual with a unique constitutional endowment that has been and continues to be influenced by the child's social and cultural environment. Regardless of age groupings, the teacher varies the curriculum according to individual and group developmental needs.

In a developmental preschool each child is encouraged to be the active partner in the learning process—to be the actor, the doer, the initiator. Children determine their own curriculum rather than being expected to fit into a preset, lockstep curriculum. The ideas come from the child, and the teacher recognizes and helps the child put them into purposeful activities. Thus, the teacher must know each child in the group well and the children must trust the teacher enough to accept guidance.

In planning a curriculum, the main consideration is placed on the needs, interests, and capacities of individual children rather than emphasizing the program as an entity in itself (Lindberg & Swedlow, 1976; Moore & Kilmer, 1973; Read & Patterson, 1980; Schulman, 1967; Todd & Heffernan, 1977; Weber, 1971). The teacher creates a consistent yet flexible framework within which he/she is available at all times for helping children succeed in the learning process. The teacher does not dominate the play activities or the children but rather gives the message that the classroom and its activities belong to both children and teacher. Yet the teacher has clear goals that at times are implicit in the materials and their presentation and at other times are explicitly spelled out in actions and words.

## THE IMPORTANCE OF PLAY

The importance and value of play for the preschool child's social, emotional, and cognitive development have been basic tenets of the developmental preschool. Play can provide a rich variety of experience and at the same time is immediately satisfying and enjoyable in itself—thus furnishing the child's immediate incentive for carrying out the exploration, experimentation, and skill-learning involved in play. In young children, play takes on an increasingly symbolic elaboration. In early dramatic play, the child acts out many of his/her notions about how things are or might be, and, through the reactions of others, the child corrects or expands the ideas and feelings he is grappling with—a move that, repeated many times, ultimately leads to increasingly accurate perception and understanding of objective reality (Singer & Singer, 1979). Dramatic play around conflictful and anxiety-ridden themes can help not only in symbolic-cognitive-affective resolution of intrapsychic conflicts, but may free energy for more impersonal cognitive tasks (Axline, 1969; Erikson, 1963; Freud, A., 1970; Gould, 1972; Murphy, 1956; Peller, 1971; Sarnoff, 1976; Singer, 1973).

From the beginning of the century, there has been a stable corps of advocates for play who have had considerable impact on the preschool movement (such as, Dewey, Isaacs, and Griffiths among others), but recently (as the present volume attests) there has been a flood tide of empirical studies of various dimensions of play (Fein, 1981).

Our study of play has been based on observational data gathered at a university demonstration preschool.[1] We have focused on the dimension of pretend play that we have called role enactment (Arnaud & Curry, 1973b, 1973d; Curry & Arnaud, 1974, p. 273) which we have defined as follows: Role enactment occurs when the child transforms himself or herself in pretend play into a person

[1]Arsenal Family & Childrens Center, formerly of the University of Pittsburgh.

or object other than himself/herself, as indicated by the child's verbal and/or motoric enactment of his/her perception of that role.

Recent empirical studies, reviewed in Fein's (1981) exemplary article, affirm that there is a developmental progression in the ability to engage in pretend play that seems to reach a crescendo during the preschool years. Yet, we have observed, both directly in the classroom, on film (Arnaud & Curry, 1973a through 1973e), and/or videotape and indirectly (through numerous student observations and consultations with teachers), that there are tremendous variations in both the quality and quantity of pretend play in nursery schools, day care centers, and Head Start classrooms. Such variation cannot be explained solely on the basis of socioeconomic status, socio–cultural background, or the child's prior experience (Fein, 1981). This variation speaks to the importance of both the physical and human environment in supporting and facilitating what appears to be a genuine developmental process.

The focus of this paper is on the facilitation of pretend play, with realization that the capacity for play will depend on the child's developmental stage, previous experience, emotional state, and the climate provided for play. Three aspects of play facilitation shall be considered: through the environment, through adults, and through peers. Each form of facilitation has a different emphasis according to the growing child's developing abilities and interests.

Although we recognize the commonalities of behavior in children's developmental progression, we also stress that the great variability of play styles that arises from individual differences among children clearly modifies and buffers their environmental encounters (Abrams & Neubauer, 1976; Jennings, 1975; Singer & Singer, 1979; Wolf & Gardner, 1978). In the following three sections, we shall deal with commonalities in children's play. Next, cultural differences and similarities are focussed on. In the last section we discuss some individual differences.

## FACILITATION OF PRETEND PLAY THROUGH THE ENVIRONMENT[2]

The importance of the physical environment for depthful play has been well established. The professional literature on environmental design has been accumulating both within and outside the field of child development. VanderVen's review of this literature (VanderVen, 1977) gives a comprehensive survey of the available literature on this extensive subject. Several excellent publications (Day & Sheehan, 1975; Dittman, 1968; Harms, 1970; Kritchevsky, Prescott, & Walling, 1969) deal with environmental design based on developmental principles.

[2]Material from this section is visually available in the film by Arnaud & Curry (1974) as well as described in Arnaud and Curry (1976).

The two latter groups of authors also provide guidelines and check lists to facilitate the evaluation of preschool settings.

Preschool texts (Lindberg & Swedlow, 1976; Moore & Kilmer, 1973; Read & Patterson, 1980; Todd & Heffernan, 1977) include as a matter of course sections on room arrangement, toy selection, and optimal use of space under the explicit assumption that the physical environment significantly influences children's activities.

Numerous research reports dealing with particular aspects of the preschool environment are available. For example, Fein (1981) reports on studies on the effect of realistic versus nonrealistic objects on the child's play, and Mueller and Vandell (1979), in a review of peer interactions in infancy and toddlerhood, discuss the effects of toys on social interactions. Specifically, Pulaski (1973) studied the effects of structured versus unstructured toys on the level of the child's make-believe play and found at a statistically significant level "a greater variety of themes in response to unstructured toys [p. 9]." Elder and Pederson (1978) noted a developmental difference between 2 and 3½-year-olds with the younger children needing more realistic toys and the older children being able to play with objects that did not closely resemble the referential object.

From our experience in implementing a curriculum based on the child's intent urge to play (Curry, 1974), in consulting with Head Start and Title XX Day Care Centers, and in filming in a variety of cultural settings (Arnaud & Curry, 1975, 1976), it has become clear that teachers explicitly or implicitly facilitate the depth and satisfaction of pretend play through the selection and presentation of materials and through the use of space. The following environmental principles have been derived from the literature and from our own studies.

Rooms should be arranged for convenience, visibility, and accessibility of materials to children. Young children need predictability, confidence that the same materials will be found in the same place, yet benefit from occasional rearrangements that are novel enough to be intriguing, but not so different as to be overwhelming (Hunt, 1961). The clarity of the environment should suit the children's perceptual level, with arrangements orderly, simple, attractive, and easily grasped by eye and by hand.

Areas for different activities should be clearly defined and out of main traffic patterns, in order to permit ongoingness, reduce distracting stimuli, and protect play from an inadvertent invasion by other groups. For instance, no matter how well the blocks are set up, if the area is used by too many children at the same time, the play can become disorganized and frustrating. All areas should be in the teachers' range of vision, so that all adults in the classroom can supervise several areas. Lack of such visibility can, of necessity, force a teacher to declare areas or activities "out of bounds" if they cannot be supervised.

Provision should be made for toys and materials that appeal to specific ages and that lend themselves to symbolization of the children's experience. These include:

1. Models of things used in adult activities, which give children a chance to act out what they see as significant for adults whom they admire or fear—for example, phones, cars, cooking and housekeeping tools, and dress-up clothes.
2. Toy models or replicas of things that are emotionally meaningful to children and through which they can symbolize their own experiences and fantasies—such as toys that illustrate appearance and disappearance (e.g., kitten in the kegs); child-size toy beds, doll carriages, baby bottles, domestic and wild animal toys; dress-up clothes for adult roles such as firemen and doctor; glamorous gowns and veils. The introduction of specific toys (e.g., crutches) is warranted when children have life experiences that highlight the need for the use of such objects.
3. For older children, the props provide costuming possibilities for a wide array of both real and remote, mythic beings—crowns, cloaks, long sweeping garments. The children may manufacture many of these products themselves.

Further environmental principles include:

1. The availability of duplicate materials for younger children to accommodate their great difficulty in sharing and postponing and their strong impulses to imitate what they see other children doing.
2. An array of miniature life toys will encourage symbolization of experience that is one step removed from the children's directly acting it out themselves—Erikson's (1963) microspheric level of play (e.g., family figures, community helpers, tame and wild animals, small vehicles, doll house furniture).
3. Unstructured materials that lend themselves to many uses to give scope to imagination and improvision (e.g., sand, blocks, clay, paper and crayons, paint, play dough, and water).
4. The teacher's permission and encouragement for toys to be used in a multiplicity of ways, (e.g., the use of toy sinks as racing cars).

The two following sections deal with play facilitation by adults and by peers. They are based on the conviction that no matter how inviting the physical environment might be, the human beings in that environment make the difference between sterile, perfunctory play or fragmented, disorganized play, and play that is zestful and engrossing.

## FACILITATION BY ADULTS

The roots of play and learning begin in the earliest relationships, as the parent and/or care-giving person foster playfulness by initiating play ideas, by responding to the child's early efforts at pretend, by pointing out play possibilities among available toys, and by letting the child know he/she approves of the child's play ideas. The importance of the mother in the play of young children has been written of extensively, with Anna Freud's (1965) developmental line from play to work exemplifying the view that the earliest play has its root in the mother/child dyad. Current literature supports this view, with many authors agreeing on the importance of attachment (Ainsworth, 1978; Bowlby, 1969) and the importance of interactive play between mother and child (Dunn & Wooding, 1977; Fein, 1979; Garvey, 1977; Lewis, 1979; Ross & Kay, 1980; Sachs, 1980; Singer, 1973) and between father, mother, and child (Clarke-Stewart, 1978). The very early interaction between infant and mother has been scrutinized by Brazelton and Als (1979) who delineate four stages of organization in parent–infant interaction that culminate in the beginning of object play at approximately four or five months; Brazleton and Als feel that achievement of the latter phase is the "real test of attachment": "At the point where the mother or nurturing parent can indeed permit the *baby* to be the *leader or signal giver,* when the adult can recognize and encourage the baby's independent search for and response to environmental or social cues and games—to initiate them, to reach for and play with objects, etc.—the small infant's own feeling of competence and of voluntary control over his environment is strengthened [p. 366]."

In their review of the literature on infant interactions, Mueller and Vandell (1979) discuss various studies that deal with parent/infant and infant/infant relationships. They hypothesize that it is possible that parent/infant relationships follow one path whereas peer relations follow another. Eckerman, Whatley, and Kutz (1975), who studied normal home-reared children at ages 10 to 12 months, 16 to 18 months, and 22 to 24 months, spoke of how mother–child interactions influence interactions between peers and how interactions with peers may contribute in their own right to early social development. In our view the role of parents in social development is a crucial one affecting social relationships with peers and with meaningful adults outside the family.

Gradually the young child is able to use the teacher in a similar way. In encouraging play of very young children, the teacher may notice and use techniques reminiscent of those of a play-invested parent. A number of studies (Christie, 1982; Rosen, 1974; Saltz, Dixon, & Johnson, 1977) have been sparked by Smilansky's (1968) seminal work on the facilitation of sociodramatic play in disadvantaged Israeli preschool children. Investigators have found that adult facilitation of children's dramatic play can increase the quality and quantity of the play of American disadvantaged child (Freyberg, 1973) and can influence social roles and ability to conserve (Fink, 1976), language development (Lovinger, 1974), problem solving (Rosen, 1974), cognitive functioning and impulse control (Saltz, Dixon, & Johnson, 1977), and creative thinking (Feitelson & Ross, 1973).

We advocate some specific ways in which adults can facilitate play: With two year olds, the teacher helps the children become more aware of each other, interprets aloud what the other child is doing, and helps them begin to interact with each other. In Arnaud and Curry (1974) the teacher arbitrates between toddlers, explaining to each what the other is doing. For example, after one snatches the other's blocks and forms a circle with them, she points out that the blocks could be a circle, says that the first child had been using them as an airplane hangar, and clarifies that a hangar is like a garage.

Further, the adult encourages play through structuring the environment, providing props, and reinforcing play when it occurs through attention, comment, and open approval, as well as occasionally providing an idea or suggesting an elaboration. The adult needs also to accommodate to the slow, deliberate pace of some 2-year-olds in their play, for in spite of the claim that 2-year-olds have short attention spans they clearly can become immersed and even entrenched in an activity. They will resist being hurried by a schedule that does not take into account their seemingly erratic timing, which includes as well easy distractibility. Two-year-olds are so acutely tuned to adult approval and modeling and to other children's activities that they will easily disrupt and/or be diverted from an embryonic play sequence if a competing activity floats into their awareness.

With 3-year-olds, the teacher becomes an unequivocally central figure. (This is in contrast to the importance of parents and siblings to toddlers, who have not yet been exposed to group life outside the home, and to the growing influence of peers for 5- and 6-year-olds.) Thus, in the preschool years the teacher continues to model and sustain play by close attentiveness, approval, and selective reinforcement. She may also occasionally enter into a play role to get things going. (When Donald persistently wailed to be cared for as a helpless baby, he was ignored by his erstwhile playmates, who had changed from being "Mommy" and "Daddy" to being puppies. The teacher offered to nurture him and suggested he might be the baby puppy in the others' game, an idea picked up with alacrity by the other children.)

In a nonintrusive manner, the adult clarifies what is going on by helping the children clarify who they are pretending to be (e.g., "Who's going to drive the car to the haunted house?"), calling them by their role names (e.g., "Mommy, your son needs some help."), and helping the children listen to and hear each other (e.g., "Did you hear Robin asking you for more tickets?").

All of these tactics help sustain play, as does a well-timed commentary, "Hey, Dad, you forgot to say 'goodbye' to the baby," as a forgetful "Dad" wanders out of the play area. The adult may also help by channeling nonproductive behavior (e.g., "Yes, Batman does race in his Batcar, but it looks like he needs a garage for his car too. Maybe you can help each other build garages for your cars."). The elaboration of play sequences often becomes short-circuited by a teacher who is made anxious by play that *could* get out of hand; rather than furthering the play to a higher level, such a teacher may divert the players (e.g., "It's juice time."), invoke superego sanctions (e.g., "That's not a nice thing to do."), or issue a flat edict (e.g., "No superhero play indoors."). In these cases, potentially high-level play never gets off the ground.

Channeling becomes a major adult function with the high energy level and strong emotionality of the 4- and 5-year-old. It can be done by the adult demonstrating the usefulness of words (e.g., "Tell him you don't want your building knocked down. You *both* need it for a train station."), keeping the play moving (e.g., "What happens after the witch goes to sleep?"), sharing ideas (e.g., "Hey kids, Perry has a good idea! Tell them about it, Perry."), and helping a recalcitrant child hear what the others are saying (e.g., "Listen, Nat, they are trying to tell you how to fix those tracks").

Four-year-olds and some fives may still have difficulty in distinguishing between imagination and reality, particularly when fear and aggressive impulses are aroused. Perhaps because older preschoolers are more aware of the world beyond school and home and the disasters that can occur, particularly through television and radio, they have exaggerated fears of nameless dangers lurking outside their familiar confines. Such fantasies and fears may spill over onto many aspects of life, both waking and sleeping. Children need help in assessing what is reality and what is fantasy without being robbed of the chance to express their fantasies and deal with them through play, discussion, or art in order to master or dispel them. By sharing their fantasies with the accepting, encouraging adult and with each other, children gradually learn to differentiate reliably between what is real and what is imaginary.

The further differentiation and cognitive comprehension of what is real and what is pretend makes it possible for older preschoolers to play out quite fearful themes, but such play is seldom sustainable without anxious disruption before middle childhood. When the distinction between reality and fantasy becomes blurred, the adult must step in and alleviate the anxiety if it is proving disruptive (e.g., "She's just pretending that's poison."). Affects, however, are acknowledged and accepted (e.g., "I know that noise frightened you. Let's go see what is was."), and the effects one's emotions have on others are also clarified, acknowledged, and accepted (e.g., "When you screamed at her, it scared her. Could you tell her why she made you so mad?"). Confronting feeling in both an empathic and matter-of-fact manner is useful in increasing children's empathy for one another, as well as helping them see that there are other points of view.

Another dimension of the adult's role is that of arbitrator and at times referee to solve the inevitable spats so that they do not disrupt play or devastate children's feelings (e.g., "When he tore your picture it was an accident. Then you tore his on purpose, and you both feel bad. Maybe you could start again, because those were really interesting pictures."). All teacher interventions involve a focused awareness of how play episodes are developing and sensitivity to children's individual reactions to the unfolding situation.

## FACILITATION BY PEERS

The importance of peers in children's social development has been of interest since the 1930s (Bridges, 1933; Buehler, 1930; Isaacs, 1933, 1972). Recently there has been a renewed and growing appreciation of the importance even very young children have for one another (Asher & Gottman, 1981; Lewis & Rosenblum, 1975). Eckerman et al. (1975) reported the progression of infants (ages 10 to 12 months) from involvement with mother to interaction with inanimate object and peers increasing until peer social play predominated by age 2. Bronson (1975), in contrast, did not find an increase in social play in her longitudinal study of children from 12 to 24 months. This discrepancy in research results has been noted by Mueller and Vandell (1979) who posit that peer relationships follow a developmental line separate from parent/child relations. In an ongoing study of toddler play and social interactions (Jennings & Curry, 1982), we are finding that 2-year-olds' capacity to engage in play with peers is strongly influenced by such aspects of the environment as whether the mother is present; how familiar the child is with the other children, the teachers, and the physical setting; and the length of time provided for children to become acclimated before undertaking the necessary preliminary negotiations leading to playing together. These environmental and experiential conditions are not clearly delineated in many of the studies previously cited.

Much of the play of 2-year-olds appears to be parallel or tangential to that of other twos. There are suggestions in the literature (Freud & Dann, 1951; Mueller & Vandell, 1979) that early peer contact may be as potent a force in social development as are parents and siblings. We certainly see with twos that there is intense watchfulness of each other, with an almost compulsive tendency to imitate (Jennings & Curry, 1982). Reflections of this watchfulness may not be readily apparent; it is usually from parent reports that we learn just how aware a child has been of the other children in the toddler group. Once the child is home again, he may talk animatedly of all the other children's activities and even do a run-through of the school events that were seemingly ignored or observed impassively. Therefore, the presence of peers may encourage a child to new forms of play, in effect expanding his or her play repertoire, but this seldom occurs until or unless the child is thoroughly familiar with the setting and the adults and children in it.

By age 3, children are obviously very aware of each other and will moderate their egocentric stance and possessiveness in order to maintain the good will of other children, even if in a somewhat quixotic and arbitrary fashion (''Okay, you can come to my party, but you have to wear running shoes.''). Lewis, Young, Brooks, & Michaelson (1975) write of the importance of daily experience with peers as fostering the development of specific response repertoires between friends. Garvey (1974), in her study of the properties of social play, noted the abilities of preschool children to engage in spontaneous dyadic social play. Jennings and Suwalsky (1982) found that by 4 years of age children were capable of engaging in complex interactions with their peers. Gottman and Parkhurst (1980), in their study of friendships of children in ages ranging from 2 years 11 months to 6 years 1 month, were impressed with how intensely concerned young children are about their social relationships, and the extent to which preschool youngsters will accommodate to the wishes of others to keep a play relationship going. They, in fact, conclude that young children (3 to 5 years) may be more competent than older children and adults in their social relationships.

In our experience, 3-year-olds seem awestruck by bolder, braver, or more experienced peers, and can be seen carefully watching and sometimes even mirroring the other child's affect—for instance, rocking in silent mirth at a group of energized, happy players—and may replicate the activity after the more experienced children have finished and left the play area. Although these tentative tendrils of interest can be nurtured by adults, by age 3 children will themselves persist in pursuing children whose play ideas parallel their own interests and concerns. (For several weeks after starting nursery school, Jim, a shy inarticulate 3-year-old, faithfully shadowed another shy, but more experienced peer until he grew brave enough to get on the other end of the seesaw with her one day. With her acceptance of his overture, he then felt free to acknowledge openly his wish to be her cohort.)

Budding friendships, where children enjoy and really want to please each other, result in children being willing to accommodate to each other through words and behavior. Friendships in preschool seem built on individual and mutual needs (e.g., the timid child who basks in the approval of the class bully who in turn softens her behavior to keep her faithful minion). Friendships seem to shift but also stabilize when children discover common developmental concerns (witness the intensity with which children play cooperatively around nurturance and caretaking, as well as around frightening themes of body damage, bad dreams, or wild animals).

By age 4 and 5, children are extremely sensitive to each other and acutely attuned to what interests, pleases, or provokes another child. The wish to be included, as well as the impulse to exclude, is strong—it sometimes seems that a child can feel defined as a group member only by excluding someone else (Curry & Arnaud, 1974, p. 276).

With increasing awareness of the payoff that satisfying, shared pretend play can offer, the primacy of who can or cannot play gives way to more relaxed and invested social give and take. Now a child will relinquish an entrenched position in order to keep the goodwill of play companions and to keep the play flowing (see *The City Builders* [Arnaud & Curry, 1973a] where two kindergarteners argue, compromise, and modify their own ideas while creating complex, interlocking block structures). The relief that comes from being able to play out common developmental concerns with others who are also experiencing them is palpable in young children. It serves as a motivating force that keeps children engaged in pretend play episodes even when their own wishes and ideas get thrust aside by other players (Rather than leaving the play when her leadership role as actor/cook was preempted by a group of doctors and patients, Sally compromised by setting up a diner near their hospital setting where the others could come on their "coffee breaks.").

## USE OF CULTURALLY RELEVANT MATERIALS

Feitelson (1977) in her cross-cultural review of children's play noted that: "not only were there great differences in the quality of representational play among children growing up in different societies, but that in some societies this mode of play was non-existent. The style of play in any one society was by no means a random occurrence but was closely linked to its social makeup and the role of young children in it [p. 9]." She went on to describe factors that affected the quality of representational play in various cultures; these factors were spaces designated for play, time allocated as legitimate play time, and play objects that are "familiar, permanent, and freely available whenever needed [p. 12]."

In connection with filming the play of children in various parts of the country,[3] we have been able to study similarities and differences in pretend play among five groups—semirural Appalachian children in Eastern West Virginia, Mexican-Americans in Texas, southern Black children in Texas, Native American children in Montana, and city children of mixed socioeconomic background in Western Pennsylvania (Arnaud & Curry, 1975, 1976). Children in all these age groups engaged in dramatic play, the vigor and intensity of which, however, was greatly influenced by the degree of environmental and interpersonal facilitation offered to the children.

Overall, far more commonalities than differences were evident in the play of the five groups. They all played out the following themes: nurturance and domestic play around food preparation and feeding; family relationships and roles such as mother–baby interactions and the roles of fathers, siblings, and occasionally grandparents; representation of the child's physical and human environment (usually with blocks and miniature life toys). Four out of the five groups played out relationships between medical personnel and patients, as well as aggressive, frightening creatures or happenings.

In spite of the distinct commonalities that emerged, there were also clear differences in play styles, emphases, and cultural content. There was no blurring between groups—each had its pervasive styles and moods so that, for instance, if a sophisticated play observer looked at some unused film footage, there would be a high probability he or she could identify the children's cultural group. The children in the five groups also built quite different representations of their surroundings (e.g., coal mines, farms, corrals, super highways, cities, and rural villages) and enacted different adult occupations related to their own experiences (e.g., animal auctioneers and butchers, miners, rural medical clinic personnel, Native American dancers). In addition to the usually available, rather homogenous preschool equipment that could be adapted to a variety of purposes, toys specifically tapping into a child's culture seemed to elicit intense play. For

---

[3]Carried out under Grant No. OEG-0-70-1833 awarded by the U.S. Office of Education.

example, children in a coal-mining community needed no help in using the blocks to build coal tipples and miniature railroads leading to the mines, but their role enactment became more vivid and sustained when mining caps and lunch buckets were added to the toys.

Thus, it may add a new dimension of richness to a child's pretend play if props or toys are provided that reflect aspects of the child's environment that are specific to his culture and experience. The addition of a Native American doll family of mother, father, and baby to a predominantly Native-American center increased the level of dramatic play markedly, even though the traditional miniature life black and white family figures had been available consistently. It is even possible to use toys that would ordinarily seem too advanced or inappropriate for preschool children—such as the introduction of tiny beads, fine needles, and thread to Native American 3- and 4-year-old children, who not only showed great interest in them but proved amazingly adept for their age in doing the beadwork that is so valued among their parents.

## INDIVIDUAL USES OF PRETEND PLAY

Up to now we have been talking about the commonalities of children's play according to age and experience. Now we would like to turn to variations in play styles and content that reflect the child's individuality. For instance, there are individual differences in the representational modes used by children as a vehicle for pretense, with some children preferring the sociodramatic mode; others expressing their pretend ideas through construction materials such as blocks, sand, or clay; and still others using various art materials. Some children use all these modes and more, but others have stable preferences for a particular form of expression.

The literature on play styles supports our position that individual children approach play by using different modes. Abrams and Neubauer (1976) and Jennings (1975) have studied children who were either object or person oriented and have discussed the implication of that orientation on the children's social and intellectual development. Wolf and Gardner (1978) described such children as "patternists" and "dramatists" and found that the style of approaching media and relating to others is clearly evident by age 2. In a later study (Shotwell, Wolf, & Gardner, 1979) they report that by age 3½ "the child's increasing elaboration of each style launches a period of complementarity, whereby children favoring one stylistic approach master the rudiments of the other style: dramatists often elaborate narratives to a point where they can make use of attribute-mapping skills, while patterners' classifications and constructions become articulate enough to imply events [p. 139]." In a similar vein Singer and Singer (1979) describe high- and low-fantasy children as having differing play modes.

For many children, their play ideas flourish when they are shared with another child or group of children. Other children may find relief and refuge in the solitary use of miniature life toys in intense dramatizations that appear to be relaxing and fulfilling. The adult should respect these individual expressive differences and show this respect by having available materials and areas that support the individual child's preferred approach.

One can often see, too, that individual teachers have a preference for one expressive mode, and through modeling and reinforcement subtly influence play in one direction (e.g., the teacher whose classroom is vibrant with dramatic play or decorated with ingenious art projects and block building). This is not to be taken as a criticism of such teachers, but as a reminder of the power of a teacher in a preschool class.

Preschoolers are deeply invested and interested in the basic life processes: birth, death, intactness of one's body, loss and restitution, love, hate, and the intricacies of human relationships. Not all children will be working on the same issues at the same time, but occasionally a play theme will surface around which several children's interests will coalesce. At other times, a child needs privacy to work on his or her concerns in solitary fashion but with the support of an empathic adult.

A child may need to abreact a specific experience to which other children have difficulty relating. For example, the kindergarten children were frightened by the impulsive darting about and shouting of one boy, "Put him in the tank! Put him in the tank!" It finally occurred to the teacher that he might be referring to jail, and this was confirmed when the mother reported that the boy had indeed been briefly confined to jail along with a carload of relatives with a drunken driver. The teacher then supplied the space, privacy, and toys for the child to play out his experience in more depth without frightening the other children who could neither relate to or empathize with his startling experience.

On the other hand, most children seem intrigued with hospital play even without having had direct experience with hospitalization. Such play taps into the children's developmental concerns about body injury. One kindergarten class, for example, developed an intricate setup with patients, doctors, nurses, and visiting relatives and with some apparent knowledge of hospital procedures such as temperature taking, eye tests, staff coffee breaks, etc. An exciting excursion into fantasy took place when the unsuspecting "patient" was welcomed home with a meal that contained poison that resulted in another emergency hospitalization. The teacher provided the props and the tacit approval to play out such an aggressive theme with the children's confidence that she would not let the play get out of hand.

It has been our experience that given the proper climate and adult permission children will abreact traumatic events (both real and imagined) and at times seem to master these within a group situation. At other times it may take individual play sessions to achieve such mastery. Here are two examples: When a 5-year-old girl's brother was killed in an accident, the impact of the uncontrollable weeping of familiar adults at the funeral home seemed to be one aspect of the trauma that was especially frightening to the little girl. With a close neighborhood friend, who also attended the kindergarten, she climbed into a rocking boat and both children repetitively and somewhat mockingly sobbed and flung their heads about, almost in a parody of uncontrollable grief. This gave the teacher the opportunity to acknowledge how frightening it is, not only to have someone die violently, but also to witness the loss of control of the adults.

Another little girl, age 3, after the sudden death of her father, repetitively threw a teddy bear from the top of the slide on to the ground and soon got the other children to join in her intense activity. It was a game of loss and rescue in which the teddy bear was tossed away, picked up and cuddled and comforted, and then tossed away again. (Although the group play supplied some comfort, this child eventually benefitted from a series of individual play sessions with a skilled play therapist.)

Occasionally there is a group trauma (e.g., earthquake, flood, airplane accident, death of a national leader, witnessing violent and frightening events), following which the children may engage in repetitive play in the group. In previous work (Brown, Curry, & Tittnich, 1971) we reported the reaction of preschool children to an accident that occurred outside the kindergarten play yard. There a workman suffered a fatal fall from a high light pole, a fall which all the kindergarten children and one 3-year-old witnessed, but which none of the 4-year-olds directly observed. The reaction of the various age groups were carefully recorded and reported. With active encouragement and permission—first to talk about and then play out this common group trauma—the children did so in both age-typical ways and with individual variations. The 5-year-olds were able to use play almost immediately and continued to do so for the remainder of the school year. There were sex differences, with boys seemingly more disorganized and impelled to act out repetitive jumping and falling play themes. With teacher intervention and channeling, the jumping and falling play moved to intense space play that became increasingly elaborated during the year. The girls were more interested in restorative play, such as nursing, and at the end of the year were able to involve the boys in military hospital play where wounded soldiers were treated by solicitous nurses.

The 4-year-olds, who had not directly seen the accident but had siblings and parents who had, delayed dramatizing the accident for almost a month, during which time they displayed more than the usual amount of aggressive and destructive play. A month later they developed a play theme around the injury of one child who was rescued by others as ambulance drivers. This play was repeated throughout the remainder of the school year. The youngest child (age 3) and the least mature 4-year-old were disorganized by the event, a finding reflected in the authors' statement (Brown, Curry, & Tittnich, 1971): "the limits of fantasy and reality are less clearly defined for younger children and less manageable [p. 38]."

More recently in a somewhat analgous situation a teacher fainted in the presence of her preschool class. Subsequently she was diagnosed as having a fatal illness and the children were told this. These children, who were younger than our kindergarten class, reacted with some similar behaviors: that is, the boys reacted with aggressive play themes while the girls intensified their baby-caring play. Group play in general became almost nonexistent or at best was fragmentary and disorganized. After a delay of several weeks, as with our 4-year-olds, the entire group got caught up in intensive, repetitive hospital play that seemed to bring about group cohesion and some relief from the high level of tension that had permeated the classroom.

When the trauma is too severe for children to master, play may become perseverative and seemingly obligatory without any relief or evidence of mastery (A. Freud, 1946). Some of the kidnapped children of Chowchilla (Terr, 1979) displayed this kind of compulsive play, which had to be stopped by caring adults when they realized the repetition was not alleviating, but instead seemed even to be intensifying, the children's anxieties. Caretaking adults must be alert in diagnosing when play is play and when it is repetition without tension release.

## SUMMARY

With a greater emphasis currently in preschools on "back to basics," the respect for pretend play as a major developmental task and attribute of preschool children seems to be on the wane. Yet, empirical data are now supporting what developmentalists and early childhood educators have been advocating since the beginning of the preschool movement. In this article we reaffirm the importance of teachers' appreciating the child's capacity for depthful pretend play, utilizing and even extending this capacity by planned modes of facilitation, and being willing to be an advocate for the child's right to do what he does best.

## REFERENCES

Abrams, S., & Neubauer, P. Object orientedness: The person or the thing. *Psychoanalytic Quarterly*, 1976, *45*, 73–99.

Ainsworth, M. D. S *Patterns of attachment*. Hillsdale, N.J.: Lawrence Erlbaum Associates, 1978.

Arnaud, S. H., & Curry, N. E. *The city builders*. Valhalla, N.Y.: Campus Film Distributors Corp., 1973. (Film) (a)

Arnaud, S. H., & Curry, N. E. *Concept instancing of role enactment*. Valhalla, N.Y.: Campus Film Distributors Corp., 1973. (Film) (b)

Arnaud, S. H., & Curry, N. E. *The moat monster*. Valhalla, N.Y.: Campus Film Distributors Corp., 1973. (Film) (c)

Arnaud, S. H., & Curry, N. E. *Role enactment in children's play: A developmental overview.* Valhalla, N.Y.: Campus Film Distributors Corp., 1973. (Film) (d)

Arnaud, S. H., & Curry, N. E. *What happens when you go to the hospital.* Valhalla, N.Y.: Campus Film Distributors Corp., 1973. (Film) (e)

Arnaud, S. H., & Curry, N. E. *The facilitation of children's dramatic play.* Valhalla, N.Y.: Campus Film Distributors Corp., 1974. (Film)

Arnaud, S. H., & Curry, N. E. *Play and cultural continuity:*
*Part I: Appalachian children*
*Part II: Southern black children*
*Part III: Mexican-American children*
*Part IV: Montana Indian children.*
*Valhalla, N.Y.: Campus Film Distributors Corp., 1975–1976. (Films)*

Arnaud, S. H., & Curry, N. E. *Study guide for eight films on Pittsburgh children's spontaneous dramatic play.* Pittsburgh: Arsenal Family & Children's Center of the University of Pittsburgh, 1976.

Asher, S. R., & Gottman, J. M. (Eds.). *The development of children's friendships.* New York: Cambridge University Press, 1981.

Axline, V. *Play therapy.* New York: Ballantine, 1969.

Bowlby, J. *Attachment and loss* (Vol. 1). New York: Basic Books, 1969.

Brazelton, T. B., & Als, H. Four early stages in the development of mother–infant interaction. In A. J. Solnit, R. S. Eissler, A. Freud, M. Kris, & P. B. Neubauer (Eds.) *Psychoanalytic study of the child* (Vol. 34). New York: International Universities Press, 1979.

Bridges, K. M. B. A study of social development in early infancy. *Child Development,* 1933, *4,* 36–49.

Bronson, W. C. Developments in behavior with age mates during the second year of life. In M. Lewis & L. A. Rosenblum (Eds.), *Friendship and peer relations.* New York: Wiley, 1975.

Brown, N. S., Curry, N. E., & Tittnich, E. How groups of children deal with common stress through play. In G. Engstrom (Ed.), *Play: The child strives toward self-realization.* Washington, D.C.: National Association for the Education of Young Children, 1971.

Buehler, C. *The first year of life.* New York: John Day, 1930.

Christie, J. F. Sociodramatic play training. *Young Child,* 1982, *37,* 25–32.

Clarke-Stewart, K. A. And daddy makes three: The father's impact on mother and young child. *Child Development,* 1978, *49,* 466–478.

Curry, N. E. Dramatic play as a curricular tool. In D. Sponseller (Ed.), *Play as a learning medium.* Washington, D.C.: National Association for the Education of Young Children, 1974.

Curry, N. E., & Arnaud, S. H. Cognitive implications of children's spontaneous role play. *Theory into Practice,* 1974, *8,* 273–277.

Day, D., & Sheehan, R. Elements of a better preschool. *Young Children,* 1975, *30,* 15–23.

Dittman, L. (Ed.). *Early child care.* New York: Atherton, 1968.

Dunn, J., & Wooding, C. Play in the home and its implications for learning. In B. Tizard & D. Harvey (Eds.), *Biology of play.* Philadelphia: Lippincott, 1977.

Eckerman, C. O., Whatley, J. L., & Kutz, S. L. Growth of social play with peers during the second year of life. *Developmental Psychology.* 1975, *11,* 42–49.

Elder, J. L., & Pederson, D. R. Preschool children's use of objects in symbolic play. *Child Development,* 1978, *49,* 500–504.

Erikson, E. H. *Childhood and Society* (2nd ed.). New York: Norton, 1963.

Fein, G. G. Play with actions and objects. In B. Sutton-Smith (Ed.), *Play and learning.* New York: Gardner Press, 1979.

Fein, G. G. Pretend play in childhood: An integrative review. *Child Development,* 1981, *52,* 1095–1118.

Feitelson, D. Cross-cultural studies of representational play. In B. Tizard & D. Harvey (Eds.), *Biology of play*. Philadelphia: Lippincott, 1977.
Feitelson, D., & Ross, G. S. The neglected factor—play. *Human Development*, 1973, *16*, 202–223.
Fink, R. S. Role of imaginative play in cognitive development. *Psychological Reports*, 1976, *39*, 895–906.
Freud, A. *The ego and the mechanisms of defense*. New York: International Universities Press, 1946.
Freud, A. *Normality and pathology in childhood: Assessment of development*. New York: International Universities Press, 1965.
Freud, A. The symptomalogy of childhood. In R. S. Eissler, A. Freud, H. Hartmann, M. Kris, & S. L. Lustman (Eds.), *Psychoanalytic Study of the Child* (Vol. 25). New York: International Universities Press, 1970.
Freud, A., & Dann, S. An experiment in group upbringing. In R. S. Eissler, A. Freud, H. Hartmann, & E. Kris (Eds.), *Psychoanalytic Study of the child* (Vol. 6). New York: International Universities Press, 1951.
Freyberg, J. T. Increasing the imaginative play of urban disadvantaged kindergarten children through systematic training. In J. L. Singer (Ed.), *The child's world of make-believe*. New York: Academic Press, 1973.
Garvey, C. Some properties of social play. *Merrill–Palmer Quarterly*, 1974, *20*, 163–180.
Garvey, C. *Play*. Cambridge, Mass.: Harvard University Press, 1977.
Gottman, J. M., & Parkhurst, J. T. A developmental theory of friendship and acquaintanceship processes. In W. A. Collins (Ed.), *Minnesota symposia on child psychology* (Vol. 13). Hillsdale, N.J.: Lawrence Erlbaum Associates, 1980.
Gould, R. *Child studies through fantasy*. New York: Quadrangle Books, 1972.
Harms, T. Evaluating settings for learning. *Young Children*, 1970, *25*, 304–308.
Hunt, J. McV. *Intelligence and experience*. New York: Ronald Press, 1961.
Isaacs, S. *Social development in young children*. New York: Schocken, 1972 (Originally published, 1933).
Jennings, K., & Curry, N. E. *Toddler social play*. Paper presented at the annual conference of the Association for Anthropological Study of Play, London, Ontario, April 1, 1982.
Jennings, K. D. People versus object orientation, social behavior, and intellectual abilities in preschool children. *Developmental Psychology*, 1975, *11*, 511–519.
Jennings, K. D., & Suwalsky, J. T. D. Reciprocity in the dyadic play of three and a half year old children. In J. Loy (Ed.), *The paradoxes of play*. West Point, N.Y.: Leisure Press, 1982.
Kritchevsky, S., Prescott, E., & Walling, L. S. *Planning environments for young children: Physical space*. Washington, D.C.: National Association for the Education of Young Children, 1969.
Lewis, M. The social determination of play. In B. Sutton-Smith (Ed.), *Play and learning*. New York: Gardner Press, 1979.
Lewis, M., & Rosenblum, L. (Eds.). *Friendship and peer relations*. New York: Wiley, 1975.
Lewis, M., Young, G., Brooks, J., & Michaelson, L. The beginning of friendship. In M. Lewis & L. Rosenblum (Eds.), *Friendship and peer relations*. New York: Wiley, 1975.
Lindberg, L., & Swedlow, R. *Early childhood education*. Boston: Allyn & Bacon, 1976.
Lovinger, S. L. Socio-dramatic play and language development in preschool disadvantaged children. *Psychology in the Schools*, 1974, *11*, 313–320.
Moore, S. G., & Kilmer, S. *Contemporary preschool education: A program for young children*. New York: Wiley, 1973.
Mueller, E., & Vandell, D. Infant–infant interactions. In J. Osofsky (Ed.), *Handbook of infant development*. New York: Wiley, 1979.
Murphy, L. B. *Personality in young children* (Vol. 1). New York: Basic Books, 1956.

Peller, L. E. Models of children's play. In R. E. Herron & B. Sutton-Smith (Eds.), *Child's play.* New York: Wiley, 1971.

Pulaski, M. A. Toys and imaginative play. In J. L. Singer (Ed.), *The child's world of make-believe.* New York: Academic Press, 1973.

Read, K., & Patterson, J. *The nursery school and kindergarten* (7th ed.). New York: Holt, Rinehart & Winston, 1980.

Rosen, C. E. The effects of sociodramatic play on problem-solving behavior among culturally disadvantaged preschool children. *Child Development,* 1974, *45,* 920–927.

Ross, H., & Kay, D. The origin of social games. In K. Rubin (Ed.), *Children's play.* San Francisco: Jossey–Bass, 1980.

Sachs, J. Role of adult–child play in language development. In K. Rubin (Ed.), *Children's play.* San Francisco: Jossey–Bass, 1980.

Saltz, E., Dixon, D., & Johnson, J. Training disadvantaged preschoolers on various fantasy activities: Effects on cognitive functioning and impulse control. *Child Development,* 1977, *48,* 367–380.

Sarnoff, C. *Latency.* New York: Aronson, 1976.

Schulman, A. S. *Absorbed in living children learn.* Washington, D.C.: National Association for the Education of Young Children, 1967.

Shotwell, J. M., Wolf, D., & Gardner, H. Exploring early symbolization: Styles of achievement. In B. Sutton-Smith (Ed.), *Play and learning.* New York: Gardner Press, 1979.

Singer, J. L. *The child's world of make-believe: Experimental studies in imaginative play.* New York: Academic Press, 1973.

Singer, J. L., & Singer, D. The values of the imagination. In B. Sutton-Smith (Ed.), *Play and learning.* New York: Gardner Press, 1979.

Smilansky, S. *The effects of sociodramatic play on disadvantaged preschool children.* New York: Wiley, 1968.

Terr, L. C. Children of Chowchilla: A study of psychic trauma. *In Psychoanalytic study of the child* (Vol. 34). New York: International Universities Press, 1979.

Todd, V. E., & Heffernan, H. *The years before school: Guiding preschool children* (3rd ed). New York: Macmillan, 1977.

Weber, L. *The English infant school and informal education.* Englewood Cliffs, N.J.: Prentice–Hall, 1971.

Wolf, D., & Gardner, H. Style and sequence in early symbolic play. In M. Franklin & N. Smith (Eds.), *Early Symbolization.* Hillsdale, N.J.: Lawrence Erlbaum Associates, 1978.

VanderVen, K. (Ed.). Environmental design for young children. *Children in Contemporary Society,* 1977, *11*(1). (A special issue)

# 16 Play Therapy in Counseling Settings

Louise F. Guerney
*The Pennsylvania State University*

## Introduction

There is no school of therapy that does not employ play or play settings for diagnosis and/or treatment. As Kanner (1948) points out in his classic work: "The richness of child play offers an invitation to make therapeutic use of it. It's self-expressive nature suggests its use for the combined purpose of revealing children's feelings and allowing the child to approach reality via the quasi-reality of his own creation [p. 230]." Play methods function, according to Kanner (1948), to enrich the knowledge of the patients' feelings and attitudes, but most of all, for therapy, the play situation offers a "unique opportunity for the development of a therapeutic relationship [p. 233]" between the child and a . . . therapist. "The child learns from his play experiences that his anxieties and guilt need not be so overwhelming as they have been. He acts them out, 'releases' them, in a setting detached from everyday life and in the presence of an adult who does not berate, threaten or reject [p. 234]."

Herein lies a second feature of the employment of play in child treatment—the opportunity it provides for the furthering of a therapeutic relationship between child/children and adult. The play situation permits the adult to enter the exclusive domain of children filled with objects acknowledged as theirs only. In so doing, the adult demonstrates to the child that the ways of the child are recognized, accepted, and indeed primary, which serves as a great power equalizer between parent and adult. One has only to observe a 200-lb therapist sitting on a child-sized chair or acting as a horse, or lying on the floor helping to find missing building pieces sought by the child, to appreciate the value of the play setting as an equilizer. The equilization of power results in the reduction of threat to the child (Axline, 1947).

The world of play is not a threatening one; it is a most positive, growth-inducing experience. By associating play with psychological issues, the threat of being examined and treated is enormously reduced, permitting the child to be unguarded in expression of content and free and open to new relationships and behaviors. The interest of the counselor in therapeutic play is in the child's verbal and nonverbal expressions in relation to the counselor and the objects present and in the resulting opportunities for the child to develop self-understanding, self-acceptance, and self-mastery. Ordinarily hidden and threatening content is brought to the surface in the nonthreatening interpersonal atmosphere of the play session.

Play is employed in counseling settings for two purposes: diagnosis and treatment of the entire array of childhood emotional and behavior disorders. Today counseling is not confined only to traditional counseling settings—clinics and hospitals. School psychologists and counselors provide play therapy in the schools (Nickerson, 1973), and paraprofessionals work with children using play therapy techniques for reducing problem behaviors in day-care or headstart settings (Andronico & B. Guerney, 1969; Brody, 1978). For this chapter, we include play for therapeutic purposes, addressing the setting as a secondary issue.

In its relatively short history, play for therapeutic purposes probably has been more widely employed than any other treatment approach for children. A recent survey of the treatment practices of members of the Clinical Child Psychology Section of the APA (Tuma & Pratt, 1982) revealed that members (nearly all psychologists) utilized play therapy with 44% of their preschool-aged cases and with 53% of school-aged children, ages 5–10. For children 11 years and older, the method dropped out completely. The lesser use of therapy with the preschool children no doubt reflects the view that their parents require counseling more than the children require direct treatment (Tuma & Pratt, 1982). As children are seen as more responsible for their own behavior, use of therapy strategies involving them directly tends to increase.

In relation to diagnosis, play is regarded as a more natural means of expression than conversation (Buros, 1975) lacking the guardedness that is likely to be generated when questions or tests are presented. So convinced are counseling professionals of the value of play as the natural modality for child expressions and performances that many standardized psychological tests contain toys and appear as much like games as possible (Buros, 1978).

Many approaches have been developed for accomplishing these ends—most of which parallel schools of therapy and methods of diagnosis for adults. In this chapter, after a brief history of play in counseling settings, we shall examine the principles and major methods of play in therapeutic work and, secondly, for diagnostic purposes. We will also look at the evidence for the value of play approaches as interventions.

## HISTORY OF PLAY IN COUNSELING

Freud's (1938) conception of the unconscious, and its revelation through dream analysis, led to the recognition that access to mental processes creating disturbance could be gained via verbal techniques. The early analysts took only a short time to recognize the possibility of using analytic approaches for children, even Freud (1938) himself numbered some children among his patients.

Hug-Hellmuth (Kanner, 1948; Klein, 1955) seems to be recognized by child analysts as the person who introduced play into psychoanalysis. Her method consisted of observing the child at play and translating every move into the analyst's set of symbols, primarily directed at repressed hostile and sexual wishes toward the parents. For example, when a little boy took his gun and said, "Puff-Puff!" this meant to Hug-Hellmuth that he nurtured patricidal wishes (Kanner, 1948, p. 230).

Klein asserted (1959), based on her work starting in the 1920s, that successful analysis is not readily possible with young children because "their relation to reality is a weak one . . . they do not as a rule feel ill [p. 28]" and most important of all, they cannot as yet give, or cannot give in a sufficient degree, those associations of speech that are the principal analytic treatment of adults. Klein goes on to say that the differences between the adult and child mind led her to a way to get at the child's unconscious, which she called Play Analysis, in which "the child expresses its fantasies, its wishes and its actual experiences in a symbolic way through play and games [p. 29]." Klein introduced miniature toy cars, animals, and dolls to stimulate fantasy. She believed that the child used the same symbols in play as adults do in dreams, which were thought to be the key to the unconscious. Most play activities were viewed as symbolic expressions of sexual conflict and aggression in relation to parents. Interpretations of the expressions were made to the children who then were believed to gain sufficient insight into their dynamics to understand their problems and change their inappropriate behavior.

Anna Freud (1955), coming along somewhat later, felt that the setting of the child's life was important and eschewed the approach of interpretation of adult symbolic meanings used by her earlier colleagues. She felt the context in which the child played and lived was important to understanding the meaning of play, including the case history from the parents. She saw play (Kanner, 1948) as a means of "getting acquainted with her patient, gaining his confidence, making herself liked by him [p. 231]." Only after she had acquired knowledge about the child from such observations and information did she attempt to try to understand the meaning of the child's play and communicate these to the child. By this time, the relationship would be sufficiently strong to assure that the child's libidinal impulses would not drive away the therapist, but rather that the therapist would be supportive in helping the child deal with them.

The first 20 years of child therapy were dominated by Freudian analytic practitioners, as was adult therapy. One must remember that until the time of Freud there were no verbal therapies. Psychiatry was dominated by physical approaches such as the use of magnets (Boring, 1950) and hypnotism (Wadden & Anderton, 1982) in which something was done to the patient. Verbal methods fostered a *relationship* between the therapist and patient requiring full expressive participation by the patient. Procedural refinements of provoking and analyzing verbal expression occupied the early days of psychotherapy. The therapist had the answers to the mysteries of the meaning of the expressions and thus was a most powerful authority, upon whom the patient became very dependent. Resolving this dependence then became another task for the analyst with both adults and children (A. Freud, 1955).

It was not until the rise of the Rogerian School of nondirective psychotherapy in the 1940s that a total and effective counter movement against the major principles of psychoanalysis was made. Rogers' (1942) approach was nearly the complete antithesis of the analytic approach. Axline, a student of Rogers (Axline, 1947) developed nondirective play therapy, which paralleled the Rogerian approach for adults. Its methods for therapeutically oriented play with children were equally antithetic to those of Klein and Freud, and even Adler, who had started child guidance programs (Bottome, 1957) for children and abandoned and expanded on many Freudian principles and procedures.

## THEORY

Today, nearly 40 years later, additional treatment approaches have emerged (e.g., Behavioral Therapy [Patterson, Jones, Whittier, & Wright, 1965]) but not replaced the Freudian and Rogerian. All employ play or play settings for diagnosis and/or treatment. However, with the exception of the psychoanalysts, who have their own theory of play, few therapists ascribe to a single generic theory of play. Counselors, in seeking support for the rationale and/or efficacy of their play tools and procedures, tend to pull upon various theoretical perspectives on a rather piecemeal basis (Brady & Friedrich, 1982). Most child counselors are content with the rationale that play is the child's natural form of expression and therefore the likely arena for determining the source of problems and the medium for resolving them.

### Psychoanalytic Theories of Play

Psychoanalysts offer several explanations for play that are considered relevant to their use of play in child therapy. One, that play is a "manifestation of the pleasure principle" that is interpreted to mean pleasure in achieving; two, functional pleasure—that is, play is pleasant and gratifying not for its product but for the joy of doing it (Kanner, 1948). Third, repetition compulsion (i.e., the need to act out repeatedly situations that are troublesome to the child) was introduced to explain the value of play. The process or outcome of a significant event were "incompletely absorbed" (Walder, 1976) making it impossible to put it aside; "it must be chewed again to be digested." Thus we see children repeat in their play everything that has made a big impression on them in actual life, permitting the child to master the situation or assimilate it via the repetition. "The function of play is not so much the preparation for future activities in adult life as it is the assimilation of the mass of excitations from the outer world, which affect the organism too severely or too suddenly to permit of their immediate disposal [Walder, 1976; p. 88 in Schaefer, 1976]."

Walder explains how play is different from other processes that also serve to further assimilation or pleasure. He points out that "play, as a fundamental and purposeful phenomenon is encountered only in children, that is during a period of growth, in which the traumata of life touch the ascending limb of the vitality curve . . . [there is] greatest plasticity of the psyche [Walder, 1976; p. 90 in Schaefer, 1976]." When this plasticity has dwindled . . . and when the diffuse *amorphous* psychic organism has become a structure, then, apparently, other less alluring procedures take the place of play.

## Other Theoretical Perspectives Regarding Play

According to Kanner (1948) child counselors have drawn upon the more modern concepts of psychodynamics rather than older theories based on physiology (e.g., Shiller) and phylogeny (e.g., Hall) for explaining the value of play to children. First among these would be the Catharsis Theory that considers play a safety valve for pent-up emotions. Erikson (1963) was a proponent of the catharsis value of play. The child "plays out" his conflicts. The concept of catharsis is a major one in psychotherapy, not limited to play per se. It serves as a counterforce to the mechanisms of suppression and repression that work to push troublesome thoughts and emotions out of consciousness. Once out of consciousness such responses can create problems. Methods of encouraging expression are used to prevent or remediate these processes.

The Self-Expression Theory (Kanner, 1948) purports that "play is the natural and most readily available outlet for a child's needs and feelings, which cannot, as in the adult, be worked out verbally, vocationally, and in many ways not accessible to a child [p. 229]." Kanner, referring to Baldwin, suggests that in play there is self-regulation and the control of impulses, as the child expresses wishes, love, fear, and hate without adult regulation.

In discussing theoretical bases for play therapy, Brady and Friedrich (1982) describe Vygotsky's "formulation of play which originates when a child's desires cannot be realized. The child engages in play, an imaginary form of his desires, in order to obtain immediate gratification [p. 39]." Brady and Friedrich

(1982) drawing upon psychoanalytic theory, see play as allowing a child to gain control over his thoughts and actions, and enabling the child to deal with painful or unpleasant situations and expressing emotions about these away from the real world, which would be more judgmental about them. Play allows the expression to be more indirect or displaced.

Brady and Friedrich (1982) relate play therapy also to Piaget's three developmental stages of play and postulate therapeutic cognitive–developmental benefits. They present a third developmental perspective in relation to play—that of an arousal function that they attribute to Ellis (1973). Through play the child seeks an optimal level of arousal and progresses to higher levels of play with growing maturity. Brady and Friedrich (1982) conclude that all of the models upon which play therapists draw depict play as "progressing from egocentric bodily movements to a more symbolic to more real-life social interactions [p. 40]."

## Perspectives on the Therapist

Brady and Friedrich (1982) postulate that the relationship with the therapist follows the same developmental path, progressing along the "dimensions of intimacy, social complexity, perspective-taking, and [increasing] the proportion of verbal materials to physical action" . . . "Recognizing that verbal descriptions of feelings are a complex behavior, the therapist meets the child where he is, and that most often initially is in the physical modality [p. 40]." Irrespective of the approach, they propose that play therapy progresses through four levels: Level I, Physical Interventions, Physical Presence, Nonverbal Gestures; Level II, Reflecting or Paraphrasing, Following and Attending; Level III, Third Person Interpretations, and Level IV, Direct Interpretations, that is, being able to talk about the child's *own* unique feelings as opposed to Level III, where feelings and ideas in general are the focus. "The levels of intervention vary within and between the sessions, but their nature increases in their complexity and directness as the child learns about himself through play and the interchanges that accompany the play [p. 43]."

Herein lies, in the opinion of the author, the distinguishing feature of play therapy as opposed to constructive engagement in solitary play, or play with a group of peers with or without adult supervision, or everyday play with an adult. The play therapist attends to the child's behavior and expressions in relation to the play (i.e., the play process). The classroom teacher, interested in cognitive development, may introduce play aspects to stimulate, reduce threat, or in other ways utilize the powers of play to enhance learning. However, she/he is interested ultimately in a product, as are physical educators, and even the child him/herself, in some instances. The play therapist rarely is concerned with a specific product but rather is concerned with the meaning of the acts and words in relation to the child's emotional and interpersonal psychological life. The therapist's behavior will be guided by the child's receptivity to the therapist's responses, and a genuine interactive process will ensue between the child and the therapist (Brady & Freidrich, 1982) which will be further shaped by the parameters of the play.

## Additional Perspectives on the Therapist

Before leaving perspectives on the therapist, the phenomenon of transference ought to be mentioned. Klein (1955) saw the critical tasks of the therapist as the consistent interpretations of the play content, and both the positive and negative transference feelings—that is, the positive or negative feelings toward the therapist, believed to be transferred to her/him from feelings actually experienced with other significant figures, most often the parents. Anna Freud (1955) argued instead that the positive transference alone is the important part of transference when working with children. She believed that affectional ties to the therapist must be established and remain intact in order for children to be able to work on their problems fruitfully and accept the interpretations of the therapist as valid.

Although not restricting their analysis of the therapeutic process to play therapy per se, Dollard and Miller (1950) translated concepts of psychoanalysis into learning theory terms. Explanations of therapeutic change involved the arousal of troublesome feelings in the presence of a supportive, instructive therapist (i.e., pairing a negative stimulus with a positive one) and through conditioning processes (i.e., bringing about a reduction of the negative feeling states associated with the original stimulus).

The theoretical perspective of the therapist in nondirective play therapy is so intricately a part of the developmental theory of the nondirective approach (Rogers, 1951), that they cannot be separated and will be explained when that therapy is described later in this chapter. However, it should be noted that the developmental theory of Rogers (1951) makes the assumption that the function of the therapist is the same in play therapy as in adult therapy, although different procedurally.

# PLAY APPROACHES CURRENTLY IN USE

Although there are a number of variations within the broader classifications, the author believes that play therapy approaches can be categorized best along three major dimensions. First, whether a single child is seen individually or whether a group is the context for the treatment. Second, there is a wide range in relation to the degree of structure imposed on the play activity. Third, approaches differ in the degree of directiveness or intrusiveness exercised by the therapist. If the *major* responsibility for deciding the content of the session rests with the therapist, the play therapy is called directive, or directed. If the choice of direction is left with the child, the approach would be called nondirective, client-centered (Dorfman, 1951), or child-centered (Guerney, 1982). The differences hinge on the word *major*. Many directive therapists will permit a child to choose what he or she wants to play and indeed will be open to nearly total control by the child during the session, including the analytic therapists (Klein, 1959). Some child-centered or nondirective therapists may have strict rules or provide a very limited selection of toys or activities for the children (Ginott, 1961). However, the directive therapist feels very free, even obliged by virtue of therapeutic conviction, to question the child about the play, provide interpretations, insert instructions, and organize variations as believed necessary. The child-centered therapist, on the other hand, is reactive or reflective of the child and considers modification of the child's own direction detrimental.

## Nondirective Therapy

Nondirective therapy, later renamed Client-Centered Therapy, was founded by Rogers (1942, 1951). These therapists believe, based on Rogers' Theory of Personality Development (1951), that such methods as interpretation and other techniques designed to further the therapist's perspective are counterproductive. They believe that these result in defensiveness that functions to protect the self from material it is unable to deal with. Rogerians theorize that the therapeutic process works (Axline, 1947) because:

> The behavior of the individual at all times seems to be caused by one drive, the drive for complete self-realization. This is a drive toward maturity, independence, and self-direction.
>
> The drive . . . needs ''growing ground'' to develop a well-balanced structure . . . the individual needs the permissiveness to be himself, the complete acceptance of himself—by himself, as well as by others—and the right to be an individual . . . in order to achieve a direct satisfaction of this growth impulse [p. 11].
>
> Nondirective counseling is really more than a technique. It is a basic philosophy of human capacities which stresses the ability of the individual to be self-directive . . . primary emphasis is placed upon the active participation of the self in the therapeutic growth experience [p. 27].
>
> The client directs the way in which the interview will go . . . selects the things that are important to him . . . assumes the responsibility for the decisions . . . does the interpreting . . . and in the atmosphere of mutual respect which characterizes this relationship, he charts his course of action—a positive course of action that correlates with his inner drive toward maturity [p. 28].

## Nondirective Play Therapy

Problems in adjustment that would account for a child's referral for treatment are viewed as a result of difficulties in achieving complete self-realization and developing inappropriate ways of attempting to achieve it. These difficulties could stem from handicapping conditions solely within the individual (e.g., neurological impairments) or be generated by conditions of the social environment.

The individual of any age experiencing such difficulties has the ability to solve his or her own problems and an inner striving to do so—to strive to be more mature as defined in the cultural context—as opposed to settling for the immature (Axline, 1947).

Explaining the rationale for child-centered play therapy, Axline (1947) asserts that:

> The play therapy room is good growing ground. In the security of this room where the *child* is the most important person, where he is in command of the situation and of himself . . . he suddenly feels that . . . he can look squarely at himself . . . for this is his world, and he no longer has to compete with other forces such as adult authority or . . . situations where he is not an individual in his own right. He is also treated with dignity and respect. He can say anything that he feels like saying—and he is accepted completely. He can play with the toys in any way he likes to . . . The usual adult responses are replaced by complete acceptance and permissiveness to be himself [p. 16].

Axline (1947) makes this distinction between the two views on the source of direction for the play session. "Play therapy may be directive in form, that is, the therapist may assume responsibility and direction for the child, or it may be nondirective: the therapist may leave responsibility and direction to the child [p. 9]." Only the nondirective therapies permit the child to assume unchallenged direction; this does not mean there are no limitations on behavior (Axline, 1947; Ginott, 1961). It means only that the therapist believes that persons of all ages have the most direct access to their own personal "maps" for healthy development (Rogers, 1951). The question of the comparable efficacy of nondirective versus directive therapies remains unanswered. Are the strengths for self-development best activated by the child at his/her own pace and direction, or must growth and change be orchestrated by the therapist?

Acceptance is the core of the interpersonal conditions created by the nondirective therapist. The ultimate goal is the child's acceptance of himself, which is considered a necessary component for a feeling of self-worth or adequate self-esteem. Acceptance is demonstrated via responses that show empathic understanding from the therapist in addition to the absence of negative and positive feedback. Praise is *not* given because the child must be free to deal with negative aspects of the self as well as positive ones, and thus should not be subject to *any* form of evaluation. Social consequences of one's expressions tend to shape, even inhibit, expression. The therapist's role is to help the child feel free to express, to take responsibility for his/her own expressions, and to evaluate the expressions from his own perceptual position. For example, if a child were to say that nobody liked him, the nondirective therapist would not try to convince the child that his perception was faulty, nor would the therapist try to show the child how he believes this only because he is confused, projecting, or trying to induce sympathy, etc. The therapist would accept the child's perception of the situation because the therapist believes that to challenge it would create defensiveness in the child. Defensiveness interferes with honesty and serious attempts to understand and evaluate the self. Acceptance permits the individual to look at the self squarely and own up to some needed changes. The process is described as follows. The child says to himself, "If the therapist can accept my feelings and doesn't question me or blame me for them, it's probably not so terrible to feel that way. I do not feel quite so bad about it—maybe I am a little more acceptable and/or capable than I thought." These new self-attitudes lay the groundwork for new behaviors more consistent with the emerging positive self-views.

## CHILD-CENTERED THERAPY VERSUS FREE PLAY AND LAISSEZ-FAIRE ADULT BEHAVIOR

Although the child is the source of session content, the client-centered play session differs in many ways from the kind of open play engaged in by children in a totally unstructured and unsupervised setting. An observer viewing a play therapy situation in which the child "calls the shots" and the therapist responds with reflective statements might interpret the scene erroneously as a void filled by the child. However, a definite structure exists and clear definitions of the therapist's behavior and expected child responses exist that are well known to the therapist, though not necessarily the child.

The goals are broad and not determined on a symptom basis. These are *process*-oriented goals, applicable to children with many kinds of problems. They are to:

1. encourage the examination of all aspects of the self and relationships to the world, in the way and at the rate at which the child feels able to do so.
2. reduce symptoms.
3. facilitate the acquisition of positive perceptions of the self, others, and the environment.

## DIRECTIVE THERAPIES

All therapy models for children, except for nondirective therapy, attempt (either via the therapist's behavior or the materials selected for the child, or both) to guide the child's expression according to therapist intuition, goals, or prescription. A number of the therapies have been designed expressly for specific problems, for example, reducing the separation difficulties of children experiencing parental divorce or placement changes by means of the presentation of two houses, about which the therapist encourages the child to express feelings in his life (Kuhli, 1979).

The rationale for the therapist's assumption of responsibility is related to principles of the therapeutic school or approach espoused by the therapist. Directive therapies tend to differ on two different dimensions, according to Allen (1934). Before Rogers (1942) and Axline (1947), Allen spelled out the value of acceptance of the child as and where he is in order to maximize therapeutic impact. He believed that play activity can be regarded as useful from two points of view. One stresses *content,* with play as a means of bringing out the fantasies and the unconscious desires of the child. Here, the content is the critical thing along with the release of feeling from the repressed material. The other point of view stresses the *relationship,* the value of play for providing the child with familiar tools to relate himself to the therapist. Here, the actual content of the play assumes less importance than the use the child makes of it in relating to the therapist (Allen, 1934).

Behaviorally, the choice of emphasis on content versus relationship often translates to the selection of toys and a structure that will provoke fantasy material valued by the therapist in relation to a child's problems, or the selection of toys and a structure that will create opportunities for relating to the therapist in ways presumed to be beneficial to the child's adjudged psychological needs.

It is difficult to make these two views clear without suggesting a greater exclusiveness between them than in fact exists. All therapists introduce play props that have value for stimulating productive content. The selection may influence what happens; proponents of the use of particular materials certainly believe that this is the case. Conversely, no use can be made of such props in the presence of a therapist without the reactions of the therapist influencing the child's use of them. A child cannot imagine himself or herself a baby and use baby props without processing the therapist's reactions to this. These reactions then shape the future expression of content as well as the future relationship to the therapist.

Although it is not always clear whether it was emphasis on content or relationship that was more critical to the development of the methods to be described, for the sake of imposing some order upon the play techniques to be presented, the play therapy approaches to be described in the following sections will be discussed under those headings. The reader should keep two things in mind. One, that the classification system represents only relative emphasis as perceived by the author, and two, that the number of methods presented are only a few of the many available that have been published; many more exist—published and unpublished. Those chosen tend to be more widely used or are especially exemplary of the category in which they have been placed. The reader should be aware that all of the methods presented have been demonstrated to be effective on at least a case study basis. Research on treatment efficacy in relation to the broader categories of play therapies will be presented later in the chapter.

## APPROACHES EMPHASIZING CONTENT

### Psychoanalytic Therapies

The most well-known and influential of all the content oriented treatments for children are the psychoanalytic (Kanner, 1948). These approaches were described in the history of child treatment section earlier in this chapter. The basic approach continues essentially as explicated by Anna Freud (1955). However, many developments in format and style have been added (e.g., group play techniques [Slavson & Shiffer, 1974]) which change the procedures but not the basic assumptions or perspectives.

### Release Therapy and Structural Play Therapy

The basic dynamic of Release Therapy (Levy, 1933) is the acting out principle. Interpretation is minimal or absent with the sessions devoted, sometimes entirely, to release of destructive behavior. Although there may be some free play, the method relies most heavily upon the therapist selecting material that is relevant to the child's problems. The child is encouraged to play out the scene presented.

Picking up on the work of Levy, Hambridge (Schaefer, 1976) developed Structured Play Therapy that expands the number and types of stimulus materials to permit release. The word ''structured'' in the title is meant to convey the idea of focusing the child's acting out in the selected areas deemed critical by the therapist. Hambridge describes structures for problems related to inhibition of hostility, concerns about separation, punishment and control by elders, peer problems, understanding birth, and sex differences. He also recommends using structured play to test out the significance of specific symbols to a child in drawings, dreams, or other creative activities. Hambridge cautions that the relationship with the therapist must be positive and stable if one is to have the child feel free to fully release feelings in relation to these structures.

### The Mutual Storytelling Technique

Gardner (1971) added a modern touch to the time-honored therapeutic practice of eliciting stories from children about their drawings, dolls, clay shapes, etc. In his

Mutual Storytelling Technique, tape recordings have been introduced. Children are invited to make up stories for a "TV show" staged with the help of the therapist. A structure for the stories is presented, including a demand that it be original. The therapist starts the story and the child "fills in blanks" on cue with plots and outcomes the child has constructed. The therapist retells the story with alternative outcomes in order to influence the child toward recognition that healthier adaptations are possible. Gardner believes that this can lead to children attempting the better alternatives in real life.

### Costume Play Therapy

The intent of this approach is to "revise the imaginative play of earlier years" in latency aged children who have become inhibited about utilizing play for expression. The costume technique is designed to combine the advantages of the structural method and free play, according to Marcus, the creator of the method (Marcus, 1966). The therapist is assigned a compatible role (without a costume) by the child that facilitates the child's acting out of "vital unconscious material." The therapist may interpret the play sequences in relation to past or present relationships in the child's life.

## APPROACHES EMPHASIZING RELATIONSHIP

### Theraplay

According to Jernberg (1979), the creator of the approach, the rationale of Theraplay is based on the theory of DesLauriers, which posits that a deficiency in emotionally positive infantile sensory experiences can lead to later emotional problems. The deficiency may lie in the failure of the parent to provide stimulation, or in the child's inability to process such stimulation. Having missed out on this vital stimulation the child fails to develop a sense of confidence in himself and a trust of others. The Theraplay technique is designed to provide the stimulation the child should have received and thus overcome the child's interpersonal distance. Much stimulation (e.g., tickling, stroking and other body contact) are initiated by the therapist. Sustained eye contact is vital to the method. The intent is for both child and therapist to enjoy these experiences immensely. Brody (1978) has reported increased school performance and relationship growth using the method with young children. Because of the satisfaction that both child and therapist share, Jernberg (1979) is now including parents as therapist trainees, hoping to cement the filial relationship in the process. Resistance to stimulation is expected on the part of many withdrawn youngsters. However, even those who are initially resistant typically participate fully after a few sessions in response to the therapist's warm, persistent advances.

### Fair Play Therapy

Introduced by Peoples (1979), Fair Play Therapy is an attempt to create a new role for the therapist. Peoples believes that traditional approaches place undue constraints on the therapist and in turn may result in the child's developing an inflated sense of his rights. Peoples' approach emphasizes the therapist's honest reactions to the child, engendered in relation to the ensuing play, as a means of helping the child share responsibility for interpersonal effects.

### Behavioral Approaches

Behavioral Therapies have moved into the playroom. Aimed primarily at specific problem behaviors, most notably noncompliance (Forehand & King, 1974) and hyperactivity (Patterson, Jones, Whittier, & Wright, 1965), reinforcement methods are used to try to modify unacceptable behaviors. Parents may be introduced into the playroom or reinforcement machines used. However, because the focus is on producing appropriate interpersonal responses or on self-control, the goal of improving relationships is clear, if not immediately apparent. When parents or professional therapists participate in the play setting with the child, they attempt to model (Johnson & Brown, 1969) desirable behaviors for the child and/or to respond to the child in ways that further the disruption of inappropriate behavior patterns and reinforce those responses that earn social approval.

## GROUP THERAPY APPROACHES

Both directive and nondirective therapies have developed group as well as individual formats. Although most of the methods already described under directive approaches indicate openness to or actual experience with group sessions, there are two group approaches that are so outstanding that they are nearly synonymous with the group therapy label. One is the Nondirective Group Therapy, explicated by Axline (1969) and Ginott (1961). The other is Activity Group Therapy, originated by Slavson (1947) and further developed by Shiffer (Slavson & Shiffer, 1974).

### Issues in Group Therapy

No clear-cut criteria exist for the placement of a particular child in a group as opposed to individual treatment. Ginott (1961) has mentioned ''social hunger'', or the desire to gain acceptance by his peers, as the basic criterion for group placement. He cautions against the use of groups for children who are so aggressive that they cannot be controlled from attacking other group members and children who have experienced serious traumas. The latter should be given the exclusive attention of the therapist. However, it is generally agreed that the advantage of the group format is to permit children to develop better relationships with peers as well as a therapist and to experience the kind of feedback available only from peers. It is implicit in the choice of group therapy that the child will be able to benefit from the experience in the particular group under consideration. The ego cannot be too fragile or underdeveloped, nor the child's hunger for adult nurturance too great. Even though the therapist's focus is on each individual member of the group as opposed to the group per se, interactions with the therapist must of necessity be diluted. For these reasons, it has happened in practice that recommendations for group therapy tend to be limited to more intact and/or older children. The rationale for age also relates to the psychoanalytic view that latency is a particularly important time for developing peer identifications (Slavson, 1947).

Most widely recognized as a productive approach for adolescents and preadolescents is Activity Group Therapy (Slavson, 1947). In the activity group, the members share in activities popular to children of their ages. Often these are suggested at first by the therapist, who selects activities that permit parallel play as opposed to group play because the latter requires more maturity than some members of the group are likely to have. For example, members might make clay or plastic models side by side around a table at first. Later the therapist, or group members themselves, might choose group games.

Conducting group therapy places greater demand on the therapist as well as the members. Much has been written by the therapists previously cited about group dynamics and the group process. Stages of development of the group have been identified that permit therapists to judge whether the group is progressing appropriately. Stagnation at a lower level of development can lead the therapist to introduce activities designed to integrate members, or to add or subtract members. All group therapists seem to agree that groups function best when the dynamics of individual members are balanced between acting out and inexpressiveness. Ginott (1961) recommends that a normal child in the group will hasten the normalization of the children at the extreme positions. The youngster will serve as a model and insist on more acceptable behaviors from the others.

In the Activity and other therapist-directed groups, the therapist makes interpretations to individual members and to dyads or the whole group about the way an individual is behaving in relation to the group or about the group as a functioning entity. For example, the therapist might say, "Your behavior today seems to be connected with Billy's absence. All of you seem uncomfortable and maybe a little guilty after what happened to Billy here last week. Who wants to talk about it?'' Members are encouraged to interpret to each other in their own terms. Group interpretations tend to be more concerned with group interaction but can be directed to content shared by the group (e.g., interpreting the sexual symbols involved in their response to clay or crawling through play tunnels).

Nondirective groups function quite similarly to activity groups except for the omission of interpretation. The therapist responds empathically to each child and to the group when reactions are common to all or most members. Members spontaneously acquire the ability to be empathic with each other. The degree of self-direction possible for an individual member would, of course, necessarily be restricted to a certain extent because of the presence of others. Group problem-solving is engaged in with the therapist as facilitator.

Both directive and nondirective methods impose greater structure when dealing with groups. More rules and limits are necessary, which are frequently developed by group members through mutual problem-solving. The number of activities may be limited for practical reasons.

## THE USE OF LIMITS IN PLAY THERAPY

All play therapists, nondirective or directive, individual or group, have some boundaries on the physical expression of the child clients. With the exception of the more intrusive therapies, for example, Fair Play (Peoples, 1979) and Theraplay (Jernberg, 1979), limits are imposed primarily to protect child, therapist, and property from destructive action. More intrusive therapies may impose demands in relation to nondestructive behaviors as well in order to structure experiences consistent with their goals. For example, in Theraplay, the child would not be permitted much distance from the therapist.

A study by Ginott and Lebo (1961) indicated that, regardless of therapeutic perspective, the most frequently used limits, beyond those on physical aggression, are on running in and out of the playroom, remaining beyond the play period, and undressing. Limits are considered to have therapeutic value beyond that of their basic housekeeping function. Adherence to limits, if made the child's responsibility as it usually is, helps the child develop self-controls and accept responsibility for his/her own behavior (Axline, 1947). They also assist in maintaining a tie to reality in juxtaposition to the fantasy behaviors that may be generated in the play content.

### Structure of the Play Approach

Structure already has been referred to in relation to a number of the therapy descriptions given. However, because it is a dimension of play therapy (Kaczkowski, 1979), it requires a separate, if brief, explanation.

Structure refers to the form of interaction and the physical dimensions of the play sessions. It would include such variables as the type and number of toys, the amount of space provided, the relative rigidity or flexibility of the activities available, and the type and degree of therapist involvement.

The structure is imposed by the therapist. It does not just happen, although the range of structuring possibilities is often automatically limited by the activity provided. For example, in the Mutual Storytelling Technique (Gardner, 1971) or Battling Tops (Goldberg, 1980) a rigid structure is imposed on the phsycial aspects of the session by the focus on a single activity. A flexible structure would be one that provides a number of activity choices, including staying in a playroom or going out onto a playground. The term *rigid* has no perjorative meaning. It refers only to the degree to which a certain structure is adhered to. Of course, variations in structure relate to the therapist's belief in the therapeutic value of the structure being fixed or variable.

The structure imposed on the interpersonal interactions may also be rigid or flexible. Unlike any other published therapist, Ginott (1961) believed that the child should draw exclusively upon his/her own resources for fantasizing, etc. Therefore he imposed a rigid structure that permitted no therapist participation in play. He maintained an active, verbal, warm, attentive but nonetheless "only an observer" role. At the other extreme, Theraplay structures activities to maximize therapist/child physical interaction by providing brushes for hair brushing, etc.

There is no empirical evidence that one type of structuring is more beneficial to progress than another. Because the structure is often so functionally related to other features of the play, as in the case of the Battling Tops game (Goldberg, 1980), it becomes very difficult to examine structure as an independent variable.

## PLAY MATERIALS

Toys are generally conceded to be the special property of children. Their presence announces to children that the sessions will be on their terms. The toys are a statement to the child about the therapist's willingness to sacrifice an adult orientation and enter the child's domain.

All schools of play therapy believe that expressive behaviors will be to some extent a function of the materials as well as the emotional needs of the child. For example, if a child is carrying on a fantasy play session in which he is desirous of defeating an adult authority figure, he is more likely to construct Western "good guy versus bad guy" kinds of scenarios if ropes, cowboy hats, etc. are present than if they are not. On the other hand, many other kinds of fantasies can promote the same theme, for example, school equipment where the teacher authority figure can be properly humiliated in a fantasy classroom scenario.

Therefore, the client-centered therapists do not become too concerned about the properties of toys, but acknowledge, as did Ginott (1961), that they cannot be ignored. Playroom materials have "behavior propelling" qualities of their own. However, as a relationship-oriented therapist, Ginott's response was to call for those kinds of toys that he believed facilitated the *process,* as opposed to stimulating specific content. He recommended that toys be those that tend to:

1. Elicit acting-out behavior but not evoke hyperactivity—paint would qualify but not fingerpaint, because of the high stimulation properties of the latter.
2. Permit reality testing.
3. Allow the child to express his/her needs symbolically.
4. Encourage catharsis and insight.

Gardner (1971) has expressed the view that distance from the realities that generate anxiety must be provided in order for children to be able to face the threat of the content that may be troubling them. Therefore, in his view the play objects provided should serve that purpose.

For general play therapy (i.e., not structured around the use of certain play objects), the list generally includes the following items: a doll family and doll house with a few pieces of furniture in scale; clay; crayons and/or water paints and paper; two toy telephones; toy animals; soldiers; cars; baby doll; nursing bottle; hand puppets representing family members; water and water implements (scoops, funnels, etc.); a sandbox, and a raised stage area for spontaneous drama presentations.

Although the kinds of toys employed have remained relatively stable over the years, there seems to be a continuous striving among play therapists to find a play object or modality that will serve as *the* stimulus capable of awakening in the child the responses that will be most immediately therapeutically productive, or as Kanner (1948) labeled it, "a short-cut to insight."

As a consequence, and as already noted earlier, many single object-oriented techniques have been developed (e.g., Battling Tops [Goldberg, 1980]) along with highly structured media for expression, for example, Mutual Storytelling (Gardner, 1971), or the "Suitcase Story," a story for children involved in extra-family placement about a suitcase that moves around a great deal, in order to foster identification (Wenger, 1982).

The search for materials seems to accelerate at the preadolescent period because of the greater inhibition children generally experience at this time. As stated by Hawkey (Schaefer, 1976), "Children of this age often think when they first come to the clinic that they are too old to play with toys. On the other hand, they may not be mature enough to be treated through dream analysis and discussion of problems alone [p. 370]." Hawkey's response was to introduce puppets and puppet drama for this age group. Although he kept clay and drawing materials in the room also, he did not include the usual younger child objects. Woltmann (1972) has also reported great success with puppets in both individual and group therapy for preadolescents.

Other formats have been introduced for older children, for example, allowing children to play in the therapist's office, stimulating fantasies of more adult roles (Dorfman, 1951), outfitting a playroom with office equipment (Durfee, 1952), and costume therapy (Marcus, 1966).

## Research on Play Objects

A few studies have been conducted on play materials; the more significant ones will be referred to later. Unlike the studies of play objects conducted by developmentalists, e.g., ([Fein (1975), Pulaski (1973), and Smilansky (1968)]), therapists report few differences in the response of children to play objects based on sociocultural factors. Probably this results from the use of different dependent variables, namely those related to meaningful expression as opposed to those of cognitive development.

Lebo (1956) was able to demonstrate empirically that toys included in general playroom fare encouraged less expressiveness in older than younger children. He concluded that the inappropriateness of the usual toys might be responsible for the belief that typical play therapy is ineffective with children entering their teens. "The toys do not encourage them to verbalize . . . they seem to feel that such toys are beneath them and the playroom is not theirs [p. 236]."

Regardless of whether toys were age-appropriate or inappropriate, Fishbein (1974) found that boys 4–12 were more aggressive than girls when both were offered the types of toys generally found in the playroom. Beiser (1955), an analytically oriented therapist, studied the therapeutic value of toys with children ages 2 through 12. She tabulated the occurrence of child fantasy and/or relevant interpretations (from the therapist) to the number of times toys were played with. She found that highest on the list for generating relevant responses from both child and therapist were the doll family, soldier, gun, clay, and paper and crayons. She found that blocks, ball, scissors, paste, and a pencil ranked lowest. Lebo (1956) had a similar list of nonproductive toys in relation to the amount of verbalization produced.

## Use of Nonprofessionals as Therapists

Probably the greatest innovation in play therapy has been the introduction of nonprofessionals to provide the therapy, operating under the supervision of highly skilled professional play therapists. Nonprofessionals come from many sources and levels of professionalization, from Head Start aides (Andronico & Guerney, 1969) to professionals in nonpsychotherapeutic fields, (e.g., teachers [Guerney & Flumen, 1970]). Undergraduate psychology students have been trained to provide therapy under the supervision of graduate students (Reif & Stollak, 1972; Stollak, Scholom, Green, Schreiber, & Messe, 1975). Parents have been trained to work with their behaviorally and emotionally disordered children (Forehand & King, 1974; Guerney, 1964; Guerney, L., 1976) and their learning disabled children (Guerney, L., 1979; Jernberg, 1979; Johnson & Brown, 1969). Hornsby and Applebaum (1978) utilize parents as therapists even with autistic children, a most challenging group even for professionals.

The process and outcomes are essentially the same as when professionals conduct the play sessions, irrespective of problem severity. (See the section on research later in this chapter.) The value of using nonprofessionals is threefold—first, in the role of supervisor of the nonprofessionals, the limited, expensive time of the professional is put to its highest and best use; second, the relationship with the child is ongoing, enduring, and relevant in the case of parents, teachers, and aides, facilitating transference of changed attitudes and behaviors to life with them outside of the playroom; third, the relationship between the child and the adult who is significantly in his daily life is dealt with directly. Frequently, problems in these relationships can be primary or at least secondary factors in the presenting disorders.

## DIAGNOSTIC USES OF PLAY

Interest in spontaneous play for diagnosis of emotional and behavior disorders has not been as intense on the part of child counselors as for therapeutic purposes. Straight interview techniques have long been known to be unproductive with children (Kanner, 1948). Other methods for encouraging the child to "reveal his personality" have had to be devised. The child clinicians have responded with the development of rather controlled or situational play techniques to meet their need for more appropriate diagnostic tools, for example, the School Play Kit of Shuman and Leton (1965) which contains a miniature classroom with figures to be placed by the child, used to assist in diagnosing the nature and conditions of school maladjustment. Levy (1933) set up a standardized play situation for the study and treatment of sibling rivalry. Conn (1939) reported the use of specific scene settings containing furniture and dolls who represented various characters in the child's life. Murphy (1964) described the use of many miniature toys that were designed to elicit fantasy as a substitute for the free associations that children (in psychoanalysis) could not be instructed to supply.

### Semi-Projective Tests

To a certain extent before and at an accelerated pace after World War II, another tack was being developed as an alternative to the structured play scene approach previously noted. The techniques to be described are considered semiprojective because a structure has been provided reducing the degree of freedom of the child to project from his own viewpoint. In semiprojective use of playlife activities, a starting stimulus is presented by the clinician with an invitation to continue with the subject's own thoughts, wishes, etc. Most common among these are pictures with scenes that the children describe or construct. In the Michigan Apperception Test, figures are placed in and out of cardboard settings. The Children's Apperception Test (CAT) (Buros, 1978) consists of 10 scenes of animal families or family subunits (e.g., child and father) which focus on specific dynamics. Presumably the child identifies with the figures and is thus able to project his own thoughts and feelings onto the animals depicted. Animals are a favorite because it is believed that they provide a protective distance for the child and are easier to identify with than human figures (Buros, 1978).

Along the same lines as the CAT are the Blacky Pictures (Buros, 1978) and the Missouri Children's Picture Series (Buros, 1978). The latter depict a clear protagonist and antagonist but the rest of the detail is sketchy enough to allow projection.

A parallel development was the construction of drawing tests that permit children to draw their own pictures and then make up stories about the figures drawn. Most notable among these are the Machover Figure Drawing Test (Buros, 1978) and the Goodenough–Harris Drawing Test (GHDT) (Buros, 1978). The latter test has had various modifications from its original format, which was intended to measure intelligence. As a personality measure, drawing the figure of the opposite sex and talking about the figures have been added (Buros, 1978). More recently the H-T-P (House-Tree-Person) Test has been added to these drawing tests, with the additional features of a house and tree. Relative proportions of these objects, presumed to represent in analytic symbols the mother (house), father (tree), and person (the child), are of importance to the clinician in determining family relationships (Buros, 1978).

There are literally scores of semiprojective, playlife diagnostic techniques described in the Buros Mental Measurements Yearbook volume on personality (Buros, 1978); only a few of the most frequently used were mentioned here. It should be noted that these kinds of instruments are viewed as minimally threatening to the child because the child is generally not aware that the innocuous tasks are revealing information about his dynamics to the examiner.

Finally, it should be noted that few validity studies on these semiprojective tests have been conducted and that those that have been done have been minimally supportive of their value for revealing personality dynamics (Buros, 1975). Their real value may be to permit the child to verbalize his feelings in the presence of the clinician, because many of the personality evaluations are intended to be followed by treatment.

## RESEARCH ON PLAY THERAPY: PROCESS, RESEARCH

Because the difference between the directive and nondirective views has been such a central issue to play therapists, much of the process research has been framed in terms of the relationship of therapist behaviors to therapeutically valued child responses. The nondirective therapists have contributed the bulk of the research information.

## Nondirective Process Studies

Before Axline published *Play Therapy* in 1947, studies had already been conducted on child and therapist verbal and nonverbal session behaviors that analyzed their frequency, type, and sequential order for both therapist and child (Landisberg & Snyder, 1946). They found that less than 10% of therapist responses were simple acceptance (e.g., yes and umhum), contrary to the then prevailing notion that nondirective therapy consisted of little more than simple acceptance. Children were found to release significant feelings primarily through action as opposed to verbal expression. These productive responses were preceded 84% of the time by reflective responses by the therapist—57% of which were empathizing with the children's verbally or nonverbally expressed feelings. Later studies (Moustakas & Schalock, 1955) confirmed the same pattern of nondirective therapist session behaviors and its relationship to child responses.

The play therapists' belief in fantasy for helping to control anxiety and master internal and external strivings has been demonstrated empirically in nontherapy contexts by a number of researchers (e.g., Singer, 1974; Yawkey, 1980). Addressing fantasy productions in play sessions per se, Reif and Stollak (1972) were able to demonstrate significant relationships between therapist acceptance and permissiveness and high levels of fantasy expression on the part of the children. A control group of children, whose "therapists" were untrained in play therapy of any type and followed their own concepts gleaned from reading and intuition, expressed significantly less fantasy. Reif and Stollak speculated that fantasy occurs most easily in the absence of compelling external stimulation and that the permissive atmosphere created by the nondirective play therapist permits the children to be more responsive to their own needs and internal states, encouraging fantasy about them.

*Research on Child Behavior Changes during Nondirective Therapy.* Many studies involving elaborate coding of child behavior in the sessions have confirmed that there is a predictable pattern in the behavior of children over a series of sessions (Finke, 1947; Landisburg & Snyder, 1946; Lebo, 1952; Moustakas & Schalock, 1955). Although coding systems varied to a certain extent, most used a variation of Finke's (1947). Regardless of system, all addressed the same core variables—the amount of verbalizing irrespective of content; verbal and nonverbal expressions of aggression, dependence, affection, fear, mastery behaviors, and negative and positive verbal statements about the self, others, and the physical world. Although the researchers have disagreed about the number of distinct stages that should be identified (Finke, 1947; Moustakas, 1973), all of the records of coded behavior indicate that the process follows a regular pattern of content, most observable with disturbed children, but also apparent with normal children (Moustakas & Schalock, 1955). In the first stage, the emotions of troubled children are diffuse and undifferentiated—generally negative, out of proportion in relation to the realities to which they are tied, and exaggerated. After a period of exploration, these negative feelings emerged as expressions of hostility, anxiety, and regression. In Stage 2, the same feelings may be expressed but they are more clearly directed—more specific, more reality oriented. In Stage 3, less negative and more ambivalent feelings are expressed. In the final stage, positive feelings begin to emerge, and these are very realistic. Positive attitudes and negative attitudes become differentiated and more moderate. Positive statements about the environment, the self, and others emerge. Mastery behaviors are undertaken at this time.

The relationship aspects of the therapy parallel this content process. The child builds up positive feelings toward the therapist and tries out previously risky behaviors in the newfound security of the accepting relationship (e.g., motor skill building [Moustakas, 1973]).

It is important that the reader understand that in nondirective therapy the therapist does not modify his behavior in relation to the child. The therapist's repertoire consists of the same empathic, structuring, and limit-setting behaviors throughout the entire series of sessions. The difference in child behavior at different points in the process is a function of the child's own response to the sustained, growth-furthering interpersonal environment.

An interesting variation in the study of process was reported by L'Abate (1979). One room equipped with typical playroom aggressive toys and a second equipped with constructive games of chance and skill, drawing equipment, two-player games like dominoes, etc. were monitored electronically to measure the amount of time spent on the activities in the "Aggression Room" versus the "Constructive Room." L'Abate (1979) identified in boys, 5–14 years old, a three-stage pattern in the therapy process over 15 sessions which parallels that described by Finke (1947) and Moustakas (1973), which he labeled "(1) exploration; (2) aggression; and (3) construction [p. 153]."

In relation to parents as therapists, B. Guerney (1976) identified a similar process over an average of 30 play sessions. As parents became more empathic, permitted more self-direction, and demonstrated complex involvement with their children's therapeutic play, the amount of aggression and dependency decreased, although not uninterruptedly downward. Leadership (assertiveness) increased in the children.

*Process in Directive Therapies.* With the exception of the behavioral therapists (e.g., Johnson & Brown [1969] and Forehand & King [1974]) empirical studies of changes in the child's and/or therapists' behavior throughout the therapy process have not been reported. Dealing with very specific behaviors, the behavioral therapists are able to demonstrate rapid declines of undesirable behaviors in the play sessions and a complete increase in desirable behaviors. When parents are used as the primary therapists the same process and outcomes are found (Johnson & Brown, 1969; Forehand & King, 1974).

## OUTCOME RESEARCH

### Outcome of Nondirective Therapies

*Individual Therapy.* As with process studies, the nondirective therapists have been more active in studying outcome, although the number of studies in recent years has been relatively few. Some of the early studies that were unusually sound methodologically for clinical studies are mentioned here. Early studies with control groups demonstrated the efficacy of individual therapy with children by showing increases on personality and sociometric measures (e.g., Cox [1953]). Bills (1950), using an own control design, was able to demonstrate that children with reading problems and personality problems, as adjudged by tests and teachers, respectively, improved significantly in reading performance after play therapy. A study by Dorfman (1958) utilized both an own control and no-treatment comparison group design and demonstrated significant changes on personality and adjustment measures that were maintained or even increased at follow-up. Seeman, Barry, and Ellinwood (1964) achieved very positive results with children rated lowest in school on teacher ratings scales and personality tests. Children were randomly assigned to treatment or control conditions. Children in the experimental group improved on all measures including ratings of reputation and amount of aggression expressed. A more recent study in West Germany (Schmidtchen & Hobrucker, 1978) added a placebo group to the no-treatment control design. Significant changes were shown for the experimental group in removing symptoms and increasing self-concept.

### Outcomes of Directive Play Therapies with Individual Children

The reported research in directive therapies has consisted primarily of case studies demonstrating the value of the given approach for a particular type of child problem (e.g., phobias, tics, elimination difficulties and other problems whose presence or absence are relatively easily ascertained). Typically these case reports contain little if any quantitative information, with the exception of the behavioral therapists who present baseline data and final status and frequently follow-up data (Johnson & Brown, 1969; Forehand & King, 1974). Pre–post test scores on an individual (Chase, 1968) or group of patients given the same treatment for similar symptoms have also been reported (Hare-Mustin, 1975).

Of the nonbehavioral directive methods included in this chapter, the Theraplay (Jernberg, 1979) method has reported the greatest number of pre–post quantitative studies in relation to the greatest number of childhood problems, as well as for developmental enhancement in instances of incapacitation (e.g., blindness). Increases in IQ on standard intelligence tests have been reported on a case study basis by Jernberg (1979) and her colleagues (Brody, 1978).

## Outcome Studies with Groups

Since Fleming and Snyder (1947), who showed gains for a treatment group over a no-treatment control group, nondirective therapists have been able to demonstrate positive changes through group play therapy with maladjusted children. Fisher (1953) and Moulin (1970) demonstrated the effectiveness of nondirective group therapy with groups of academic underachievers.

Abramowitz (1976) examined group therapy outcome studies conducted with children and observed that the results were inconclusive. However, only 28% of the treatment groups she examined were play therapy groups. According to Abramowitz, only one-third of all approaches yielded generally positive results. She did not analyze success rate according to the type of therapy offered or the conditions of the study (e.g., the presence of control or comparison groups). However, a scrutiny of her tables for design conditions and use of play therapy indicates that when *any* type of play therapy was utilized as a treatment or comparison condition that some positive changes occurred in the play condition in all but 2 of 12 studies. In four studies, improvement was demonstrated on the personality measures but not on such measures as intelligence. These figures exceed the overall success rate she reported. However, the author must agree with Abramowitz' conclusion that the quality of the data base must be improved if genuinely meaningful judgements are to be made about the efficacy of group methods with children, whether they be play or any other.

## Outcome Studies with Nonprofessional Therapists

*College Students.* Using trained versus untrained undergraduate students, Stollak, Scholom, Green, Schreiber, and Messe (1975) randomly assigned children with problems to one of the two therapist conditions for therapy or "just to play" with an untrained student, considered a placebo condition. Stollak et al. were able to demonstrate very significant decreases in the problem behaviors of treatment children, as reported by parents and teachers naive about the condition in which the children had been placed. No such changes occurred for any of the control children.

*Teachers.* Guerney and Flumen (1970) trained teachers to administer play therapy to withdraw children from their classes. Classroom raters who did not know the identity of the treatment children indicated that specific classroom social behaviors of the treatment children were significantly improved over those of a comparable group of untreated children.

*Parents.* Guerney and Stover (1971) reported significant pre–post behavioral changes in 41 children who had participated in Filial Therapy (B. Guerney, 1964, 1976) which utilizes parents to serve as nondirective play therapists. The mothers of these children conducted approximately 30 weekly home play sessions and supervised sessions at the treatment site. Children improved significantly more than a comparable group of nontreatment children over a similar time span (Oxman, 1971). Three years later 36 remained improved (L. Guerney, 1975).

Sywulak (1977), using a sample of 19 mothers and fathers and an own control design, demonstrated that parental acceptance increased steadily over a 4 month treatment period spent in Filial Therapy. Also, the children experienced a significant decrease in problem behaviors. Sensue (1981) continued to study the same group of parents at 6 months and up to 3 years later. Gains increased at 6 months and remained as high at 3 years. Parents' scores on acceptance of their children were higher than those of a comparable group of parents whose children had never experienced problems. As a group, the children, originally behaviorally or emotionally disordered, were no different from normative samples and peers who had not had problems.

In the behavioral approaches, parents as therapists in play programs have been able to demonstrate significant gains in targeted behaviors, which then transferred to the home and continued, in some instances, to increase even more after 1 year (Forehand & King, 1974; Johnson & Brown, 1969).

## OVERVIEW AND FUTURE DIRECTIONS

In this chapter, different perspectives on the nature of the therapeutic process have been examined in relation to the behavior of the play therapist. Comparable information about the effects of these differing emphases and methods is impossible to obtain because of the dearth of research, particularly in relation to process phenomena. In regard to outcome, no definitive differential effectiveness studies have yet appeared in spite of a nearly 40 year history of the existence of the two opposing positions.

The problems in attempting to conduct serious investigations of differential treatment effectiveness in treatment settings, particularly where children are involved, remain as difficult to surmount as they have ever been. Until such tests can be conducted regarding comparative efficacy, using adequate designs, practicing clinicians have three choices open to them. Those more scientifically disposed use the methods that have been proven effective in solid experimental tests, which in play therapy would be the nondirective approach. Others espouse the approach based on the theory of personality and/or change or communication that they believe in, whether it is supported or not. Or, they can become "eclectic." If done correctly, becoming eclectic means developing a conceptually integrated blend of more than one approach, for example, Filial Therapy (Guerney, 1964; L. Guerney, 1976) which integrates Rogerian and behavioral principles and procedures. More typically, the eclectic practitioner merely picks and chooses features from among treatment methods he has been exposed to, constructing an amalgam devoid of a sound theory base and/or empirical evidence for its potential effectiveness. This tends to result in a quest for techniques that it is hoped will provide instant reduction of problems. The efficacy of these techniques generally cannot be established beyond positive therapeutic effects for a single client, class of clients, or a single problem.

That this situation has become more or less permanent in the field of play therapy is evidenced by the age of the well-controlled studies, few of which are less than 25 years old. The fantasy of a single approach that will work flawlessly with all problems or at least for given groupings of problems and clients will probably remain unfulfilled. However, attempting to show the superiority of a single approach empirically may not prove to be as fruitful as isolating from the many approaches the common elements associated with desirable treatment effects. Early nondirective play therapy researchers started to do this but seem to have stopped prematurely. Thus, no core conditions necessary for producing therapeutic change have been defined, operationalized, and universally accepted as has happened for adult therapy (Carkhuff, 1969).

Because clinical research in counseling settings does appear to be chronically rare, it might be productive for clinicians to make better use of relevant findings from other disciplines. A resurgence of interest in play appears to have occurred among developmental researchers (Fein, 1975; Yawkey, 1980) who study the relationship of play conditions and materials to child verbal and nonverbal responses. To test the possibilities of transferring elements identified as productive in their studies, e.g., encouraging fantasy expression, in order to attain related treatment goals, might prove fruitful. The laboratory researcher in turn would acquire information about the transferability and generalizability of these variables to applied situations.

A number of promising developments have arisen in play therapy in recent years. The use of nonprofessionals, including parents, to serve as play therapists opens up the possibility of using the play methods for improving the quality of significant real-life relationships. The use of undergraduates (Reif & Stollak, 1972) and parents (Guerney & Stover, 1971) have been researched both for process and outcome, with positive results.

There is a parallel movement oriented toward broadening the application of play therapy methods for developmental enhancement. One is even labeled Developmental Play (Brody, 1978) and is applied in preschool groups utilizing nonprofessional therapists. Although thus far these developmental approaches rely on pre–post case studies for proof of their efficacy, these efforts indicate that the normalization of children and the attainment of certain developmental goals through play methods are becoming of interest to clinicians. This is a refreshing change from the clinical writings of 50 years ago that were preoccupied with the perfecting of details of a particular type of interpretation for a particular type of personality abberation.

## REFERENCES

Abramowitz, C. Group psychotherapy with children. *Archives of General Psychiatry,* 1976, *33,* 320–326.

Allen, F. Therapeutic work with children. *American Journal of Orthopsychiatry,* 1934, *4,* 193–202.

Andronico, M., & Guerney, B. A psychotherapeutic aide in a headstart program. *Children,* 1969, *16,* 14–22.

Axline, V. *Play therapy.* Cambridge, Mass.: Houghton Mifflin, 1947.

Axline, V. *Play therapy* (Rev. Ed.). New York: Ballatine Books, 1969.

Beiser, H. Play equipment for diagnosis and therapy. *American Journal of Orthopsychiatry,* 1955, *15,* 761–770.

Bills, R. E. *Non-directed play therapy with retarded readers. Journal of Consulting Psychology,* 1950, *14,* 140–149.

Boring, E. G. *A history of experimental psychology,* New York: Appleton–Century, 1950.

Bottome, P. *Alfred Adler.* New York: Vanguard Press, 1957.

Brady, C., & Friedrich, W. Levels of intervention: A model for training in play therapy. *Journal of Clinical Child Psychology,* 1982, *11,* 39–43.

Brody, V. Developmental play: A relationship-focused program for children. *Child Welfare,* 1978, *57,* 591–599.

Buros, O. (Ed.). *The sixth mental measurements yearbook.* Highland Park, N.J.: Gryphon Press, 1975.

Buros, O. (Ed.). *The eighth mental measurements yearbook* (Vol 2). Highland Park, N.J.: Gryphon Press, 1978.

Carkhuff, R. *Helping and human relationships* (Vols. I & II). New York: Holt, Rinehart and Winston, 1969.

Conn, J. The child reveals himself through play—The method of the play interview. *Mental Hygiene,* 1939, *23,* 49–69.

Cox, F. Sociometric status before and after play therapy. *Journal of Abnormal and Social Psychology,* 1953, *48,* 354–356.

Dollard, J., & Miller, N. *Personality and psychotherapy.* New York: McGraw–Hill, 1950.

Dorfman, E. Play therapy. In C. Rogers (Ed.), *Client-centered therapy.* Boston: Houghton Mifflin Co., 1951.

Dorfman, E. Personality outcomes of client-centered child therapy. *Psychological Monographs,* 1958, *72*(3, Whole No. 456).

Durfee, M. B. Use of ordinary office equipment in play therapy. *American Journal of Orthopsychiatry,* 1952, *12,* 495–503.

Ellis, M. *Why people play.* Englewood Cliffs, N.J.: Prentice–Hall, 1973.

Erikson, E. H. *Childhood and society.* New York: Norton, 1963.

Fein, G. G. A transformational analysis of pretending. *Developmental Psychology,* 1975, *11,* 291–296.

Finke, H. *Changes in the expression of emotionalized attitudes in six cases of play therapy.* Unpublished masters thesis, University of Chicago, 1947.

Fishbein, C. *The relationship between age-related toys and therapeutic expression in non-directive play therapy.* Unpublished masters thesis, The Pennsylvania State University, 1974.

Fisher, B. Group therapy with retarded readers. *Journal of Educational Psychology,* 1953, *360,* 356–360.

Fleming, L., & Snyder, W. Social and personal changes following non-directive group play therapy. *American Journal of Orthopsychiatry,* 1947, *17,* 101–116.

Forehand, R., & King, E. Pre-school children's noncompliance: Effects of short term behavior therapy. *Journal of Community Psychology,* 1974, *2,* 42–44.

Freud, A. *The psycho-analytical treatment of children.* New York: International Universities Press, 1955.

Freud, S. *Basic writings.* New York: Modern Library, 1938.

Gardner, R. *Therapeutic communication with children: The mutual story telling technique.* New York: Science House, 1971.

Ginott, H. *Group psychotherapy with children.* New York: McGraw–Hill, 1961.

Ginott, H., & Lebo, D. Play therapy limits and theoretical orientation. *Journal of Consulting Psychology,* 1961, *25,* 337–340.

Goldberg, T. Battling tops: A modality in child psychotherapy. *Journal of Clinical Child Psychology,* 1980, *9,* 206–209.

Guerney, B. Filial therapy: Description and rationale. *Journal of Consulting Psychology,* 1964, *28,* 303–310.

Guerney, B. Filial therapy used as a treatment method for disturbed children. *Evaluation,* 1976, *3,* 34–35.

Guerney, B., & Flumen, A. Teachers as psychotherapeutic agents for withdrawn children. *Journal of School Psychology,* 1970, *8,* 107–113.

Guerney, B., & Stover, L. *Filial therapy: Final report on MH 1826401.* State College, PA, 1971, mimeograph, p. 156.

Guerney, L. A follow up study on filial therapy. Symposium paper presented at the annual convention of the Eastern Psychological Association, New York, April 1975.

Guerney, L. Filial therapy program. In D. H. Olson (Ed.), *Treating relationships.* Lake Mills, Ia.: Graphic Publishing, 1976.

Guerney, L. Play therapy with learning disabled children. *Journal of Clinical Child Psychology,* 1979, *8,* 242–244.

Guerney, L. Client-centered (non-directive) play therapy. In C. Schaefer & K. O'Connor (Eds.), *Handbook of play therapy.* New York, Pa.: Wiley, 1982.

Hare-Mustin, R. Treatment of temper tantrums by a paradoxical intervention. *Family Process,* 1975, *14,* 481–485.

Hornsby, L., & Applebaum, A. Parents as primary therapists: Filial therapy. In L. Arnold (Ed.), *Helping parents help their children.* New York: Brunner/Mazel, 1978.

Jernberg, A. M. *Theraplay.* San Francisco: Jossey–Bass, 1979.

Johnson, S., & Brown, R. Producing changes in parents of disturbed children. *Journal of Child Psychology and Psychiatry,* 1969, *10,* 107–121.

Kaczkowski, H. Group work with children. *Elementary School Guidance and Counseling,* 1979, *14,* 44–51.

Kanner, L. *Child psychiatry.* Springfield, Ill.: Charles C. Thomas, 1948.

Klein, M. The psychoanalytic play technique. *American Journal of Orthopsychiatry,* 1955, *55,* 223–227.

Klein, M. *The Psycho-analyses of Children.* London: Hogarth Press, Ltd., 1959.
Kuhli, L. The use of two houses in play therapy. *American Journal of Orthopsychiatry,* 1979, *49,* 431–435.
L'Abate, L. Aggression and construction in boys' monitored play therapy. *Journal of Counseling and Psychotherapy,* 1979, *2,* 137–158.
Landisberg, S., & Snyder, W. Nondirective play therapy. *Journal of Clinical Psychology,* 1946, *2,* 203–213.
Lebo, D. The relationships of response categories in play therapy to chronological age. *Child Psychiatry,* 1952, *20,* 330–336.
Lebo, D. Age and suitability for non-directive therapy. *Journal of Genetic Psychology,* 1956, *89,* 231–238.
Levy, D. Hostility patterns in sibling rivalry. *American Journal of Orthopsychiatry,* 1933, *3,* 266–275.
Levy, D. Release therapy. In C. Schaefer (Ed.), *Therapeutic use of child's play.* New York: Aronson, 1976.
Marcus, I. Costume play therapy. *American Academy of Child Psychiatry Journal,* 1966, *5,* 441–451.
Moulin, E. K. The effects of client-centered group counseling play media on the intelligence, achievement, and psycholinguistics of underachieving primary school children. *Elementary School Guidance Counselor,* 1970, *5,* 85–98.
Moustakas, C. *Children in play therapy* (Rev. ed.). New York: Aronson, 1973.
Moustakas, C., & Schalock, H. An analysis of therapist–child interaction in play therapy. *Child Development,* 1955, *26,* 143–157.
Murphy, L. *Methods for the study of young children.* New York: Basic Books, 1964.
Nickerson, E. The application of play therapy to a school setting. *Psychology in the Schools,* 1973, *10,* 362–365.
Oxman, L. *The effectiveness of filial therapy: A control study.* Unpublished doctoral dissertation, Rutgers University, 1971.
Patterson, G., Jones, R., Whittier, J., & Wright, M. A behavior modification technique for the hyperactive child. *Behavioral Research and Therapy,* 1965, *2,* 217–226.
Peoples, C. Fair play therapy: A new perspective. *Journal of Psychology,* 1979, *102,* 113–117.
Pulaski, M. Toys and imaginative play. In J. Singer (Ed.), *The child's world of make-believe.* New York: Academic Press, 1973.
Reif, T., & Stollak, G. *Sensitivity to young children: Training and its effects.* East Lansing, Mich.: Michigan State University Press, 1972.
Rogers, C *Counseling and psychotherapy.* Boston: Houghton Mifflin, 1942.
Rogers, C. *Client-centered therapy.* Boston: Houghton Mifflin, 1951.
Schaefer, C. *Therapeutic use of child's play.* New York: Aronson, 1976.
Schmidtchen, S., & Hobrucker, B. The efficiency of client-centered play therapy. *Praxis Der Kinderpsychologie and Kinderpsychiatrie,* 1978, *1,* 64–66.
Seeman, J., Barry, E., & Ellinwood, C. Interpersonal assessment of play therapy outcomes. *Psychotherapy: Theory, Research, and Practice,* 1964, *1,* 64–66.
Sensue, M. E. *Filial therapy follow-up study: Effects on parent acceptance and child adjustment.* Unpublished doctoral dissertation, The Pennsylvania State University, 1981.
Shuman, W., & Leton, D. A narrative study of diagnostic techniques in school play. *Psychology in the Schools,* 1965, *2,* 359–364.
Singer, J. (Ed.). *The child's world of make believe.* New York: Academic Press, 1974.
Slavson, S. *The practice of group therapy.* New York: International Universities Press, 1947.
Slavson, S., & Shiffer, M. *Group psychotherapies for children.* New York: International Universities Press, 1974.

Smilansky, S. *The effects of sociodramatic play on disadvantaged preschool children.* New York: Wiley, 1968.

Stollak, G., Scholom, A., Green, L., Schreiber, J., & Messe, L. Process and outcome of play encounters between undergraduates and clinic-referred children: Preliminary findings. *Psychotherapy: Theory, Research, and Practice,* 1975, *13,* 327–331.

Sywulak, A. E. *The effect of filial therapy on parental acceptance and child adjustment.* Unpublished doctoral dissertation, The Pennsylvania State University, 1977.

Tuma, J., & Pratt, J. Clinical child psychology practice and training: A survey. *Journal of Clinical Child Psychology,* 1982, *11,* 27–34.

Wadden, T., & Anderton, C. The clinical use of hypnosis. *Psychological Bulletin,* 1982, *91,* 215–243.

Walder, R. Psychoanalytic theory of play. In C. Schaefer (Ed.), *Therapeutic use of child's play.* New York: Aronson, 1976.

Wenger, C. The Suitcase Story: A therapeutic technique for children in out-of-home placement. *American Journal of Orthopsychiatry,* 1982, *52,* 353–355.

Woltmann, A. Puppetry as a tool in child psychotherapy. *International Journal of Child Psychiatry,* 1972, *1,* 84–96.

Yawkey, T. An investigation of imaginative play and aural language development in young children, five, six, and seven. In D. Williamson (Ed.), *Play in human settlements.* London, England: Croonhelm Publishers, 1980.

# 17 Play in Hospital Settings

Rosemary Bolig
*Ohio State University*

Play is children's way of making sense of the world, of integrating thought and feeling, while concurrently causing action on the world and bending reality to fulfill needs. Play is an alliance with the environment, a delicate balance or mutual exchange of control, stimulation, and imagination. Without play it appears that children's potential for learning and mastery may be limited (Chance, 1979).

Any brief and intense stress, for example, a spanking, may render normally functioning children "playless." The combined physiological and psychological stresses of illness and hospitalization, however, place extreme demands upon children's capacities to utilize play to maintain equilibrium, to comprehend, or to cope. In the absence of familiar persons, objects, and routines and with the real or perceived threat of injections, medications, and procedures many children while hospitalized cannot spontaneously play.

Although scientific validation of play and various facilitative approaches is currently lacking, play and related activities is increasingly recognized as essential to children's and adolescent's effectively coping with the experience of being hospitalized (Association for the Care of Children's Health, 1979). What play is and what conditions are necessary for it to continue to occur under stress are differently perceived (McCue, Wagner, Hansen, & Rigler, 1980). In some hospitals any activity or action that appears pleasurable and goalless is labeled play; in others, there is a distinction made between experiences that are adult selected and directed, and those that are child motivated and controlled. Conditions for play to occur vary from provision of toys to elaborate play and activity programs with professional staff whose primary concern is the psychosocial, recreational, and educational needs of hospitalized, and frequently outpatient, children and their families.

Likewise, views of the functions of play vary from diversionary to cathartic to mastery to learning. The following quotations from health care practitioners exemplify the diversity of perceptions of the values of play:

1. The most obvious use of play is as a simple occupation to take the child's mind off the distressing events around him [Lindquist, Lind, & Harvey, 1977, p. 164].
2. What does the child in hospital specially need from his play? He is away from home in a strange and sometimes frightening environment, surrounded by people he does not know and experiences he cannot understand. His need to play out his problems and anxieties is urgent and demanding [Harvey & Hales-Tooke, 1972, p. 27].
3. Play restores, in part, normal aspects of living and prevents further disturbances. Also, it provides the child with the opportunity to recognize his life; thus it reduces anxiety and establishes a sense of perspective [Petrillo & Sanger, 1972, p. 97].
4. Play is basic to the ways in which children learn about themselves and the world around them. Through directed play activities the child can better understand the experiences of the hospital and communicate his fears and understandings of the various aspects of his illness and required treatment [Azarnoff & Flegal, 1975, p. 3].

In many hospital settings play and other activities are intended to serve multiple functions. Implications for facilitation of play or programming (e.g., role of the adult, types of toys and materials, interaction with peers), however, often appears to be derived from the prevalent institutional philosophy on the functions and/or importance of play.

Thus, this chapter attempts to describe the state of the art of play in hospital settings. This description is prefaced with a brief review of the effects of hospitalization on children and ameliorative approaches that includes play or organized play/activity programs.

It should be noted that although many of the elements of play to be described in this chapter share some of the characteristics of nondirective play therapy as described by Axline (1966) and are presumed to provide similar curative functions, they are intended to be utilized with normally functioning children who are situationally in distress and/or unable to play. Confrontation, interpretation, intrusion, and other highly directive techniques would rarely if ever be utilized by the persons (e.g., nurses, play specialists,[1] volunteers) who generally are

[1]The term *play specialist* is used to identify persons with educational backgrounds of child development, education, psychology, or related fields whose primary function is to facilitate play, activities, and other related experiences. A variety of terms (e.g., play leader, play therapist, child-life worker) are currently employed for persons performing this function.

involved in the day-to-day facilitation of play and play programs in hospital settings. Hospitalized children with more enduring behavioral or personality problems or children who do not respond to various teaching and nondirective play techniques utilized would in most instances be referred to clinicians or clinical specialists.

## THE IMPACT OF HOSPITALIZATION

### Overview

With the information provided by more than 40 years of cumulative data, social scientists and practitioners clearly recognize that hospitalization is an inherently stressful experience for children and their families. Most children as well as many adults evidence symptoms of distress while hospitalized. Children may cling and cry, become listless and silent, regress and/or resist and struggle (Gellert, 1958). Bowlby (1969) and Robertson (1953) identified three stages—protest, despair, and denial—that children typically progress through during hospitalization. These reactions, however, are more likely to occur in the absence of parents (Robertson & Robertson, 1971).

Degree of distress and how rapidly children regress and progress has been found to be related to children's age or developmental level, prehospital personality, and coping style, and what actually happens to them in the hospital (e.g., the nature of illness, presence of parents, preparation, play, types of procedures). Children between the ages of 7 months to 4 or 5 years generally exhibit the most observable distress during hospitalization. High dependency on significant adults for need gratification, level of cognitive development, separation or maternal deprivation, misconceptions, anxieties aroused, and sensory/motor deprivation are but a few of the theoretical explanations offered for young children's reactions.

Although there is ample evidence that most children, especially those under the age of 4 or 5, are distressed while hospitalized, there has been continual controversy over whether hospitalization, particularly in the early years, has any long-term sequelae. Most early studies (Jessner, Bloom, & Waldfogel, 1952; Prugh, Staub, Sands, Kirshbaum, & Lenihan, 1953) found evidence of distress months and years after hospitalization. Because they have lacked control groups or failed to control extraneous variables, these studies have frequently been criticized (Goslin, 1978). With more sophisticated methodologies, Douglas (1975) and Quinton and Rutter (1976) found no long-term effects following *single* hospitalizations of *less* than a week. However, multiple or recurrent admissions did appear to be related to subsequent disorders in behavior and school-related problems. Although it may be possible, therefore, to conclude that more than one hospitalization may have long-term effects, Rutter (1981) contends that chronic family adversity, related to more frequent hospitalizations of children, should be considered.

Rutter (1981) hypothesizes that a "first admission must in some way sensitize the child so that he is more likely to suffer the next time [p. 193]." Early admissions may increase a child's vulnerability to later stress and perhaps most in children who have an ambivalent relationship with their parents. There is, however, some evidence that vulnerability may be decreased. Some children appear to improve behaviorally following hospitalization (Shore, Geiser, & Wolman, 1965). Rutter (1981) states: "Presumably, it matters whether the child emerges from the first stress with improved coping mechanisms, enhanced self-esteem or a more effective physiological response [p. 196]."

Children may be more resilient than earlier believed, and brief, isolated hospitalizations may not be necessarily "traumatic." Nevertheless, hospitalization must be considered a "crisis" as both opportunity and danger exist for coping, adaption, and continued learning (Goslin, 1978).

## Ameliorative Approaches

Approaches to ameliorate the impact of hospitalization and increase children's abilities to cope have resulted from the identification of factors contributing to psychological upset (Vernon, Foley, Sipowicz, & Schulman, 1965). Although there is conceptual and programmatic overlap, the concern for separation has resulted in allowing parents more opportunity to visit and to "room-in." The concern for unfamiliarity and children's conceptions has precipitated the development of preparation programs, materials, and films, whereas the concern of sensorimotor restrictions and deprivation has supported the implementation of play and activities programs.

Of these three ameliorative approaches, parent involvement and preparation have received the most empirical support. Brain and Maclay (1968), Couture (1976), and Fagin (1964) have found that the continual presence (rooming-in) of a parent, usually the mother, contributes significantly to less upset following hospitalization. Branstetter (1969) found, however, that the presence of a parent or parent substitute were both equally more effective in reducing distress than no consistent adult. Most preparation studies in which professionals prepared children have found that although anxiety was not always reduced in the hospital, there were significantly positive long-term effects, particularly for older children (Rie, Boverman, Grossman, & Natividad, 1968; Visitainer & Wolfer, 1975; Wolfer & Visitainer, 1975).

Goslin in her 1978 review of the research states that at present it appears that parent involvement is more effective in reducing negative effects in preschool-age children than is preparation alone, whereas preparation strategies are effective for school-age children.

To date, there has been little research on the effects of participation in play and activities programs (Bolig, 1980; Goslin, 1978; Hodapp, 1982). Prugh et al.'s (1953) investigation of improved ward management versus traditional ward management included the availability of an activities program as one of the conditions in improved ward management. Although children experiencing improved ward management evidenced less upset than those subjected to the traditional approach, there is no way of gauging the influence of play or activities. Bopp (1967) also investigated the effects of two conditions: play/activities program and no preparation and restricted visiting. She found no significant posthospitalization differences, but, like Prugh et al.'s (1953) study, there were several confounding variables. Johnson (1969) compared children in isolation who received individualized play sessions with children who did not and found no significant differences from parents' perspectives.

Bolig (1980), however, found that the more time children spent in a supervised play/activities program, the more internal (i.e., locus of control) they became. This finding suggests that play, activities, and/or the relationships established through play can contribute to an increased perception of control of events and reinforcements. Theoretically, children who became more internal may be able to cope more effectively with subsequent events by being more active, inquiring, and demanding of the environment than previously. Case studies (Byers, 1972, Erikson, 1958; Noble, 1967) have shown play sessions effective in reducing anxiety associated with specific procedures. Field studies by Hall (1977) and Stacey, Dearden, Pill, and Robinson (1970) suggest more generalized reduction of anxiety through participation in play and activities.

## DEFINING PLAY IN HOSPITALS

Since the 1930s play and recreation as stimulation or activity has been the most frequently mentioned method of mitigating upset associated with sensorimotor restrictions or deprivation (Vernon et al., 1965). Gellert (1958) hypothesized that anxiety is aroused when there are physical limitations that interfere with activity. This view, based on a combination of stimulation, arousal, and relaxation theories, continues to contribute to a generalized definition of play in hospitals, that is, that any action or activity of children that appears pleasurable or goalless is play. Furthermore, any action or activity is often presumed to reduce anxiety.

The integration of other theoretical orientations (e.g., cognitive) has begun to provide both a more comprehensive perspective on the functions of play and a framework for descriminating play, and its various forms, from other experiences. Therefore, it is important to emphasize that until recently throughout the hospitalized child literature that "play" often referred to any activity, whether it be entertainment, recreation, or instruction, in which children engaged. Increasingly, however, health-care practitioners have begun to utilize criteria such as the following by Neuman (1971) in defining play for hospitalized children.

Play is:

—Internally controlled: i.e., the child controls the process and the objectives.
—Intrinsically motivated: i.e., the child chooses to participate.
—Actively engaging: i.e., the child uses actions and words in participating.
—Internally real: i.e., the child suspends external reality in order to establish rules, procedures, roles, content, and outcome.
—Pleasurable: i.e., the child smiles, laughs, and is relaxed [p. 8–9].

The Association for the Care of Children's Health, a multidisciplinary organization whose focus is the psychological needs of hospitalized children, adolescents, and their families, regards play as but one of several interrelated strategies including activities, other experiences, and interpersonal relationships that can facilitate the primary goals of: (1) minimizing stress and anxiety for the child and adolescent; (2) providing essential life experiences; and (3) providing opportunities to retain self-esteem and appropriate independence (ACCH, 1979). Although play is generally recognized as vital to coping, particularly for the young child, actual provisions for and facilitation of "play" varies considerably from setting to setting, as do provisions for other activities and experiences.

## ELEMENTS OF PLAY IN HOSPITAL SETTINGS

The following elements, although heretofore have often been termed "play," are variously found in hospitals and most frequently when there are play or activity programs with consistent, trained, paid staff. The degree to which each element is developed and integrated, the frequency of each element's occurrence, the role of the "adult" (i.e., play specialist, nurse, volunteer, teacher) in each element, and the manner in which each element is presented and the functions it is presumed to serve varies from hospital to hospital and from program to program. Philosophies of how children learn and cope are significant factors in whether or not specific elements are included, in what combinations, and in what manner. Ages of children served, nature of their illnesses, as well as number of staff, educational backgrounds of staff (or volunteers), and space also influence selection of and combinations of elements. Although in some hospitals the development and/or implementation of certain elements are a cooperative effort among play/activities staff, nursing staff, and/or other groups, in other institutions, one group is totally responsible for specific elements.

### Preparation

Preparation exists in many forms from prehospitalization tours or parties to individualized instruction and/or explanation of and manipulation of materials prior to a specific procedure. Puppets, films, body outlines, dolls, and miniature hospital toys as well as ''real'' hospital equipment such as syringes, masks, and IVs are variously utilized in helping children to become familiar with objects, roles, and procedures as well as to anticipate and to understand impending events. Films and objects for older children often are stimuli for discussion, and opportunity is provided for them to ask questions and express feelings. For younger children, during their play and related verbalizations, the adult may add facts and sequence events, perhaps through role playing. The role of the adult varies from participator to instructor—from facilitating expression of feelings to organizing the experience conceptually.

## Play

As in preparation, there are several subelements of play that are variously anticipated and facilitated. There are continuities across subelements: The adult is generally a nondirective facilitator, and children generally control the process and the content.

*Free Play.* During the hours that the playroom is open and supervised, time is alloted for children to choose to participate in a variety of activities or to choose from a variety of play materials. Dependent on the nature of the activities and the needs of children, the adult may be instructor or facilitator. Dramatic and sociodramatic play on themes common to young children (e.g., house, store) may be encouraged. Water play, painting, stories, and other types of activities commonly enjoyed by young children are other choices.

*Hospital Play.* Real and play medical equipment is provided to stimulate individual or group pretense play. Although hospital equipment is often consistently available in playrooms and may be spontaneously chosen by older children and facilitated by the adult (e.g., the play specialist or nurse), such play is frequently planned by organizing the materials in the playroom or transporting them to children who are unable to participate in the playroom. The adult generally is nondirective in hospital play. His or her presence, however, is often essential for younger children to explore or play comfortably with objects that are anxiety producing.

*Individualized Play.* When children are isolated, critically ill, or in such distress that they cannot participate in group activities, the adult takes toys and activities to the child. Often the adult may begin by playing for the child, moving objects about, and verbalizing roles. Eventually, the child is encouraged to be a more active participant.

*Play Session.* Materials and objects are selected that have unique meaning to the individual (e.g., syringes, catheter). Under the nondirective guidance of the adult (in this case, either the nurse or play specialist) the child is encouraged to express disorganized emotions and to reverse roles. Although the play session shares characteristics of hospital or individualized play, it is generally conducted following procedures or events that have been particularly upsetting to the child.

## Activities

Experiences that are planned, organized, and directed by an adult in which the child is physically or verbally actively engaged but in which there are adult-chosen goals (and occasionally a product) are activities. Examples of activities would include arts and crafts and making play dough. Although expression of feelings or unique utilization of the materials or ''play'' is not discouraged, the focus is on doing or participating. The adult, although responsive to individual needs, concentrates the children's attention on the activity (e.g., ''Jaime, here are some triangles for your collage.'')

## Recreation

Experiences that are loosely structured and organized by the adult but in which both the adult and the child play relatively passive or participant roles are recreation. Examples are playing a game together such as pool or Candyland, listening to records, playing the piano, and looking at magazines. Recreation experiences are intended to be relaxing; voluntary participation is thus essential. General discussion with other children or with the adult either while playing a game or in and of itself is also encouraged.

## Entertainment

Entertainment is preplanned, adult-organized experiences, such as films, puppet shows, clowns, and magic shows, in which children are passive participants (e.g., watching, listening) and which are intended to amuse, relax, or divert. Although the adult may utilize entertainment experiences as a basis for later discussions or for play, they are typically isolated from other elements of planned or spontaneous programming.

## Education

The process of continuing to acquire knowledge and to develop new relationships in thinking through direct experiencing is often an implicit goal in activities or play. Naming colors and shapes, grouping objects, concept formation, and experimenting with physical properties of objects are activities frequently facilitated in certain types of programs. Informing children of names of hospital equipment, basic medical terminology, and reasons for hospitalization are educational components of preparation. Whether or not expression of feelings is facilitated, preparation—individual and group—includes education.

However, the opportunity and encouragement of continuing with "school work" is a readily identifiable example of the education element. Many well-developed play/activity programs integrate math, science, and other academic subjects into group or individualized programming for school-age children. In these instances, education or academics is the *means* for providing a more normal environment, for achieving positive self-esteem, and for continuing to feel in control rather than the goal itself. The children's hospital experiences are often used as a basis for their "learning." Writing a poem or story about hospital experiences, interviewing staff, or drawing a map of the hospital are but a few examples of cognitive–affective learning activities.

Hospital teachers may be assigned to children's hospital by local boards of education. Their primary function is to tutor children who are hospitalized more than a specific period of time (e.g., 6 weeks) in academic subjects. Some hospital teachers are aware of and sensitive to children's psychosocial and medical needs and thus also engage in activities and play as appropriate to the individual. Others concentrate totally on subject matter. This variance is related to the degree to which hospital teachers are integrated into the multidisciplinary team and/or cooperatively work with the play/activities staff.

In hospitals in which many or all of the aforementioned elements exist, but usually only where there is a play program in which the adults are *maximally* responsive to individuals, discrimination between elements may be difficult. The control in an activity, for example, may be allowed (or encouraged) to shift from the adult to the child. Thus, making a real pizza may be the activity, but if children spontaneously take on roles of "pizza maker" and "customer," the play specialist can facilitate what is now play.

In many instances, however, it is possible to discriminate elements on the basis of an adult-to-child continuum as follows:

The degree to which the adult controls the process.
The degree to which children are engaged (physically and verbally).
The degree to which the adult controls selection of objects.
The degree to which children are permitted (or encouraged) to deviate.
The degree to which the adult selects materials and/or encourages expression of ideas and feelings about hospitalization and procedures.
The degree to which children are permitted (or encouraged) to express preference, ideas, and/or feelings.

The elements of preparation, play, activities, entertainment, recreation, and education in various combinations are most frequently provided for inpatients. Types of materials utilized, expectations for the level of and form of participation, and the role of the adult varies dependent on the ages of children (in many hospitals, from infancy through adolescence) as well as limitations imposed by the intensity of children's illnesses or physical restrictions. However, there are many outpatient programs in which free play, hospital play, and activities are the most frequent elements. Prehospitalization tours may also include hospital play. In some hospitals siblings are permitted to participate in activities, free play, and hospital play, especially as such elements occur in supervised playrooms.

## CONDITIONS FOR PLAY

Under severe psychological and/or physiological stress, children do not play. The demands of survival bind children to necessity (Schiller, 1954). The impact of illness, procedures, and hospitalization in general can be observed by changes in children's play as well in other behaviors. In protest, children do not play or seek comfort from objects. In despair, they engage in self-stimulatory behavior. During denial they begin to manipulate, explore, and functionally play with toys and objects. By ambivalence/rapprochement, they begin to use objects and toys symbolically and creatively. When children have reached reestablishment, they are able to begin to involve whole selves in dramatic or social dramatic play.

Although changes in play behaviors are increasingly recognized as symptomatic of the distress children experience, it is often assumed that children will begin to play "naturally" when homeostatis is reestablished. Yet play contributes to equilibrium and to attachment, which in turn enhances play and its optimal utilization (Rutter, 1981). The theoretical and practical implications of discerning the respective functions of play and attachment, the synergistic relationship between the two, and their respective contributions to mastery often underlies the issues of what are the *necessary* and *sufficient* conditions for play to occur in hospital settings. In some settings, provision of toy objects is viewed as sufficient; in others, parent presence or case assignment of nurses is viewed as sufficient. In others, play programs have been developed.

It is, however, a combination of conditions, similar to those cited by Chance (1979) for children in other settings that provides an optimal environment. These conditions are particularly important for hospitalized children (and their families) because of the institutionalized atmosphere, the limits on children's physical and psychological mobility, and their resultant dependency on adults. First, there must be a child-oriented atmosphere. Mobiles, colorful murals, tricycles and wagons in the halls, and playrooms are symbols of such an atmosphere and signal to children (and their families) that play and other child activities are acceptable. Allowing and encouraging children to be mobile as possible (e.g., roaming halls in wheelchairs, finding a lap in the nurses station), to be as independent as is feasible, to express feelings, and to interact with others, however, is critical to a child-oriented atmosphere. Second, toy objects and creative materials must be available to mobile children as well as bedridden, isolated, or severely ill children. Toys should vary in their degree of inherent structure and realism (Fein, 1979). When provided by adults, toys should be selected to match interests and developmental as well as situational needs of individual children. A distraught 3-year-old might find finger paintings too fluid, whereas the structure of a puzzle may be comforting (Wolfgang, 1977; Wolfgang & Bolig, 1979). Hospital toys (e.g., a miniature hospital, doctor and nurse puppets) and real hospital objects such as masks, gowns, and dressing, which are associated with specific anxieties of hospitalization, are essential (Gilmore, 1966). Novelty must be provided (Chase, 1979). Mobiles should be changed, different and intriguing toys and materials brought to children, various toys put out on tables in the playroom, and different activities planned. Although novelty is important, especially for isolated or long-term children, it is equally important that some familiar toys remain consistently available. In the playroom, well-liked toys and areas, such as dolls, stuffed animals, the housekeeping corner, the block area, should remain available as well as hospital toys and objects.

The third condition for play in hospital settings is the presence of a trusted, *permission-giving,* and responsive adult. In the absence of such a person, most young children cannot play. Also, older children often initially need the presence of such an adult, or at least until they establish peer relationships. Provision of play objects or play areas is not enough to stimulate play (Provence & Lipton, 1962). Even in normal settings, "while children show a certain amount of play spontaneously it drops off as time goes by unless there is some sort of active adult intervention [Singer, 1979, p. 49]." Harvey (1966) found that when supervised play was provided, children engaged in "settled activities" for an average of 39.4 minutes, whereas in the absence of the play/activities specialist, children engaged in settled activities for an average of 3.8 minutes.

Who is the trusted, responsive, permission-giving adult? Is it the parent, the nurse, the volunteer, or the play specialist? Or do they, in the combination of their roles, provide the optimal conditions for play? From many studies (Brain & Maclay, 1968; Fagin, 1964) and from attachment theory, it appears that separation is a significant factor in young children's responses during and following hospitalization. Longitudinal studies have found that, although children whose parents are present may exhibit more symptoms of distress during hospitalization than children whose parents are not continuously present, following hospitalization such children evidence significantly fewer behavioral symptoms of distress. Because parents' presence appears to provide psychological security for *expression* of anxiety, earlier mastery, and subsequently less repression typically is the result.

Innumerable studies have found that a consistent, warm, responsive substitute can diminish the effects of separation (Rutter, 1981). Foster grandparents and volunteers have been suggested to provide "T.L.C." and nurturance. Nursing case rather than task assignment has been instituted in some hospitals in order that children will have fewer nurses to relate to, and through greater consistency, develop attachments.

Although there is some evidence that these approaches are effective in helping children cope, a critical issue is whether the mere presence of a parent or a nurturing, consistent, substitute or case assignment of nurses although perhaps necessary for basic psychological security is sufficient for continued stimulation, learning, and mastery through play. Parents, or significant others, if not too distressed themselves, often can perform at least some of the aspects of adequate "mothering" essential to attachment and play: nurturing or taking care of physical needs, warmth, acceptance, responsiveness, and consistency (Rutter, 1981).

Most parents are adequate "mothers," that is, capable of nurturing, responding, *and* stimulating. When their children are hospitalized, however, many parents are anxious and change their behaviors toward their children. They are often uncertain of what they can or cannot do with or for their children. They may assume a sick room role: quiet, soothing, holding, and reassuring. For these parents, "permission" to continue or resume play with their children is often granted through the existence of play program and play specialists (Hall, 1977). Seeing other children engaged in normal activities and play, having a variety of toys and materials available, obtaining suggestions from the play specialist is often necessary but sufficient for those parents to continue to play with their children. The relationships of their children with the play specialist and other children provides additional opportunity for socialization, independence, and mastery. However, some parents, who are normally adequate nurturers and players, are in such distress that they cannot play with their children. At times they are not capable of continuing to soothe, touch, or reassure. The play specialist as well as other staff may temporarily take on some of their functions, while modeling and instructing parents on ways to continue nurturing, responding, stimulating, and playing.

Other parents have not been adequate nurturers and/or stimulators prior to hospitalization of their children. As children with emotional disturbances are more likely to be hospitalized than other children, it is probable that a considerable number of children admitted have preexistent adjustment and personality problems related to anxious attachment. These children, and children who have had recent change or trauma in their lives or who have had not previous, pleasant brief separations from their parents, often are most vulnerable (Wolff, 1981). It is unrealistic to assume that parents who have not been adequate parents in the past will be able to provide the necessary conditions for psychological security and thus for play during hospitalization without institutional support and intervention.

The identification of children (with families) who have inadequate relationships may provide the opportunity for a variety of interventions. However, in these situations play specialists may need to assume some nurturing as well as stimulating functions of a parent. Most play specialists are not involved in basic physical care except for feeding. However, a warm, acceptive, and responsive play specialist who is relatively consistent and adapts his or her behaviors to the individual child often becomes the object of secondary attachment for children whose parents are not present or who are temporarily unable to nurture and play. Whereas Tisza, Hurwitz, and Arzonoff (1970) found that it took 3 days for young children to form a relationship with the play specialist in order for them to begin to play, some case studies have indicated that far less time is often necessary. Bowlby (1969) and Maccoby and Masters (1970) have also found that anxiety, illness, fear, and fatigue tend to increase attachment behavior.

The nursing profession has increasingly recognized the value of play for hospitalized children and encouraged its use both as a diagnostic and as a therapeutic tool. Whether most children are able to establish and develop an attachment to nurses who may at times cause them distress (Rutter, 1981), and whether nurses are able or permitted to play are significant issues. Hall (1977) notes that although all the nurses in the wards they sampled "agreed that play was part of a nurse's duties, very few were seen playing spontaneously with children [p. 34]." The primary role of nurses is the physical care of children and it often appears that play is secondary. Spontaneous play with children is generally engaged in only after attending to children's physical needs. Organized play in which nurses regularly engage, in some hospitals, is either as a part of preparation or as an individualized play session.

Although these conditions—a "child-oriented" atmosphere; toys, hospital objects, and creative materials; a permission-giving adult—in combination are necessary for hospitalized children to play, they may not be sufficient. Individual differences of children to play prior to hospitalization influence their ability to play during hospitalization. However, in a setting in which children are situationally handicapped, sufficiency may reside in the capacity of adults to provide stimulus, reinforcement, surprise, intensity, and variety while responding consistently to the individuals actions, words, needs, thoughts, and fantasies.

It would be ideal if all adults who work with children in hospital settings could have the unique combination of personality characteristics; knowledge of how children learn, grow, and feel; flexibility of thinking; and responsiveness essential to being an effective player. But play specialists, whose primary function is the psychosocial needs of children, should be expected to possess such a configuration of knowledge, traits, and skills. In so doing, they can significantly contribute to children's interaction with the environment through play. They can become advance organizers, stimuli screeners, engagers, and expanders. As such, play specialists appear critical both to children's continuation of development and to their total health care.

## PLAY/ACTIVITY PROGRAMS

Play has been cited in the literature on the effects of hospitalization since the 1930s as important to hospitalized children for stimulation, diversion, and mastery. It has only relatively recently begun to be viewed as essential, however, at least as evidenced by the development of organized programs of play, activities, and other experiences. Play/activities program staff, as no other continually available persons, have the training, time, and permission to focus on children's psychosocial and educational needs. According to Larsen (1980) the common care of play/activities program work is: "the provision of supervised opportunities for children to explore, manipulate, learn, create, express themselves and benefit from supportive relationships [p. 3]."

The evolution of provisions for play, from merely giving toys to hospitalized children to formalized programs with paid, trained, consistent staff, has to some extent paralleled the merging theoretical formulations on the functions of play. Play research, and specifically the conditions necessary for play to occur (Chance, 1979), the role of adults in children's play (Singer, 1973; Smilansky, 1968), and the relationship of play and attachment have also contributed to play program development. An increased knowledge of the differential effects of "maternal" deprivation and sensorimotor deprivation has also begun to provide a firmer rationale for the existence of play/activities programs (Rutter, 1981). Nevertheless, although play specialists are increasingly articulating their functions, little empirical research has been conducted. As play or play programs may be regarded as secondary or supplementary to other ameliorative efforts, especially unrestricted visiting of parents for young children, critical questions regarding who can or does play most optimally with children and under what conditions as indicated in the previous section will continue to need to be addressed (Hall, 1977).

However, at present there are approximately 260 programs in the United States and Canada that focus on psychosocial, educational, and recreational needs of hospitalized and often outpatient children (ACCH, 1981). Although the title "child life" is increasingly used (Mather & Glasrud, 1981) and is the title by which the Association for the Care of Children's Health (1979) refers to such programs, recreation therapy, children's activities, recreation, play therapy, and patient activities are common titles (McCue et al., 1980).

More than half of the programs have been developed since the late 1960s; the earliest currently existing program was established in 1917 (Rutkowski, 1978). The first formal meeting of child life professionals in 1965, and the ensuing foundation of the multidisciplinary Association for the Care of Children in Hospitals in 1968, appear to have been major catalysts (Larsen, 1980). The association, now the Association for the Care of Children's Health, continues to be the primary advocate for play/activity programs as well as for other ameliorative efforts.

A few programs listed in the *Directory of Child Life Activity Programs* (AACH, 1981) have no paid staff, relying entirely on volunteers. Where there are paid staff (varying from one to 18 full-time and 7 part-time staff), recreation therapy, followed closely by child development and education are the primary educational backgrounds of the staff (Mather & Glasrud, 1981; McCue et al., 1980). However, child development is the predominant background of program directors (Rutkowski, 1978).

The Association for the Care of Children's Health in a *Child Life Activity Study Section Position Paper* (1979) states the general purpose of child life programs:

> Child Life Programs in health care settings strive to promote optimum development of children, adolescents and families, to maintain normal living patterns and to minimize psychological trauma. As integral members of the health care team in both the ambulatory care and inpatient settings, child life staff provide opportunities for gaining a sense of mastery, for play, for learning, for self-expression, for family involvement and for peer interaction [p. 1].

The title child life often, but not exclusively, denotes a more comprehensive approach to programming than other titles (Mather & Glasrud, 1981, McCue et al., 1980). Play (normative and therapeutic), activities, education, and the maintenance or development of interpersonal relationships are viewed as essential to coping and mastery. Further, child life program staff are frequently involved in prehospital and preprocedural education (McCue et al., 1980), and to a somewhat lesser degree in supporting parents, such as through facilitating parent support or discussion groups (Rutkowski, 1978). Training and supervising volunteers and student interns is often a function of child life programs.

Most programs entitled child life, or programs with other titles that serve a similar variety of functions, appear to be advocates for children and their families in medical settings—encouraging changes in policies and practices, such as unrestricted visiting and parent presence during stressful events (ACCH, 1979). Staff become "culture brokers," explaining and interpreting the culture of children and families to medical and nursing staff and hospital administrators (Johnson, 1981).

## Variations in Play Programs

It is, however, increasingly evident to practitioners and researchers that there is great variation in programs, despite sharing similar goals. McCue et al. (1980) state:

> Two general areas of program philosophy seem to emerge. One philosophy seems to emphasize diversionary or distraction activities as its major focus . . . The other

> philosophical orientation focuses on providing for the full-range of psychological, social, and intellectual needs of pediatric patients in a medical setting [p. 19].

There are many factors that contribute to play/activity program variations as noted in Fig. 17.1. Whether the program is a separate department or an extension of another (e.g., nursing, occupational therapy), the length of time the program has been in existence, the number of and educational backgrounds of staff, and the institution's acceptance and support are but a few of the factors cited as contributing to program variation.

Many of the factors may not be within the perceived immediate control of the program. For example, the amount of space alloted to play areas may determine whether programming can be conducted with groups or whether most activities will be done with individual children in their rooms. Alternatively, if there is a large number of children per staff member, most programming, if there is space,

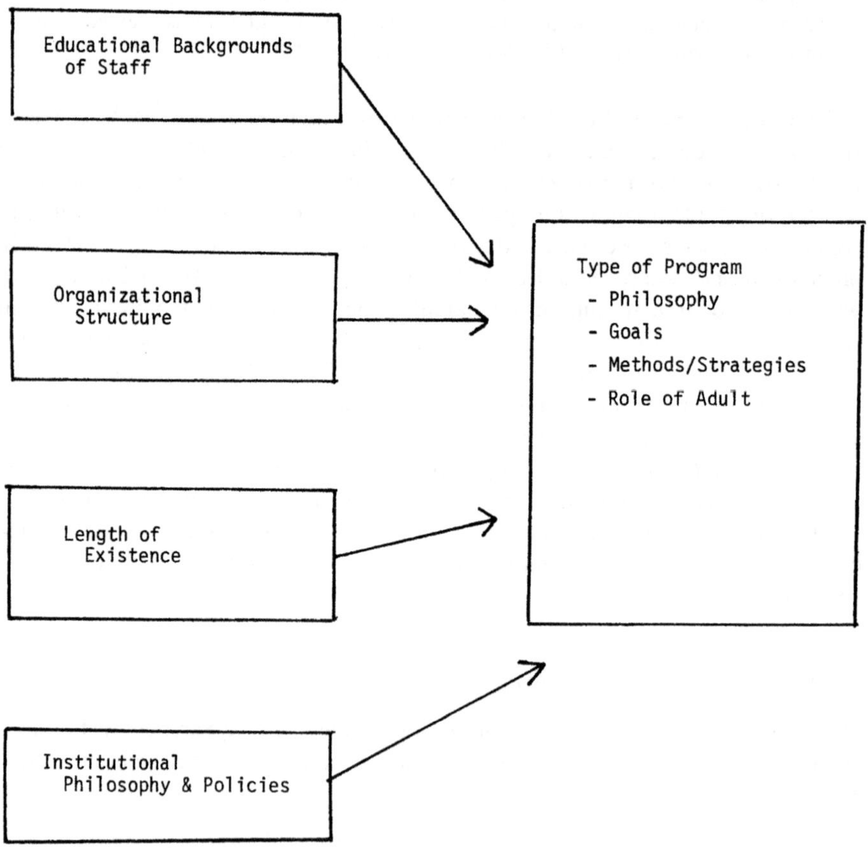


FIG. 17.1 Factors influencing program variation.

may be done with groups with little opportunity for individualized experiences. Far more important, however, than the environment factors are the *beliefs* about children: how they grow, learn, and cope with stress and what approaches assist them in this process. Some institutions, and indeed some programs, appear to believe that diverting children, through entertainment and activities, is most helpful. Happy faces on bandaids, gifts when admitted, puppet shows and parties, whether or not functional for children, often help adults feel better in that they have provided ''childlike'' experiences. Other programs concentrate on the potential meaning of hospitalization to children and provide multiple opportunities for children to express their feelings and thus master them through exploration of and play with hospital materials.

Differences between programs, in philosophy and theoretical basis that may not be articulated, and strategies may not be apparent to the untrained observer. Children engaged in fingerpainting in one setting may act and react very much like children fingerpainting in another setting. But the manner in which this activity is presented, the expectations for children's performance, the adult's interactions, as well as the rationale for the experience being chosen will vary from program to program. There is also considerable within program variation, from staff member to staff member, from activity to activity, but indepth observation also will reveal significant philosophical variation from program to program.

## Typology of Hospital Play Programs

The following typology has been developed to guide observers and serve as a basis for further inquiry. Although each program type may include the ''elements'' previously described, it is the degree of concentration of specific elements or combination of elements concurrent with the range of adult roles and strategies that discriminates one program from another. Program types can be viewed on a continuum as illustrated in Fig. 17.2 from those in which goals and strategies are diffuse with little or no individualization or recognition of the psychosocial impact of hospitalization to those in which there are specific goals and strategies utilized in concentrating on the individual's mastery of the feelings aroused through his or her unique experiences. It should be noted that the titles attached to the types do not necessarily imply that existant programs that have

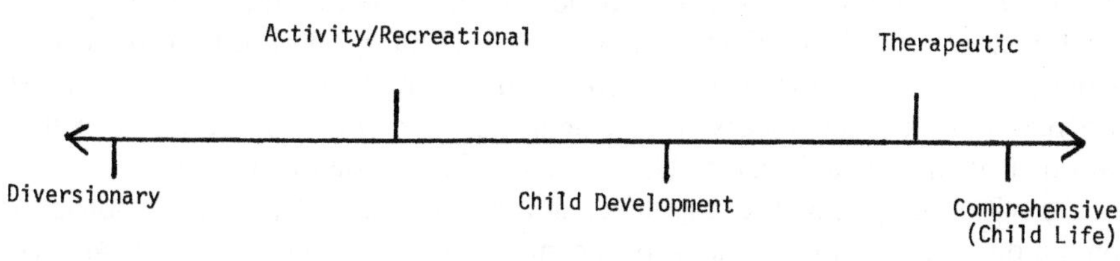


FIG. 17.2 Continuum of play/activity programs.

that title or similar one (e.g., Patient Activities, Pediatric Recreation) necessarily share a philosophical orientation. However, Mather and Glasrud (1981) found that programs that are entitled "child life" tend to have more comprehensive functions, while integrating the child development and therapeutic types, described herein.

*Diversionary Model.* The primary processes for achieving the goal of reducing children's anxiety is through distraction and avoidance in the diversionary model. By giving children toys, by occasionally providing activities in which content is unrelated to the hospital experience and in which there is often a product, and by entertaining them (e.g., puppet shows, films, clowns), children are intended to be distracted from events impinging upon their lives. Although a combination of several theories of play (e.g., surplus energy and relaxation) may provide some basis for this approach, rather it appears to reflect beliefs about children that have little current validity from child development or play research or specific research on hospitalized children. One belief is that confrontation with concepts, objects, and experiences related to the current environments will increase anxiety. A second and more pervasive belief is that toys (materials) are sufficient stimulus for play. Although play may occur spontaneously if relationships between children or between children and adults have been sufficiently established, it is neither planned for nor viewed as important to children's learning, expression, or mastery.

The diversionary model is on the furtherest end of the continua (Fig. 17.2) of model types. Its goals, strategies, and theoretical base is most diffuse; is it the least individualized, does not provide the conditions necessary for play to occur, nor does it meet ACCH's (1979) criteria for adequate programming. Whereas every other program type includes some elements that are diversionary, few pure diversionary programs exist when there are trained, paid, and consistent staff whose primary function is to assist with children's psychosocial needs. However, in hospitals where nursing staff only occasionally open the play area for activities or arrange for a party or where inconsistent volunteers are in charge of activities, a diversionary approach may result.

*Activity/Recreation Model.* The activity/recreation model is based on three premises. First, *doing* is essential for maintenance of function and skills; second, doing *simultaneously* reduces stimulation or stress and is thus "relaxing" and "refreshing"; third, participation must be voluntary. Relaxation–recreation, arousal, and stimulation theories provide the theoretical basis for this model, whereas psychosocial theory supplements it: by being active on and in their world, it is anticipated that children also obtain a sense of mastery.

Activities are planned for age-level abilities and interests, but the emphasis is on the doing rather than content or meaning. Most activities are adult directed, and there are frequently many planned group activities (e.g., arts and crafts, cooking, stories). Although play is not discouraged, there is often not sufficient time, representational materials, or adult facilitation for it to occur. Social interaction, whether while engaged in an activity or in and of itself, is also emphasized. Being with others is viewed as "refreshing." Thus, playing games, such as cards or Monopoly, playing the piano, or listening to records with the adult or other children is encouraged.

*Child Development Model.* In the child development model, based on the integration of psychosocial and cognitive theories, activities, play, and relationships are viewed as essential for the continuation of development as well as for mastery. An emphasis is placed on "normalization," which includes creating a physical and affective environment that is familiar and thus psychologically safe. Although multiple opportunities for exploration and play with hospital materials, either self-selected or teacher facilitated, is an essential element, such experiences are not the major focus. Activities similar to those found in nursery schools, such as planting seeds, listening to stories, creative art, and free play, are equally emphasized.

When children cannot participate with others in a group, the adult individually interacts with children. However, playing with and sharing experiences with other children is seen as normal and essential for imitation, mastery, and continued social development and is thus encouraged whenever possible.

The adult's role varies with the nature of the activity and needs of individual children. In general, however, the adult is nondirective in play while occasionally modeling and participating. The underlying belief of the child development model is when children are provided the necessary conditions for play (including a consistent, permission-giving adult who assumes various roles), a variety of creative and real materials, and relationships with other children, they will be able to continue to be independent, express feelings through actions and words, and thus generally master and cope with the environment.

*Therapeutic Model.* The therapeutic model, based primarily on psychoanalytic theories, begins with the assumption that children in the hospital are in psychological distress because of anxieties aroused (e.g., mutilation, castration, separation) through the specific nature of their illness and the procedures and unfamiliarity of the setting. A variety of activities are planned, for groups or for individuals, in which there is a focus on expression of feelings. Creative art, puppets, dolls, micro hospital toys, and books are selected and utilized for their symbolism. Play, especially with hospital objects, is seen as essential for catharsis and mastery. Group play with hospital objects or hospital sociodramatic play is frequently planned as well as spontaneously facilitated. However, in this model social experience is secondary to psychological needs; thus there is a concentration on the individual. Individualized play and play sessions with individual children are central elements. Depending on the training of the adult and the needs of the individual children, play sessions are either nondirective or directive. Either nonspecific or specific materials (e.g., hospital equipment or micro hospital toys) are selected as having significance for the individual. Through expressing disorganized emotions, repeating painful experiences, and reversing roles, play assists the child in mastery. The content of each session supplies the adult with additional insight into the child's feelings and perceptions and thus to the nature of the subsequent encounter.

*Comprehensive Model: Child Life.* The comprehensive model is best described as an integration of the child development and therapeutic models. Although emphasizing the continuation of opportunities and supports for normal development, the comprehensive model also individualizes activities and play and provides multiple experiences with hospital objects while concentrating on expression of feelings and mastery. The adult roles in this model are varied and maximally responsive to individual, group, and situational needs. However, what is unique about this model is that its functions and goals extend beyond the children. An important goal is to "maintain the child's relationship with parents and family members [ACCH, 1979, p. 1]." Parents, and other family members, are therefore encouraged to be a part of the children's activities and play. Concern and support for parents—helping them to express their feelings and needs—is an informal but essential aspect of the comprehensive model. Occasionally, child life staff may facilitate parent support or education groups.

There is currently no empirical data to suggest that variation in programs is related to different outcomes in children or that one type is more effective than others in "minimizing stress and anxiety" or in "retaining self-esteem and appropriate independence [ACCH, 1979, p. 1]." It would appear that programs that provide a diversity of experiences, with ample opportunity for self-expression, exploration, and play with consistent permission-giving adults who vary their roles and who are able to individualize their strategies as necessary, might be most effective.

## CONCLUSION

From the earliest recognition of children's distress during and following hospitalization, many contributing factors have been suggested including separation or maternal deprivation, cognitive or developmental level, prehospital personality, sensorimotor deprivation, and what occurs during hospitalization (Vernon et al., 1965; Wolff, 1981). Three major ameliorative efforts have emerged from the identification of these factors—play/activities, preparation, and parent involvement. The degree to which each ameliorative approach has been developed and integrated into the primary functions of hospitals serving children is variable.

In some settings parents are allowed to visit much more frequently than in the past. In others, parents are encouraged to room-in and to continue their nurturing roles (Arzonoff & Hardgrove, 1981; Hardgrove & Dawson, 1972). Some hospitals have extensive preparation strategies, from prehospitalization tours to individualized preparation for specific procedures, whereas others provide little or no preparation (Droske & Francis, 1981). Provision for play in some hospitals is merely the presence of toys or occasional entertainment; in others there are organized play programs with professional staff (Wilson, 1979).

In most hospitals, full development of any one approach appears to precipitate or to be contingent upon the evolution of the others. For example, it would be unusual that a hospital would have an organized, diversified, vital, and integrated play program and *not* provide preparation and facilitate parent involvement. Hospital administrators, physicians, nurses, social workers, and play specialists are increasingly aware that whereas each ameliorative effort can contribute to reducing children's distress, that a synthesis of the three provides the most optimal environment for children (and their families) to continue to learn, to master, and to cope effectively during hospitalization (ACCH, 1979).

## REFERENCES


Association for the Care of Children's Health (ACCH). *Child life activity study section position paper*. Washington, D.C.: Association for the Care of Children's Health, 1979.

Association for the Care of Children's Health (ACCH). *Directory of child life activity programs in North America*. Washington, D.C.: Association for the Care of Children's Health, 1981.

Axline, V. M. *Play therapy*. New York: Ballantine Books, 1966.

Arzonoff, P., & Flegal, S. *A pediatric play program*. Springfield, Ill.: Charles C. Thomas, 1975.

Arzonoff, P., & Hardgrove, C. *The family in child health care*. New York: Wiley, 1981.

Bolig, R. *The relationship of personality factors to responses to hospitalization in young children admitted for medical procedures*. Unpublished doctoral dissertation, The Ohio State University, 1980.

Bopp, J. *A hospital play program, unrestricted visiting and rooming-in: Their effects upon children's posthospital behavior*. Unpublished master's thesis, Michigan State University, 1967.

Bowlby, J. *Attachment and loss (Vol. II): Separation anxiety and anger*. New York: Basic Books, 1969.

Brain, D., & Maclay, I. Controlled study of mothers and children in hospital. *British Medical Journal*, 1968, *5587*, 278–280.

Branstetter, E. The young child's response to hospitalization: Separation anxiety or lack of mothering care? In M. V. Baty (Ed.), *Communicating Nursing Research*, Boulder, Colo.: WISCH, 1969.

Byers, M. L. Play interviews with five-year-old boy. *Maternal–Child Nursing Journal*, 1972, *1*(2), 133–141.

Chance, P. *Learning through play*. Piscataway, N.J.: Johnson & Johnson Baby Products Co., 1979.

Chase, P. In P. Chance, *Learning through play*. Piscataway, N.J.: Johnson & Johnson Baby Products Co., 1979.

Couture, C. *The psychological response of young children to brief hospitalization and surgery: The role of parent–child contact and age.* Unpublished doctoral dissertation, Boston University, 1976.

Douglas, J. Early hospital admissions and later disturbance of behavior and learning. *Developmental Medical and Child Neurology,* 1975, *17,* 456–480.

Droske, C., & Francis, S. *Pediatric diagnostic procedures with guidelines for preparing children for clinical tests.* Toronto: Wiley, 1981.

Erikson, F. Play interviews with four-year-old hospitalized children. *Monographs of the Society for Research in Child Development,* 1958, *23* (3, Serial No. 69).

Fagin, C. M. The case for rooming-in when young children are hospitalized. *Nursing Science,* 1964, *2,* 324–333.

Fein, G. G. In P. Chance, *Learning through play.* Piscataway, N.J.: Johnson & Johnson Baby Products Co., 1979.

Gellert, E. Reducing the emotional stresses of hospitalization for children. *American Journal of Occupational Therapy,* 1958, *12,* 125–129.

Gilmore, J. The role of anxiety and cognitive factors in children's play behavior. *Child Development,* 1966, *37,* 397–416.

Goslin, E. Hospitalization as a life crisis for the preschool child: A critical review. *Journal of Community Health,* 1978, *3,* 321–346.

Hall, D. J. *Social relations and innovation: Changing the state of play in hospitals.* Boston: Routledge & Kegan Paul, 1977.

Hardgrove, C. B., & Dawson, R. B. *Parents and children in the hospital: The family's role in pediatrics.* Boston: Little, Brown, 1972.

Harvey, S. *United Kingdom Committee for the World Organization for Early Childhood - Play in hospital.* London: E. T. Heron & Co., 1966.

Harvey, S., & Hales-Tooke, A. Play in the hospital from 0 to 5 years. In S. Harvey & A. Hales-Tooke (Eds.), *Play in hospital.* London: Faber & Faber, 1972.

Hodapp, R. M. Effects of hospitalization on young children: Implications of two theories. *Children's Health Care,* 1982, *10,* 83–86.

Jessner, L., Bloom, G., & Waldfogel, S. Emotional implications of tonsilectomy and adenoidectomy on children. In *The psychoanalytic study of the child* (Vol. F). New York: International Universities Press, 1952.

Johnson, J. M. *The effects of a play program on hospitalized children.* Unpublished master's thesis, The Ohio State University, 1969.

Johnson, M. Rituals of the hospital culture. In P. Azarnoff & C. Hardgrove (Eds.), *The family of child health care.* New York: Wiley, 1981.

Larsen, C. The child life profession: Today and tomorrow. In *Child life activities: An overview.* Washington: Association for the Care of Children's Health, 1980.

Lindquist, I., Lind, J., & Harvey, S. Play in hospital. In V. Bruner (Ed.), *Biology of play.* Levenham, England: Lavenham Press, 1977.

Maccoby, E. E., & Masters, J. C. Attachment and dependency. In P. H. Mussen (Ed.), *Manual of child psychology.* New York: Wiley, 1970.

Mather, P. H., & Glasrud, P. H. Child life workers: Who are they and what are they doing? *Children's Health Care,* 1981, *10,* 11–15.

McCue, K., Wagner, M., Hansen, H., & Rigler, D. A survey of a developing health care profession: Hospital "play" programs. In *Child life activities: An overview.* Washington, D.C.: Association for the Care of Children's Health, 1980.

Neuman, E. *The elements of play.* New York: MSS Information Corp., 1971.

Noble, E. *Play and the sick child.* London: Farber & Farber, 1967.

Petrillo, M., & Sanger, S. *Emotional care of hospitalized children: An environmental approach.* Philadelphia: Lippincott, 1972.

Provence, S., & Lipton, R. E. *Infants in institutions.* New York: International Universities Press, 1962.

Prugh, D., Staub, E., Sands, H., Kirshbaum, R., & Lenihan, E. A study of the emotional reactions of children and families to hospitalization and illness. *American Journal of Orthopsychiatry,* 1953, *23,* 70–106.

Quinton, D., & Rutter, M. Early hospital admissions and later disturbances of behavior: An attempted replication of Douglas's findings. *Developmental Medical and Child Neurology,* 1976, *18,* 447–459.

Rie, H., Boverman, H., Grossman, B., & Natividad, O. Immediate and long-term effects of interventions in prolonged hospitalization. *Pediatrics,* 1968, *41,* 755–764.

Robertson, J. Some responses of young children to loss of maternal care. *Nursing Times,* 1953, *10,* 30–35.

Robertson, J., & Robertson, J. Young children in brief separation: A fresh look. *Psychoanalytic Study of the Child,* 1971, *26,* 264–315.

Rutkowski, J. A survey of child life programs. *Journal of the Association for the Care of Children in Hospitals,* 1978, *6,* 11–16.

Rutter, M. *Maternal deprivation reassessed.* New York: Penguin, 1981.

Schiller, F. *On the aesthetic education of man.* (R. Suell, Trans.) New Haven: Yale University Press, 1954.

Shore, M., Geiser, R., & Wolman, H. Constructive uses of a hospital experience. *Children,* 1965, *12,* 3–8.

Singer, J. L. (Ed.). *The child's world of make believe: Experimental studies of imaginative play.* New York: Academic Press, 1973.

Smilansky, S. *The effects of socio-dramatic play on disadvantaged pre-school children.* New York: Wiley, 1968.

Stacey, M., Dearden, R., Pill, R., & Robinson, D. *Hospitals, children, and their families.* Boston: Routledge & Kegan Paul, 1970.

Tisza, V. B., Hurwitz, I., & Arzonoff, K. The use of a play program by hospitalized children. *Journal of American Academy of Child Psychology,* 1970, *9,* 515–531.

Vernon, D., Foley, J., Sipowicz, R., & Schulman, J. *The psychological responses of children to hospitalization and illness.* Springfield, Ill.: Charles C. Thomas, 1965.

Visitainer, M., & Wolfer, J. Psychological preparation for surgical pediatric patients: The effect on children's and parents' stress responses and adjustment. *Pediatrics,* 1975, *56,* 187–202.

Wilson, J. M. Child life. In P. J. Valletutti & F. Christopolos (Eds.), *Preventing physical and mental disabilities: Multidisciplinary approaches.* Baltimore: University Park Press, 1979.

Wolfer, J., & Visintainer, M. Pediatric surgical patients' and parents' stress responses and adjustments. *Nursing Research,* 1975, *24,* 224–255.

Wolff, S. *Children under stress.* New York: Penguin, 1981.

Wolfgang, C. H. *Helping aggressive and passive preschoolers through play.* Columbus, O.: Merrill, 1977.

Wolfgang, C. H., & Bolig, R. Play techniques for preschool children under stress. *Journal of the Association for the Care of Children in Hospitals,* 1979, *7,* 3–10.

# 18 Creative Dramatic Play and Language Comprehension

Peter A. Williamson
Steven B. Silvern
*Auburn University, Alabama*

Late in the second decade of the twentieth century a young scientist observed the verbal interactions of children. These observations led this scientist, Jean Piaget, and others into complex studies of the relationship between children's thought and language. As in other areas of competence Piaget showed that children progressed from a limited self-centered use of language to a broad-based other-centered use of language (1926).

Language for the young child is an extremely personalized form of expression. This is most easily found in the undifferentiated speech of the toddler where the single word sentence "Bye" may mean everything from "You can't leave!" to "Get me out of this car seat!" After the age of 4, however, when the child's language begins to sound like adult language, it is more difficult to witness the personalized nature of expression that continues to exist in the child's speech. Nevertheless, elements of personalized speech remain throughout the elementary school years. Such elements include the overuse of an undifferentiated pronoun. For example, in explaining how to wind a clock, the child might say, "First you turn it around, and then you turn it a few times." The first "it" may refer to the clock and the second "it" may refer to the winding stem at the back of the clock. Another such element is syntactical error. For example, Miss Jones may say, "Billy, why don't you ask Jennifer to let you use a pencil?" Billy then says to Jennifer, "Miss Jones said for you to give me a pencil."

While we have been discussing children's expressive language, the same personalization of speech holds true for receptive language. This is most commonly seen in sharing time (formerly known as "show and tell"). For very young children no connection is made between what one child has to say and following comments. When speech is personalized, there is no concept of ''sticking to the subject.'' Older children begin to see a connection between comments, but at best the connection is tenuous. For example, one child might say, ''My cat had kittens.'' A second will follow with, ''My cat was run over by a truck.'' And a third will ''continue'' the subject with ''My dad has a truck.'' The personalization of language allows the child to select a word out of context and use that word as the topic rather than the entire content that had been expressed.

## LANGUAGE IS TIED TO THOUGHT

The work exploring the relationship between thought and language is voluminous, and a review of same is beyond the scope of this chapter. The interested reader may refer to an excellent text by Bloom and Lahey (1978) or any of several works by Sinclair.

The purpose of the present section is to explore the origin of personalized speech described previously. From what has already been discussed, one may have determined that the relationship between thought and language will be viewed from a Piagetian perspective; that is, thought leads language. The form of expression is dictated by the individual's form of thought. This concept is easily demonstrated at an adult level; we do not lead conversations about things we do not know (except politics, religion, and education), but we readily engage in conversations about things in which we are knowledgeable. Further, it is easy to spot someone who does not follow this ''rule.'' We find his expression empty, and ''He doesn't know what he is talking about.'' Although empty communication is easily spotted in adults, we generally have difficulty identifying empty communication in children. One of the authors was confined in a car on a long trip with a ''gifted'' 10-year-old child. The child had been studying the Voyager bypass of Saturn and was eager to share what he had learned. The conversation follows:

Adult: What was the purpose of Voyager?
Child: To fly past Saturn and send pictures of the planet to Earth.
Adult: You mean that someone in the satellite took pictures and mailed them to earth?
Child: No. The camera was operated electronically and the pictures were sent by telemetry.
Adult: How does that work, telemetry?
Child: Telemetry is the process they use to send the pictures.
Adult: Yes, but how do they send the pictures? Do they put them in an envelope, or what?

Child: No, they don't put them in an envelope!
(condescendingly) They use telemetry.
Adult: But what is that? What is telemetry?
Child: You mean you don't know what telemetry is?
Adult: No.
Child: Telemetry is the way they send pictures back from space.
Adult. Oh!

Other adults, trapped in the same vehicle on the same long journey, were impressed with the child's knowledge. However, examination of the conversation shows that the child was defining by function (Bruner, Oliver, & Greenfield, 1966), demonstrating understanding at a preoperational level. Although the child was using big words and talking about an abstract subject, his level of thought did not allow him to go beyond a preoperational understanding.

Because thought leads language, characteristics of levels of thought should be evident in the child's expressive and receptive language.

## Preoperational Thought

Thought at the preoperational level is characterized by:

A focus on one's own point of view (egocentrism).
Intuition.
Centering on a single event or variable.
Animism.

Understanding of language, then, is limited by these characteristics. Because of egocentrism, events are related to direct personal experience. Because of intuition, causality is not recognized. For example, in a study of levels of comprehension (Silvern & Williamson, 1980) children were asked if the protagonist of a story was wise. The question required children to analyze the cause of several events and then respond, no the character was not wise. Further questioning would indicate whether or not children understood the causality of the story. One 5-year-old responded that Petunia the silly goose was not wise. When asked why, the child said, "Because ducks don't have teeth." Centering on a single event or variable allows children to ignore context and causality and integrate an event or variable into their own point of view. This gives adults the impression that children are not paying attention or that they do not know how to listen. Finally, animism allows children to accept fantasy as an explanation for events. For example, in response to the question, "Did Max really sail to where the wild things are?", the response is obviously yes. However, this is not a lack of comprehension, rather it is a willingness, an ability, to accept fantasy as an explanation.

### Concrete Operational Thought

Thought at the concrete operational level is characterized by an:

Ability to take another's point of view.
Understanding of causality *based on experience.*
Ability to coordinate multiple events and variables.

Because of these abilities, children's comprehension seems more adultlike, with a singular exception. The understanding of causality must be grounded in experience. Although concrete operational children no longer use intuitive logic, they are not yet capable of formal logic. This middle area of logic can only exist if the child has direct, active experience with the ideas and events in question. In addition, simply telling, or giving information, does not substitute for direct, active experience. In fact, lack of experience provides for more preoperational than concrete operational thought.

This is an opportune point for identifying a major pitfall encountered when working with children in the area of language comprehension. The period of concrete operations has been identified as occurring at about the age of 7. Therefore, older elementary children must be concrete operational, right? Wrong. Because concrete thought is dependent on experience, it can only emerge after experience. So, concrete thought will emerge dependent on the specific content (events and variables) being addressed. It is, then, possible for a gifted 10-year-old to use language *preoperationally* when dealing with telemetry and *concretely* when dealing with batting averages.

Young children will demonstrate preoperational and concrete operational thought, dependent on their direct, active experience. Included in the concept of experience is social interaction. Action on objects alone is not sufficient for comprehension. Sharing the experience with peers, parents, and teachers is also required. Sharing provides the child the opportunity to integrate the experience with other well-developed understandings.

## THE RELATIONSHIP OF PLAY TO LANGUAGE COMPREHENSION

From the Piagetian perspective, language is dependent on thought. Children's thought is dependent on experience and social interaction. One of the most prevalent events in early childhood that provides both experience and social interaction is play. Piaget, himself, identified the representational function provided by play (Piaget, 1973).

The natural outgrowth of this thinking is the hypothesis that play is facilitative to children's aural language comprehension. That is, children who are allowed to play what they hear will have a better understanding of what they hear and, therefore, will recall more of what they have heard. Playing out a story forces children to do several things. First, the children become actively involved in the experience. They are no longer just hearing words; they are recreating events. Second, to recreate the events physically, the children must create mental representations of the events. Third, the children must engage in social interaction to coordinate their play. This social interaction acts further to help children create mental representations of the events.

Saltz and Johnson (1974), Saltz, Dixon, and Johnson (1977), and Pellegrini and Galda (1982) have demonstrated that play is indeed facilitative for children's comprehension of stories. Saltz and Johnson and Saltz et al. trained young children to act out fairy tales. They also trained children in sociodramatic play. After a long training period the children were tested on a picture-sequencing task. Children did *not* play as a part of this task. Results indicated that the play-training condition positively affected children's story sequencing relative to the other conditions.

Pellegrini and Galda (1982) used a brief play training period and a task where children acted out the story of *Little Red Cap*. After acting out the story the children were given a multiple-choice comprehension test as well as a free-recall test. In both the test and free-recall tasks, children who acted out the story performed better than children who discussed the story and children who drew a picture of the story.

These studies give positive evidence that play facilitates children's story comprehension. However, these studies give no indication as to what aspects of the play situation were important in comprehension.

## PLAY COMPONENTS AFFECTING COMPREHENSION

Over the past 5 years the authors have engaged in several studies that provide indirect evidence for components that seem to be essential for a successful play experience. This section presents summaries of those studies and attempts to identify components of play situations that seem to facilitate comprehension.

Yawkey and Silvern (1979) read individual children a story entitled *The Biggest Bear*. After the story the children and the experimenter engaged in play, play with puppets, or no activity (control). Comprehension was tested using a modified cloze technique. Results indicated that children who played recalled more of the story than children who used puppets. However, there was no difference in comprehension between the play and control groups.

Results may have been affected by children's familiarity with the story. In a follow-up study Silvern (1980) compared a play condition with a picture condition and two control conditions. Individual children were read a 10-sentence laboratory-generated story. After the story the children in the play condition played out the story with the experimenter. Results indicated no significant differences between the four conditions.

The Saltz studies and the Pellegrini and Galda study used familiar stories and achieved positive results for play, where Silvern found no positive results for play. Also, all the studies had the experimenter involved in the children's play. However, Silvern's studies had individual children playing, whereas the other studies had children playing in groups. Also, Silvern did not provide any training experiences where the other studies did. Silvern, Williamson, and Waters (in press) read children a series of 10 laboratory-generated stories over a period of 10 weeks. The children listened to the stories in groups of five. There were five conditions. In one condition the children played out the story. In a second condition the children played out the story using puppets. Pictures were shown to the children in the third condition. The remaining two conditions were controls. The dependent variable was the number of correct responses on a multiple-choice comprehension test given after each story. Over the 10-week period, children in the play condition gained the most in comprehension. The picture condition, however, was still the best mediating condition with no significant differences between the other conditions. These findings seem to indicate that children need experiences in playing in order for play to be facilitative. However, playing in groups without experimenter did not create the significant differences found in other studies.

Silvern, Williamson, Taylor, Surbeck, and Kelley (1982) read children six stories that were judged to be unfamiliar to the children. Half the children played out the stories and half the children discussed the stories afterward. Although the experimenter did not play with the experimental group, she did take the role of "director." That is, the experimenter made sure that all the parts were enacted, that the entire story was played out, and that the play went smoothly. The dependent variable was the number of correct responses on a multiple-choice comprehension test taken after listening to a laboratory generated story. Similar to Saltz and Johnson and Saltz et al. the children did *not* play as part of the criterion measure. Children in the play condition performed significantly better on recall than children in the discussion condition.

In a follow-up study, Williamson, Silvern, Taylor, Surbeck, and Kelley (1982) had half the children listen to unfamiliar stories and half the children listen to familiar stories. In addition, in half the play conditions the experimenter acted as a director and in half the conditions the experimenter acted as a facilitator (i.e., helped the children to solve problems that were in the way of playing but did not assist in the play). The same dependent variable was used as in the previous study. The children did *not* play during the criterion task. Once again the children in the play condition displayed better recall than children in the discussion condition. There was no main effect for kind of story or for type of adult (facilitator vs. director). There was, however, an adult interaction by story interaction. Children in the unfamiliar-story adult-directive situation performed better than children in the familiar-story adult-directive situation. However, children in the familiar-story adult-facilitative condition performed better than children in the familiar-story adult-directive situation.

These findings point to several recommendations regarding the use of play for story comprehension. First, it appears that children should have experience playing out stories before play becomes an effective device. Second, children should play out stories in small groups. Third, it is not necessary for the teacher to engage in the children's play. But, if the story is unfamiliar, the teacher should help direct the playing (not necessarily play out a role). Fourth, children should begin playing with familiar stories and work toward unfamiliar stories. Fifth, teachers should be less directive when children are playing familiar stories. Sixth, it seems that comprehension does not depend directly on play; that is, the children do not have to act out a specific story to comprehend it. Rather, many experiences with playing out stories seem to assist children's comprehension.

The remainder of this chapter is devoted to practical suggestions as to how teachers may want to use play in their classrooms.

## CLASSROOM PROCEDURES FOR CREATIVE DRAMATICS

Before getting into specifics, however, we need to stress one critically important point—the inclusion of play in a curriculum needs to be viewed as a long-term, serious, and regular commitment on the part of classroom teachers for it to be effective. Our research demonstrates quite clearly and simply that the more opportunities children have to play, the higher quality the play. Not only does the quality of the play itself improve, so too do the spin-offs in both the cognitive and socioemotional domains. Many publications directed at teachers include sections that could be labeled "activities for rainy Fridays" and specify a number of isolated time fillers. Too often, it is these activities that teachers employ with their children in an irregular disjointed manner and then assume they are incorporating play in the curriculum. In our view this approach falls far short of the mark and is really no approach at all.

What then do we mean by a long-term, serious, and regular approach to the incorporation of play in an early childhood curriculum? Let's consider these, one at a time, from both the child's and the teacher's points of view. For the child "long term" means, quite simply, the duration of a particular school year. For the teacher this definition is necessary but not sufficient. Acceptance of a long-term commitment implies an initial belief in the value of play as well as ongoing experimentation over the course of a career to develop this value to the highest degree possible. In this sense the approach to play is really no different than any other curriculum area. For instance, a teacher who initially commits himself or herself to the value of a discovery approach to mathematics does so initially based on research findings as well as his or her own philosophy. As long as he or she adheres to this commitment, it is likely that he or she will become better at it. His or her math program will hopefully be more successfully implemented in the third year than the first, in the fifth year than the third, and so on. So too, with play.

From the child's point of view, play is quite serious business. An observation of children arguing over a rules infraction on the playground will attest to this. Children are generally not accustomed, however, to playing within the context of the classroom and initial attempts may prove unsatisfactory. This is where the attitude of the teacher is critical. The teacher must view play as a serious endeavor and work conscientiously to develop the quality of the children's interactions. To the extent that he or she is able to convey this viewpoint to the students, will they develop the attitude that play is serious business in the classroom and not just at recess time.

From a student's point of view, if a teacher does something infrequently and unpredictably, it comes across as something he or she probably does not value greatly. On the other hand, if the students know that come hell or high water creative dramatics will occur at 12:15 every Monday, Wednesday, and Friday, they cannot escape the conclusion that the teacher considers it important. There is no magical number that distinguishes regular from irregular, but we would think that for young children, especially, fewer than three times a week is less than regular.

## KEY COMPONENTS OF CREATIVE DRAMATICS

The procedure that we describe here has several key components that we have found makes it realistic to accomplish as well as being in accord with sound educational principals. Let us start with an example.

Setting: Ms. Smith's second-grade classroom in late September. Ms. Smith's highest reading group has just completed reading a version of *The Three Little Pigs,* and this will be their first attempt at recreation through creative dramatics. Before beginning to play, Ms. Smith asks the children to identify all the characters in the story. She lists these on the board or on chart paper. She then asks the children to tell her all the parts of the story that they will act out. These too she jots down on the board. If a key part is omitted, she prompts and prods until the children remember. If they are unable to, she finally provides it herself. Next, she asks the children to choose a part to play. Because there are eight children in her group, she ends up with six pigs and two wolves—two children for each of the parts. She then tells the children that she will narrate the story and as she does so, they are to act out the appropriate action as their character. The play proceeds.

We assume that the reader will be struck by the fact that this scenario is hardly a revolution in terms of teaching technique. Let us highlight some of the key components, however, as background for demonstrating how creative dramatics can develop over the course of the year. First, Ms. Smith did herself a favor by starting small with her most advanced children. Too often when we are conceptualizing an innovative teaching technique for our classrooms, we think it will not be fair unless we can do it for all our children at once. This idea coupled with our own feelings of uncertainty when trying something new often overwhelms us to the point where we will not try it at all. In our example, Ms. Smith too wants her whole class to reap the possible benefits of creative dramatics, and she is a bit uncertain about her own ability to do a good job because this is her first attempt at introducing it in her classroom. For Ms. Smith, however, creative dramatics is not a gimmick that has to be perfect for everyone, all at once. Instead, she has made a long-term commitment to its incorporation in her classroom and has a long-term plan. For the children's sake she wants to begin with those who are most likely to be able to handle something new. Additionally, she wants some time to iron out any wrinkles before introducing it to the rest of the class. So she starts *small.*

Second, because this is the first time Ms. Smith has used creative dramatics, she chooses a story with which the children are familiar. She does so because she assumes the children probably know this story by heart and will experience success in being able to identify the characters and the event in the story. She wants the student's first experience with creative dramatics to be successful as well as enjoyable.

Third, Ms. Smith is very directive with the group. She is aware of the research that suggests that the teacher's role can be less directive when children are enacting a familiar story. Obviously, over time, she wants to move toward a more facilitative nondirective role and allow the children to do more and more on their own—but not at first. Ms. Smith remembers when she introduced learning centers into her room 2 years ago. Although her long-range intent was for the children to operate as independently as possible in the various centers, at first she was quite directive. She literally had to train the children in: (1) how to choose a center; (2) how to move from one center to another; (3) how to use the materials in each center; etc. In fact, it was only after a number of weeks of progressively less direct supervision that the students could begin using the centers as productively as she had originally intended.

As she considered introducing creative dramatics, Ms. Smith was aware of the long-term benefits cited earlier. She also knew that these were not going to be achieved by simply turning the kids loose with the directions of "Go play." She had to train her students in some of the mechanics of reenacting a story until it becomes second nature. Some of the mechanical features were highlighted in her first session: identifying characters, reviewing the events to be enacted, choosing a part, and dramatizing.

Let us return to Ms. Smith's classroom. Setting: March of the same school year. By this time all her groups of children are involved in creative dramatics, at least to the point where we left the highest group in September. Ms. Smith has been experimenting and feeling her way with the highest group as to how quickly she can be increasingly nondirective. To this point she has found that with books or stories that are unfamiliar to the children she needs to be much more directive than with familiar stories. The novelty or difficulty of the unfamiliar stories seem to be enough of a mental load for the children that they still need the security of the teacher to provide them with the mechanical framework. When working with familiar material, however, the students seem increasingly at ease with taking more responsibility.

Today they have just completed reading a version of *Goldilocks and the Three Bears*. Before sending them off to do the reenactment, Ms. Smith asks the students what they need to do. Various children volunteer that they need to identify the characters, make sure they know all the important events, choose a part, gather some props, and act it out for the rest of the class. Satisfied that the children understand the framework, Ms. Smith asks what they will do if there is disagreement—for instance, if several kids want to be Goldilocks. The children respond again with several alternatives: talk about it, remember who had the lead part most recently, see if it is all right to have more than one Goldilocks. The children then go about the task of preparing while Ms. Smith observes and is available for questions. Only one conflict arises—it seems that Rodney wants to include a fourth bear with some funny lines, which of course is not in the original story. The students ask Ms. Smith if this is allowed. She responds that this is something for them to decide but if they think this addition is a positive one they can surely include a fourth bear. After 5 minutes more the children tell Ms. Smith that they are ready. Ms. Smith asks the rest of the class to put down their work for a moment and turn to watch the performance. The class does so and the play proceeds with the fourth bear, who indeed has some very funny lines, included.

Let us look for a moment at how this example derives developmentally from the first. Perhaps the most striking feature is that the kids are so much more independent of Ms. Smith than they were in September. This has occurred because they thoroughly understand the framework of how to proceed (i.e., identify the characters, go over the events). The reasons they can do this on their own at this point is because Ms. Smith has led them through this process each and every time they have begun creative dramatics. This process is so ingrained by this time in the year that Ms. Smith no longer needs to lead them through it herself. Notice that she does ask them to verbalize the procedure before going off to plan the play. In a short time this verbalization will probably no longer be necessary.

Ms. Smith has been directing a good deal of her energy at helping the children find ways of resolving conflicts as they arise, as they inevitably do. Ms. Smith has been attempting to teach the children strategies for conflict resolution so that they could employ these strategies to find solutions on their own. To this point she has surely made a good deal of progress. Earlier in the year the children would come to her as the final arbiter every time a disagreement arose, and she found herself making decisions that she felt the children could make for themselves. Thus, she has provided the children various questions to consider when conflicts arise (e.g., "Who had the lead most recently?") and to the extent possible made the children solve their own problems by employing these questions as a guide. In this respect, Ms. Smith believes that people become good decision makers only by making decisions and then living with the consequences. What people do need help in is developing criteria or strategies for making sound decisions and relying less and less on some outside all-knowing authority.

A particularly interesting phenomenon occurs in this scenario—the question of the addition of a character who is not in the original story. Until this time every play has been a literal reenactment with virtually no adaptation. Some may view this as undesirable and indicative of children's lack of understanding of a story. Such a possibility exists and teachers need to pay close attention. In the case of Ms. Smith's class, however, this does not seem to be the case. If it were a case of misunderstanding, then surely it would have occurred countless times in the past. The timing of this adaptation represents not a misunderstanding but instead a breakthrough of sorts. The strong possibility exists that the children are so familiar with the story and increasingly comfortable with their dramatic abilities that they are now able to go beyond the literal reenactment and, in fact, add something of their own that fits in the context of the story but adds a new dimension. This adaptation is to be encouraged, not stymied.

A final component to be highlighted in this example is the casual atmosphere encouraged by Ms. Smith. This reenactment is not intended to be a Broadway production. Instead, it is to be regarded as an ongoing and regular part of the children's curriculum. The students take only about 10 minutes to get the play together and are not to rehearse in a formal sense. This aspect is critical—it is the process of the planning and the informality of the production that leads to increased abilities in the cognitive and social areas, not the repetition of several rehearsals. Moreover, and in very practical terms, the schedule of a teacher's day does not allow for two to three formal productions per week—there would be time for little else. Additionally, the teacher reinforces the low-key atmosphere she intends for creative dramatics by having the "audience" remain where they are, watch, and then return to what they were doing.

We think these examples demonstrate several of the key components of an approach to the use of creative dramatics as well as the decision-making processes that a classroom teacher must address as she proceeds. For the sake of clarity of presentation as well as space limitations we have used reading groups for examples of the thinking a teacher must go through in the implementation of creative dramatics. We think reading groups are a logical place for many teachers to begin but ask the reader not to be limited by our examples. For instance, the children in our example at this point in the year can no doubt make very productive use of a creative dramatics center—a place where they can go with no direct teacher supervision. The teacher instead stocks the center with materials with which she wants the children to become involved. They know the framework for the interaction. Social studies units, science investigations, and even vocabulary development and work on math skills are additional areas where we have seen creative dramatics make impacts on children's learning.

The common characteristic that we have observed in teachers who successfully used creative dramatics in the classroom is that they do not regard it as a gimmick but rather view it as a long-term, serious, and regular commitment.

## ACKNOWLEDGMENTS

Studies by the authors reported herein were supported by the Auburn University grant-in-aid program and the Auburn University School of Education Research grant program.

## REFERENCES

Bloom, L., & Lahey, M. *Language development and language disorders.* New York: Wiley, 1978.

Bruner, J., Oliver, P., & Greenfield, P. *Studies in cognitive growth.* New York: Wiley, 1966.

Pellegrini, A. D., & Galda, L. The effects of thematic-fantasy play training on the development of children's story comprehension. *American Educational Research Journal,* 1982, *19,* 443–452.

Piaget, J. *The language and thought of the child.* New York: Harcourt, Brace, 1926.

Piaget, J. *Psychology of intelligence.* Totowa, N.J.: Littlefield Adams, 1973.

Saltz, E., Dixon, D., & Johnson, J. Training disadvantaged preschoolers on various fantasy activities: Effects on cognitive functioning and impulse control. *Child Development,* 1977, *48,* 367–380.

Saltz, E., & Johnson, J. Training for thematic fantasy play in culturally disadvantaged children: Preliminary results. *Journal of Educational Psychology,* 1974, *66,* 623–630.

Silvern, S. B. Play, pictures, and repetition: Mediators in aural prose learning. *Educational Communication and Technology,* 1980, *28,* 134–139.

Silvern, S. B., & Williamson, P. A. *The effects of text elaborations on children's aural language comprehension.* A paper presented at the annual meeting of the Developmental Psychology Section of the British Psychological Society, Edinburgh, Scotland, September 1980.

Silvern, S. B., Williamson, P. A., Taylor, J. B., Surbeck, E., & Kelley, M. F. *The effects of self-directed dramatization on story recall.* A paper presented at the annual meeting of the American Educational Research Association, New York, March, 1982.

Silvern, S. B., Williamson, P. A., & Waters, B. Play as a mediator of comprehension: An alternative to play training. *Educational Research Quarterly,* (in press).

Williamson, P. A., Silvern, S. B., Taylor, J. B., Surbeck, E., & Kelley, M. F. *Young children's story recall as a product of play, story familiarity and adult intervention.* A paper presented at the annual meeting of the American Educational Research Association, New York, March 1982.

Yawkey, T. D., & Silvern, S. B. *An investigation of imaginative play and language growth in five, six, and seven year-old children.* A paper presented at the annual meeting of the American Educational Research Association, San Francisco, April 1979.

# 19 Effects of Realistic and Unrealistic Props on Symbolic Play

Bruce L. Mann
*Cornell University*

Although Dewey (1944) first directed the attention of educators to imaginative play as a medium of teaching subjects lying beyond the scope of direct physical response, not until 1962 did serious scientific interest in make-believe play appear. In *Play, Dreams and Imitation in Childhood,* Jean Piaget (1962) detailed an intimate link between symbolic play and the development of representational, preoperational intelligence. The educational potential of make-believe play, however, did not become clear until Smilansky's (1968) attempt to use a form of symbolic play, sociodramatic play, to increase school-related abilities among disadvantaged preschoolers. The literature review first focuses on experimental studies assessing the effectiveness of symbolic play educational programs. Secondly, previous research investigating a specific component of symbolic play programs, the realism of the toys used as props in the children's pretense, is described.

## SYMBOLIC PLAY AS A PRESCHOOL INSTRUCTIONAL STRATEGY

Smilansky (1968) provided 400 four-year-olds with a daily sociodramatic play lesson. Sociodramatic play, as used by Smilansky, involves either events that are common in the lives of young children (e.g., visiting the doctor, going to the store) or events in which a group of preschoolers had participated together (e.g., visiting the police station, visiting the fire station). A second group of 400 four-year-olds were provided with an identical preschool experience, except instead of a period of sociodramatic play these subjects engaged in nature activities (e.g., going on a hike, collecting leaves, incubating eggs). A third group of 400 preschoolers spent the time in various arts and crafts activities (e.g., cutting and pasting). Smilansky found that the sociodramatic play treatment lead to superior performance on a variety of verbal measures: (1) average number of words spoken in 15 minutes; (2) sentence length; (3) play-related speech; and (4) vocabulary.

Since Smilansky's (1968) landmark study there have been many published accounts of preschool training programs that use symbolic play. Empirical documentation of the value of symbolic play is most impressive in regard to perspective taking skills (Burns & Brainerd, 1979; Golomb & Cornelius, 1977; Iannotti, 1978; Saltz, Dixon, & Johnson, 1977). Considerable evidence also exists that training leads to the development of verbal abilities (Lovinger, 1974; Saltz, Dixon, & Johnson, 1977; Saltz & Johnson, 1974; Yawkey, Jones, & Hrncir, 1979); control over impulsivity (Manosevitz, Fling, & Prentice, 1977; Singer, 1966; Saltz, Dixon, & Johnson, 1977); and number recognition and set theory (Yawkey, Jones, & Hrncir, 1979).

The dependent variables used in this study were recall of stories and divergent thinking. Recall was assessed in two ways. The first method required subjects to respond verbally to questions about story content. The second asked subjects to order pictures depicting story events in the proper sequence. For verbal recall of stories Yawkey and Silvern (1979) found significant effects for symbolic play in facilitating immediate recall of stories. They provided subjects with either a symbolic play or nonplay experience in conjunction with a story and then assessed recall of the story. Saltz and Johnson (1974) and Saltz, Dixon, and Johnson (1977) looked at the effectiveness of symbolic play in regard to increasing performance on tests of the second dependent variable used in this study, sequential recall. The 1974 study found 1 year of symbolic play training to significantly increase sequential memory performance, whereas the 1977 study found the same but only for older subjects.

The third dependent variable used in this study was divergent thinking. Several researchers, notably Hutt and Bhavnani (1976), Singer (1966), Pulaski (1970), MacKinnon (1962), Johnson (1976), and Lieberman (1977) have found evidence linking play to creativity. The most convincing studies were performed by Dansky and Silverman (1973, 1975). In both studies Dansky and Silverman divided their 5-year-old subjects into three groups and provided each with a different experience prior to the administration of an alternate uses test. A "play group" was allowed to interact spontaneously with a roomful of toys; an "imitation group" was asked to repeat the experimenter's actions; and a control group was given a box of crayons and four sketches and permitted to color the sketches as they wished. The results conformed to their hypothesis that the information registered during playful activity tends to increase the number of alternate uses suggested for a set of objects.

The mediating variable intervening between symbolic play and the development of these symbolic abilities is thought to be the acquisition of imagery skills. Singer and Singer (1977) clearly describe this relationship; imagery skills are believed to play a vital role in later vocabulary growth, because words associated with pictures in the mind are remembered more easily than entirely abstract terms. Thus, symbolic play leads to the development of imagery skills, which leads to growth in representationally based activities.

Several researchers have investigated whether training in mental imagery facilitates recall. Levin (1972) showed that 6-year-old subjects who were instructed to generate a mental interaction involving paired associate items outperformed their control counterparts by so much that there was little overlap in the distributions. Wolff and Levin (1972), however, found that although the performance of 8-year-olds was improved by imagery instructions, the performance of 5-year-olds was not. Instructions to engage in *overt* imagery behaviors did have a strongly facilitative effect on recall for 5-year-olds (Wolff, Levin, & Longobardi, 1972) and even 3-year-olds (Levin, McCabe, & Bender, 1975). Lastly, Lesgold, McCormick, and Golinkoff (1975), using a procedure similar to that used in this study, showed that children in an imaging training group performed better than the control subjects on recall after both groups had listened to a story.

The research to be reported here is part of a larger research effort (Mann, 1981) that explored the effectiveness of symbolic play as an instructional strategy for preschoolers. This chapter examines the role of abstract unrealistic prop imagery, compared to concrete realistic prop imagery as components of a symbolic play lesson.

## REALISTIC PROPS VERSUS UNREALISTIC PROPS

In *Play, Dreams and Imitation in Childhood,* Piaget (1962) pointed to symbolic play as a crucial mechanism in the transition from sensorimotor to preoperational thought. According to Piaget, make-believe play is the earliest symbolic behavior engaged in by the young child and usually appears in the latter half of the second year of life. The basic concept is that when the child pretends his or her pretense forms a symbol for what is being pretended. For example, when Piaget's 18-month-old daughter, Lucien, rested her head on her cloth comfortor and pretended to go to sleep, the comfortor served as a symbol for a pillow. Furthermore, Piaget contended that Lucien needed a concrete visible prop to symbolize her thought about going to sleep because she lacked a cognitively based representational system able to bring the thought to consciousness covertly. In other words, Lucien needed to externalize her thoughts in the form of behaviors and props to bring to mind persons, actions, or events in their absence. By the age of 6 or 7 her representational system will have developed to the point where she can recall past events or contemplate wishes for the future without the use of external cues. At this point symbolic play disappears from the behavioral repertoire. Daydreams and a variety of other common thinking activities serve the purposes that symbolic play had earlier fulfilled.

The abstract symbolic nature of make-believe play has been the major reason for using it as an instructional medium for facilitating the development of preschool representational abilities. Yet, only three studies have examined the hypothesis that the more abstract the child's make-believe, the greater the enhancement of representational skills. In other words, that by increasing the difficulty of imagining and portraying an event, teachers can help children become more adept at symbolizing events in their absence. Two of those studies (Pulaski, 1970, is the third), Saltz and Johnson (1974) and Saltz, Dixon, and Johnson (1977) varied the abstractness of the make-believe themes being enacted by their preschool subjects. Both studies contrasted sociodramatic role play with the less realistic "thematic-fantasy" play (primarily enacting fairy tales). The results they obtained were mixed; in the latter study significant differences were found on only three of six dependent variables.

Although Saltz, Dixon, and Johnson (1977) refer to Piaget (1962) for theoretical support, Piaget never indicated that the themes of symbolic play become more fantasylike across development. However, Piaget did note a developmental progression from an initial reliance on the visual and tactile similarities between the signifying prop and the object being signified, to a point at which the signifying prop need only subtly suggest the imagined object. Indeed the research indicates a within-individual continuity of fantasy themes that is more dependent on personality variations than on maturation. For example, a given child's play will tend to express a preference for adventure plots, perhaps cowboys and Indians, and this preference will remain stable across many years. However, the form in which the stories are expressed is likely to change with age. The 3-year-old may be incapable of playing cowboys and Indians without using a rocking horse to sustain the play imagery. The child at 4 need simply grab a broom to sustain the horse image, whereas the 5-year-old need only neigh and gallup to get the pretense underway.

Smilansky (1968) found a continuity of themes across the limited age range (3 to 5 years) of her subjects. At the same time she noted a five-level developmental progression in the way her subjects used objects as signifiers in their play. The first level involves simple manipulation of toys. Taking a toy telephone as an example, this stage involves the mere examination and manipulation of the telephone as a physical object (hard plastic, with a dial you can stick a finger into, and that makes a clicking noise when spun). This level is followed by the use of miniature replicas of objects in exactly the same way as adults use them, and for the purpose of mastering the object-related behaviors. Now the child knows what each part of the telephone is used for, and appropriate behaviors are rehearsed. In the third stage, miniature replicas are used as aids in sustaining a certain role. The child now uses the toy telephone to support his role as Daddy at the office. From this level the child's dependence on the prop as a means of relating the child to his role lessens. At the fourth level the child uses unrealistic props as aids in sustaining a role. Now the child needs only a stick that serves as a telephone. The fifth stage involves a progressively larger use of verbal descriptions and assertions to define and support the pretense. Smilansky found that her lower-socioeconomic status subjects were usually at levels 1 and 2, whereas middle-class subjects were usually at levels 3 through 5.

Empirical documentation for this developmental progression is growing. Greta Fein (1975), in a now classic study, defined the conditions under which 2-year-olds could use more and less realistic props in a given make-believe action sequence. On the assumption that there is a developmental progression from single transformations of objects to multiple transformations of objects, Fein asked her subjects to make a realistic or unrealistic toy horse drink from a realistic or unrealistic toy cup. She found that her 2-year-old subjects could enact the sequence if only one of the unrealistic props were used (single transformations). When both of the toys were unrealistic (multiple transformations), subjects were unable to perform the sequence. Fein and Robertson (1974) observed the play of children 20 to 26 months of age with both high- and low-realism toys and found that the younger subjects engaged in more symbolic play when provided with highly realistic than with less realistic toys. For the older subjects, toy realism was not as potent a factor. Fein and Robertson concluded that the ability to play with low-realism toys increased with age.

Based on Piaget's observations and Fein's experimental work, McCune-Nicolich (Nicolich, 1977) designed a study to assess the symbolic maturity of five children by examining their use of representation in symbolic play. The children ranged between 14 and 27 months of age, and were videotaped in their homes for 6 to 11 months. Like Smilansky, McCune-Nicolich identified five levels of symbolic transformations in make-believe. The earliest level, "Presymbolic Schemes," involves simple awareness of an object's appropriate functions. "Auto-Symbolic Schemes" come next and involves pretense at self-related activities, such as eating from an empty spoon. At the third level, "Single Scheme Symbolic Games," the child extends the symbolism beyond his own actions, either by including other actors as recipients of action (e.g., child feeds doll) or by pretending to be another person, an animal, or an object. The fourth state involves "Multi-Scheme Combinations," sequential acts such as stirring a pot, putting food in a dish, and then feeding the doll. Only at the fifth level, "Planned Symbolic Games," is the child capable of substituting low-realism objects to signify a different object. McCune-Nicolich believes that the fifth level indicates a clear advance in symbolic maturity, and she writes that "rather than being dependent on external stimulation as in earlier pretending, the child generates the relevant property mentally prior to the external actions [p. 96]." She found that her subjects progressed through the symbolic levels at various paces but in a set order. Only with advancing age did children become capable of employing low-realism props in their play.

Two additional studies provide strong support for the notion of an age-related increase in the capacity to substitute objects in make-believe play. Elder and Pederson (1978) asked children 2 to 3.5 years of age to play with toys, either low or high in realism, or with no toys. They found that the younger the child, the more dependent he or she was on the similarities between the original object and the signifying toy. Their results suggested at least three levels of transformations involving a similar substitute, a dissimilar substitute, and no object present. Most recently, Ungerer, Zelazo, Kearsley, and O'Leary (1981) found that 18-month-olds rarely (6%) substitute low-realism props in symbolic play; however by 34 months such behavior is fairly commonly observed (44% of subjects). Furthermore, Ungerer et al. found that when substitution symbols first emerged, they incorporated objects whose functions were ambiguous (e.g., blocks, cloth). Only later were objects with clear functions (e.g., cups, spoons) used as substitutes for different objects. The older the child, they concluded, the more capable he or she was of overriding the conflicting cues provided by the objects with unambiguous functions.

The developmental progression from high- to low-realism props in symbolic play is now widely accepted by the research community. One indication of that acceptance is the tendency for research to take the progression as a given and examine second-level questions. Watson and Fischer (1977) looked at differences in the ability to substitute agent and recipient objects in play. Fenson and Ramsay (1980) showed how themes become more elaborated as children become capable of imaginary sequences. McGhee, Ethridge, and Benz (1981) assessed childrens' preferences for high- versus low-realism toys at different ages, and Jackowitz and Watson (1980) assessed the role of physical versus functional similarity between signifiers and signified. Virtually unresearched, however, is whether training with low-realism props would succeed better than training with high-realism props in facilitating the growth of symbolic skills. Children do seem to become progressively more capable of employing unrealistic props in their symbolic play. A reasonable conclusion is that attainment of this higher level of play must reflect a correspondingly higher level of symbolic cognition and that training directed at this higher level of cognition might speed the growth of imaging abilities.

Only Pulaski (1970) has directly attempted to investigate the hypothesis that certain cognitive abilities might be more facilitated by symbolic play employing unrealistic props than by symbolic play employing realistic props. After providing her 6- to 8-year-old subjects with a brief period of free play in a room containing either realistic or unrealistic toys, Pulaski asked them to make up a play about a given theme. Her findings favored the unrealistic toy condition on the divergent thinking variables and on ability to sequentially organize stories.

Thus, evidence exists supporting not only the idea that play that employs less realistic toys is a more advanced behavior than symbolic play with more realistic toys, but also that this finding has useful educational implications. This chapter evaluates the different effects of using unrealistic as opposed to realistic props in facilitating verbal recall of a story, sequential recall of a story using pictures, and divergent thinking. Secondly, the different effects of the two-prop conditions on the subjects' behavior during the rehearsal is examined. The two hypotheses are as follows:

1. The treatment employing the abstract unrealistic props will prove superior on the dependent variables to the treatment employing the realistic props.
2. The quality of subjects' symbolic play performances during the rehearsal will be predictive of the quality of their performance on the dependent tasks. In other words, the better a subject's enactment of the story during the rehearsal, the more accurate his later recall should be.

## Experiment

### *Subjects*

Forty subjects, 22 boys and 18 girls, were chosen for participation. Subjects were drawn from three preschools in the Ithaca, New York, area. The subjects were all from middle-class homes and ranged in age from 42 to 63 months, with a mean age of 55.5 months. Each subject was seen on four occasions, no more than 15 days apart; each subject received each of four rehearsal treatments. The subjects were seen in groups of four at a time.

### *Procedure*

An experimental design with three basic procedural phases was used. On four separate occasions, subjects first heard a story, then participated in a rehearsal of the story, and then were tested on their recall of the story. Their ability to problem solve creatively, within the story context, was also measured. Thus, a given subject heard four different stories, participated in four types of rehearsal, and answered four series of questions. During the two symbolic play rehearsals (the only rehearsal conditions we are concerned with here) observations were recorded characterizing the quality of each subject's play behavior. The next three sections describe in detail each of the procedural phases: stories, rehearsal, and assessment.

*Stories.* In the first phase of the experiment a story was read to the group of four subjects. As each subject was seen four times, it was necessary to find four different stories. The stories chosen were grouped into a single book, *The Adven-*

*tures of Mole and Troll,* written by Tony Johnston and illustrated by Wallace Tripp. These stories were chosen for the following reasons:

1. The stories were age appropriate. Vocabulary was simple, and for each page of text there was a page of illustration.
2. All the stories were written in the same style by the same author.
3. The stories were similar in length, each being between 480 and 520 words long, and taking between 12 and 15 minutes to read.
4. Each of the stories involved the same characters and had identical plot formats. In each of the stories: (1) a problem arises; (2) an attempt is made to resolve the problem; (3) the attempted solution fails; and (4) a new solution is tried and is successful.

*Rehearsal Treatments.* As mentioned, each subject performed the experiment four times, each time experiencing a different form of story rehearsal. On the first two occasions subjects were administered an observation rehearsal treatment and an imitation rehearsal treatment (counterbalanced). In the observation treatment subjects watched the experimenter as he played out the story using the realistic props. In the imitation condition subjects imitated the experimenter as he played out the story, again with the realistic props. These two sessions constituted a brief training period for the behaviors that the children were expected to perform independently during the two symbolic play rehearsal conditions (also counterbalanced) administered during the third and fourth sessions.

The two forms of symbolic play rehearsal differed only in the realism of the props used to signify the story characters. Each rehearsal condition began with instructions reminding the children of the earlier observation and imitation conditions during which they had watched and imitated the experimenter. Then, subjects were requested to play out the story by themselves (e.g., "Show me what happened in the story using these toys.") The only procedural difference in the administration of the two symbolic play treatments other than the differences in the props themselves was that introducing the props was a lengthier process for the unrealistic prop condition. In the realistic prop condition the toys were presented to the children and precautions were taken to ascertain that subjects understood the relation of the dolls to the fictional Mole and Troll characters. The unrealistic prop condition called for a two-step process. First the relationship between the realistic props and the fictional characters was explained, and, secondly, the relationship between the unrealistic and realistic props was explained. Using the Mole character as an example, first the realistic Mole doll was compared to the pictures of Mole in the story, and subjects were told that the Mole doll was to represent the Mole character. Then the unrealistic Mole doll was paired with the realistic Mole doll, and subjects were told that the unrealistic doll was to represent the realistic doll. Regardless of rehearsal condition, each child was tested to ascertain that he or she could match the props to the characters the props signified. Then the initial scene from the story was set up, and subjects were requested to play out the story.

If subjects appeared stuck on a certain scene from the story, they were prodded with questions as to what came next in the story. Generally this was enough to prolong the play. However, on four occasions the group had to be told which event they should enact next. Although somewhat constrained by the events in the story, subjects often jumped from one scene to another, missing much of the detail in between. Subjects frequently replayed their favorite scenes several times or used the dolls to enact completely different plots, sometimes from previous Mole and Troll stories.

The length of the rehearsal period was set after the two initial sessions. A minimum of 3 minutes was predetermined, and by 4 minutes the children had sometimes played out the story twice and all were growing either bored or rowdy. Thus, throughout the data collection phase, the rehearsal treatments lasted at least 3 minutes and went as long as 4 minutes. Play was terminated either when all four subjects had ceased rehearsing the story or when 4 minutes had elapsed. Including the lengthy instructions and stage setting prior to rehearsal, the treatments took 6 to 7 minutes to complete.

During the rehearsal period observations that assessed the quality of the childrens' play were recorded on the form exhibited in Fig. 19.1. Each subject was observed for three periods of 15 seconds at different points during the rehearsal period. After 15 seconds of observation, the child's activity was given one of four descriptive classifications depending upon the highest level of play observed during that 15-second interval. The categories were:

1. Inattentive to props: This category includes all behavior which completely ignores the props (e.g. getting up and walking away, sitting still and looking around the room).
2. Exploration of the props: This category corresponds to Smilansky's (1968) first level of simple manipulation of objects. It includes behavior which is focused on the props but not symbolically (e.g., feeling the doll's hair, unsnapping the doll's clothes, throwing the doll on the floor).
3. Symbolic enactment with the props: This category describes symbolic behavior with the props where the pretense involves anything other than the plot of the Mole and Troll story just heard.
4. Symbolic enactment of the proper Mole and Troll story: All observations were recorded by the primary experimenter; hence no reliability coefficient was determinable. As the categories were clear-cut and did not require subtle discriminations, interobserver reliability was not seen to be an issue.

### *Assessment*

Three dependent variables were examined: simple verbal recall, sequential recall using pictures depicting story events, and divergent problem solving.

SCHOOL ______________________ SUBJECTS ______________ DATE ________ VISIT # _______

TREATMENT ____________ STORY ___________ ASSESSMENT ORDER __________

*PLAY INVOLVEMENT*

| SUBJECTS | 15 | 30 | 45 | 60 | 75 | 90 | 105 | 120 | 135 | 150 | 165 | 180 |
|---|---|---|---|---|---|---|---|---|---|---|---|---|
| | | | | | | | | | | | | |

*COMMENTS*

SUBJECT _______

SUBJECT _______

SUBJECT _______

SUBJECT _______

0=Inattention to Props
1=Exploration of Props
2=Non-story Symbolic Play
3=Symbolic Play of Story

FIG. 19.1 Observation form.

*Simple Recall.* This variable was assessed by a set of questions for each story which addressed the subjects' recall of specific story events. The questions were verbally administered and the answers were audiotaped for later transcription and analysis. The choice of questions was based on the analysis of the story formats that have already been described. Four questions were asked requesting identification of: (1) the problem situation; (2) the initial resolution; (3) reasons for failure; and (4) the final resolution of the problem.

Often questions had to be worded in several different ways so as to ascertain whether the subjects merely failed to understand what information was requested of them or truly could not remember the information. Prompts were used if a child indicated no memory or gave a partial response. In scoring the responses, points were subtracted if prompts were needed, however not if questions were repeated. The distinction was that prompts added new information to the original question, whereas repetitions did not. Sometimes the new information was provided by an inflection of tone or voice; at other times information from the story was added.

Each question was worth three points. This figure was arrived at to permit the child prompts and errors before he scored zero on a question. Partial credit was given for incomplete responses, and points were subtracted where prompts were needed to arrive at the correct answer. One point was substracted for wrong answers if the correct answer was given at a later point. Thus the range of possible scores ranged from 0 to 12. Interscorer reliability, based on the first 25 transcripts, was a quite satisfactory .90 as determined by Kendall's tau.

*Sequential Recall.* Four pictures from a story were laid before the subjects in a predetermined order that correlated 0.0 with the correct order. The pictures were carefully made copies of illustrations from the Mole and Troll stories. Each picture represented one of the four events basic to each story's format. Subjects were told that these four pictures were from the story just read and then were requested to examine each picture carefully. Subjects were then asked to point to the picture that they saw first in the story. After making their choice, subjects were alternatively asked, "Which of these pictures that are left was the first one that you saw," and Which of these pictures came next?. As for the simple recall task, the rationale for phrasing the question in several ways was to maximize the probability that subjects understood what was expected of them. In this case it seemed to matter little which way the question was phrased; those children who possessed the ability to order understood the question regardless of its wording; whereas those subjects unable to order understood neither form in which the question was phrased. Frequently this latter group went from left to right, merely identifying the order in which the pictures had been placed before them.

Upon completion of this task, the order in which subjects had arranged the pictures was noted and later transformed into a single score derived by calculating the Spearman Rank Order Correlation between the subject's order and the correct one.

*Divergent Problem Solving.* For each story a single question requested that subjects suggest solutions to the central problem of the story. It was deemed desirable that the problem-solving situation be made maximally relevant to the child, and the question always began, "Pretend that you are in situation X. How else might you solve the problem?" Special attention was made to reinforce verbally all efforts at solution so as to ensure that subjects did not feel that requests for more solutions implied the inadequacy of their initial response. Requests for additional solutions usually halted when subjects indicated that they could think of no other solutions. On occasion, subjects began to scan the room randomly, enumerating different objects regardless of the objects suitability for the purposes it was to be put to in the problem-solving situation. This behavior also terminated requests for additional solutions.

Responses were taped for later transcription, and scores were derived for each subject on the dimensions of fluency, flexibility, and originality. The "Composite Divergent Problem Solving" score reported here is the summation of these three scores. Subjects' fluency scores indicate the total number of acceptable responses given. Flexibility refers to the number of categories of acceptable solutions suggested by subjects, and originality refers to the statistical rarity of the solutions offered. To calculate the originality score, all acceptable solutions were weighted by the frequency of their occurrence. The weights for all the responses made by a given subject were then added together and divided by the total number of responses. The obtained originality values indicate the average rarity of a subject's responses. Those responses that occurred more than three times across the entire sample received one point for originality. Responses occurring two or three times received two points, and responses occurring only a single time received three points for originality. Again, the score reported here, the "Composite Divergent Problem Solving" score, is simply a summation of a subject's scores on fluency, flexibility and originality.

### *Data Collection*

Data were collected on 40 separate occasions over a 4-month period (January to April, 1980). All data collection tasks were performed by the experimenter, and each session lasted 1 hour. A complete series of four sets of data were collected for 33 subjects, three sets for six subjects, and two sets for only one subject. A session was run if a minimum of three of the four subjects in a group were present. No attempt was made to retest absentees on a later date. This decision was based on the reasoning that the group atmosphere was an integral part of the treatments, and results from a one-to-one session are impossible to compare.

At the outset it was hoped that each group would be assessed four times separated by 7 to 10 days; however that goal was proved unrealistic. Sessions were canceled for a variety of reasons. At no point were sessions separated by more than 15 days.

### *Results*

The two hypotheses of concern were: (1) the rehearsal treatment employing the unrealistic props will prove superior in facilitating performance on the dependent variables to the rehearsal treatment employing the realistic props; and (2) the quality of a subject's symbolic play performance during the rehearsal period would be predictive of his performance on the subsequent dependent variable tasks. The first hypothesis was tested by comparing the mean scores obtained for simple recall, sequential recall, and divergent thinking following a period of play with the realistic props, as opposed to a period of play with the unrealistic props. A $t$ test (see Table 19.1) found the difference between the treatments to be nonsignificant for all three dependent variables.

The second hypothesis was examined by correlating (Pearson Product-Moment) the observation scores assessing the quality of a subject's play with his or her scores on the later tasks. As seen in Table 19.2, a curious pattern of correlations was obtained.

Four points should be noted:

1. All the correlations are positive. The lowest correlation, that between a subject's score on the sequential recall measure and his unrealistic prop symbolic play observation score, was .16.

2. Within the symbolic play conditions there is a great amount of consistency across the three dependent variables. This stability suggests that the behaviors observed for each type of symbolic play possess a characteristic effect upon later task performance. For the realistic prop condition the correlations varied

TABLE 19.1
T tests comparing realistic versus unrealistic symbolic play treatments on simple and sequential recall

| *Dependent Variable* | *Treatment* | *N* | $\bar{X}$ | *SD* | *t* | *df* |
|---|---|---|---|---|---|---|
| Simple recall | Realistic symbolic play | 40 | 9.50 | 2.16 | .991 | 78 |
| | Unrealistic symbolic play | 40 | 9.95 | 1.83 | .991 | 78 |
| Sequential recall | Realistic symbolic play | 40 | .55 | .59 | .000 | 78 |
| | Unrealistic symbolic play | 40 | .55 | .41 | .000 | 78 |
| Composite divergent | Realistic symbolic play | 40 | 3.61 | 3.37 | .060 | 78 |
| Thinking score | Unrealistic symbolic play | 40 | 3.66 | 3.57 | .060 | 78 |

TABLE 19.2
Pearson product–moment correlations between observation scores and dependent variable scores

| *Dependent Variables* | *Realistic Prop Symbolic Play* | *Unrealistic Prop Symbolic Play* |
|---|---|---|
| Simple recall | .6096* | .1773 |
| Sequential recall | .4165* | .1617 |
| Composite divergent | .4124* | .1910 |

* = $p < .001$

from .41 to .61. For the unrealistic prop condition the correlations varied between .16 and .19.

3. The correlations between observation scores and the three dependent variables for the realistic prop condition were all statistically significant ($p < .001$).

4. The correlations between observation scores and dependent variables for the unrealistic prop condition were all statistically nonsignificant.

### *Discussion*

A simple explanation for this pattern of correlations might be that the subjects were less capable of playing out the stories with the unrealistic props than they were with the realistic props and thus were not as able to rehearse effectively. If the subjects in the unrealistic prop condition were unable to rehearse effectively, then one would not expect their attempts at rehearsal to predict their performance on the subsequent tasks. This explanation, however, falls short on two counts. First, as seen in Table 19.1, the unrealistic prop rehearsal condition produced task means at least as substantial as the realistic prop condition. Secondly, mean observation scores for the two symbolic play treatments did not differ significantly, as determined by a *t* test (see Table 19.3). Although difficult to characterize a subject's pattern of activity from the group mean score, it is of interest to note that the overall mean is over six (maximum = 9) for both rehearsal conditions. Thus the average subject spent at least part of the rehearsal period symbolically enacting the story, regardless of the type of props he was given. In summary, despite facilitating later task performance at least as much as did symbolic play with realistic props, and despite differing very little in adherence to rehearsal instructions, that adherence did not predict later task performance nearly as well for the unrealistic prop as for the realistic prop condition.

Reconciliation of these findings requires a look at the assessment instrument and its suitability for describing the behaviors expected to occur during the different treatments. Clearly, a measure used to record observed behavior is more capable of describing the sum of a subject's activity when the activity of interest is primarily behavioral, as opposed to cognitive, in nature. The rationale

TABLE 19.3
T test comparing realistic and unrealistic imagery symbolic play on observation scores

| *Treatment* | *N* | $\bar{X}$ | *SD* | *t* | *df* |
|---|---|---|---|---|---|
| Realistic imagery symbolic play | 40 | 6.850 | 1.56 | .6543 | 78 |
| Unrealistic imagery symbolic play | 40 | 6.625 | 1.51 | .6543 | 78 |

underlying the design of the unrealistic prop condition, however, was to force subjects to rely to a greater extent upon their own powers of imaging and concept formation than was necessary in the realistic prop condition. Thus, for the unrealistic prop condition, the activity of interest was covert and less available for observation and measurement. If the manipulation of prop imagery was correctly conceptualized, one would not expect the behavioral observations to have as high a predictive value in the unrealistic prop condition as compared to the realistic prop condition.

In short, the manipulation of prop imagery appears to have been successful in producing the intended types of rehearsal behavior. For the rehearsal condition using the realistic props, the degree of success with which subjects were observed to enact the stories predicted both their ability to recall the stories and their ability to think creatively about the story's central conflict situation. The failure of those same behaviors to predict performance when unrealistic props were employed strongly suggests an increased involvement of covert cognitive processes at work. Overtly the behaviors associated with each of the play treatments were very similar. However, in the unrealistic imagery condition an unobserved process accounted for the resulting successful task performance. What was overtly occurring that caused successful performance is unclear. All that might be inferred is that use of unrealistic props involved greater use of the covert representational skills involved in concept formation and divergent thinking. Use of unrealistic props seems to have forced subjects to rely upon their imaging capacities to a greater extent than did the realistic props.

This conclusion possesses practical implications of substantial importance. The use of unrealistic props required the children to deal with the stories on a more covert level. Over the long term, symbolic play with unrealistic props might reasonably be expected to facilitate the development of representational thought better. Thus, although on a one-lesson basis the prop-realism component of this study did not significantly influence task scores, this study does support the assertion made by Saltz and Johnson (1974) that more abstract forms of symbolic play are more educationally facilitative than less abstract forms. However, the abstractness of the theme or plot being enacted is not important. Of relevance is the abstractness of the symbol whereby those themes are expressed. By manipulating the signifying prop's realism, educators can provide preschoolers with experiences in the realm of representational thought.

Children $2\frac{1}{2}$ to 4 years of age should be provided with highly realistic props to support and sustain the symbolic enactments. Once the ability to represent thoughts in terms of concrete highly suggestive imagery has matured, children should be encouraged to use less realistic props in their pretense. Further research is necessary in determining norms as aids to teachers in facilitating this transition; however, teachers should watch the symbolic enactments of each child to gauge his readiness for more unrealistic props. Also, instructional materials need to be developed that ease the transition from concrete to abstract imagery, perhaps by breaking the process into the five stages that were described earlier (Smilansky, 1968).

Preschool teachers should be encouraged to follow story reading with a period of symbolic play. Teachers should participate in these structured periods of symbolic play in order to extend the enactments; however, the children should be left free to develop their own technique of signifying events and concepts. Moreover, play with unrealistic props is at least as useful as play with elaborate and expensive props. This creates the unusual situation where higher-quality education can be offered at a lower cost. For example, a set of the realistic toys used in this study cost nine times the price of an unrealistic set. Ideally, the preschool environment should possess sets of simple materials that can be used to suggest a variety of pretend actions upon a variety of pretend environments.

Commercially purchased beanbag dolls were used as unrealistic props in this study. One might do just as well, however, using self-made puppets. Hand puppets can be made with paper bags, socks, popsicle sticks, potatoes, balls, yogurt cartons, or clothespins. In conjunction with scraps of wood for use as vehicles, boxes of all sizes, and an easily constructed puppet stage, a great diversity of make-believe themes can be portrayed. Alternatively clay or play dough can be used to mould figures. Tape placed on the floor to signify rooms, roads, or towns also adds to a flexible make-believe environment. These suggestions possess the additional merit of requiring children to construct the prop images they want, adding constructive types of play (Piaget, 1962) experiences to make-believe experiences. Future research is needed to assess the effect of long-term use of unrealistic props on children's ability to recall and think about prior experiences.

## REFERENCES

Burns, S. M., & Brainerd, C. J. Effects of constructive and dramatic play on perspective taking in very young children. *Developmental Psychology*, 1979, *15*, 501–521.

Dansky, J., & Silverman, I. Effects of play on associative fluency in preschool children. *Developmental Psychology*, 1973, *9*, 38–43.

Dansky, J., & Silverman, I. Play: A general facilitator of associative fluency. *Developmental Psychology,* 1975, *11,* 104.

Dewey, J. *Democracy and education.* New York: Macmillan, 1944.

Elder, J. L., & Pederson, D. R. Preschool children's use of objects in symbolic play. *Child Development,* 1978, *49,* 500–504.

Fein, G. G. A transformational analysis of pretending. *Developmental Psychology,* 1975, *11,* 291–296.

Fein, G. G., & Robertson, A. *Cognitive and social dimensions of pretending in two-year-olds.* New Haven, Conn.: Yale University, 1974. (ERIC Document Reproduction Service No. ED IL9806)

Fenson, L., & Ramsay, D. S. Decentration and integration of the child's play in the second year. *Child Development,* 1980, *51,* 171–178.

Fink, R. S. Role of imaginative play in cognitive development. *Psychological Reports,* 1976, *39,* 895–906.

Golomb, C., & Cornelius, C. Symbolic play and its cognitive significance. *Developmental Psychology,* 1977, *13,* 246–252.

Hutt, C., & Bhavnani, R. Predictions from play. In J. Bruner, A. Jolly, & K. Sylva (Eds.), *Play: Its role in development and evolution,* New York: Basic Books, 1976.

Iannotti, R. J. Effects of role-taking experiences on role taking, empathy, altruism, and aggression. *Developmental Psychology,* 1978, *14,* 119–124.

Jackowitz, E. R., & Watson, M. W. Development of object transformations in early pretend play. *Developmental Psychology,* 1980, *16*(6), 543–549.

Johnson, J. The relations of divergent thinking and intelligence test scores with social and non-social make-believe play of preschool children. *Child Development,* 1976, *47,* 1200–1203.

Lesgold, A. M., McCormick, C., & Golinkoff, R. M. Imagery training and children's prose learning. *Journal of Educational Psychology,* 1975, *67,* 29–34.

Levin, J. R. When is a picture worth a thousand words? In *Issues in imagery and learning: Four papers* (Theoretical Paper No. 36). Madison, Wis.: Wisconsin Research and Development Center for Cognitive Learning, 1972.

Levin, J. R., McCabe, A. E., & Bender, B. G. A note on imagery inducing motor activity in young children. *Child Development,* 1975, *46,* 263–266.

Lieberman, J. N. *Playfulness: Its relationship to imagination and creativity.* New York: Academic Press, 1977.

Lovinger, S. L. Sociodramatic play and language development in preschool disadvantaged children. *Psychology in the Schools,* 1974, *11,* 313–320.

MacKinnon, D. W. The nature of creative talent. *American Psychologist,* 1962, *17,* 484–495.

Manosevitz, M., Fling, S., & Prentice, N. Imaginary companions in young children: Relationships with intelligence, creativity and waiting ability. *Journal of Child Psychology and Psychiatry,* 1977, *18,* 73–78.

Mann, B. L. *An experimental investigation of the value of symboic play as an instructional strategy for preschoolers.* Unpublished doctoral dissertation, Cornell University, 1981.

McGhee, P. E., Ethridge, O. L., & Benz, N. A. *Effect of level of toy structure on preschool children's pretend play.* Paper presented at the annual meeting of the Association for the Anthropological Study of Play, Fort Wroth, April 1981.

Nicolich, L. M. Beyond sensorimotor intelligence: Assessment of symbolic maturity through analysis of pretend play. *Merrill–Palmer Quarterly,* 1977, *23,* 89–99.

Piaget, J. *Play, dreams and imitation in childhood.* New York: Norton, 1962.

Pulaski, M. A. Play as a function of toy structure and fantasy predisposition. *Child Development,* 1970, *41,* 531–537.

Saltz, E., Dixon, D., & Johnson, J. Training disadvantaged preschoolers on various fantasy activities: Effects on cognitive functioning and impulse control. *Child Development,* 1977, *48,* 367–379.

Saltz, E., & Johnson, J. Training for thematic-fantasy play in culturally disadvantages preschoolers: Preliminary results. *Journal of Educational Psychology,* 1974, *66,* 623–630.

Singer, D. G., & Singer, J. L. *Partners in play: A step-by-step guide to imaginative play in children.* New York: Harper & Row, 1977.

Singer, J. L. *Daydreaming: An introduction to the experimental study of inner experience.* New York: Random House, 1966.

Smilansky, S. *The effects of sociodramatic play on disadvantaged children.* New York: Wiley, 1968.

Ungerer, J. A., Zelazo, P. R., Kearsley, R. B., & O'Leary, K. Developmental changes in the representation of objects in symbolic play from 18 to 34 months of age. *Child Development,* 1981, *52,* 186–195.

Watson, M. W., & Fischer, K. W. A developmental sequence of agent use in later infancy. *Child Development,* 1977, *48,* 828–836.

Wolff, P., & Levin, J. R. The role of overt activity in children's imagery production. *Child Development,* 1972, *43,* 537–547.

Wolff, P., Levin, J. R., & Longobardi, E. T. Motoric mediation in children's paried-associate learning: Effects of visual and tactual contact. *Journal of Experimental Child Psychology,* 1972, *14,* 176–183.

Yawkey, T. D., & Silvern, S. B. *An investigation of imaginative play and language growth in five, six and seven-year-old children.* Paper presented at the Annual Meeting of the American Educational Research Association, 1979.

Yawkey, T. D., Jones, K. C., & Hrncir, E. J. *The effects of imaginative play and sex differences on mathematics, playfulness, imaginativeness, creativity, and reading capacities in 5-year-old children.* Paper presented at Annual Meeting of the Northeastern Educational Research Association, 1979.

# Author Index

Numbers in *italics* denote pages with complete bibliographic information.

## C

## I



## J



## K

N



O

## T



## U, V, W

## Y, Z

# Subject Index